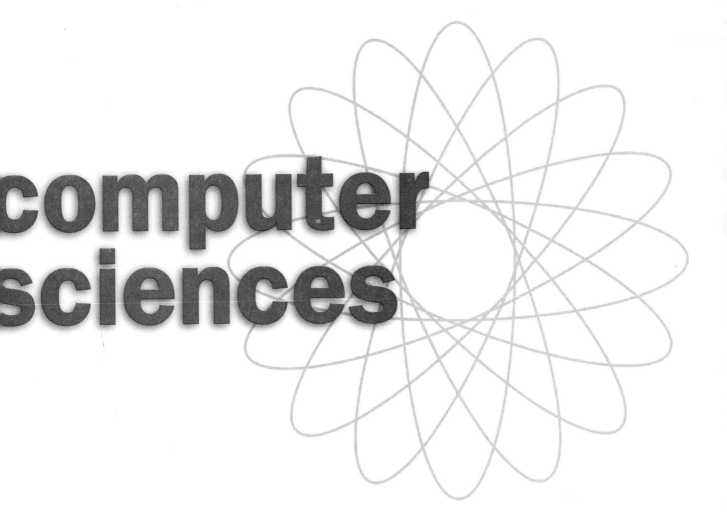

computer
sciences

computer sciences

VOLUME 2
Software and Hardware

Roger R. Flynn, Editor in Chief

MACMILLAN
REFERENCE
USA™

THOMSON
GALE

New York • Detroit • San Diego • San Francisco • Cleveland • New Haven, Conn. • Waterville, Maine • London • Munich

Macmillan Reference USA
300 Park Avenue South
New York, NY 10010

Gale Group
27500 Drake Rd.
Farmington Hills, MI 48331-3535

Library of Congress Cataloging-in-Publication Data
Computer sciences / Roger R. Flynn, editor in chief.
            p.   cm.
      Includes bibiographical references and index.
      ISBN 0-02-865566-4 (set: hardcover : alk. paper) —
      ISBN 0-02-865567-2 (Volume 1: Foundations: Ideas and People : alk. paper) —
      ISBN 0-02-865568-0 (Volume 2: Software and Hardware : alk. paper) —
      ISBN 0-02-865569-9 (Volume 3: Social Applications : alk. paper) —
      ISBN 0-02-865570-2 (Volume 4: Electronic Universe : alk. paper)
      1. Computer science. I. Flynn, Roger R., 1939-
QA76 .C572   2002
004—dc21
                                                            2002000754

Printed in the United States of America
1 2 3 4 5 6 7 8 9 10

Preface

The science of computing has come a long way since the late 1930s, when John Vincent Atanasoff and Clifford Berry began work on the first electronic digital computer. One marvels to see how the science has advanced from the days of Charles Babbage, who developed the Difference Engine in the 1820s, and, later proposed the Analytical Engine. Computer science was and continues to be an intriguing field filled with interesting stories, colorful personalities, and incredible innovations.

Ever since their invention, computers have had a profound impact on society and the ways in which humans conduct business and financial matters, fight wars and maintain peace, provide goods and services, predict events (e.g., earthquakes, the weather, global warming), monitor security and safety, and a host of other applications too numerous to mention. Plus, the personal computer revolution, beginning in the 1980s, has brought computers into many homes and schools. This has helped students find new ways to prepare reports, conduct research, and study using computerized methods. In the new millennium, the role that computers play in society continues to grow.

The World of Computer Science

In preparing this encyclopedia, I came across references to the early work on the IBM System/360 series of computers, which featured capacities of 65,000 to 16 million bytes (4 byte-words) of main storage and disk storage of several million to tens or hundreds of million bytes. At the same time, I opened the Sunday paper in February of 2002 and scanned the ads for personal computers, announcing memories of several hundred million bytes and disk storage of gigabytes. The cost of the 360 series ranged from fifty to several hundred thousand dollars to more than a million. Prices for the computers advertised in my Sunday paper ranged from several hundred dollars to a few thousand. The IBM 360 series was released in 1964. If a similar breakthrough occurred in education or automobile manufacturing (a factor of 1000, on the conservative side), a year in college would cost $20, as would a good model car! This, of course, is not the case.

However, computer hardware is not the entire story. Machines all need software, operating systems, applications software, and the like. While a person was hard pressed to get a line drawing or a bar chart on the screen 25 years ago, someone today has a choice of presentation software (slides or projections of the computer screen), desktop publishing, spreadsheets, and the like, much of which comes bundled with the system.

In fact, today one can purchase, for a few thousand dollars, more equipment and software than the Department of Information Science and

Telecommunications at my school (the University of Pittsburgh) or, for that matter, the entire university, could buy, when I first arrived in 1974. This is, indeed, an extraordinary era to have been a part of and witnessed. However, this does not happen in a vacuum. In this encyclopedia we aim to detail the people, activities, products, and growth of knowledge that have helped computer science evolve into what it is today.

Volume Breakdown

The organization of this encyclopedia reflects the history and application of the field. Our first volume in this series is dedicated to the history of computing. Its subtitle is *Foundations: Ideas and People*. The second volume describes *Software and Hardware*, while the third addresses *Social Applications*. The fourth is appropriately subtitled the *Electronic Universe* as it looks at such developments and inventions as the Internet, ubiquitous computing (embedded computing), and miniaturization.

While the intent is to give an exhaustive view of the field, no encyclopedia of this size, or, for that matter, ten times its size, could provide a complete rendering of the developments, events, people, and technology involved. Hence, the four volumes provide a representative selection of the people, places, and events involved. The encyclopedia was developed from a U.S. point of view, but we trust that the articles herein are not intentionally biased and, hopefully, do justice to innovations and contributions from elsewhere in the world. A brief look at each volume of the encyclopedia follows.

Volume 1

Volume I discusses the foundations of computer science, including computing history and some important innovators. Among the people are American inventor Herman Hollerith (1860–1929), the designer of punched card and punched card equipment; English mathematician Charles Babbage (1791–1871), the inventor of the Difference Engine and the proposed Analytical Engine, a precursor of the stored program computer; English noblewoman Ada Byron King, the Countess of Lovelace (1815–1852), the first "computer programmer"; American executive Thomas J. Watson Sr. (1874–1956), early chief of the IBM Corporation; and American mathematician Grace Hopper (1906–1992), who helped in the development of COBOL (COmmon Business Oriented Language) and developed one of its predecessors, FLOW-MATIC, and is the person who allegedly coined the term "computer bug."

Within Volume 1, various groups and organizations are discussed. These include the Association for Computing Machinery (ACM), which brings together people from around the globe to exchange ideas and advance computer science; the Institute of Electrical and Electronic Engineers (IEEE), which serves as the world's largest technical professional association, with more than 350,000 members; and the IBM Corporation, Apple Computer Inc., and the Microsoft Corporation, which all contributed to the start of the personal computer (PC) revolution. Among the more general articles the reader will find those concerning topics such as early pioneers, featuring primarily American and European scientists and their work; language generations, focusing on the evolution of computer languages; and computer generations, discussing early machines such as the ENIAC (Electronic

*Explore further in Hollerith, Herman; Babbage, Charles; Lovelace, Ada Byron King, Countess of; Watson, Thomas J., Sr; and Hopper, Grace.

*Explore further in Association for Computing Machinery; Institute of Electrical and Electronic Engineers (IEEE); IBM Corporation; Apple Computer, Inc.; Microsoft Corporation; Early Pioneers; Generations, Languages; and Generations, Computers.

Numerical Integrator and Computer) and the EDVAC (Electronic Discrete Variable Automatic Computer).

Finally, other articles of general interest in Volume 1 concern the history and workings of supercomputers; the development of the mouse; the question of computer security; the beginnings of the Internet; and the basics of digital and analog computing. The government's role is explained in articles on the U.S. Census Bureau and funding research projects. In addition, mathematical tools such as the binary number system and the slide rule as well as innovations such as France's Minitel are also featured.

*Explore further in Supercomputers; Mouse; Security; Internet; Digital Computing; Analog Computing; Census Bureau; Government Funding, Research; Binary Number System; Slide Rule; Minitel.

Volume 2

Volume 2 describes software and hardware. Articles cover topics from system analysis and design, which is the cornerstone of building a system, to operating systems, compilers, and parallel processing, which discuss some of the technical aspects of computing. Telecommunication subjects range from network design to wireless technology to ATM transmission, while application-oriented articles include pattern recognition, personal digital assistants (PDAs), and computer music. Essays concerning software products include object-oriented languages, client/server technology, invasive programs, and programming.

*Explore further in System Analysis; Systems Design; Operating Systems; Compilers; Parallel Processing; Network Design; Wireless Technology; ATM Transmission; Pattern Recognition; Personal Digital Assistants; Music, Computer; Object-Oriented Languages; Client/Server Systems; Invasive Programs; and Programming.

Among the people featured in Volume 2 are John Bardeen (1908–1991), Walter H. Brattain (1902–1987), and William B. Shockley (1910–1989), inventors of the transistor; English mathematician George Boole (1815–1864), developer of Boolean logic; and Alexander Graham Bell (1847–1922), inventor of the telephone. Rounding out Volume 2 are the technical aspects of hardware-related topics, including coding techniques, digital logic design, and cellular technology.

*Explore further in Bardeen, John, Brattain, Walter H., and Shockley, William B.; Boole, George; Boolean Algebra; Bell, Alexander Graham; Coding Techniques; Codes; Digital Logic Design; and Cellular Technology.

Volume 3

In Volume 3, the emphasis is on social applications. From fashion design to meteorology, the use of computers impacts our everyday lives. For example, computer technology has greatly influenced the study of biology, molecular biology, physics, and mathematics, not to mention the large role it plays in air traffic management and aircraft flight control, ATM machines and magnetic stripe cards for shopping and business. Businesses, large and small, have significantly benefited from applications that track product growth, costs, and the way products are managed. Volume 3 essays also explore the computer's role in medical image analysis and legal systems, while our use of computers in everyday life and our means of interacting with them are addressed in subjects such as library applications and speech recognition.

*Explore further in Fashion Design; Weather Forecasting; Biology; Molecular Biology; Physics; Mathematics; Aircraft Traffic Management; Aircraft Flight Control; ATM Machines; Magnetic Stripe Cards; Project Management; Economic Modeling; Process Control; Productivity Software; Integrated Software; Image Analysis: Medicine; Legal Systems; Library Applications; Speech Recognition.

Volume 3 addresses our aesthetic and intellectual pursuits in areas such as composing music, playing chess, and designing buildings. Yet the advancements of computer sciences go much further as described in articles about agriculture, geographic information systems, and astronomy. Among the people featured in the volume are American inventor Al Gross (1918–2001), the "father of wireless"; Hungarian mathematician Rózsa Péter (1905–1977), promoter of the study of recursive functions; and American author Isaac Asimov (1920–1992), famed science fiction writer who wrote extensively about robots.

*Explore further in Music Composition; Chess Playing; Architecture; Agriculture; Geographic Information Systems; Astronomy; Gross, Alfred J.; Péter, Rózsa; Asimov, Isaac.

Volume 4

Volume 4 delves into our interconnected, networked society. The Internet is explored in detail, including its history, applications, and backbone. Molecular computing and artificial life are discussed, as are mobile computing and encryption technology. The reader will find articles on electronic banking, books, commerce, publishing, as well as information access and overload. Ethical matters pertaining to the electronic universe are also addressed.

Volume 4 extends our aesthetic interest with articles on photography and the use of computers in art. Readers will learn more about how cybercafes keep friends and family connected as well as the type of social impact that computers have had on society. Data gathering, storage, and retrieval are investigated in topics such as data mining and data warehousing. Similarly, Java applets, JavaScript, agents, and Visual Basic are featured.

Among the people highlighted in Volume 4 are Italian physicist Guglielmo Marconi (1874–1937), inventor of wireless communications; American engineer Claude E. Shannon (1916–2001), a pioneer of information theory; and Soviet mathematician Victor M. Glushkov (1923–1982), who advanced the science of cybernetics.

The Many Facets of Computer Science

Computer science has many interesting stories, many of which are told in this volume. Among them are the battle between John Atanasoff and John Mauchley and J. Presper Eckert Jr. over the patent to the electronic digital computer and regenerative memory, symbolized and embodied in the lawsuits between Sperry-Rand (Mauchley-Eckert) and Honeywell (Atanasoff) and Sperry-Rand (Mauchley-Eckert) and CDC (Atanasoff). The lawsuits are not covered here, but the principal actors are. And there is Thomas J. Watson's prediction, possibly apocryphal, of the need ("demand") for 50 computers worldwide! Plus, Ada Byron King, Countess of Lovelace, became famous for a reason other than being British poet Lord George Gordon Byron's daughter. And German inventor Konrad Zuse (1910–1995) saw his computers destroyed by the Allies during World War II, while Soviet mathematician Victor M. Glushkov (1923–1982) had an institute named after him and his work.

Scientific visualization is now a topic of interest, while data processing is passé. Nanocomputing has become a possibility, while mainframes are still in use and e-mail is commonplace in many parts of the world. It has been a great half-century or so (60 some years) for a fledgling field that began, possibly, with the Abacus!

Organization of the Material

Computer Sciences contains 286 entries that were newly commissioned for this work. More than 125 people contributed to this set, some from academia, some from industry, some independent consultants. Many contributors are from the United States, but other countries are represented including Australia, Canada, Great Britain, and Germany. In many cases, our contributors have written extensively on their subjects before, either in books or journal articles. Some even maintain their own web sites providing further information on their research topics.

Explore further in Internet: History; Internet: Applications; Internet: Backbone; Molecular Computing; Artificial Life; Mobile Computing; Cryptography; E-banking; E-books; E-commerce; E-journals and E-publishing; Information Access; Information Overload; Ethics; Copyright; and Patents.

Explore further in Photography; Art; Cybercafe; Social Impact; Data Mining; Data Warehousing; Java Applets; JavaScript; Agents; Visual Basic.

Explore further in Marconi, Guglielmo; Shannon, Claude E.; Glushkov, Victor M.

Explore further in Zuse, Konrad.

Explore further in Data Processing; Nanocomputing; Mainframes; E-mail; Abacus.

Most entries in this set contain illustrations, either photos, graphs, charts, or tables. Many feature sidebars that enhance the topic at hand or give a glimpse into a topic of related interest. The entries—geared to high school students and general readers—include glossary definitions of unfamiliar terms to help the reader understand complex topics. These words are highlighted in the text and defined in the margins. In addition, each entry includes a bibliography of sources of further information as well as a list of related entries in the encyclopedia.

Additional resources are available in the set's front and back matter. These include a timeline on significant events in computing history, a timeline on significant dates in the history of programming and markup and scripting languages, and a glossary. An index is included in each volume—Volume 4 contains a cumulative index covering the entire *Computer Sciences* encyclopedia.

Acknowledgments and Thanks

We would like to thank Elizabeth Des Chenes and Hélène Potter, who made the project possible; Cindy Clendenon; and, especially, Kathleen Edgar, without whose work this would not have been possible. Also thanks to Stephen Murray for compiling the glossary. And, I personally would like to thank the project's two other editors, Ida M. Flynn and Ann McIver McHoes, for their dedicated work in getting these volumes out. And finally, thanks to our many contributors. They provided "many voices," and we hope you enjoy listening to them.

Roger R. Flynn
Editor in Chief

Measurements

Data Unit	Abbreviation	Equivalent (Data Storage)	Power of Ten
Byte	B	8 bits	1 byte
Kilobyte	K, KB	$2^{10} = 1,024$ bytes	1,000 (one thousand) bytes
Megabyte	M, MB	$2^{20} = 1,048,576$ bytes	1,000,000 (one million) bytes
Gigabyte	GB	$2^{30} = 1,073,741,824$ bytes	1,000,000,000 (one billion) bytes
Terabyte	TB	$2^{40} = 1,099,511,627,776$ bytes	1,000,000,000,000 (one trillion) bytes
Petabyte	PB	$2^{50} = 1,125,899,906,842,624$ bytes	1,000,000,000,000,000 (one quadrillion) bytes

Time	Abbreviation	Equivalent	Additional Information
femtosecond	fs, fsec	10^{-15} seconds	1 quadrillionth of a second
picosecond	ps, psec	10^{-12} seconds	1 trillionth of a second
nanosecond	ns, nsec	10^{-9} seconds	1 billionth of a second
microsecond	μs, μsec	10^{-6} seconds	1 millionth of a second
millisecond	ms, msec	10^{-3} seconds	1 thousandth of a second
second	s, sec	1/60 of a minute; 1/3,600 of an hour	1 sixtieth of a minute; 1 thirty-six hundredths of an hour
minute	m, min	60 seconds; 1/60 of an hour	1 sixtieth of an hour
hour	h, hr	60 minutes; 3,600 seconds	
day	d	24 hours; 1,440 minutes; 86,400 seconds	
year	y, yr	365 days; 8,760 hours	
1,000 hours		1.3888... months (1.4 months)	$1,000 \div (30 \text{ days} \times 24 \text{ hours})$
8,760 hours		1 year	365 days $\times$ 24 hours
1 million hours		114.15525... years	$1,000,000 \div 8,760$
1 billion hours		~114,200... years	$1,000 \times 114.15525...$
1 trillion hours		~114,200,000 years	$1,000 \times 114,200$

Length	Abbreviation	Equivalent	Additional Information
nanometer	nm	10^{-9} meters (1 billionth of a meter)	~ 4/100,000,000 of an inch; ~ 1/25,000,000 of an inch
micrometer	μm	10^{-6} meter (1 millionth of a meter)	~ 4/100,000 of an inch; ~ 1/25,000 of an inch
millimeter	mm	10^{-3} meter (1 thousandth of a meter)	~ 4/100 of an inch; ~ 1/25 of an inch (2/5 $\times$ 1/10)
centimeter	cm	10^{-2} meter (1 hundredth of a meter); 1/2.54 of an inch	~ 2/5 of an inch (1 inch = 2.54 centimeters, exactly)
meter	m	100 centimeters; 3.2808 feet	~ 3 1/3 feet or 1.1 yards
kilometer	km	1,000 meters; 0.6214 miles	~ 3/5 of a mile
mile	mi	5,280 feet; 1.6093 kilometers	1.6×10^3 meters

Volume	Abbreviation	Equivalent	Additional Information
microliter	μl	1/1,000,000 liter	1 millionth of a liter
milliliter	ml	1/1,000 liter; 1 cubic centimeter	1 thousandth of a liter
centiliter	cl	1/100 liter	1 hundredth of a liter
liter	l	100 centiliters; 1,000 milliliters; 1,000,000 microliters; 1.0567 quarts (liquid)	~ 1.06 quarts (liquid)

Base 2 (Binary)	Decimal (Base 10) Equivalent	Approximations to Powers of Ten
2^0	1	
2^1	2	
2^2	4	
2^3	8	
2^4	16	
2^5	32	
2^6	64	
2^7	128	10^2; 100; one hundred; 1 followed by 2 zeros
2^8	256	
2^9	512	
2^{10}	1,024	10^3; 1,000; one thousand; 1 followed by 3 zeros
2^{11}	2,048	
2^{12}	4,096	
2^{13}	8,192	
2^{14}	16,384	
2^{15}	32,768	
2^{16}	65,536	
2^{17}	131,072	
2^{18}	262,144	
2^{19}	524,288	
2^{20}	1,048,576	10^6; 1,000,000; one million; 1 followed by 6 zeros
2^{21}	2,097,152	
2^{22}	4,194,304	
2^{23}	8,388,608	
2^{24}	16,777,216	
2^{25}	33,554,432	
2^{26}	67,108,864	
2^{27}	134,217,728	
2^{28}	268,435,456	
2^{29}	536,870,912	
2^{30}	1,073,741,824	10^9; 1,000,000,000; one billion; 1 followed by 9 zeros
2^{31}	2,147,483,648	
2^{32}	4,294,967,296	
2^{33}	8,589,934,592	
2^{34}	17,179,869,184	
2^{35}	34,359,738,368	
2^{36}	68,719,476,736	
2^{37}	137,438,953,472	
2^{38}	274,877,906,944	
2^{39}	549,755,813,888	
2^{40}	1,099,511,627,776	10^{12}; 1,000,000,000,000; one trillion; 1 followed by 12 zeros
2^{50}	1,125,899,906,842,624	10^{15}; 1,000,000,000,000,000; one quadrillion; 1 followed by 15 zeros
2^{100}	1,267,650,600,228,229,401,496,703,205,376	10^{30}; 1 followed by 30 zeros
2^{-1}	1/2	
2^{-2}	1/4	
2^{-3}	1/8	
2^{-4}	1/16	
2^{-5}	1/32	
2^{-6}	1/64	
2^{-7}	1/128	1/100; 10^{-2}; 0.01; 1 hundredth
2^{-8}	1/256	
2^{-9}	1/512	
2^{-10}	1/1,024	1 /1000; 10^{-3}; 0.001; 1 thousandth

Base 16 (Hexadecimal)	Binary (Base 2) Equivalent	Decimal (Base 10) Equivalent	Approximations to Powers of Ten
16^0	2^0	1	
16^1	2^4	16	
16^2	2^8	256	2×10^2; 2 hundred
16^3	2^{12}	4,096	4×10^3; 4 thousand
16^4	2^{16}	65,536	65×10^3; 65 thousand
16^5	2^{20}	1,048,576	1×10^6; 1 million
16^6	2^{24}	16,777,216	
16^7	2^{28}	268,435,456	
16^8	2^{32}	4,294,967,296	4×10^9; 4 billion
16^9	2^{36}	68,719,476,736	68×10^9; 68 billion
16^{10}	2^{40}	1,099,511,627,776	1×10^{12}; 1 trillion
16^{-1}	2^{-4}	1/16	
16^{-2}	2^{-8}	1/256	
16^{-3}	2^{-12}	1/4,096	$1/4 \times 10^{-3}$; 1/4-thousandth
16^{-4}	2^{-16}	1/65,536	
16^{-5}	2^{-20}	1/1,048,576	10^{-6}; 1 millionth
16^{-8}	2^{-32}	1/4,294,967,296	$1/4 \times 10^{-9}$; 1/4-billionth
16^{-10}	2^{-40}	1/1,099,511,627,776	10^{-12}; 1 trillionth

Base 10 (Decimal)	Equivalent	Verbal Equivalent
10^0	1	
10^1	10	
10^2	100	1 hundred
10^3	1,000	1 thousand
10^4	10,000	
10^5	100,000	
10^6	1,000,000	1 million
10^7	10,000,000	
10^8	100,000,000	
10^9	1,000,000,000	1 billion
10^{10}	10,000,000,000	
10^{11}	100,000,000,000	
10^{12}	1,000,000,000,000	1 trillion
10^{15}	1,000,000,000,000,000	1 quadrillion
10^{-1}	1/10	1 tenth
10^{-2}	1/100	1 hundredth
10^{-3}	1/1,000	1 thousandth
10^{-6}	1/1,000,000	1 millionth
10^{-9}	1/1,000,000,000	1 billionth
10^{-12}	1/1,000,000,000,000	1 trillionth
10^{-15}	1/1,000,000,000,000,000	1 quadrillionth

Sizes of and Distance to Objects

Sizes of and Distance to Objects	Equivalent	Additional Information
Diameter of Electron (classical)	5.6×10^{-13} centimeters	5.6×10^{-13} centimeters; roughly 10^{-12} centimeters
Mass of Electron	9.109×10^{-28} grams	roughly 10^{-27} grams (1 gram = 0.0353 ounce)
Diameter of Proton	10^{-15} meters	10^{-13} centimeters
Mass of Proton	1.67×10^{-24} grams	roughly 10^{-24} grams (about 1,836 times the mass of electron)
Diameter of Neutron	10^{-15} meters	10^{-13} centimeters
Mass of Neutron	1.673×10^{-24} grams	roughly 10^{-24} grams (about 1,838 times the mass of electron)
Diameter of Atom (Electron Cloud)	ranges from 1×10^{-10} to 5×10^{-10} meters;	$\sim 10^{-10}$ meters; $\sim 10^{-8}$ centimeters; $\sim 3.94 \times 10^{-9}$ inches (roughly 4 billionth of an inch across or 1/250 millionth of an inch across)
Diameter of Atomic Nucleus	10^{-14} meters	$\sim 10^{-12}$ centimeters (10,000 times smaller than an atom)
Atomic Mass (Atomic Mass Unit)	1.66×10^{-27} kilograms	One atomic mass unit (amu) is equal to 1.66×10^{-24} grams
Diameter of (standard) Pencil	6 millimeters (0.236 inches)	roughly 10^{-2} meters
Height (average) of Man and Woman	man: 1.75 meters (5 feet, 8 inches) woman: 1.63 meters (5 feet, 4 inches)	human height roughly 2×10^0 meters; 1/804.66 miles; 10^{-3} miles
Height of Mount Everest	8,850 meters (29,035 feet)	~ 5.5 miles; roughly 10^4 meters
Radius (mean equatorial) of Earth	6,378.1 kilometers (3,960.8 miles)	$\sim 6,400$ kilometers (4,000 miles); roughly 6.4×10^6 meters
Diameter (polar) of Earth	12,713.6 kilometers (7,895.1 miles)	$\sim 12,800$ kilometers (8,000 miles); roughly 1.28×10^7 meters (Earth's diameter is twice the Earth's radius)
Circumference (based on mean equatorial radius) of Earth	40,075 kilometers (24,887 miles)	$\sim 40,000$ kilometers (25,000 miles) (about 8 times the width of the United States) (Circumference = $2 \times \pi \times$ Earth's radius)
Distance from Earth to Sun	149,600,000 kilometers (92,900,000 miles)	$\sim 93,000,000$ miles; ~ 8.3 light-minutes; roughly 10^{11} meters; roughly 10^8 miles
Distance to Great Nebula in Andromeda Galaxy	2.7×10^{19} kilometers (1.7×10^{19} miles)	~ 2.9 million light-years; roughly 10^{22} meters; roughly 10^{19} miles

Timeline: Significant Events in the History of Computing

The history of computer sciences has been filled with many creative inventions and intriguing people. Here are some of the milestones and achievements in the field.

c300-500 BCE	The counting board, known as the ancient abacus, is used. (Babylonia)
CE 1200	The modern abacus is used. (China)
c1500	Leonardo da Vinci drafts a design for a calculator. (Italy)
1614	John Napier suggests the use of logarithms. (Scotland)
1617	John Napier produces calculating rods, called "Napier's Bones." (Scotland)
	Henry Briggs formulates the common logarithm, Base 10. (England)
1620	Edmund Gunter devises the "Line of Numbers," the precursor to slide rule. (England)
1623	Wilhelm Schickard conceives a design of a mechanical calculator. (Germany)
1632	William Oughtred originates the slide rule. (England)
1642	Blaise Pascal makes a mechanical calculator, which can add and subtract. (France)
1666	Sir Samuel Morland develops a multiplying calculator. (England)
1673	Gottfried von Leibniz proposes a general purpose calculating machine. (Germany)
1777	Charles Stanhope, 3rd Earl of Stanhope, Lord Mahon, invents a logic machine. (England)
1804	Joseph-Marie Jacquard mechanizes weaving with Jacquard's Loom, featuring punched cards. (France)
1820	Charles Xavier Thomas (Tomas de Colmar) creates a calculating machine, a prototype for the first commercially successful calculator. (France)
1822	Charles Babbage designs the Difference Engine. (England)
1834	Charles Babbage proposes the Analytical Engine. (England)
1838	Samuel Morse formulates the Morse Code. (United States)
1842	L. F. Menabrea publishes a description of Charles Babbage's Analytical Engine. (Published, Italy)

1843	Ada Byron King, Countess of Lovelace, writes a program for Babbage's Analytical Engine. (England)
1854	George Boole envisions the Laws of Thought. (Ireland)
1870	William Stanley Jevons produces a logic machine. (England)
1873	William Thomson, Lord Kelvin, devises the analog tide predictor. (Scotland)
	Christopher Sholes, Carlos Glidden, and Samuel W. Soule invent the Sholes and Glidden Typewriter; produced by E. Remington & Sons. (United States)
1875	Frank Stephen Baldwin constructs a pin wheel calculator. (United States)
1876	Alexander Graham Bell develops the telephone. (United States)
	Bell's rival, Elisha Gray, also produces the telephone. (United States)
1878	Swedish inventor Willgodt T. Odhner makes a pin wheel calculator. (Russia)
1884	Dorr Eugene Felt creates the key-driven calculator, the Comptometer. (United States)
	Paul Gottlieb Nipkow produces the Nipkow Disk, a mechanical television device. (Germany)
1886	Herman Hollerith develops his punched card machine, called the Tabulating Machine. (United States)
1892	William Seward Burroughs invents his Adding and Listing (printing) Machine. (United States)
1896	Herman Hollerith forms the Tabulating Machine Company. (United States)
1901	Guglielmo Marconi develops wireless telegraphy. (Italy)
1904	John Ambrose Fleming constructs the diode valve (vacuum tube). (England)
	Elmore Ambrose Sperry concocts the circular slide rule. (United States)
1906	Lee De Forest invents the triode vacuum tube (audion). (United States)
1908	Elmore Ambrose Sperry produces the gyrocompass. (United States)
1910	Sperry Gyroscope Company is established. (United States)
1912	Frank Baldwin and Jay Monroe found Monroe Calculating Machine Company. (United States)
1914	Leonardo Torres Quevado devises an electromechanical calculator, an electromechanical chess machine (End Move). (Spain)
	Thomas J. Watson Sr. joins the Computing-Tabulating-Recording Company (CTR) as General Manager. (United States)

1919	W. H. Eccles and F. W. Jordan develop the flip-flop (memory device). (England)
1922	Russian-born Vladimir Kosma Zworykin develops the iconoscope and kinescope (cathode ray tube), both used in electronic television for Westinghouse. (United States)
1924	The Computing-Tabulating-Recording Company (CTR), formed in 1911 by the merger of Herman Hollerith's Tabulating Machine Company with Computing Scale Company and the International Time Recording Company, becomes the IBM (International Business Machines) Corporation. (United States)
1927	The Remington Rand Corporation forms from the merger of Remington Typewriter Company, Rand Kardex Bureau, and others. (United States)
1929	Vladimir Kosma Zworykin develops color television for RCA. (United States)
1931	Vannevar Bush develops the Differential Analyzer (an analog machine). (United States)
1933	Wallace J. Eckert applies punched card machines to astronomical data. (United States)
1937	Alan M. Turing proposes a Theoretical Model of Computation. (England)
	George R. Stibitz crafts the Binary Adder. (United States)
1939	John V. Atanasoff devises the prototype of an electronic digital computer. (United States)
	William R. Hewlett and David Packard establish the Hewlett-Packard Company. (United States)
1940	Claude E. Shannon applies Boolean algebra to switching circuits. (United States)
	George R. Stibitz uses the complex number calculator to perform Remote Job Entry (RJE), Dartmouth to New York. (United States)
1941	Konrad Zuse formulates a general-purpose, program-controlled computer. (Germany)
1942	John V. Atanasoff and Clifford Berry unveil the Atanasoff-Berry Computer (ABC). (United States)
1944	The Colossus, an English calculating machine, is put into use at Bletchley Park. (England)
	Howard Aiken develops the Automatic Sequence Controlled Calculator (ASCC), the Harvard Mark I, which is the first American program-controlled computer. (United States)
	Grace Hopper allegedly coins the term "computer bug" while working on the Mark I. (United States)
1946	J. Presper Eckert Jr. and John W. Mauchly construct the ENIAC (Electronic Numerical Integrator and Computer),

the first American general-purpose electronic computer, at the Moore School, University of Pennsylvania. (United States)

J. Presper Eckert Jr. and John W. Mauchly form the Electronic Control Company, which later becomes the Eckert-Mauchly Computer Corporation. (United States)

1947

John Bardeen, Walter H. Brattain, and William B. Shockley invent the transistor at Bell Laboratories. (United States)

J. Presper Eckert Jr. and John W. Mauchly develop the EDVAC (Electronic Discrete Variable Automatic Computer), a stored-program computer. (United States)

1948

F. C. Williams, Tom Kilburn, and G. C. (Geoff) Tootill create a small scale, experimental, stored-program computer (nicknamed "Baby") at the University of Manchester; it serves as the prototype of Manchester Mark I. (England)

1949

F. C. Williams, Tom Kilburn, and G. C. (Geoff) Tootill design the Manchester Mark I at the University of Manchester. (England)

Maurice V. Wilkes develops the EDSAC (Electronic Delay Storage Automatic Calculator) at Cambridge University. (England)

Jay Wright Forrester invents three dimensional core memory at the Massachusetts Institute of Technology. (United States)

Jay Wright Forrester and Robert Everett construct the Whirlwind I, a digital, real-time computer at Massachusetts Institute of Technology. (United States)

1950

J. H. Wilkinson and Edward A. Newman design the Pilot ACE (Automatic Computing Engine) implementing the Turing proposal for a computing machine at the National Physical Laboratory (NPL). (England)

Remington Rand acquires the Eckert-Mauchly Computer Corporation. (United States)

1951

Engineering Research Associates develops the ERA 1101, an American commercial computer, for the U.S. Navy and National Security Agency (NSA). (United States)

The UNIVAC I (Universal Automatic Computer), an American commercial computer, is created by Remington Rand for the U.S. Census Bureau. (United States)

Ferranti Mark I, a British commercial computer, is unveiled. (England)

Lyons Tea Co. announces Lyons Electronic Office, a British commercial computer. (England)

1952

UNIVAC I predicts election results as Dwight D. Eisenhower sweeps the U.S. presidential race. (United States)

Remington Rand Model 409, an American commercial computer, is originated by Remington Rand for the Internal Revenue Service. (United States)

Remington Rand acquires Engineering Research Associates. (United States)

1953 The IBM 701, a scientific computer, is constructed. (United States)

1954 The IBM 650 EDPM, electronic data processing machine, a stored-program computer in a punched-card environment, is produced. (United States)

1955 Sperry Corp. and Remington Rand merge to form the Sperry Rand Corporation. (United States)

1957 Robert N. Noyce, Gordon E. Moore, and others found Fairchild Semiconductor Corporation. (United States)

Seymour Cray, William Norris, and others establish Control Data Corporation. (United States)

Kenneth Olsen and Harlan Anderson launch Digital Equipment Corporation (DEC). (United States)

1958 Jack Kilby at Texas Instruments invents the integrated circuit. (United States)

1959 Robert N. Noyce at Fairchild Semiconductor invents the integrated circuit. Distinct patents are awarded to both Texas Instruments and Fairchild Semiconductor, as both efforts are recognized. (United States)

1960 The first PDP-1 is sold by Digital Equipment Corporation, which uses some technology from the Whirlwind Project. (United States)

The UNIVAC 1100 series of computers is announced by Sperry Rand Corporation. (United States)

1961 The Burroughs B5000 series dual-processor, with virtual memory, is unveiled. (United States)

1964 The IBM/360 family of computers begins production. (United States)

The CDC 6600 is created by Control Data Corporation. (United States)

1965 The UNIVAC 1108 from Sperry Rand Corporation is constructed. (United States)

The PDP-8, the first minicomputer, is released by Digital Equipment Corporation. (United States)

1968 Robert N. Noyce and Gordon E. Moore found Intel Corporation. (United States)

1969 The U.S. Department of Defense (DoD) launches ARPANET, the beginning of the Internet. (United States)

1970 The PDP-11 series of computers from Digital Equipment Corporation is put into use.(United States)

The Xerox Corporation's Palo Alto Research Center (PARC) begins to study the architecture of information. (United States)

1971   Ken Thompson devises the UNIX Operating System at Bell Laboratories. (United States)

Marcian E. (Ted) Hoff, Federico Faggin, and Stanley Mazor at Intel create the first microprocessor—a 4-bit processor, 4004. (United States)

1972   Seymour Cray founds Cray Research Inc. (United States)

Intel releases the 8008 microprocessor, an 8-bit processor. (United States)

1974   Intel announces the 8080 microprocessor, an 8-bit processor. (United States)

Motorola Inc. unveils the Motorola 6800, its 8-bit microprocessor. (United States)

Federico Faggin and Ralph Ungerman co-found Zilog, Inc., a manufacturer of microprocessors. (United States)

1975   Bill Gates and Paul Allen establish the Microsoft Corporation. (United States)

The kit-based Altair 8800 computer, using an 8080 microprocessor, is released by Ed Roberts with MITS (Model Instrumentation Telemetry Systems) in Albuquerque, New Mexico. (United States)

MITS purchases a version of the BASIC computer language from Microsoft. (United States)

The MOS 6502 microprocessor, an 8-bit microprocessor, is developed by MOS Technologies, Chuck Peddle, and others, who had left Motorola, (United States)

1976   Gary Kildall creates the CP/M (Control Program/Monitor or Control Program for Microprocessors) Operating System of Digital Research; this operating system for 8-bit microcomputers is the forerunner of DOS 1.0. (United States)

Steven Jobs and Stephen Wozniak found Apple Computer, Inc. and create the Apple I. (United States)

Seymour Cray devises the Cray-1 supercomputer. (United States)

Commodore Business Machines acquires MOS Technologies. (Canada)

1977   The Commodore PET (Personal Electronic Transactor) personal computer, developed by Jack Tramiel and Chuck Peddle for Commodore Business Machines, features the 6502 8-bit Microprocessor. (Canada)

The Apple II personal computer from Apple Computer, Inc., is released featuring a 6502 microprocessor. (United States)

The TRS-80 personal computer from Tandy Radio Shack, equipped with the Zilog Z80 8-bit microprocessor from Zilog, is unveiled. (United States)

1978 Intel announces the 8086 16-bit microprocessor. (United States)

Digital Equipment Corporation launches the VAX 11/780, a 4.3 billion byte computer with virtual memory. (United States)

1979 Intel presents the 8088 16-bit microprocessor. (United States)

Motorola Inc. crafts the MC 68000, Motorola 16-bit processor. (United States)

1980 Tim Patterson sells the rights to QDOS, an upgrade operating system of CP/M for 8088 and 8086 Intel microprocessors, 16-bit microprocessor, to Microsoft. (United States)

1981 The IBM Corporation announces the IBM Personal Computer featuring an 8088 microprocessor. (United States)

The Microsoft Operating System (MS-DOS) is put into use. (United States)

The Osborne I, developed by Adam Osborne and Lee Felsenstein with Osborne Computer Corporation, invent the first portable computer. (United States)

1982 Scott McNealy, Bill Joy, Andy Bechtolsheim, and Vinod Khosla found Sun Microsystems, Inc. (United States)

1984 The Macintosh PC from Apple Computer Inc., running with a Motorola 68000 microprocessor, revolutionizes the personal computer industry. (United States)

Richard Stallman begins the GNU Project, advocating the free use and distribution of software. (United States)

1985 The Free Software Foundation is formed to seek freedom of use and distribution of software. (United States)

Microsoft releases Windows 1.01. (United States)

1986 Sperry Rand and the Burroughs Corporation merge to form Unisys Corporation. (United States)

1989 SPARCstation I from Sun Microsystems is produced. (United States)

1991 Tim Berners-Lee begins the World Wide Web at CERN. (Switzerland)

Linus Torvalds builds the Linux Operating System. (Finland)

Paul Kunz develops the first web server outside of Europe, at the Stanford Linear Accelerator Center (SLAC). (United States)

1993	Marc Andreesen and Eric Bina create Mosaic, a web browser, at the National Center for Supercomputing Applications (NCSA), University of Illinois-Urbana Champaign. (United States)
1994	Marc Andreesen and James H. Clark form Mosaic Communications Corporation, later Netscape Communications Corporation. (United States)
	Netscape Navigator is launched by Netscape Communications Corporation. (United States)
1995	Java technology is announced by Sun Microsystems. (United States)
1996	World chess champion Garry Kasparov of Russia defeats Deep Blue, an IBM computer, in a man vs. computer chess matchup, four to two. (United States)
1997	IBM's Deep Blue defeats world chess champion Garry Kasparov in a rematch, 3.5 to 2.5. (United States)
	An injunction is filed against Microsoft to prohibit the company from requiring customers to accept Internet Explorer as their browser as a condition of using the Microsoft operating system Windows 95. (United States)
1998	America OnLine (AOL) acquires Netscape. (United States)
	Compaq Computer Corporation, a major producer of IBM compatible personal computers, buys Digital Equipment Corporation. (United States)
	America OnLine (AOL) and Sun form an alliance to produce Internet technology. (United States)
1999	Shawn Fanning writes code for Napster, a music file-sharing program. (United States)
	The Recording Industry Association of America (RIAA) files a lawsuit against Napster for facilitating copyright infringement. (United States)
2000	Zhores I. Alferov, Herbert Kroemer, and Jack Kilby share the Nobel Prize in Physics for contributions to information technology. Alferov, a Russian, and Kroemer, a German-born American, are acknowledged for their contributions to technology used in satellite communications and cellular telephones. Kilby, an American, is recognized for his work on the integrated circuit. (Sweden)

Timeline: The History of Programming, Markup and Scripting Languages

The history of computer sciences has been filled with many creative inventions and intriguing people. Here are some of the milestones and achievements in the field of computer programming and languages.

CE c800	al-Khowarizmi, Mohammed ibn-Musa develops a treatise on algebra, his name allegedly giving rise to the term algorithm.
1843	Ada Byron King, Countess of Lovelace, programs Charles Babbage's design of the Analytical Engine.
1945	Plankalkul is developed by Konrad Zuse.
1953	Sort-Merge Generator is created by Betty Holberton.
1957	FORTRAN is devised for IBM by John Backus and team of programmers.
	FLOW-MATIC is crafted for Remington-Rand's UNIVAC by Grace Hopper.
1958	LISP is produced by John McCarthy at Massachusetts Institute of Technology.
1960	ALGOL is the result of work done by the ALGOL Committee in the ALGOL 60 Report.
	COBOL is formulated by the CODASYL Committee, initiated by the the U.S. Department of Defense (DoD)
1961	JOSS is originated by the RAND Corporation.
	GPSS (General Purpose Simulation System) is invented by Geoffrey Gordon with IBM.
	RPG (Report Program Generator) is unveiled by IBM.
	APL (A Programming Language) is designed by Kenneth Iverson with IBM.
1963	SNOBOL is developed by David Farber, Ralph Griswold, and Ivan Polonsky at Bell Laboratories.
1964	BASIC is originated by John G. Kemeny and Thomas E. Kurtz at Dartmouth.
	PL/I is announced by IBM.
	Simula I is produced by Kristen Nygaard and Ole-Johan Dahl at the Norwegian Computing Center.
1967	Simula 67 is created by Kristen Nygaard and Ole-Johan Dahl at the Norwegian Computing Center.

	LOGO is devised by Seymour Papert at the MIT Artificial Intelligence Laboratory.
1971	Pascal is constructed by Niklaus Wirth at the Swiss Federal Institute of Technology (ETH) in Zurich.
1973	C developed by Dennis Ritchie at Bell Laboratories.
	Smalltalk is invented by Alan Kay at Xerox's PARC (Palo Alto Research Center).
1980	Ada is developed for the U.S. Department of Defense (DoD).
1985	C++ is created by Bjarne Stroustrup at Bell Laboratories.
1986	SGML (Standard Generalized Markup Language) is developed by the International Organization for Standardization (ISO).
1987	Perl is constructed by Larry Wall.
1991	Visual Basic is launched by the Microsoft Corporation.
	HTML (HyperText Markup Language) is originated by Tim Berners-Lee at CERN (Organization Europeene pour la Recherche Nucleaire).
1993	Mosaic is created by Marc Andreesen and Eric Bina for the National Center for Computing Applications (NCCA) at the University of Illinois-Urbana Champaign.
1995	Java is crafted by James Gosling of Sun Microsystems.
	A written specification of VRML (Virtual Reality Markup Language) is drafted by Mark Pesce, Tony Parisi, and Gavin Bell.
1996	Javascript is developed by Brendan Eich at Netscape Communications co-announced by Netscape and Sun Microsystems.
1997	VRML (Virtual Reality Modeling Language), developed by the Web3D Consortium, becomes an international standard.
1998	XML (Extensible Markup Language) is originated by a working group of the World Wide Web Consortium (W3C).

Contributors

Tom Abel
Penn State University, University Park, PA

Martyn Amos
University of Liverpool, United Kingdom

Richard Archer
Pittsburgh, PA

Pamela Willwerth Aue
Royal Oak, MI

Nancy J. Becker
St. John's University, New York

Mark Bedau
Reed College, Portland, OR

Pierfrancesco Bellini
University of Florence, Italy

Gary H. Bernstein
University of Notre Dame, Notre Dame, IN

Anne Bissonnette
Kent State University Museum, Kent, OH

Kevin W. Bowyer
University of Notre Dame, Notre Dame, IN

Stefan Brass
University of Giessen, Germany

Barbara Britton
Windsor Public Library, Windsor, Ontario, Canada

Kimberly Mann Bruch
San Diego Supercomputer Center, University of California, San Diego

Ivan Bruno
University of Florence, Italy

Dennis R. Buckmaster
Pennsylvania State University, University Park, PA

Dan Burk
University of Minnesota, Minneapolis, MN

Guoray Cai
Pennsylvania State University, University Park, PA

Shirley Campbell
University of Pittsburgh, Pittsburgh, PA

Siddharth Chandra
University of Pittsburgh, Pittsburgh, PA

J. Alex Chediak
University of California, Berkeley, CA

Kara K. Choquette
Xerox Corporation

John Cosgrove
Cosgrove Communications, Pittsburgh, PA

Cheryl L. Cramer
Digimarc Corporation, Tualatin, OR

Anthony Debons
University of Pittsburgh, Pittsburgh, PA

Salvatore Domenick Desiano
NASA Ames Research Center (QSS Group, Inc.)

Ken Doerbecker
Perfection Services, Inc.; WeirNet LLC; and FreeAir Networks, Inc.

Judi Ellis
KPMG, LLP, Pittsburgh, PA

Karen E. Esch
Karen Esch Associates, Pittsburgh, PA

Ming Fan
University of Notre Dame, Notre Dame, IN

Jim Fike
Ohio University, Athens, OH

Ida M. Flynn
University of Pittsburgh, Pittsburgh, PA

Roger R. Flynn
University of Pittsburgh, Pittsburgh, PA

H. Bruce Franklin
Rutgers University, Newark, NJ

Thomas J. Froehlich
Kent State University, Kent, OH

Chuck Gaidica
WDIV-TV, Detroit, MI

G. Christopher Hall
PricewaterhouseCoopers

Gary Hanson
Kent State University, Kent, OH

Karen Hartman
James Monroe Center Library, Mary Washington College, Fredericksburg, VA

Melissa J. Harvey
Carnegie Mellon University, Pittsburgh, PA

Albert D. Helfrick
Embry-Riddle Aeronautical University, Daytona Beach, FL

Stephen Hughes
University of Pittsburgh, Pittsburgh, PA

Bruce Jacob
University of Maryland, College Park, MD

Radhika Jain
Georgia State University, Atlanta, GA

Wesley Jamison
University of Pittsburgh at Greensburg

Sid Karin
San Diego Supercomputer Center, University of California, San Diego

Declan P. Kelly
Philips Research, The Netherlands

Betty Kirke
New York, NY

Mikko Kovalainen
University of Jyväskylä, Finland

Paul R. Kraus
Pittsburgh, PA

Prashant Krishnamurthy
University of Pittsburgh, Pittsburgh, PA

Marina Krol
Mount Sinai School of Medicine, New York, NY

Susan Landau
Sun Microsystems Inc., Mountain View, CA

Nicholas C. Laudato
University of Pittsburgh, Pittsburgh, Pennsylvania

George Lawton
  Eutopian Enterprises
Cynthia Tumilty Lazzaro
  Pinnacle Training Corp., Stoneham, MA
Joseph J. Lazzaro
  Massachusetts Commission for the Blind, Boston, MA
John Leaney
  University of Technology, Sydney, Australia
Robert Lembersky
  Ann Taylor, Inc., New York, NY
Terri L. Lenox
  Westminster College, New Wilmington, PA
Joyce H-S Li
  University of Pittsburgh, Pittsburgh, PA
Michael R. Macedonia
  USA STRICOM, Orlando, FL
Dirk E. Mahling
  University of Pittsburgh, Pittsburgh, PA
Cynthia J. Martincic
  St. Vincent College, Latrobe, PA
Michael J. McCarthy
  Carnegie Mellon University, Pittsburgh, PA
Ann McIver McHoes
  Carlow College, Pittsburgh PA
Genevieve McHoes
  University of Maryland, College Park, MD
John McHugh
  CERT™ Coordination Center, Software Engineering Institute, Carnegie Mellon University, Pittsburgh, PA
Donald M. McIver
  Northrop Grumman Corporation, Baltimore, MD
Maurice McIver
  Integrated Databases, Inc., Honolulu, HI
William J. McIver, Jr.
  University at Albany, State University of New York
Trevor T. Moores
  University of Nevada, Las Vegas
Christopher Morgan
  Association for Computing Machinery, New York, NY
Bertha Kugelman Morimoto
  University of Pittsburgh, Pittsburgh, PA
Tracy Mullen
  NEC Research Inc., Princeton, NJ

Paul Munro
  University of Pittsburgh, Pittsburgh, PA
Stephen Murray
  University of Technology, Sydney, Australia
Carey Nachenberg
  Symantec Corporation
John Nau
  Xceed Consulting, Inc., Pittsburgh, PA
Paolo Nesi
  University of Florence, Italy
Kai A. Olsen
  Molde College and University of Bergen, Norway
Ipek Özkaya
  Carnegie Mellon University, Pittsburgh, PA
Bob Patterson
  Perfection Services, Inc.
Robert R. Perkoski
  University of Pittsburgh, Pittsburgh, PA
Thomas A. Pollack
  Duquesne University, Pittsburgh, PA
Guylaine M. Pollock
  IEEE Computer Society; Sandia National Laboratories, Albuquerque, NM
Wolfgang Porod
  University of Notre Dame, Notre Dame, IN
Anwer H. Puthawala
  Park Avenue Associates in Radiology, P.C., Binghamton, NY
Mary McIver Puthawala
  Binghamton, NY
Sudha Ram
  University of Arizona, Tucson, AZ
Edie M. Rasmussen
  University of Pittsburgh, Pittsburgh, PA
Robert D. Regan
  Consultant, Pittsburgh, PA
Allen Renear
  University of Illinois, Urbana-Champaign
Sarah K. Rich
  Pennsylvania State University, University Park, PA
Mike Robinson
  Sageforce Ltd., Kingston on Thames, Surrey, United Kingdom
Elke A. Rudensteiner
  Worcester Polytechnic Institute, Worcester, MA

Frank R. Rusch
  University of Illinois at Urbana-Champaign
William Sherman
  National Center for Supercomputing Applications, University of Illinois at Urbana-Champaign
Marc Silverman
  University of Pittsburgh, Pittsburgh, PA
Munindar P. Singh
  North Carolina State University, Raleigh, NC
Cindy Smith
  PricewaterhouseCoopers, Pittsburgh, PA
Barry Smyth
  Smart Media Institute, University College, Dublin, Ireland
Amanda Spink
  Pennsylvania State University, University Park, PA
Michael B. Spring
  University of Pittsburgh, Pittsburgh, PA
Savitha Srinivasan
  IBM Almaden Research Center, San Jose, CA
Igor Tarnopolsky
  Westchester County Department of Laboratories and Research, Valhalla, NY
George A. Tarnow
  Georgetown University, Washington, DC
Lucy A. Tedd
  University of Wales, Aberystwyth, Wales, United Kingdom
Umesh Thakkar
  National Center for Supercomputing Applications, University of Illinois at Urbana-Champaign
Richard A. Thompson
  University of Pittsburgh, Pittsburgh, PA
James E. Tomayko
  Carnegie Mellon University, Pittsburgh, PA
Christinger Tomer
  University of Pittsburgh, Pittsburgh, PA
Upkar Varshney
  Georgia State University, Atlanta, GA
Jonathan Vos Post
  Webmaster <http://magicdragon.com>

Tom Wall
Duke University, Durham, NC

Brett A. Warneke
University of California, Berkeley, CA

Patricia S. Wehman
University of Pittsburgh, Pittsburgh, PA

Isaac Weiss
University of Maryland, College Park, MD

Martin B. Weiss
University of Pittsburgh, Pittsburgh, PA

Jeffrey C. Wingard
Leesburg, VA

Victor L. Winter
University of Nebraska at Omaha

Charles R. Woratschek
Robert Morris University, Moon Township, PA

Peter Y. Wu
University of Pittsburgh, Pittsburgh, PA

William J. Yurcik
Illinois State University, Normal, IL

Gregg R. Zegarelli
Zegarelli Law Group, P.C.

Table of Contents

computer
sciences

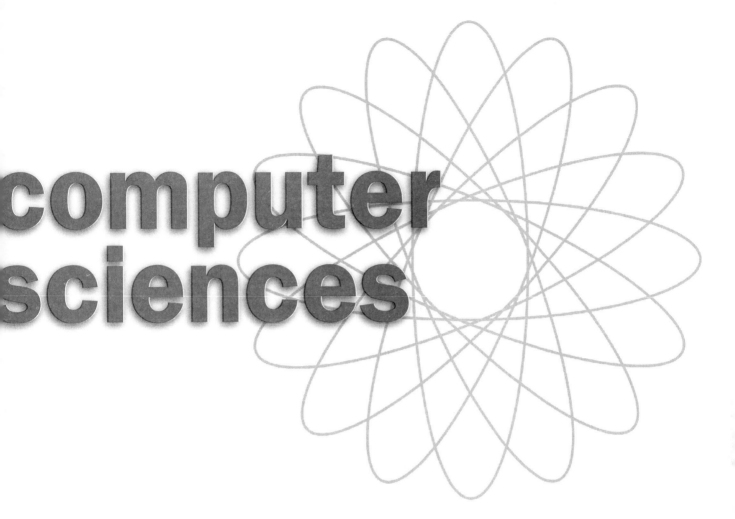

Algol-60 Report

The Algol-60 report was written between 1959 and 1960 by a team of programming language experts consisting of editor Peter Naur and several educators and practitioners from Europe and the United States. The purpose of the report was to develop a complete description of an international **algorithmic** language for expressing numerical processes in a form suitable for translation into computer programming languages. It was not intended to be a programming language, although it was subsequently implemented as a language and became popular in Europe.

Many versions of the Algol programming language were implemented in the 1960s and early 1970s. It also led to the development of several other programming languages, such as Pascal, implemented by Niklaus Wirth in the early 1970s, and C.

The report introduced the notions of a reference language, a publication language, and a hardware representation. The reference language was the standard for the report, compiler writers, and hardware implementation. It dictated the form of the language and its **syntax**. The publication language used the reference language with minor adjustments for publication variations across countries and printing and writing variations such as the handling of subscripts, superscripts, and other notation. The hardware representation took into consideration the characteristics of the machine. The reference language was the defining language, and the publication language and hardware representation had to be translatable into it.

The purpose of the report and the language was to give an unambiguous representation to various computer concepts—in particular, algorithm design, or ALGOrithmic Language 1960. A subsequent version, Algol68, was not as popular or widely implemented as Algol-60, although it was more powerful.

Algol is a structured language, incorporating while statements, if-then-else-statements, and other constructs that implement selection, iteration, basic statements, block structure, and recursion. Although it was developed only a few years after FORTRAN (FORmula TRANslator), released in 1957 by IBM, it incorporated features missing from FORTRAN—namely the recursion and the structured language—and was a major advance in the programming arena.

algorithmic pertaining to the rules or procedures used to solve mathematical problems—most often described as a sequence of steps

syntax a set of rules that a computing language incorporates regarding structure, punctuation, and formatting

Thomas Kurtz (pictured here) and John Kemeny worked to simplify computer language so that college students could learn it quickly. The result was BASIC, which became popular worldwide.

compilers programs that translate human-readable high-level computer languages into machine-readable code

One of the descendants of Algol and FORTRAN was BASIC (Beginner's All-purpose Symbolic Instruction Code) language, developed by John Kemeny and Thomas Kurtz of Dartmouth University. BASIC was a sort of format-statement-free version of FORTRAN for interactive and beginning computing. BASIC enjoyed a long reign from the 1970s to the 1980s and has recently been implemented in a quite different form, Visual Basic.

A descendent of Algol was Pascal, which also enjoyed a long reign as a popular language for implementing data structures and studying **compilers**. It was not a production language, but a teaching tool. C was a system's language and led to the development of C++, an object-oriented language that is still popular.

The Algol language was described in a notation called Backus normal or Backus-Naur form (BNF). The notation was suggested by John Backus, who based it on a notation by E. L. Post, a famous logician in the 1930s. It was similar to the notation developed by Noam Chomsky in 1957 for linguistics, which was used to implement grammars. A grammar is a succinct, unambiguous way of describing languages. The use of a formal notation in language theory was a major advance.

The evolution of programming languages was striking, but not as stunning as the evolution of compiler theory. Shortly after the Algol-60 report, several compiler theorists used the grammar notation to implement compilers in an "automatic" fashion. These compilers were known as compiler-compilers. Similar efforts were the development of Lex, a lexical analyzer, and Yacc ("Yet another compiler-compiler") at Bell Laboratories in the mid-1970s.

Understanding Programming Language

English grammar has certain constructs, such as a noun phrase, which is composed of other constructs, such as a noun and a modifier. Programming languages have constructs such as while-statements, and arithmetic expressions. These constructs are indicated by special symbols called the nonterminal or meta symbols of the language.

The symbols that actually appear in the language are called terminal symbols. The terminology comes from the data structures, or parse trees, used to implement the language.

An example is:

E-->E+T

    T

T-->T*F

    F

F-->(E)

    id

    num

This grammar indicates that an arithmetic expression, E, consists of other arithmetic expressions and terms, T, added together (E-->E+T). A term, T, is composed of a term times a factor, F, so that T-->T*F. Finally, a factor, F, is the most basic expression, consisting of parenthesized expressions (the parenthesized E), identifiers (user-defined identifier or variables), id, and numeric constants (num). The grammar gives the form of the arithmetic expressions.

The example gives a flavor of the notation. The items on the left of the arrow are composed of the items on the right. In this case, the E, T, and F are the meta-symbols. The other symbols, +, *, (,), and, in this case, id and num, appear in the language. They are the words of the language. In this case, E is the start symbol or first non-terminal symbol. It is the most general expression being defined. Although the notation may seem awkward at first, it is useful in language design, compiler theory, and implementation.

The development of grammars in computer science gave a great impetus to programming language design and implementation. SEE ALSO ALGORITHMS; PROCEDURAL LANGUAGES; PROGRAMMING.

Roger R. Flynn

Bibliography

Naur, Peter, ed. "Revised Report on the Algorithmic Language Algol-60." *Communications ACM* 6, no. 1 (1963): 1–17.

Wexelblat, Richard L., ed. *History of Programming Languages*. New York: Academic Press, 1981.

Algorithms

The word "algorithm" comes from the name of the ninth-century Persian mathematician Mohammed al-Khowarizmi. He wrote a widely read book entitled *Kitab al jabr w'al-muqabala* (*Rules of Restoration and Reduction*). This book describes many procedures for the manipulation of decimal numbers.

Today, the term **algorithm** is used to describe a wide variety of procedures from the sequence of steps executed for the manipulation of integers to the series of actions involved in searching databases and the Internet.

An algorithm can be described informally or with mathematical rigor. Informally, it might be described as a basic set of steps that must be performed to reach a predetermined result. For example, in grade school, students learn to multiply two integers by carrying out a repetitive sequence of activities. If they proceed carefully according to the directions, they will eventually compute the product.

algorithm a rule or procedure used to solve a mathematical problem— most often described as a sequence of steps

According to the more rigorous definition of an algorithm, the sequence of steps that are carried out must have five important features: finiteness, definiteness, input, output, and effectiveness.

Finiteness means that an algorithm is guaranteed to terminate after a finite number of steps as long as the integers are finite in length. When multiplying two integers, for example, the rules of the procedure will cause one to reach a point where no other steps are possible. For large integers, this might take a long time.

Definiteness means that each step in the sequence is clear and unambiguous. A cake-baking algorithm, for example, usually fails in this regard. Different cooks may define a dash of salt in slightly different ways.

Greek mathematician Euclid outlined theories in geometry and logic.

Input means that zero or more values are available to the algorithm before it begins execution. For example, multiplication of two integers begins with the two integers. Long division begins with the divisor and the dividend. Searching the Internet begins with a collection of web pages and addresses.

Output means that one or more quantities are the result of the algorithm's execution of the inputs. In the case of long division, the results are the quotient and remainder. In the case of an Internet search, the result might be a collection of web pages or addresses.

Effectiveness means that each of the steps of the algorithm must be completed in some finite length of time.

All general-purpose digital computers, both past and present, execute algorithms. The algorithm is as central to computer technology as recipes are to the functioning of a gourmet restaurant. Without recipes, whether written on paper or stored in the mind of the chef, nothing gets cooked. Without algorithms, the whole notion of general-purpose digital computers makes little sense and nothing gets computed.

It is difficult to imagine doing multiplication or other tasks without algorithms. For example, try multiplying 3 by 5. Now, without using a calculator, multiply 3,456 by 2,139 without executing a repetitive sequence of steps.

The person or machine executing an algorithm need not be aware of the explanation or mathematical proof of why the algorithm works. Useful computations can be performed mechanically without any understanding of why the sequence of steps is guaranteed to produce the correct result.

History of Algorithms

Algorithms are not new. One of the oldest algorithms known is that of Greek mathematician Euclid (fl. 300 B.C.E.). Euclid's algorithm was designed to compute the greatest common divisor of two positive integers. For example, the greatest common divisor of 40 and 24 is 8 because 8 is the largest integer that divides 40 and 24 evenly. The greatest common divisor of 34,512 and 2,341,200 can also be found by using the repetitive procedure that Euclid's algorithm provides.

In 1937 the British mathematician Alan Turing (1912–1954) wrote a very important paper that introduced a simple mathematical device. His intention, in part, was to provide a formal and rigorous definition of algorithm. This mathematical formalization allowed Turing to prove statements about the capabilities and limitations of algorithms. It turns out, for example, that there are well-defined problems that have no algorithmic solution. The theory of algorithms is still an active area of research.

Algorithm discovery, enhancement, and implementation play increasingly important roles in modern life. New algorithms (sometimes called search engines) are being developed to search the Internet in ways that will allow people to gain useful information from a large and broad collection of data. Hardware algorithms are being improved to speed up the rate of instruction execution in modern machines. Software engineers implement algorithms as computer programs, which are used in an ever-widening variety of devices from hand-held personal data assistants to Internet browsers. SEE ALSO BOOLEAN ALGEBRA; DESIGN TOOLS; PROCEDURAL LANGUAGES; PROGRAMMING.

Michael J. McCarthy

Bibliography

Knuth, Donald E. *The Art of Computer Programming*, 3rd ed. Reading, MA: Addison-Wesley, 1997.

Assembly Language and Architecture

When they hear the term architecture, most people automatically visualize a building. However, architecture can also refer to a computer system. Architecture can also be defined as an interconnected arrangement of readily available components. A computer systems architect takes a collection of parts and organizes them so that they all work together in an optimal way. More than one way exists to put a computer system together from constituent parts, and some configurations will yield a computer system that is better at a particular task than other configurations, which might be better at something else. For example, consider a computer system for use by human users to support activities in managing their work in an office environment—composing documents, storing them, and printing them out. This computer system architecture would be completely different from that of a computer system designed to deal with a task like guiding a rocket in flight.

Even though there are many different ways of structuring computer systems so that they can be matched to the jobs for which they are responsible, there is surprisingly little variation in the nature of the fundamental building blocks themselves. Most conventional computer systems are comprised of a **central processing unit (CPU)**, the part of a computer that performs computations and controls and coordinates other parts of the computer; some memory—both **random access memory (RAM)** and **read only memory (ROM)**; secondary storage to hold other programs and data; and lastly, interconnecting pathways called **buses**. The part that makes a computer different from many other machines is the CPU. Memory devices, storage units, and buses are designed to act in a supporting role, while the principal player is the CPU.

Often people studying the essential nature of a CPU for the first time struggle with some of the concepts because it is not like any other machine they know. A car engine or sewing machine has large moving parts that are easier to analyze and understand, while a CPU does not have moving parts to observe. However, by imagining moving mechanisms, one can gain a better understanding of what happens down inside those black ceramic packages.

The fundamental component of a CPU is an element called a register. A register is an array of flip-flop devices that are all connected and operate in unison. Each flip-flop can store one **binary** bit (a 0 or 1) that the CPU will use. Registers can be loaded up with bits in a parallel operation and they can then shift the bits left or right if needed. Two registers can be used to hold collections of bits that might be added together, for example. In this

central processing unit (CPU) the part of a computer that performs computations and controls and coordinates other parts of the computer

random access memory (RAM) a type of memory device that supports the nonpermanent storage of programs and data; so called because various locations can be accessed in any order (as if at random), rather than in a sequence (like a tape memory device)

read only memory (ROM) a type of memory device that supports permanent storage of programs

buses groups of related signals that form interconnecting pathways between two or more electronic devices

binary existing in only two states, such as "on" or "off," "one" or "zero"

case, corresponding bits in each register would be added together with any carried bits being managed in the expected way—just as would be done by a person manually, using pencil and paper.

Registers tend to vary in size from one processor to another, but are usually eight, sixteen, thirty-two, or sixty-four bits in width. This means that they are comprised of that particular number of flip-flop devices. Some registers are set aside to hold specific types of information, like memory addresses or instructions. These are known as special purpose registers. In addition, there are general purpose registers that hold data that are to be used in the execution of a program.

CPUs contain another set of elements that are very similar to registers, called buffers. Buffers, like registers, are constructed from groups of flip-flops, but unlike registers, the information contained within them does not change. Buffers are simply temporary holding points for information while it is being transferred from one place to another in the CPU, while registers actually hold information as it is being operated on.

The part of the CPU that actually carries out the mathematical operations is called the arithmetic and logic unit (ALU). It is more complex than the registers and handles operations like addition, subtraction, and multiplication, as well as operations that implement logic functions, like logical "or" and "and" functions.

The most complex part of the CPU and the one that requires the most effort in design is the control unit. Registers, buffers, and arithmetic and logic units are all well-documented building blocks, but the control unit is more mysterious. Most manufacturers keep the design of their control units a closely guarded secret, since the control unit manages how the parts of the CPU all work together. This part of the CPU influences the architecture. The control unit is constructed to recognize all of the programming instructions that the CPU is capable of carrying out. When all these instructions are written down in a document that the manufacturer provides, it is known as the instruction set of that particular CPU. All instructions that the processor understands are to be represented as a sequence of bits that will fit into the registers. The control unit responds to the instructions by decoding them, which means that it breaks them down into sub-operations, before getting the ALU and registers to carry them out. Even a relatively simple instruction like subtracting a number in one register from some number in another register, requires the control unit to decode and manage all the steps involved. This would include loading the two registers with the numbers, triggering the ALU to do the subtraction, and finding somewhere to store the difference.

Although it is possible for human users to construct programs as correct sequences of binary bits for the processor to execute, this is very intensive and error-prone. Actually creating a program in this way is known as writing a program in machine code because these sequences of bits are the codes that the CPU machine knows and understands. When programmable computers were first being developed in the mid-twentieth century, this was the only means of programming them. Human programmers were soon looking for a less laborious way of getting the machine code to the CPU. The answer was to represent each of the machine code instructions

ASSEMBLY LANGUAGE LIVES

While almost no commercial software developer would consider writing programs in assembly language because of the extraordinarily intensive labor it requires, assembly language is not dead. There are groups of dedicated programmers collaborating on projects involving assembly language so as to attain the maximum possible run-time performance from the hardware. For example, the "V2 Operating System" is completely implemented in assembly language.

by shortened words, rather than the sequence of bits. For example, a command to the CPU to add two numbers together would be represented as a short human-readable instruction like "ADD A, B" where A and B are the names of two registers. This would be used instead of a confusing list of binary bits and tends to make programming much easier to comprehend and execute. The short words used to represent the instructions are called **mnemonics**. The programmer can write the program in a computer language known as assembly language using mnemonics. Another program called an **assembler** translates the assembly language mnemonics into the machine code, which is what the CPU can understand.

Other computing languages can be developed that are even more amenable to human use. These languages can be translated to assembly language and then to machine code. That way, human programmers can concentrate more on making sure that their programs are correct and leave all of the drudgery of translation to other programs.

No two assembly languages are exactly alike and most differ markedly from one another in their **syntax**. Since assembly language is quite close to the particular instructions that the CPU understands, the programmer must know a great deal about the particular architecture of the processor under study. However, little of this knowledge is directly transferable to processors developed by other manufacturers. The ways in which two different CPUs work might be quite similar, but there will always be some differences in the details that prevent assembly language programs from being transportable to other computers. The advantage of assembly language is that the programs constructed in assembly language are usually much smaller than programs constructed in high-level languages, they require less memory for storage, and they tend to run very fast. Many computer programs that are developed for small-scale but high-market-volume embedded systems environments (like domestic appliances and office equipment) are written in assembly language for these reasons.

Personal computers have their own type of architectures and can be programmed in assembly language. However, assembly language on these computers is usually used only in certain parts of the operating system that need to manage the hardware devices directly. SEE ALSO BINARY NUMBER SYSTEM; CENTRAL PROCESSING UNIT; OBJECT-ORIENTED LANGUAGES; PROCEDURAL LANGUAGES; PROGRAMMING.

Stephen Murray

mnemonics devices or processes that aid one's memory

assembler a program that translates human readable assembly language programs to machine readable instructions

syntax a set of rules that a computing language incorporates regarding structure, punctuation, and formatting

Bibliography

Klingman, Edwin E. *Microprocessor Systems Design*. Upper Saddle River, NJ: Prentice Hall, 1977.

Mano, M. Morris, and Charles R. Kime. *Logic and Computer Design Fundamentals*. Upper Saddle River, NJ: Prentice Hall, 2000.

Milutinovic, Veljko M., ed. *High Level Language Computer Architecture*. Rockville, MD: Computer Science Press, 1989.

Stallings, William. *Computer Organization and Architecture*. Upper Saddle River, NJ: Prentice Hall, 2000.

Tanenbaum, Andrew S., and Albert S. Woodhull. *Operating Systems Design and Implementation*. Upper Saddle River, NJ: Prentice Hall, 1997.

Triebel, Walter A., and Avtar Singh. *The 8088 and 8086 Microprocessors*. Upper Saddle River, NJ: Prentice Hall, 1991.

Uffenbeck, John. *The 8086/8088 Family: Design, Programming and Interfacing*. Upper Saddle River, NJ: Prentice Hall, 1987.

Wakerly, John F. *Digital Design Principles and Practices*. Upper Saddle River, NJ: Prentice Hall, 2000.

Asynchronous and Synchronous Transmission

Asynchronous and synchronous communication refers to methods by which signals are transferred in computing technology. These signals allow computers to transfer data between components within the computer or between the computer and an external network. Most actions and operations that take place in computers are carefully controlled and occur at specific times and intervals. Actions that are measured against a time reference, or a clock signal, are referred to as synchronous actions. Actions that are prompted as a response to another signal, typically not governed by a clock signal, are referred to as asynchronous signals.

Typical examples of synchronous signals include the transfer and retrieval of address information within a computer via the use of an **address bus**. For example, when a processor places an address on the address bus, it will hold it there for a specific period of time. Within this interval, a particular device inside the computer will identify itself as the one being addressed and acknowledge the commencement of an operation related to that address.

In such an instance, all devices involved in ensuing bus cycles must obey the time constraints applied to their actions—this is known as a synchronous operation. In contrast, asynchronous signals refer to operations that are prompted by an exchange of signals with one another, and are not measured against a reference time base. Devices that cooperate asynchronously usually include modems and many network technologies, both of which use a collection of control signals to notify intent in an information exchange. Asynchronous signals, or extra control signals, are sometimes referred to as handshaking signals because of the way they mimic two people approaching one another and shaking hands before conversing or negotiating.

Within a computer, both asynchronous and synchronous **protocols** are used. Synchronous protocols usually offer the ability to transfer information faster per unit time than asynchronous protocols. This happens because synchronous signals do not require any extra negotiation as a prerequisite to data exchange. Instead, data or information is moved from one place to another at instants in time that are measured against the clock signal being used. This signal is usually comprised of one or more high frequency rectangular shaped waveforms, generated by special purpose clock circuitry. These pulsed waveforms are connected to all the devices that operate synchronously, allowing them to start and stop operations with respect to the clock waveform.

In contrast, asynchronous protocols are generally more flexible, since all the devices that need to exchange information can do so at their own natural rate—be these fast or slow. A clock signal is no longer necessary; instead the devices that behave asynchronously wait for the handshaking sig-

address bus a collection of electrical signals used to transmit the address of a memory location or input/output port in a computer

protocols agreed understanding for the sub-operations that make up transactions; usually found in the specification of inter-computer communications

nals to change state, indicating that some transaction is about to commence. The handshaking signals are generated by the devices themselves and can occur as needed, and do not require an outside supervisory controller such as a clock circuit that dictates the occurrence of data transfer.

Asynchronous and synchronous transmission of information occurs both externally and internally in computers. One of the most popular protocols for communication between computers and peripheral devices, such as modems and printers, is the asynchronous RS-232 protocol. Designated as the RS-232C by the Electronic Industries Association (EIA), this protocol has been so successful at adapting to the needs of managing communication between computers and supporting devices, that it has been pushed into service in ways that were not intended as part of its original design. The RS-232C protocol uses an asynchronous scheme that permits flexible communication between computers and devices using byte-sized data blocks each framed with start, stop, and optional parity **bits** on the data line. Other conductors carry the handshaking signals and possess names that indicate their purpose—these include data terminal ready, request to send, clear to send, data set ready, etc.

bits the plural of bit, a single binary digit, 1 or 0—a contraction of Binary digIT; the smallest unit for storing data in a computer

Another advantage of asynchronous schemes is that they do not demand complexity in the receiver hardware. As each **byte** of data has its own start and stop bits, a small amount of drift or imprecision at the receiving end does not necessarily spell disaster since the device only has to keep pace with the data stream for a modest number of bits. So, if an interruption occurs, the receiving device can re-establish its operation with the beginning of the arrival of the next byte. This ability allows for the use of inexpensive hardware devices.

byte a group of eight binary digits; represents a single character of text

Although asynchronous data transfer schemes like RS-232 work well when relatively small amounts of data need to be transferred on an intermittent basis, they tend to be sub-optimal during large information transfers. This is so because the extra bits that frame incoming data tend to account for a significant part of the overall inter-machine traffic, hence consuming a portion of the communication **bandwidth**.

bandwidth a measure of the frequency component of a signal or the capacity of a communication channel to carry signals

An alternative is to dispense with the extra handshaking signals and overhead, instead synchronizing the transmitter and receiver with a clock signal or synchronization information contained within the transmitted code before transmitting large amounts of information. This arrangement allows for collection and dispatch of large batches of bytes of data, with a few bytes at the front-end that can be used for the synchronization and control. These leading bytes are variously called synchronization bytes, flags, and preambles. If the actual communication channel is not a great distance, the clocking signal can also be sent as a separate stream of pulses. This ensures that the transmitter and receiver are both operating on the same time base, and the receiver can be prepared for data collection prior to the arrival of the data.

An example of a synchronous transmission scheme is known as the High-level Data Link Control, or HDLC. This protocol arose from an initial design proposed by the IBM Corporation. HDLC has been used at the data link level in public networks and has been adapted and modified in several different ways since.

A more advanced communication protocol is the Asynchronous Transfer Mode (ATM), which is an open, international standard for the transmission of voice, video, and data signals. Some advantages of ATM include a format that consists of short, fixed cells (53 bytes) which reduce overhead in maintenance of variable-sized data traffic. The versatility of this mode also allows it to simulate and integrate well with legacy technologies, as well as offering the ability to guarantee certain service levels, generally referred to as quality of service (QoS) parameters. SEE ALSO ATM TRANSMISSION; NETWORKS; TELECOMMUNICATIONS.

Stephen Murray

Bibliography

Black, Uyless D. *Data Networks—Concepts, Theory and Practice.* Englewood Cliffs, NJ: Prentice Hall, 1989.

Gates, Stephen C., and Jordan Becker. *Laboratory Automation Using the IBM PC.* Englewood Cliffs, NJ: Prentice Hall, 1989.

Tanenbaum, Andrew S. *Computer Networks*, 2nd ed. Englewood Cliffs, NJ: Prentice Hall, 1989.

Internet Resources

The ATM Forum. <http://www.atmforum.com/>

ATM Transmission

Asynchronous Transfer Mode (ATM) networking is an outgrowth of efforts during the 1970s and 1980s to develop a broadband Integrated Service Digital Network (ISDN) capability. ATM provides a transport mechanism that allows digital data to be efficiently transmitted over high-speed links. Currently, most of the high-speed backbone networks throughout the world use ATM technology. It is also used to some extent as a **local area networking** technology, although the availability of low-cost 100 megabyte and gigabyte Ethernet equipment reduces its appeal for this application.

ATM technology was developed to support a blending of circuit-switching and packet-switching technologies. It is intended to support traffic that requires a fairly constant rate of data delivery, such as voice and video, as well as variable data rate traffic, such as most computer data. ATM is a connection-oriented technology. This means that a fixed path through the network must be established before data can be transmitted. In this respect, ATM is similar to earlier telephone technologies in which physical wires between switching centers were allocated for the duration of each telephone call. Establishing an ATM connection causes a **virtual channel connection** (VCC) or **virtual circuit** (VC) to be created through the ATM network between the end users of the connection.

Virtual channels can be bundled into virtual paths in much the same way that physical wires were bundled into trunk lines. Virtual channels can be either permanent virtual channels (PVCs), established manually and persisting for long periods of time, or switched virtual channels (SVCs), set up dynamically as needed and torn down when the need no longer exists.

Data traveling over a VC are divided into fixed-length packets called cells. Each cell contains forty-eight **bytes** of user data and five bytes of

local area networking using a high speed computer network that is designed for users who are located near each other

virtual channel connection an abstraction of a physical connection between two or more elements (or computers); the complex details of the physical connection are hidden

virtual circuit like a virtual channel connection, a virtual circuit appears to be a direct path between two elements, but is actually a managed collection of physical connections

bytes groups of eight binary digits; each represents a single character of text

header. Three of the header bytes are used to identify the virtual path (eight **bits**) and virtual channel (sixteen bits). One byte is used for header error checking, and the remaining eight bits are used for flow control (four bits), payload type (three bits), and priority (one bit). The small payload size benefits services such as voice and video, where timely and regular delivery are required.

ATM supports five different classes of service:

- Constant bit rate (CBR) allows the desired bit rate to be set when the virtual circuit is established; it is used for services such as uncompressed voice and video;

- Variable bit rate–non-real time (VBR–NRT) allows statistical techniques to be used to optimize network throughput when the rate at which data is available varies;

- Variable bit rate–real time (VBR-RT) is intended for applications such as compressed speech and video, where data delivery must occur at regular intervals;

- Available bit rate (ABR) is used for non-time-critical operations such as bulk file transfers that can adjust their rate of input to use available network capacity; minimum acceptable rates can be specified to ensure some service at all times.

- Unspecified bit rate (UBR) is the residual class with no guaranteed properties; it is used primarily for TCP/IP data traffic.

When an ATM connection is established, a number of parameters may be specified to ensure desired service properties such as acceptable cell loss percentage, maximum delivery time, variation in delivery time, and the variability of variable rate sources, which specify peak and average data rates and the maximum duration of a burst of peak-rate traffic. Not all parameters apply to all classes of service. Variability parameters make no sense for constant-rate connections, for example. The ability to specify both the type of service needed and parameters controlling the quality of service make ATM well suited to deliver data for multimedia applications.

The ATM Forum is a non-profit international organization dedicated to speeding the development and mass-market deployment of ATM broadband communications technologies. The forum is focused on development of interoperability specifications, promotion of industry-wide cooperation, and educational awareness of the technology's capabilities. Among its other activities, the forum defines standards for connecting other networking technologies to ATM systems. This is necessary because few if any applications use the forty-eight byte data cell payloads of ATM as their native format. A number of ATM adaptation layer (AAL) standards exist that specify the methods to be used.

AAL-1 provides for the conversion of voice and video circuits to CBR ATM virtual channels. The use of PVCs emulates fixed physical circuits and is generally wasteful of bandwidth, as few point-to-point circuits carry fixed traffic levels for long periods of time. The use of SVCs for this traffic represents an improvement, but is still far from optimum, because voice traffic is characterized by lengthy periods of silence, such as when one party is listening to the other. AAL-2 provides a VBR–RT trunking mechanism that

bits the plural of bit, a single binary digit, 1 or 0—a contraction of Binary digIT; the smallest unit for storing data in a computer

UNDERSTANDING THE TERMINOLOGY

Here is a key to some of the concepts mentioned in this article: 1) Internet Protocol (IP)—specifies the structure and handling of datagrams sent over the Internet. It is defined in RFC (Request for Comments) 791. 2) Integrated Services Digital Network (ISDN)—is a system of digital telephone connections that allows voice and/or data to be transmitted over digital circuits. 3) Motion Picture Experts Group (MPEG)—an organization that defines standards for video compression. MPEG-1 provides VCR-quality video at a data rate of about two megabits per second; MPEG-2 provides broadcast audio and video using variable data rates. 4) Request for Comments (RFC)—a series of documents that defines standards for the Internet, which are published by the RFC editor of the Internet Engineering Task Force (IETF). 5) Statistical multiplexing—a technique used in digital telephony to increase the capacity of a multi-channel system by not transmitting channels during periods of silence, such as when a party is listening rather than talking.

uses statistical multiplexing techniques to eliminate the cells that would contain silence.

Compressed video in the MPEG-2 format is accommodated by either AAL-1 or CBR AAL-5. The use of AAL-1 provides for forward error correction at the expense of increased bandwidth and delivery delay. It also allows compensation for Cell Delay Variation (CDV) and the replacement of lost cells. AAL-5 does not compensate for CDV or for bit errors, and lost cells cannot be replaced. For these reasons, AAL-1 is recommended when high video quality is needed.

Internet data traffic also travels over ATM circuits. These data typically take the form of Internet Protocol (IP) datagrams that range in length from a few bytes to thousands of bytes. At the lowest levels of the protocol stack, each datagram is treated independently, and delivery is on a best-effort basis where some loss is deemed acceptable. Higher-level **protocols** add additional information to the datagram payloads to ensure that they are delivered reliably and in the proper order, retransmitting lost datagrams as necessary. These functions are provided at the end points and are not part of the network routing structure. It would be possible to set up a VCC for a single datagram and tear it down once the packet had been delivered, but the overheads would be excessive. Instead, ATM connections are established between Internet routers. These connections are treated as equivalent to direct physical links between the routers, with the virtual circuit carrying traffic for multiple users. IP over ATM typically uses UBR AAL-5 connections. A potential problem occurs in mapping IP datagrams into ATM cell payloads, because loss of a single cell necessitates retransmission of the entire datagram. SEE ALSO ASYNCHRONOUS AND SYNCHRONOUS TRANSMISSION; NETWORK DESIGN; TELECOMMUNICATIONS.

John McHugh

protocols agreed understanding for the sub-operations that make up transactions; usually found in the specification of inter-computer communications

Internet Resources

ATM Forum. <http://www.atmforum.com>

"Speaking Clearly with ATM—A Practical Guide to Carrying Voice Over ATM." ATM Forum. <http://www.atmforum.com/index.cfm>

Bardeen, John
1908–1991

Brattain, Walter H.
1902–1987

Shockley, William B.
1910–1989

Inventors of the Transistor

John Bardeen, Walter H. Brattain, and their boss William B. Shockley at AT&T's Bell Labs in Murray Hill, New Jersey, had a job to do. AT&T needed a way to amplify voices, which tended to get "lost" in static when

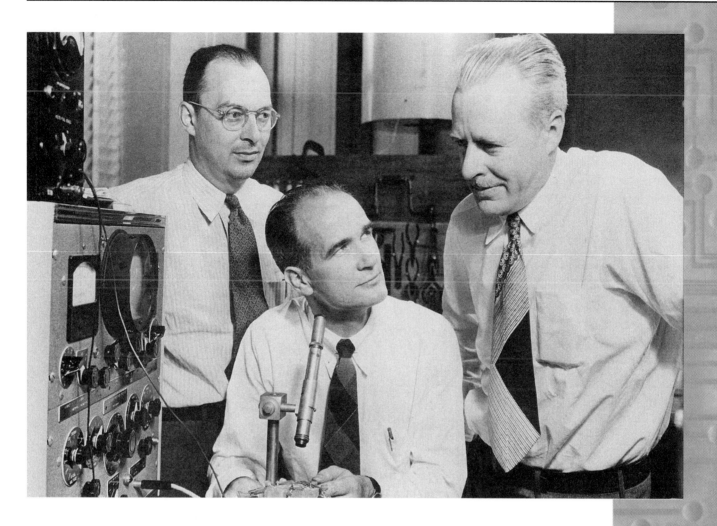

traveling through more than 1,610 kilometers (1,000 miles) of telephone lines. These physicists were intent upon inventing a device to amplify sound in order to replace bulky, fragile, and expensive **vacuum tubes**. In December of 1947, after two years of hard work, they succeeded with a piece of V-wedged **germanium** and a strip of gold foil. Even though the newly termed **semiconductor** transistor was one fiftieth of the size of vacuum tubes and drew one millionth of the electricity, they had no idea their invention would change the face of the twentieth century. The three were awarded a Nobel Prize in Physics in 1956 for their discovery.

John Bardeen

Nicknamed "Whispering John" because of his soft-spoken manner, Bardeen was born in Madison, Wisconsin, on May 23, 1908. He earned a bachelor's degree in electrical engineering in 1928, and his master's degree in 1929, both from the University of Wisconsin. He spent three years researching geophysics at the Gulf Research Laboratories in Pittsburgh, Pennsylvania. Leaving this position, he pursued studies in mathematical physics at Princeton University, receiving his Ph.D. in 1936.

Bardeen then became a junior fellow of the Society of Fellows at Harvard University. An assistant professorship at the University of Minnesota followed. After that, Bardeen worked at the Naval Ordinance Laboratories in Washington, D.C. In the fall of 1943, Bardeen left there to study solid

John Bardeen, William B. Shockley, and Walter H. Brattain changed history with their discoveries concerning the transistor.

vacuum tubes electronic devices constructed of sealed glass tubes containing metal elements in a vacuum; used to control electrical signals

germanium a chemical often used as a high performance semiconductor material; chemical symbol Ge

semiconductor solid material that possesses electrical conductivity characteristics that are similar to those of metals under certain conditions, but can also exhibit insulating qualities under other conditions

OH THE IRONY!

Ironically, the transistor in John Bardeen's automatic garage door malfunctioned as he was preparing to leave for the press conference announcing he had won the Nobel Prize. He had to get a ride to the event.

transistor a contraction of TRANSfer resISTOR; a semiconductor device, invented by John Bardeen, Walter Brattain, and William Shockley, which has three terminals; can be used for switching and amplifying electrical signals

superconductivity the property of a material to pass an electric current with almost no losses; most metals are superconductive only at temperatures near absolute zero

THE TRANSISTOR

The transistor allows the miniaturization of electronic equipment and is regarded as the nerve cell of the Information Age. Its first use was in the telephone switching machine in Englewood, New Jersey, in 1952. By the end of the twentieth century, the transistor could be found everywhere, in supercomputers, televisions, radios, toys, greeting cards, and garage door openers.

state physics at Bell Labs. Soon after the **transistor** discovery, Bardeen and Brattain disputed the implication that their boss, Shockley, was also credited with the invention.

Bardeen left Bell Labs in 1951 to become a professor of electrical engineering of physics at the University of Illinois. Once in Illinois, and along with graduate students L.N. Cooper and J.R. Schrieffer, Bardeen discovered microscopic **superconductivity** during 1956 and 1957. He was awarded a second Nobel Prize in 1972, becoming the third Nobel laureate after Marie Curie and Linus Pauling to win the coveted prize a second time.

Experts in the field have compared Bardeen's gift of physics to Wolfgang Mozart's gift of music. Bardeen influenced almost every field of physics and continued publishing papers in his field until his death. He was bestowed with numerous awards and honors representing national and worldwide recognition for his efforts. Bardeen died on January 30, 1991, at age 82, of a heart attack, in Boston, Massachusetts.

Walter H. Brattain

Brattain was born in Amoy, China, on February 10, 1902. His family moved back to the United States soon after his birth. Brattain grew up on a ranch in Washington. He earned a bachelor's degree from Whitman College in 1924 and a master's degree from the University of Oregon. He earned his Ph.D. at the University of Minnesota. His first post-graduate job was at the National Bureau of Standards, but he soon left there to get back into physics. Bell Labs hired Brattain in 1929. He interrupted his stint at Bell Labs to work on ways to detect submarines during World War II, but returned after the war.

Brattain's partnership with Bardeen, whom Brattain met through his brother, was a great success. Brattain had an excellent reputation as an experimenter. Bardeen, the theoretical physicist, watched the experiments. He would then ask Brattain to modify them to test new theories. Together, the two developed the first transistor, while working under the supervision of Shockley. Because of friction, Brattain eventually transferred out of Shockley's department, but he continued to work at Bell Labs until his retirement in 1967.

Brattain also lectured at Harvard University, the University of Minnesota, and the University of Washington. He was also awarded several honorary degrees. He viewed his accomplishments with modesty, saying he was fortunate to be in the right place at the right time. He was a member of the National Inventors Hall of Fame. Brattain died of Alzheimer's disease in Seattle, Washington, on October 13, 1987, at the age of 85.

William Shockley

Born in London, England, on February 13, 1910, Shockley grew up in Palo Alto, California. He received his bachelor's degree from California Institute of Technology and his Ph.D. from Massachusetts Institute of Technology in 1936. Then he began working at Bell Labs in New Jersey. During World War II, he directed research on anti-submarine technology for the U.S. Navy, but like Brattain, returned to Bell Labs. In 1945 he was named the director of solid state physics for Bell Labs.

Although he was not present at the first successful transistor experimentation with Bardeen and Brattain, in the weeks following that discovery, Shockley contributed a series of insights that contributed to the understanding of semiconductor materials, and developed several theories about another type of amplification device, the junction transistor. He also formulated many of the theories that allowed **silicon** chips to be mass-produced.

In 1956 Shockley left Bell Labs to form his own company, Shockley Semiconductor Laboratories, with the intent of producing silicon transistors. He established his new company near Palo Alto, California. Eventually, Shockley's abrasive management style led to the departure of several of his employees, including Gordon Moore and Robert Noyce, who then went on to establish Fairchild Semiconductors and later, the Intel Corporation. Because so many of these companies were founded in that area, the region became known as **Silicon Valley**.

Later in life, Shockley accepted an appointment at Stanford University, where he formulated several theories about genetics. He withstood substantial criticism regarding his race-based theories, especially since the subject was deemed out of his area of expertise, physics. Bardeen died of prostate cancer on August 12, 1989, at the age of 79. SEE ALSO BELL LABS; DIGITAL LOGIC DESIGN; INTEGRATED CIRCUITS; INTEL CORPORATION; TRANSISTORS; VACUUM TUBES.

Mary McIver Puthawala

silicon a chemical element with symbol Si; the most abundant element in the Earth's crust and the most commonly used semiconductor material

Silicon Valley an area in California near San Francisco, which has been the home location of many of the most significant information technology orientated companies and universities

Bibliography

Anderson, Susan Heller. "Walter Brattain, Inventor, Is Dead." *New York Times*. October 14, 1987.

Moore, Gordon E. "Solid State Physicist: William Shockley—He Fathered the Transistor and Brought the Silicon to Silicon Valley but Is Remembered by Many Only for his Noxious Racial Views." *Time*. March 23, 1999, p. 160.

United Press International. "John Bardeen, at Age 82, Was an Electronics Pioneer." *The Record, Bergen Record Corp*. January 31, 1991.

Internet Resources

John Bardeen. University of Illinois, December 5, 1995. <http://www.physics.uiuc.edu/people/jbardeen.html>

Walter Brattain. ScienCentral, Inc. and the American Institute of Physics, 1999. <http://www.pbs.org/transistor/album1/brattain/brattain2.html>

Bell, Alexander Graham

American Inventor
1847–1922

Alexander Graham Bell, best known as the inventor of the telephone, was born in Edinburgh, Scotland, on March 3, 1847. When he died in Baddeck, Nova Scotia, Canada, on August 2, 1922, he was considered one of the most successful inventors of his time.

Bell's interest in communication was stimulated by unique family circumstances. Both his grandfather and father were accomplished speech experts. Many believe Bell's father was the inspiration for Professor Henry

Onlookers watch with anticipation as Alexander Graham Bell tests out his new invention, the telephone.

visible speech a set of symbols, comprising an alphabet, that "spell" sounds instead of words

Higgins in the 1964 movie *My Fair Lady*. Having a hearing-impaired mother also made Bell conscious of the challenges of being deaf. In 1868 he began using his father's models of **visible speech** to teach deaf students phonetics, a career he resumed after emigrating with his family from Scotland to Brantford, Ontario, Canada, in 1870.

The following year he moved to Boston, Massachusetts, and taught at the Boston School for Deaf Mutes (later called the Horace Mann School). Teaching private students supplemented his income. One of these hearing-impaired students, Mabel Hubbard, later became his wife. Bell's passion for helping the disabled, particularly the sight- and hearing-impaired, remained with him throughout his life.

Although Bell experimented throughout his childhood, it was not until he moved to Boston that his interests in inventing became serious. There he decided to work on developing the multiple telegraph, which would allow several telegraphs to be sent over the same line simultaneously instead of one at a time. He received that patent in 1875. He also became fascinated with the concept of sending varying pitches, mimicking the human voice, over a wire via undulating electrical impulses, then reconstructing the pitches at the other end of the wire. After years of experimenting, he and his assistant, Thomas A. Watson, met with success. Bell's patent application for the telephone was submitted only hours before a rival, Elisha Gray, submitted his version.

In July 1877, the Bell Telephone Company was founded. The shares were divided between Bell, Watson, and two other men. As a wedding gift, Bell gave his wife, Mabel, 5,015 shares of Bell Telephone Company, keeping only ten shares for himself. Bell Telephone rapidly expanded throughout the world. While these shares provided Bell with financial security, they made his wife quite wealthy. During Bell's lifetime, Mabel repeatedly provided grants to fund his research.

The photophone, which Bell invented in 1880, worked like a telephone but used light beams instead of wire. Bell considered it one of his greatest inventions. Although the photophone's success was limited because of the lack of technology at that time, Bell's invention used the same principles as modern **fiber optic** telecommunications.

While living in Mabel's hometown of Washington, D.C. in 1882, Bell became an American citizen. Later he built a second home in Baddeck and called it Beinn Bhreagh. Much of his inventing was completed there.

After winning the Volta prize of France for the telephone, Bell invested the award money in the creation of the Volta Labs at Beinn Bhreagh. This lab produced the flat-disk record and a floating stylus to improve upon Thomas Edison's phonograph. With earnings from those patents, Bell established the Volta Bureau in 1908, which was dedicated to advancing knowledge of the deaf. He also established the American Association for the Promotion of the Teaching of Speech to the Deaf and continued being instrumental in assisting many deaf children, including Helen Keller, to overcome their disabilities.

Bell also became interested in screening children for hearing impairment. After developing the audiometer, he was honored for his accomplishments in that field with the term used for measuring the level of audible sound: the decibel.

Bell's interests were not confined to matters of speech. His father-in-law, Gardiner Hubbard, was a founding member and the first president of the National Geographic Society. When Hubbard died in 1897, Bell accepted the presidency of the society. He then underwrote the hiring of his future son-in-law to edit the association's monthly publication. Bell influenced many trademark features of the society, including the formation of grants for research expeditions. He also encouraged the inclusion of dynamic multiple-color photographs in *National Geographic Magazine*.

Bell also nurtured a fascination with flight. At Beinn Bhreagh, he experimented with kites and eventually developed and patented the tetrahedron, a four-sided triangle used in his aerial experiments. With Mabel's sponsorship, he formed the Aerial Experiment Association (AEA) with four other men. From 1908 to 1909, after the Wright Brothers flew the first

BELL'S RIVAL: ELISHA GRAY

Although most people have heard of Alexander Graham Bell, the name of rival inventor Elisha Gray (1835–1901) is not as recognizable. After growing up on a farm in Ohio, Gray worked as a carpenter to support his studies at Oberlin College, where he became interested in electrical devices. Like Bell, Gray worked on improvements to the telegraph. Bell beat Gray by only two hours when filing the patent for the telephone. Gray went on to create the TelAutograph, which transmitted writing or drawings. He demonstrated his invention at the World's Fair in Chicago in 1893. Shortly before his death, Gray began tests of an underwater signaling device.

fiber optic transmission technology using long, thin strands of glass fiber; internal reflections in the fiber assure that light entering one end is transmitted to the other end with only small losses in intensity; used widely in transmitting digital information

airplane, Bell and his associates built four airplanes. With those machines, the AEA gained patents for improving airplane designs. The AEA then sought to build a craft that could take off and land on water. In 1918 this led to the patent for the fastest watercraft of its time, the hydrofoil HD4, which reached speeds of 114 kilometers (71 miles) per hour.

In tribute to Bell's life and accomplishments, telephones across the United States were silenced for one minute during his funeral in Baddeck in 1922. SEE ALSO BELL LABS; INTERNET; TELECOMMUNICATIONS.

Mary McIver Puthawala

Bibliography

Bruce, Robert V. *Alexander Graham Bell and the Conquest of Solitude*. Ithaca, NY: Cornell University Press, 1990.

Matthews, Tom L. *Always Inventing*. Washington D.C.: National Geographic Society, 1999.

Pasachoff, Naomi. *Alexander Graham Bell: Making Connections*. Oxford: Oxford Press, 1996.

Boole, George

English Mathematician
1815–1864

George Boole was a mathematician whose work in symbolic logic laid new foundations for modern algebra, and set the stage for contemporary computer circuitry and database search strategy **syntax**. Boole was born in Lincolnshire, England, in 1815, and he died December 8, 1864, in County Cork, Ireland. He received little in the way of formal education, but he was a dedicated reader and self-taught student of languages and mathematics.

At the age of sixteen, Boole became an assistant teacher for elementary school students. By age twenty, Boole had started his own school. Dismayed at what he considered to be inadequate materials available to teach mathematics to young students, Boole undertook the serious study of mathematics on his own. In subsequent years he wrote several seminal papers on the relationship between logic and mathematics. Despite his lack of university training and connections, he managed to get his works published in *The Cambridge Mathematical Journal*, eventually winning the professional respect of other mathematicians and logicians. In 1854 he published *An Investigation of the Laws of Thought, on Which Are Founded the Mathematical Theories of Logic and Probabilities*. Considered his most influential work, this text provides the foundation for what has become known as **Boolean algebra**. Other significant works include the *Treatise on Differential Equations* (1859) and the *Treatise on the Calculus of Finite Differences* (1860).

Boole was a deeply religious man. He was influenced by the works of Sir Isaac Newton, Joseph LaGrange, and Pierre-Simon Laplace, as well as the philosopher Gottfried Wilhelm Leibnitz. Also a family man, Boole married Mary Everest, niece of Sir George Everest, for whom Mt. Everest was named. Boole and Everest married in 1855 and eventually had five daughters: Mary, Margaret, Alicia, Lucy, and Ethel.

George Boole.

syntax a set of rules that a computing language incorporates regarding structure, punctuation, and formatting

Boolean algebra a system developed by George Boole that deals with the theorems of undefined symbols and axioms concerning those symbols

Boole died of pneumonia at the age of forty-nine, when Alicia was four years old and his youngest daughter was an infant. His widow, Mary Everest Boole, made significant contributions to the field of mathematics herself, carrying on her late husband's work of helping children learn mathematics. She described her work as that of a "mathematical psychologist," and focused on understanding how children use reason and logic, physical activity, and subconscious processes to learn mathematics.

Boolean Legacies

Many mathematicians consider Boole's most significant contribution to be his Boolean algebra, which articulates a theory of relations. Boolean algebra furnishes laws of possibility among propositions. In the 1940s, early computer pioneer Claude Shannon (1916–2001) applied Boole's principles to electrical wiring and developed a mathematical theory of communication, which led to the connection between the work of George Boole and modern computer circuitry, which Boole of course could not have anticipated.

Boolean algebra is also at the center of symbolic reasoning, which is widely applied in the formation of database search statements. Often called Boolean Logic, Boole's explanation of logical operators of thought provides the foundation of computer search engine syntax. Boolean "operators" are enlisted in search statements to help online searchers to restrict or expand their search results. Boolean Logic separates concepts from each other and examines their properties relative to each other. These properties can be demonstrated through **Venn diagrams** and **syllogistic statements**.

The pragmatics of Boolean Logic are found in AND, OR, and NOT statements. Unlike in typical mathematics, AND statements limit results. For example, $2 + 3 = 5$. However, in Boolean Logic, the combination of Concept A and Concept B yields only results that contain *both* A and B. Thus, the resulting set number is less than either of the two concepts viewed singularly. This concept is often difficult for database searchers to learn to use. Accustomed to the numerical principle that adding units together yields greater results, the most common mistake of novice online searchers is to add too many variables to their search syntax, believing that more variables will provide more results. In fact, the opposite is true.

To get more results with a Boolean search, the OR statement is needed. OR statements can be tricky, however, depending on where they appear in the search statement. For example, A OR B AND C can be interpreted as (A OR B) AND C, which is likely what the searcher intends. If the search engine interprets the statement as A OR (B AND C), very different results are given. Properly placed parentheses are recommended in virtually all cases where the OR operator is employed.

The NOT operator is also a limiter, in that it restricts the search by omitting results that contain the NOT word or concept. For example, A AND B NOT C will retrieve records that contain A and B but exclude all records that contain C, even if they contain A and B.

As is evident from Boolean operators, relationships among objects or ideas may be governed by a logic that is not necessarily congruent with conventional human reasoning. What may be rational in numbers, e.g.

LIKE FATHER, LIKE DAUGHTER

Alicia Boole Stott continued in the family tradition of mathematics. She later built a reputation in the field of mathematics for her study of the visualization of geometric figures.

Venn diagrams diagrams used to demonstrate the relationships between sets of objects

syllogistic statements the essential tenets of western philosophical thought, based on hypotheses and categories

addition, does not "add up" when applied to the use of the Boolean "AND" in a search statement.

Boole was drawn to explore the depths of logical and mathematical reasoning, and the ways in which human thought comprehends the relationships among ideas. In ways Boole could never have foreseen, his intellectual interests provided the foundation for future generations of logicians and mathematicians whose work is enhanced by the computing and database searching technology people take for granted today. SEE ALSO BOOLEAN ALGEBRA; DIGITAL LOGIC DESIGN.

Tom Wall

Bibliography

Gasser, James, ed. *A Boole Anthology: Recent and Classical Studies in the Logic of George Boole.* Boston: Kluwer Academic Publishers, 2000.

MacHale, Desmond. *George Boole: His Life and Work.* Dublin: Boole Press, 1983.

Internet Resources

O'Connor, John J., and Edmund F. Robertson. "George Boole." Web site of the School of Mathematics and Statistics, University of St. Andrews, Scotland. <http://www-history.mcs.st-andrews.ac.uk/history/Mathematicians/Boole.html>

Voss, Natalie D. "George Boole." *Jones Telecommunications and Multimedia Encyclopedia.* <www.digitalcentury.com/encyclo/update/boole.html>

Boolean Algebra

In 1847 George Boole (1815–1864), an English mathematician, published one of the works that founded symbolic logic. His combination of ideas from classical logic and algebra resulted in what is called Boolean algebra.

Using variables and symbols, Boole designed a language for describing and manipulating logical statements and determining if they are true or not. The variables stand for statements that are either true or false. The symbols +, * and − represent *and*, *or*, and *not* and are equivalent to the symbols ^, ∨, and − used in the truth tables in logic. Although truth tables use T and F (for true and false respectively) to indicate the state of the sentence, Boolean algebra uses 1 and 0.

The relationship between Boolean algebra, set algebra, logic, and **binary** arithmetic has given Boolean algebra a central role in the development of electronic digital computers. Besides its many applications in the design of computers, it forms the foundation of information theory.

Truth Tables

Boolean algebra is based on propositions, which are non-ambiguous sentences that can be either true or false. One can combine these propositions in a variety of ways by using the connectives *and* and *or*, or one can negate them by preceding them with *not*. The results of these operations on propositions are dictated by the rules of Boolean algebra. For example, if one says: "I will buy green mittens," then she is actually saying that she will buy mittens and those mittens will be green. Therefore the properties of "mittens" and "green" will have to be present in all her "hand-covering" purchases. This will exclude gloves and all non-green mittens. How does this work out

binary existing in only two states, such as "on" or "off," "one" or "zero"

using truth tables? Let A represent "mittens," B represent "green." Figure 1(a) shows how the statement "mittens and green" is represented using truth tables, while Figure 1(b) shows the same statement using Boolean algebra.

A	B	A ^ B
T	T	T
T	F	F
F	T	F
F	F	F

(a)

A	B	A * B
1	1	1
1	0	0
0	1	0
0	0	0

(b)

Figure 1. The statement "mittens and green" is represented using truth tables (a) and Boolean algebra (b).

What the tables indicate is that if an item does not possess both the quality of being a mitten and the quality of being green, then it will be discarded. Only those that satisfy both qualities will be selected.

On the other hand, if one says: "I will buy gloves or mittens," then he is actually saying that he will buy mittens, or gloves, or some combination. This means that he will have a great assortment of "hand-covering" garments. Let A represent "mittens" and B represent "gloves." Figure 2(a) shows how the statement "mittens or gloves" is represented using truth tables, while Figure 2(b) shows the same statement using Boolean algebra.

A	B	A v B
T	T	T
T	F	T
F	T	T
F	F	F

(a)

A	B	A + B
1	1	1
1	0	1
0	1	1
0	0	0

(b)

Figure 2. The statement "mittens or gloves" is represented using truth tables (a) and Boolean algebra (b).

What the tables indicate is that an item will be selected if it possesses both qualities of mitten and glove, or possesses only one quality, either glove or mitten. Only those that satisfy neither quality will be discarded—for example, all red socks.

One can also say: "I will buy something to cover my hands, but not mittens." Let A represent "mittens." Figure 3(a) shows how the statement "not mittens" is represented using truth tables, while Figure 3(b) shows the same statement using Boolean algebra.

Figure 3. The statement "not mittens" is represented using truth tables (a) and Boolean algebra (b).

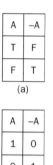

A	–A
T	F
F	T

(a)

A	–A
1	0
0	1

(b)

The tables indicate that if an item is a mitten then its negation, –A, represents a non-mitten—for example, a glove or a sock.

Computer Design

Boolean algebra can be applied to the design and simplification of complex circuits present in computers because computer circuits are two-state devices: they can be either off or on. This corresponds to the general representation of Boolean algebra with two elements, 0 and 1. To show how this works, take a look at two simple circuits, "and," and "or," which correspond to the first two sets of tables presented earlier. These simple circuits consist of a power source—a battery connected by a wire to a destination—and a lamp with two switches that control the flow of electricity. The position of a switch either allows electricity to flow from the power source to the destination, or stops it. For example, if the switch is up, or open, then electricity does not flow, and this condition is represented by a 0. However, if the switch is down, or closed, the electricity will flow, and this is represented by 1.

Figure 4 shows the diagram of a two-switch series circuit, where electricity will flow from the source to the destination only if both switches are closed. This diagram represents the *and* condition of Boolean algebra.

Figure 4. Example of a series circuit. In order for the electricity to flow from the battery to the lamp, both switches must be down or closed. This represents the "and" condition.

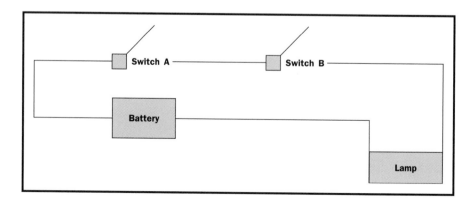

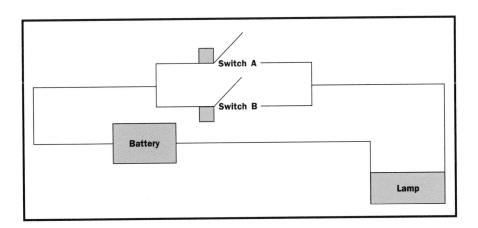

Figure 5. Example of a parallel circuit. In order for the electricity to flow from the battery to the lamp, at least one of the switches must be down or closed. This represents the "or" condition.

A circuit where electricity flows whenever at least one of the switches is closed is known as a parallel circuit. This corresponds to the *or* condition of Boolean algebra. Figure 5 shows the diagram of a two-switch parallel circuit.

To represent the *not* condition, one must remember that in this system a switch has only two possible positions, open or closed. Its complement is a switch that will have the opposite position. For example, if switch A is open, its complement will be closed and vice versa. Logic designers can use these diagrams to plan complex computer circuits that will perform the needed functions for a specific machine.

Information Theory

Boolean algebra is used in information theory because almost all search engines allow someone to enter queries in the form of logical expressions. The operator *and* is used to narrow a query whereas *or* is used to broaden it. The operator *not* is used to exclude specific words from a query. For example, if one is looking for information about "privacy in computer environments," she could phrase her query as "computer *and* privacy," or "computer *or* privacy," or even "computer *and* privacy *not* mainframes." The amount of information received from each query will be different.

The first query will retrieve fewer documents because it will only select those that contain both terms. The second will retrieve many documents because it will select those that contain "computer," those that contain "privacy," and also those that contain both terms. The last query will retrieve documents that contain both "privacy" and "computer," while anything containing the term "mainframe" will be discarded.

When using search engines, one must realize that each one will access its database differently. Typically the same search performed in more than one database will not return the same result. To do a thorough search, one must become familiar with a few of the different search engines and understand their major features, such as Boolean logic and truncation. In addition, one must check the search engine's documentation often because it can change frequently. SEE ALSO ALGORITHMS; BINARY NUMBER SYSTEM; BOOLE, GEORGE; DECISION SUPPORT SYSTEMS; DIGITAL LOGIC DESIGN.

Ida M. Flynn

Bibliography

McCullough, Robert N. *Mathematics for Data Processing*, 2nd ed. Englewood, CO: Morton Publishing Co., 2001.

Warring, Ronald H. *Logic Made Easy*. Summit, PA: TAB Books, Inc., 1985.

Whitesitt, J. Eldon. *Boolean Algebra and Its Applications*. New York: Dover Publications, Inc., 1995.

Bridging Devices

local area network (LAN) a high-speed computer network that is designed for users who are located near each other

The need for bridging devices arises with the need to communicate with computers located beyond a particular **local area network (LAN)**. Although all the clients (computers) attached to a LAN need not be located in the same room, there are limitations on the distance between clients as well as on the number of clients that can be attached to a single network segment. Bridging devices are used to overcome these limitations and facilitate communication among machines on different floors, different buildings, different cities, and different countries.

Bridging devices are available in a variety of configurations to interconnect multiple local area network segments. The choice of bridging device depends on distance, traffic volume, and complexity of the communication pathways between sites. Commonly used bridging devices include repeaters, bridges, routers, and gateways.

Repeaters

The simplest bridging device is known as a repeater. As messages travel over increasing distances, their signals become weak and distorted. A repeating device extends the distance over which clear communication can take place by regenerating messages. For example, repeaters can be used to facilitate communication among computers in a LAN that spans several floors of a building.

The LAN cable for each floor is connected to a repeater, which is sometimes called a hub. Additional cabling connects a repeater to other repeaters on adjacent floors. As messages travel from floor to floor, their signal strength is maintained because the repeaters regenerate them.

Repeaters are limited as bridging devices because they operate at the physical network layer and simply pass on all the bits that they receive. Repeaters do not distinguish between messages intended for clients on the same floor and those intended for clients on different floors. Repeaters also retransmit messages with errors and signals resulting from collisions when clients attempt to send simultaneous messages. If traffic volume is heavy, performance on the network will deteriorate.

Bridges

A device known as a bridge is used to reduce network traffic by filtering messages. Bridges, unlike repeaters, do not retransmit every signal that they receive. Bridges operate at the data link layer of the networking hierarchy. They filter messages using the hardware or MAC (medium access control) addresses of the PCs attached to the local network. A bridge retransmits

NETWORK OF NETWORKS

The Internet is often described as a network of networks. Bridging devices are the connectors that join one part of the larger network to another. Bridging devices differ in sophistication of the connection they provide, but they all contribute to the rapid movement of data that is the key to the Information Age.

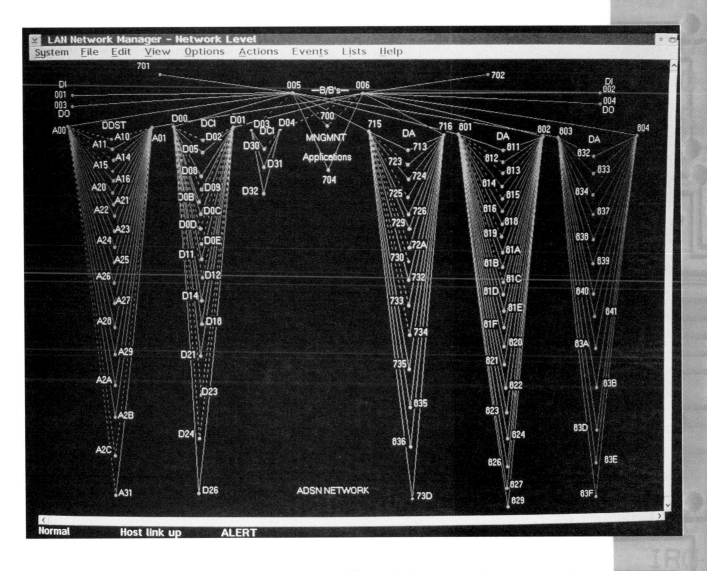

A computer screen shows the local area network (LAN) bridges that link units in a vast government agency system in the Washington, D.C. area.

only correct messages with destination addresses that fall outside the network segment from which the message originated.

A bridge, for example, can be used to connect LAN segments located in two different buildings. Although the two network segments function as a single LAN, the bridge limits traffic between buildings to messages involving client PCs actually located in different buildings. Performance for the entire LAN will be better because a pair of clients in each building will be able to exchange messages without interfering with communications in the other building. Network designers use bridges to improve performance on busy LANs by dividing the network into segments connected by bridges and assigning computers that frequently exchange messages to the same segment.

To filter messages, bridges must know the location of the client computers attached to their network segments. When a bridge receives a message, it recovers the hardware address of the sending computer and adds it to a table that associates computers with network segments. After each PC on the network has sent one message, the bridge will have a complete record of PCs and their locations.

This complete table of computers and location addresses is crucial to the operation of the bridge. Bridges compare the destination addresses in messages to their tables to determine when to retransmit a message. If the destination address belongs to the segment over which the message arrived, the destination computer has already received the message and the bridge does not need to forward the message. If the destination address does not belong to the segment over which the message arrived, the bridge will forward a copy of the message to the other network segment.

The great advantage of a bridge is that it is a plug-and-play device that requires no set-up by a network administrator. Bridges are very effective for small networks involving just a few segments. As the number of segments in a network increases, redundant multiple paths between distant LAN segments become an important issue. Redundancy in a network means alternate pathways between network locations are available in case of a failure or congestion in one part of a network. Unfortunately, the rules by which bridges operate restrict the effective pathways between network segments. Consequently, with an increase in both the number of segments in an organization's network and the need to make connections across networks (e.g., the Internet), bridges become less effective than routers as the bridging device of choice.

Routers

A router differs from a bridge because it operates at the network layer of the network model. The addresses used by routers are network addresses such as the familiar "dotted-decimal" addresses found on the Internet. Each message packet must specify a network destination address (e.g., 124.26.112.98). In a complex network with multiple alternate paths between locations, the primary task of the routers on a network is to use the destination address of a message to determine the best path between locations for a message to follow.

Packets traveling through a network are passed from router to router until they reach a router that is attached to the same local network as the destination. When a packet arrives at a router, the router first determines if it is addressed to a device on its local network. If not, the router chooses the next router to receive the packet in its progress across the network.

The data that a router will use to make its forwarding decisions are contained in a routing table. The routing table contains a list of destination addresses and the "next-hop" router appropriate for each of those destinations. The minimum set of entries in a routing table includes an address to identify devices on the router's local network and a default address for forwarding all other packets. More complex tables present alternative pathways so that a router can choose to forward a message along the most direct, the least congested, or the fastest pathway. Routers in a network are able to exchange data to update their routing tables with information about failures, congestion, or new paths in the network.

Gateways

All the routers on the Internet operate according to the **Internet Protocol (IP)**. A different kind of bridging device, called a gateway, is needed to interconnect two networks that use different network layer protocols. When an IP router communicates with an adjacent IP router, it is only necessary to package the data for the shared network protocol in a data-link layer

Internet Protocol (IP) a method of organizing information transfer between computers; the IP was specifically designed to offer low-level support to Transmission Control Protocol (TCP)

frame. However, when an IP router needs to communicate with, for example, an IBM SNA router, it will also be necessary to replace the IP network data with appropriate SNA network data.

The task of translating network layer descriptions for different networks is performed by a gateway. The gateway receives messages from one network, removes the network layer information, adds network layer information formatted for the second network, packages the message in a data-link layer frame and forwards it to the second network. SEE ALSO E-COMMERCE; INTERNET; NETWORKS; TELECOMMUNICATIONS; WORLD WIDE WEB.

Wesley Jamison

Bibliography

Comer, Douglas. *Computer Networks and Internets*, 2nd ed. Upper Saddle River, NJ: Prentice Hall, 1999.

FitzGerald, Jerry, and A. Dennis. "High-Speed LAN and Backbone Networks." In *Business Data Communications and Networking*, 6th ed. New York: Wiley, 1999.

Kurose, James, and K. Ross. *Computer Networking: A Top-Down Approach Featuring the Internet*. Reading, MA: Addison-Wesley, 1999.

Cache Memory

Cache memory refers to a fast storage buffer in the **central processing unit (CPU)** of a computer, allowing the computer to store data temporarily, making information retrieval faster and more efficient. By storing often-used data in a special memory chip rather than accessing the memory of the computer for the same information each time, cache memory helps maximize the efficiency of the CPU.

central processing unit (CPU) the part of a computer that performs computations and controls and coordinates other parts of the computer

bus a group of related signals that form an interconnecting pathway between two or more electronic devices

Typically, in order to execute a command, the processor in a computer places a numeric address for the instruction it is about to execute on the address **bus**. Once the memory subsystem senses the address, it deposits the code representing that instruction onto the data bus. The processor then collects this code from the data bus, interpreting it as a command of some sort. The execution of this instruction may involve several operations similar to the one that enabled the processor to fetch the instruction in the first place. For example, the processor may discover that the instruction it just fetched requires it to get some data from memory and then add that data to a register. Whatever the nature of the instruction, once it is complete, the processor must repeat the instruction fetching cycle for the next instruction in the program it is currently executing.

The rate at which the processor can execute instructions partly determines its perceived performance—therefore, it would help tremendously if the next instruction that the processor was going to fetch was located or retrieved for it automatically whilst it was busy executing the previous one. Cache memory allows the processor to do exactly that.

Although the simultaneous functionality discussed earlier introduces a little more complexity into the system, the benefits are significant, and most modern processors incorporate a small amount of memory within them. This block of memory, also called a cache memory, is often built into the processor core itself. Cache memory is managed by another unit, called the

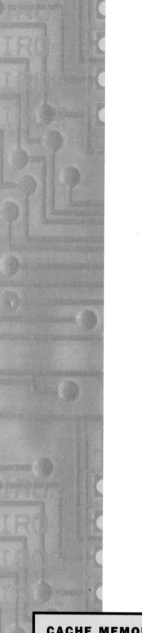

cache controller, and is implemented from high-speed, and therefore comparatively expensive, memory devices.

The intent is to increase the average speed at which a program can be executed. This is accomplished when the cache controller tries to pre-fetch blocks of instructions that are to be executed by the processor, storing them in its high-speed cache. Because the instructions are now instantly available, the processor need not wait for each instruction to be fetched in sequence before execution.

Despite their advantages, caches are not completely foolproof. Since the cache cannot know with complete certainty which instruction the processor is going to need next, it selects groups of instructions that happen to be in memory, and close to the last instruction that was executed. The cache relies on a correlation that suggests that when processors execute programs, the instructions tend to be fetched in order in memory. However, it is quite possible that the cache controller will, on some occasions, fetch blocks of instructions from the wrong place. There are several reasons why this would happen. For example, the processor may have just executed an instruction that commands it to jump to another part of the program, which might be quite distant from the current point of execution. Whenever the cache controller correctly predicts the next block of instructions needed by the processor, it is referred to as a cache hit. When the converse happens though, it is described as a miss.

A number of factors can affect the hit rate, and therefore the average speed, of program execution. For example, if the cache is large, it statistically increases the chances of it retrieving the correct pieces of information. However, it also increases the cost and complexity of the cache since it is now somewhat more difficult to manage. Caches tend to work very well when the programs that are being executed are structured as a straightforward sequence of instructions. This can be accomplished by having development tools such as compilers and interpreters take on the responsibility of organizing the memory image.

In addition to blocks of instructions, caches are applied with equal validity to blocks of data needed by programs. Many modern processors incorporate separate instruction and data caches of various sizes, depending on which combination helps optimize the performance of the processor. On a larger scale, but employing exactly the same principle, are data caches for fixed disks and for servers in a distributed network. It is possible to attach special cache units to disk drive controllers. These cache units attempt to speed up the average access time of the disk by predicting what portions might be needed next, pre-loading these into memory set aside on the disk controller based on currently accessed file(s). Similarly, when client computers are accessing a World Wide Web (WWW) server, they might store on their own disk a collection of documents and images that have been recently accessed. Then, if these documents are browsed again soon afterward, they can be reloaded from the local disk cache rather than transferring them from the server again.

Whatever the scale and implementation, caching is a statistically based approach that tries to enhance the average performance of a system by attempting to anticipate the information that will be required, and having it

CACHE MEMORIES IN NEXT GENERATION CPUs

Intel Corporation of Santa Clara, California, has indicated that there will be three levels of cache memories within their "Madison" Itanium processor, and the largest cache block will be a staggering 6 megabytes in size. This amount of memory constituted approximately the entire memory subsystem of popular microcomputers of only a decade earlier.

ready ahead of time. SEE ALSO CENTRAL PROCESSING UNIT; MAINFRAMES; MEMORY; MINICOMPUTERS; SUPERCOMPUTERS; WORLD WIDE WEB.

Stephen Murray

Bibliography

Baron, Robert J., and L. Higbie. *Computer Architecture*. Reading, MA: Addison-Wesley, 1992.

Beck, Michael, H. Bohme, M. Dziadzka, U. Kunitz, R. Magnus, and D. Verworner. *Linux Kernel Internals*, 2nd ed. Harlow, England: Addison-Wesley, 1998.

Hayes, John P. *Computer Architecture and Organization*. Tokyo: McGraw-Hill, 1979.

Laplante, Philip A. *Real-time Systems Design and Analysis—An Engineer's Handbook*. New York: IEEE Press, 1993.

Stone, Harold S. *High-Performance Computer Architecture*, 3rd ed. Reading, MA: Addison-Wesley, 1993.

Cellular Technology

The cellular phone is the latest in a long line of mobile, portable, and wireless technologies extending back to the 1930s. Military forces were among the first to use mobile radio communications. Early mobile radio equipment for the military involved large transmitters aboard military vehicles with huge antennas and high transmitter power. The large, robust military vehicles were capable of accommodating the massive, power-hungry equipment.

The first use of radio communications for civilian land vehicles was primarily by police departments. The earliest systems were one-way, where the dispatcher could broadcast to all cars the location and nature of a problem. There was no return communication and thus no verification of a response to the problem, but it was better than nothing.

The first successful installation of a large two-way police radio system was for the Connecticut State Police in 1939. This system used a newly invented type of radio called **frequency modulation** (FM). This system set the standard for mobile radio for many years.

Two-way radio installed in automobiles inspired the idea for a mobile telephone service. The first police radio was a **simplex,** or one-way, system, meaning that the mobile unit could only receive communications. The two-way police radio was a half **duplex** system in which both the mobile and base units could transmit and receive but not at the same time. Proper radio procedures were required, such as saying "over" to invite the other station to transmit, and using radio call signs. The frequency was shared by a number of users and conversations were far from private.

Ideally, a mobile telephone is a full duplex system where both stations transmit and receive simultaneously and the channel is not shared. The first full duplex mobile telephone systems were installed in large cities in the 1950s. The systems used base stations connected to the public switched telephone network (PSTN) and had a range of 60 to 80 kilometers (37 to 50 miles). Mobile telephones had a telephone number, rang like a normal telephone, and were full duplex. Because of the large area covered by the base station and the limited number of available channels or radio frequencies, the mobile phone system (MPS) quickly reached full capacity. Priority for

frequency modulation a technique whereby a signal is transformed so that it is represented by another signal with a frequency that varies in a way related to the original signal

simplex uni-directional communication over a single communication channel

duplex simultaneous two-directional communication over a single communication channel

MAKING COMMUNICATION POSSIBLE

Providing reliable communications for millions of subscribers from portable handsets is not a simple feat. Cellular technology uses sophisticated technologies to achieve this goal.

new subscribers was given to physicians and others needing emergency communications, and the waiting lists were very long.

A Texas rancher, Tom Carter, played an important role in mobile telephone history. Carter had made a simple device that would allow his private business two-way radio system to be used with his office telephone when he was out on the ranch. The telephone company refused to allow Carter to connect his device to the PSTN and Carter took the case to court. Although it took fifteen years, the Federal Communications Commission (FCC) in 1968 ruled in favor of Carter in the landmark Carterfone decision. The action opened the PSTN to radio connections as well as those for computer data and other devices.

In the 1970s Bell Telephone Laboratories began investigating a replacement system for the MPS. After the Carterfone decision, competitors were gearing up to use new technologies to provide alternative mobile telephone service. The FCC reassigned a number of under-used ultra-high frequency (UHF) television channels for a new, advanced mobile phone system (AMPS). The AMPS had considerably more channels than the older MPS and had two sets—one for the local telephone company, and a second set for a competitor.

The concept of the AMPS was to increase the reuse of the communications channels. Frequency reuse occurs when two stations occupy the same frequency or channel but are separated by such a distance that they do not interfere. The MPS used high antennas to provide a 60 to 80 kilometer (37 to 50 mile) range, but no two base stations could be closer than about 150 kilometers (93 miles) to avoid interference. In the AMPS, the height of the base station antenna and the transmitter power are limited so the range of a cell is only about 11 to 15 kilometers (7 to 9 miles). In addition, the base station controls the transmitter powers of the mobile units. This ensures that the least amount of power is used, which limits the interference and allows the channels to be reused by another cell only 20 to 30 kilometers (12 to 19 miles) away.

The cells are interconnected with wire lines or microwave radio links. When a user leaves the coverage of one cell and enters another, the new cell provides continuing communications, a process called handoff. The cell system must determine which cell is most capable of picking up the user, acquire that user, and connect the user to the correct land line. All of this is invisible to the user.

algorithms rules or procedures used to solve mathematical problems—most often described as sequences of steps

The handoff process involves a number of **algorithms** using various data from the mobile telephone. First, every cell phone handset has a digital address that is continuously transmitted. Any cell site, or base station, can positively identify signals being received even though many of the received signals are not communicating with that cell site. Cell sites continually communicate with neighboring cell sites and compare the signal quality of the mobile units being received. If a particular mobile telephone unit has a superior signal in a neighboring cell site, the handoff process begins. This has to be done with care, as certain situations can cause a signal to fade temporarily in one site while improving at another, perhaps only for a few seconds. If a handoff is initiated prematurely, it will be necessary to restore the mobile phone to the original cell site quickly.

In addition to determining which cell site is capable of providing the best communications to the mobile phone, the computer system must also switch the land lines and keep a tally of the airtime for billing purposes.

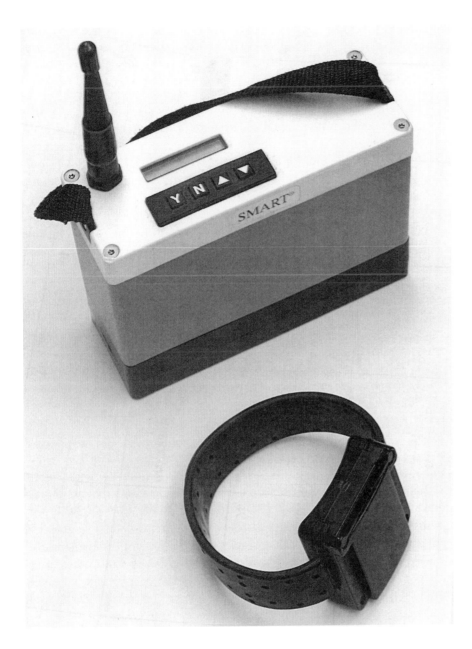

Cellular technology is also featured in these SMART system components, which are used by authorities in various states to keep track of sexual and domestic violence offenders. The ankle cuff and cellular transmitter box are used in conjunction with global positioning to report the location of the wearer.

Early cell telephone systems only allowed customers to use the system to which the user was a subscriber. Later, roaming, or using another company's cell system, was initiated. This came with very high prices and complicated billing procedures. As the cellular mobile phone system became financially successful, more cell sites were constructed, and now most of the continental United States has cell coverage. Proposed regulations would require the cell system to determine the location of a handset in emergency situations. Agreements between cellular telephone companies simplified roaming, and a customer can now travel through much of the country with no loss of service. This is called a seamless system.

AMPS uses frequency modulation (FM), which is the same technology used in the very first mobile two-way radio in 1939. FM has performed well for many years but is inferior to many digital systems. These digital systems opened up the way for more sophisticated applications—especially non-voice communications such as paging, e-mail, and Internet services. Many mobile telephones became not just telephones but personal communications systems or PCSs.

It is important for a global, seamless, wireless cell phone system to have well thought-out standards to which the cell sites adhere. With the advent of the more sophisticated digital cell systems, a large number of new standards have appeared. These include a European standard, global system for mobile (GSM), code division multiple access (CDMA), time division multiple access (TDMA), and others. The complexity of modern handsets has increased because of the need to operate with a number of different standards. The modern cellular telephone is a sophisticated, cost-effective, and worldwide communications device and promises to become more capable in the future. SEE ALSO CELL PHONES; NETWORKS; TELECOMMUNICATIONS; WIRELESS TECHNOLOGY.

Albert D. Helfrick

Bibliography

Kellogg, Steven, ed. *The Comprehensive Guide to Wireless Technology.* Fuquay-Varina, NC: APDG Publishing, 2000.

Stetz, Penelope. *The Cell Phone Handbook: Everything You Wanted to Know About Wireless Telephony (But Didn't Know Who or What to Ask).* Newport, RI: Aegis Publishing Group, 1999.

Central Processing Unit

Computers exist as a collection of interrelated components functioning together under the control of a central processor known as the central processing unit (CPU). The CPU is responsible for manipulating data and coordinating the activities of the computer's other physical components, including memory and peripherals. Instructions gathered from input interfaces are executed at the CPU, and the results delivered to output interfaces. The CPU, therefore, functions as the heart of the computer, facilitating all data processing activity.

The central processing unit is composed of several internal components needed to retrieve, store, and calculate data in a controlled fashion. Instructions enter the CPU from a computer's **random access memory (RAM)** through the **bus**. The bus is a grouping of wires that provide a physical medium for data transport between components. The instructions are decoded by the CPU's control unit, which interprets the data and sends control signals to the other components as appropriate. From here, instructions pass to the arithmetic logic unit (ALU), which performs calculations and other logical operations. The control unit and ALU depend on memory registers for the temporary storage of data and internal instructions. These registers, internal to the CPU, are similar to RAM but operate much faster and have far less storage capacity. They are used by the ALU to store calculated results until the end of an operation, and by the control unit to store instructions.

Computer instructions may be for data transfer, data manipulation, or program control. Data transfer instructions cause data to be moved between

random access memory (RAM) a type of memory device that supports the nonpermanent storage of programs and data; so called because various locations can be accessed in any order (as if at random), rather than in a sequence (like a tape memory device)

bus a group of related signals that form an interconnecting pathway between two or more electronic devices

locations without affecting content, data manipulation instructions request arithmetic or logic operations from the ALU, and program control (branch) instructions facilitate decision operations. The control unit executes these instructions sequentially from consecutive memory locations. Each memory location is represented by a unique address, which permits a program counter to keep track of the last instruction executed. When the control unit retrieves an instruction, the program counter is incremented to reflect the next memory address. Unless the control unit is executing a branch instruction that alters this program counter value, that address will be the next instruction retrieved.

As noted earlier, the ALU performs arithmetic and logic operations. Basic arithmetic operations, like addition and subtraction, are performed by an arithmetic circuit; logic operations, such as AND, OR, and XOR (exclusive OR), are performed by a logic circuit. Like all components of the CPU, the ALU operates at the **binary** level. AND, OR, and XOR are examples of Boolean operations, whereby **bits** are compared to produce a logical (yes or no) result. A better understanding of ALU operations may be gained through the study of **Boolean algebra**.

Memory access is the slowest central processing operation; therefore memory registers are the most important components in determining the performance of a CPU. A register is a group of binary storage cells, or flip-flops, each capable of storing one bit of data. A CPU will often utilize large numbers of small registers because performance and capacity are inversely proportional, meaning that many small registers are faster than fewer larger registers. The smallest memory components are generally placed the closest to central processing components in order to optimize performance for the majority of processing operations.

A clock that sends repetitive pulses throughout the components of the CPU synchronizes all of these operations. Each clock pulse triggers an action—therefore, a CPU's performance can be measured by the frequency of clock pulses. The clock, however, must not exceed the performance of the registers or the CPU cannot function. The frequency of the clock is measured in Hertz (pulses per second).

Early CPUs were constructed from **vacuum tubes**, which required a great deal of energy and physical space compared to modern construction. The Electronic Numerical Integrator and Computer (ENIAC), which became operational in 1945 using more than 18,000 vacuum tubes, is largely regarded as the first electronic computer. The **transistor** was introduced in 1948, providing a smaller, faster, more efficient and reliable alternative to the vacuum tube. In 1956 the UNIVAC (Universal Automatic Computer) was completed, the first computer to incorporate a transistor-based CPU.

Development of the integrated circuit (IC), or computer chip, began in 1958 when Texas Instruments introduced a single piece of silicon containing multiple components. The integrated circuit provides the physical basis for today's microcomputers. In 1965 Gordon Moore made a prediction, now known as Moore's Law, that the number of transistors contained on a computer chip would double every year. In fact, the number of transistors integrated onto a single chip has doubled about every eighteen months over recent years. The first ICs had less than one hundred transistors, as opposed

binary existing in only two states, such as "on" or "off," "one" or "zero"

bits the plural of bit, a single binary digit, 1 or 0—a contraction of Binary digIT; the smallest unit for storing data in a computer

Boolean algebra a system developed by George Boole that deals with the theorems of undefined symbols and axioms concerning those symbols

vacuum tubes electronic devices constructed of sealed glass tubes containing metal elements in a vacuum; used to control electrical signals

transistor a contraction of TRANSfer resISTOR; semiconductor device, invented by John Bardeen, Walter Brattain, and William Shockley, which has three terminals; can be used for switching and amplifying electrical signals

MOORE'S LAW

Gordon Moore voiced his now famous law in 1965 when he predicted how quickly computer chip technology would advance. He asserted that the number of transistors that could be contained on an integrated circuit would double each year. He was right. It was not until 1995 that Moore revised his projection. Now the number doubles approximately every 18 months to two years. With advances in transistor technology, notably the invention of the molecular transistor, Moore's Law is apt to change once again.

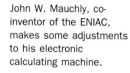

John W. Mauchly, co-inventor of the ENIAC, makes some adjustments to his electronic calculating machine.

to the more than eight million transistors now common on a single chip. Continually improving methods in IC manufacturing have led to larger numbers of smaller components, which have in turn led to faster processing.

In 1967 Fairchild Semiconductor introduced an IC that contained all of the ALU functions, but required additional circuitry to provide register storage and data control. Intel Corporation introduced the first fully functioning microprocessor in 1971. The Intel 4004 was capable of four-bit arithmetic operations and was used in a number of handheld calculators.

The 4.77 MHz sixteen-bit Intel 8086 was introduced seven years later, becoming the first generation of the popular x86 series of microprocessors and the basis for the personal computer. This line of microprocessors, including the 80286 (286), 386, 486, and Pentium (586), has evolved to include a robust complement of digital components integrated within the same IC that contains the basic CPU. In 2001 Intel introduced the 32-bit Pentium IV with a clock speed of 1.5 GHz, or 1.5 billion pulses per second.

The integration of CPU and other computer functions on the same microprocessor chip has blurred the distinction between a computer and its CPU. It is not uncommon for computer users to refer to their entire system by the name of its CPU—a practice that is not unfounded since the architecture of a CPU largely determines every other peripheral the computer can support. SEE ALSO INTEL CORPORATION; MICROCHIP.

Jeffrey C. Wingard

Bibliography

Mano, M. Morris. *Computer Systems Architecture.* Englewood Cliffs, NJ: Prentice Hall, 1982.

Sclater, Neil. *McGraw-Hill Electronics Dictionary.* New York: McGraw Hill, 1997.

Client/Server Technology

More computing power can be brought to bear on a problem in three ways. The first way is to build a computer that has a very fast processor. This was the goal of many of the early **supercomputer** efforts. The second way is to build a computer that has multiple processors working on different parts of some problem using shared memory, storage, and **input/output (I/O)**. These "parallel computing" systems were the goal of many of the later supercomputer efforts.

The third way to increase computing power dedicated to solving a problem is to use networks to link many separate computers working on different parts of the same problem. Each of the computers has its own processor, memory, storage, and I/O channels. They use a particular I/O channel—a network connection—to communicate and coordinate with each other.

Collectively, these systems are classified as distributed computing systems. The distinction between parallel and distributed computing is somewhat gray. Generally, a parallel computing system connects the cooperating components within a single system, or "box." Distributed computing connects boxes over a network. However, as networks increase in speed, the communications between components comes close to the speed of communication over a slow internal **bus**. As networks become **ubiquitous** and reliable, the term "network computing" is frequently used synonymously with distributed computing.

A distributed computing system may be thought of as a loosely coupled parallel system. Although this is true, parallel systems are generally devoted to working on problems where many similar calculations are carried out in parallel by the various components. In distributed computing systems, it is more frequently the case that the various components are optimized for different kinds of functions, which are carried out through a sequential dialog.

supercomputer a very high performance computer, usually comprised of many processors and used for modeling and simulation of complex phenomena, like meteorology

input/output (I/O) used to describe devices that can accept input data to a computer and to other devices that can produce output

bus a group of related signals that form an interconnecting pathway between two or more electronic devices

ubiquitous to be commonly available everywhere

paradigm an example, pattern, or way of thinking

server a computer that does not deal directly with human users, but instead handles requests from other computers for services to be performed

client a program or computer often managed by a human user, that makes requests to another computer for information

protocols agreed understanding for the suboperations that make up transactions; usually found in the specification of inter-computer communications

The dialog generally consists of a series of requests and responses. The dominant **paradigm** for this kind of distributed computing system is the client/server model.

In the simplest model for a client/server system, one of the components, a **server** process, is started on a given computer and runs in an endless loop waiting for a connection from a **client**. The client process is started on another computer, and it makes a request, which is sent across the network and processed by the server. A response is formulated. The response is then sent back to the client. The client may then disconnect from the server or make another request. At some point, the client terminates its connection to the server and the server returns to a "wait state" listening for a connection from another client.

Network and application **protocols** are essential for client/server systems to work. A networking protocol, like a diplomatic protocol, simply de-

Sun Microsystems President Ed Zander unveiled his company's new line of servers in 1996. The servers were designed to take the place of minicomputers and mainframes.

fines the conventions that will be used in an interaction. Three classes of protocols are required. The first is an addressing protocol that allows one component to specify the other component with which it wishes to communicate. Although there are numerous addressing protocols, the dominance of the Internet has, for all practical purposes, made the Internet Protocol (IP) the **de facto** addressing protocol.

de facto as is

The second class of protocols applies to protecting the quality of networked communication. Since a message from one computer to another must be transmitted as a series of packets, there must be some agreement on what to do if a packet that is part of a message is lost or is corrupted. This protocol must also address how to put the packets back together at the destination should they arrive out of order.

This protocol also addresses issues of synchronization between the two sides—e.g. how many packets should be sent before waiting to see if they have arrived safely, and how long should the sender keep a record of sent packets in the event that one needs to be resent. There are many different ways that this exchange might be managed, but again, the dominance of the Internet has made the Transmission Control Protocol (TCP) the dominant protocol for controlling communications quality.

Finally, the client and the server must have a protocol which governs the nature of the dialog in which they will engage. This third type of protocol defines the nature of the relationship between the client and the server. The names of some of these protocols are well known even if the underlying nature of the dialog they define is not. The relationship between World Wide Web browsers and web servers is defined by the HyperText Transfer Protocol or HTTP. The process by which files are transferred is defined by the File Transfer Protocol or FTP. The exchange of mail is defined by the Simple Mail Transfer Protocol or SMTP. These protocols are defined as "standards."

Client/Server Paradigms

The preceding section described a simple model for a client server interaction, where a server accepts a connection from a single client, handles the exchange, and then closes the connection to wait for a new one. This is called an **iterative** client server model. It is also possible for the server to be constructed to handle multiple requests simultaneously. This model is called a **concurrent** client server model.

The astute reader will recognize that if the server program is running on a machine with a single processor, it is not really possible to handle requests concurrently. The use of the term concurrent here refers to the overall handling of connections between the clients and the server. In a concurrent model, the server creates copies of the main process. Each copy is dedicated to handling the request from a single client, with the original process returning immediately to listen for additional connections. Depending on the nature of the interaction between the client and the server, this design may be more or less efficient than the iterative design.

For example, if the connection between the client and the server consists of a single request and response, and if the processing of the request by the server is very efficient and quick, the overhead of creating a copy of

iterative describes a procedure that involves repetitive operations before being completed

concurrent pertaining to simultaneous activities, for example simultaneous execution of many computer programs

multitasking the ability of a computer system to execute more than one program at the same time; also known as multiprogramming

the server process and then of shutting it down will make the handling of requests less efficient. However, if the exchange between the client and the server involves multiple requests and responses and if the client is operating in conjunction with human input, the server will spend a lot of time waiting for the client to make a request and very little of its time actually handling the request. In this case, the **multitasking** capability of the operating system can be used to shift back and forth between the various server processes, handling the requests from the various clients in a timely fashion. Thus, from the point of view of the clients, the server is handling the various requests concurrently.

Other client/server model variations involve the preallocation of server processes such that there are multiple copies of the server listening for a request at the same address. Each request is processed iteratively by one of the servers, but multiple processes can be running in parallel handling these requests. This is the model most frequently employed by web servers.

It is also possible to design a server that will open multiple connections to a number of different clients. The one server then checks and handles communications from all of these clients in some "round-robin" fashion. This model is frequently used for applications like chat rooms, where the information presented by one client is then broadcast to all the clients.

Client/server systems may be chained or linked with a server to one client being a client to another server. Additionally, a client may simultaneously connect to multiple servers for different services. As an example of the first model, consider a client that makes a connection to a server to process a purchase order. The server may understand all the rules about who may make orders, and how an order is to be processed, but the actual recording of the order may be handled by another process that would place the order into a database.

This is the model for most three-tier client server systems. The client handles the user interface which processes requests to a middleware server. This intermediate server applies rules and checks on the data. When satisfied, the middleware server makes a connection as a client to another server, which controls a database. The database server is only responsible for storing the data, assuming that the middleware server has done the necessary checking.

More Sophisticated Models for Clients and Servers

Over the years, it has become clear that the process of defining protocols for clients and servers is a difficult task, and not fully consistent with modern programming techniques. In addition, the process of locating the address at which a server is listening for clients has become more complicated as the number of client/server applications has grown.

These and other problems associated with client/server design and implementation have been addressed by new layers of protocols. The most well known of these is the Remote Procedure Call (RPC) protocol, which was developed to insure protocol consistency between pairs by automating much of the basic structural code, and by establishing a mechanism for registration and finding of server processes through a shared directory service.

While RPC worked for procedural languages, a model was also needed for object-oriented programming languages. Remote Method Invocation (RMI) fills this need in a similar fashion.

Beyond these efforts, more recent developments include mechanisms for standardizing more of the basic functionality of the interaction, allowing for servers to be located across multiple machines, and for managing the various services that are running. These models, generally classified as distributed application servers, include the Common Object Request Broker Architecture (CORBA), Distributed Component Object Model (DCOM), JavaSpaces and JINI, and E'Speak to name a few.

Design Issues

Client/server systems endeavor to optimize per-problem performance, multiple-problem throughput, and reliability, among other things. New problems arise for the programmer, however, because techniques used for writing stand-alone serial programs often fail when they are applied to distributed programs.

In building a system, the programmer must address a variety of issues such as **data partitioning**, **task partitioning**, task scheduling, **parallel debugging**, and **synchronization**. In addition, the programmer has to understand that interconnection **bandwidth** and message latency dominate the performance of distributed and parallel systems. There is no clear-cut way to predict what the performance of a new system will be. Therefore, it is difficult to predict what the benefits of a distributed or parallel system will be prior to an investment of time and effort. Finally, the design of the server in a client/server system requires particular attention to a number of issues, including process synchronization, global state, reliability, distributed resource management, deadlock, and performance evaluation. SEE ALSO ASSEMBLY LANGUAGE AND ARCHITECTURE; INFORMATION TECHNOLOGY STANDARDS; NETWORKS; OPERATING SYSTEMS.

Michael B. Spring

data partitioning a technique applied to databases (but not restricted to them) which organizes data objects into related groups

task partitioning the act of dividing up work to be done so that it can be separated into distinct tasks, processes, or phases

parallel debugging specialized approaches to locating and correcting errors in computer programs that are to be executed on parallel computing machine architectures

synchronization the time domain ordering of events; often applied when events repeatedly occur simultaneously

bandwidth a measure of the frequency component of a signal or the capacity of a communication channel to carry signals

Bibliography

Ananda, Akkihebbal L., and B. Srinivasan. *Distributed Computing Systems: Concepts and Structures.* Piscataway, NJ: IEEE Computer Society Press, 1991.

Beeri, Catriel, Philip A. Bernstein, Nathan Goodman. "A Model for Concurrency in Nested Transactions Systems." *The Journal of the ACM* 36, no. 2 (April 1989): 230–269.

Ben-Ari, M. *Principles of Concurrent and Distributed Programming.* New York: Prentice Hall, 1990.

Black, Uyless. *TCP/IP and Related Protocols*, 3rd ed. New York: McGraw-Hill, 1998.

Brewer, Eric, et al. "A Network Architecture for Heterogeneous Mobile Computing." *IEEE Personal Communications*, October 1998.

Comer, Douglas, and David Stevens. *Internetworking with TCP/IP*, vols. 1 and 2. Upper Saddle River, NJ: Prentice Hall, 1994.

———. *Internetworking with TCP/IP*, vol. 3. Upper Saddle River, NJ: Prentice Hall, 1996.

Mullender, Sape, ed. *Distributed Systems*, 2nd ed. Reading, MA: Addison-Wesley, 1993.

Orfali, Robert, and Dan Harkey. *Client/Server Programming with Java and CORBA*, 2nd ed. New York: John Wiley and Sons Inc., 1998.

Codes

The first widely used character code was the Morse Code, developed in 1838 by Samuel F. B. Morse (1791–1872). This two-symbol, dot-and-dash code is capable of representing the characters of the alphabet by varying the number of symbols between one and four. If one considers the symbols to be similiar to **bits**, then the number character set, 0 to 9, uses 1 to 5 bits.

In 1874 Jean-Maurice Émile Baudot (1845–1903) received a patent for a printing telegraph. He also introduced a code using 5 bits per character. Five bits can be combined in 32 different ways, enough for uppercase letters and a few control characters. To include the number set, Baudot devised a shift to another level, much as the Cap Lock on a keyboard. The shift provides the number set, punctuation symbols, and control character representations for the 32 separate, 5-bit combinations. The control characters include the carriage return and the line feed. All the control characters are present in either letter or figure shift mode. The letters were in the lower shift mode and the figures in the upper shift mode. Early teletype ma-

bits plural of bit, a single binary digit, 1 or 0—a contraction of Binary digIT; the smallest unit for storing data in a computer

More than 100 years after its invention, the Morse Code was still in use. During World War II, for example, Air Corps cadets at the Tuskegee Institute learned Morse Code during U.S. Army training.

chines punched the messages into paper tapes and read tapes to send messages. Later, machines were designed to print out the messages in character form. Some teletypes for the hearing impaired in use today are based on the Baudot code.

Early computers used a version of Baudot's code called ITA$_2$, a 6-bit code that had more control and format characters in addition to the uppercase letter and the ten numeric characters. The increase to 6 bits, or 64 combinations, eliminated the need for the shift control to switch from letter to numeric characters. There was no urgency to improve the character code by adding lowercase letters and more punctuation symbols, as computers were considered calculation machines. By the late 1950s, computers were used more widely for commercial purposes. The variation in the control character set from system to system was a drawback. The American Standards Association (ASA) developed a standardized code. The ASA is composed of various corporations, including IBM, AT&T, and an AT&T subsidiary, Teletype Corporation—manufacturer of the most widely used communications equipment.

In 1963 the first version of American Standard Code for Information Interchange (ASCII) was introduced. IBM waited until the 1980s to use it, while AT&T's immediate acceptance of it made ASCII the standard for communications. This new code was based on 7 bits, allowing for 128 characters in the character code table. This initial version did not have a lowercase letter set. It did include all the COBOL (COmmon Business-Oriented Language) graphics characters based on the earlier FIELDATA code used by the military, added more control characters such as a linefeed, and simplified some of the transmission control codes. Collating problems were solved by separating the number set from the letter set in the table, and ordering the letter set to allow collating by letter using simple arithmetic comparisons.

The next version of ASCII in 1967 included the lowercase letter set, FORTRAN graphic characters, square bracket, curly braces, and others. Control character changes were made and a small set of international characters was added. The control characters were relocated in the first half of the table. This version of ASCII remained the standard for thirty years.

Meanwhile, back at IBM, a different character code came into use. Why? Perhaps because the origin of IBM goes back to Herman Hollerith (1860–1929), the **punched card**, and the 6-bit character code. The early IBM mainframes used a 6-bit character code, or Binary Coded Decimal Interchange Code (BCDIC). In 1964 a **proprietary** code, Extended Binary Coded Decimal Interchange Code (EBCDIC), was created for use on IBM/360 **mainframe** computers. This 8-bit code was an extension of the earlier code. It included most of the characters in the ASCII code but with differing bit-string representations. For example, the ASCII representation of M is 01001101; the EBCDIC representation of M is 11010100.

Multiple versions of EBCDIC character code sets had to be created as the mainframe market spread throughout the world. Another difficulty arose when translating from or into ASCII. Because there was a difference in the character sets, the translation was slow and error-prone. The general trend is to convert EBCDIC data files into ASCII or other non-proprietary code formats.

punched card a paper card with punched holes which give instructions to a computer in order to encode program instructions and data

proprietary a process or technology developed and owned by an individual or company, and not published openly

mainframe large computer used by businesses and government agencies to process massive amounts of data; generally faster and more powerful than desktop computers but usually requiring specialized software

In the 1980s, the growth of international business generated interest in a multilingual character code. The International Organization for Standardization (ISO) and a group of American computer firms started on methods to produce a universal character code set. Unicode, which gives a unique number to each character, resulted from merging the two efforts. It is still evolving and currently uses a single 256-by-256 grid that supports 65,236 character points and unifies similar characters, especially within the Asian languages. Unicode is supported by multiple industries and companies ranging from Apple Computer, Inc., IBM Corporation, and Hewlett Packard to Oracle, Microsoft Corporation, and Sun Microsystems. It is supported by operating systems and browsers. Unicode is capable of transporting data through many platforms without data corruption. SEE ALSO BINARY NUMBER SYSTEM; CODING TECHNIQUES; GENERATIONS, LANGUAGES.

Bertha Kugelman Morimoto

Internet Resources

Searle, Steven J. "A Brief History of Character Codes in North America, Europe, and East Asia." University of Tokyo. 1999. <http://tron-web.super-nova.co.jp/characcodehist.html>

Verstraete, Anthony A. "Data Communication: Early History and Evolution In-Depth." January 1998. <http://www.smeal.psu/misweb/datacomm/id/history1.html>

Coding Techniques

Representation of information is a fundamental aspect of all communication from bird songs to human language to modern telecommunications. In the case of digital storage and transmission of information, mathematical analysis has led to principles that drive the design of symbolic representations. For example, it has let a **binary code** be defined as a mapping from a set of source symbols, or source *alphabet*, to unique bit strings. A familiar example is the standard American Standard Code for Information Interchange (ASCII) code (see Table 1) in which each character from a standard keyboard is represented as a 7-bit sequence.

ASCII is an example of a *block code*, where each symbol is represented by a fixed-length "block" of n **bits**. Given a number of symbols (K) to encode in binary form, a number of bits (n) is chosen such that there are enough binary patterns of that length to encode all K symbols. With n bits, 2^n unique strings exist, and so we choose the smallest integer n that satisfies $K < 2^n$. Thus a 3-bit code can represent up to eight symbols, a 4-bit code can be used for a set of up to 16 symbols, etc.

Because of its universal use, the ASCII code has great advantages as a means of storing textual data and communicating between machines. On the face of it, the ASCII design seems perfectly reasonable. After all, a common language is central to communication. However, ASCII lacks certain properties desirable in a code. One of these is *efficiency* and the other is *robustness*.

Efficiency

Knowledge of symbol probabilities can be exploited to make a code more efficient. Morse code, the system of dots and dashes used for telegraph trans-

binary code a representation of information that permits only two states like one or zero

bits the plural of bit, a single binary digit, 1 or 0—a contraction of Binary digIT; the smallest unit for storing data in a computer

TABLE 1. THE 7-BIT ASCII CODE

Symbol	Code	Symbol	Code	Symbol	Code	Symbol	Code
NUL	0000000		0100000	@	1000000	`	1100000
SOH	0000001	!	0100001	A	1000001	a	1100001
STX	0000010	"	0100010	B	1000010	b	1100010
ETX	0000011	#	0100011	C	1000011	c	1100011
EOT	0000100	$	0100100	D	1000100	d	1100100
ENQ	0000101	%	0100101	E	1000101	e	1100101
ACK	0000110	&	0100110	F	1000110	f	1100110
BEL	0000111	'	0100111	G	1000111	g	1100111
BS	0001000	(	0101000	H	1001000	h	1101000
TAB	0001001	)	0101001	I	1001001	i	1101001
LF	0001010	*	0101010	J	1001010	j	1101010
VT	0001011	+	0101011	K	1001011	k	1101011
FF	0001100	,	0101100	L	1001100	l	1101100
CR	0001101	-	0101101	M	1001101	m	1101101
SO	0001110	.	0101110	N	1001110	n	1101110
SI	0001111	/	0101111	O	1001111	o	1101111
DLE	0010000	0	0110000	P	1010000	p	1110000
DC1	0010001	1	0110001	Q	1010001	q	1110001
DC2	0010010	2	0110010	R	1010010	r	1110010
DC3	0010011	3	0110011	S	1010011	s	1110011
DC4	0010100	4	0110100	T	1010100	t	1110100
NAK	0010101	5	0110101	U	1010101	u	1110101
SYN	0010110	6	0110110	V	1010110	v	1110110
ETB	0010111	7	0110111	W	1010111	w	1110111
CAN	0011000	8	0111000	X	1011000	x	1111000
EM	0011001	9	0111001	Y	1011001	y	1111001
SUB	0011010	:	0111010	Z	1011010	z	1111010
ESC	0011011	;	0111011	[	1011011	{	1111011
FS	0011100	<	0111100	\	1011100	|	1111100
GS	0011101	=	0111101	]	1011101	}	1111101
RS	0011110	>	0111110	^	1011110	~	1111110
US	0011111	?	0111111	_	1011111	α	1111111

mission in the early days of electric communication, made use of such knowledge. By representing the more frequent letters in common English with shorter dash-dot sequences, the average time to transmit a character is reduced in a message whose character statistics are consistent with the assumed frequencies (see Table 2).

Consider codes in which the number of bits assigned to each symbol is not fixed, and let l_i denote the number of bits in the string for the ith symbol s_i. In such a *variable length code*, it makes sense to assign shorter bit strings to symbols that tend to occur more frequently than average in typical use. Hence, an efficient code can be designed by making l_i a function of a

TABLE 2. MORSE CODE

Symbol	Code	Symbol	Code	Symbol	Code
A	. -	N	- .	0	- - - - -
B	- . . .	O	- - -	1	. - - - -
C	- . - .	P	. - - .	2	. . - - -
D	- . .	Q	- - . -	3	. . . - -
E	.	R	. - .	4	. . . . -
F	. . - .	S	. . .	5	. . . . .
G	- - .	T	-	6	- . . . .
H	. . . .	U	. . -	7	- - . . .
I	. .	V	. . . -	8	- - - . .
J	. - - -	W	. - -	9	- - - - .
K	- . -	X	- . . -	period	. - . - . -
L	. - . .	Y	- . - -	comma	- - . . - -
M	- -	Z	- - . .		

TABLE 3. TWO CODES ON FOUR SYMBOLS

Symbol	Probability	Code I	Code II
a	0.5	00	0
b	0.25	01	10
c	0.125	10	110
d	0.125	11	111
Average Length		2	1.75

symbol's probability, p_i. Let the efficiency of a code be measured as the average number of bits per symbol, L_{avg}, weighted by the probabilities [Eq. 1].

$$L_{avg} \equiv \sum_{i=1}^{K} p_i l_i \qquad [1]$$

The example that follows illustrates the increase in efficiency offered by a variable length code. Consider a set of four symbols a, b, c, and d with corresponding probabilities $p_a = 0.5$, $p_b = 0.25$, $p_c = p_d = 0.125$. Two codes are listed in Table 3, with the average lengths for each computed according to Equation 1. Note that the average length computed for Code II depends on the probability distribution, whereas the average number of bits per symbol for an n-bit block code is obviously n, regardless of the probabilities. Which code would be more efficient if the four symbols all have the same probability? (They would be equally efficient, both two bits long for each symbol.)

A potential problem with variable length codes is that an encoded string of symbols may not be uniquely decodeable; that is, there may be more than one interpretation for a sequence of bits. For example, let the symbol set {a,b,c} be encoded as $a = 0$, $b = 10$, $c = 01$. The sequence 010 could be interpreted as either *ab* or *ca*, thus this code is *not* uniquely decodeable. This problem does not occur with all variable length codes. *Huffman Codes* are uniquely decodeable codes that are generated based on symbol probabilities.

The entropy of a probability distribution (denoted H and defined in Equation 2) is the lower bound for L_{avg}. That is, for a given set of probabilities $p_1, p_2, \ldots p_K$, the most efficient uniquely decodeable code must satisfy:

$$L_{avg} \geq H \equiv \sum_{k=1}^{K} p_k \log_2 \frac{1}{p_k} \qquad [2]$$

Robustness

A principle of redundancy underlies the design of *error correcting codes*. By using more bits than are actually required to represent a set of symbols uniquely, a more robust code can be generated. If the code is designed such that any two legal codewords differ in at least 3 bits, then the result of "flipping" the value of any bit (that is, converting a 1 to a 0 or vice versa) will result in a string that remains closer to the original than it is to any other codeword. Similarly, if the minimum distance is 5 bits, double errors can be reliably corrected, with a 7-bit minimum distance, triple errors can be corrected, etc. A very simple illustration of this principle is the case of two symbols. In each of the four codes in Table 4, the symbol A is represented by a set of 0s, and B is represented by a block of 1s. For codes of increasing blocksize, more errors can be tolerated. For example, in the case of the 5-bit double-error correcting code, the received sequence 10100 would be interpreted as an A.

TABLE 4. SIMPLE ERROR CORRECTING CODES

Symbol	Unique encoding	Single error correcting	Double error correcting	Triple error correcting
A	0	000	00000	0000000
B	1	111	11111	1111111

The codes noted in Table 4 are *inefficient*, in that they require many bits per symbol. Even the single error correcting code in Table 4 uses three times as many bits than are necessary without error correction. Much more efficient error-correcting codes are possible. The code in Table 5 is an example of a family of codes developed by Richard Hamming. It is a representation of a set of 16 symbols using 7 bits per symbol. While 4 bits would be sufficient to represent each of the symbols uniquely, this 7-bit code designed by Hamming guarantees the ability to correct a single bit error in any 7-bit block. The Hamming code is designed such that any two codewords are different in at least 3 bits. Hence, if one bit is altered by a storage or transmission error, the resulting bit string is still closer to the original codeword than it is to any of the other 15 symbols. Thus, this code is robust to single errors. Note that if two errors occur in the same block, the code fails.

TABLE 5. A 7-BIT HAMMING CODE

Symbol	Codeword	Symbol	Codeword
A	0000000	I	1000101
B	0001011	J	1001110
C	0010110	K	1010011
D	0011101	L	1011000
E	0100111	M	1100010
F	0101100	N	1101001
G	0110001	O	1110100
H	0111010	P	1111111

Conclusion

The primary framework for symbolic representation of information is human language, which has evolved over a period spanning more than 100,000 years. But only the past century has seen the application of mathematical principles to the design of encoding schemes. In combination with high-speed electronic signal transmission, the result is a system that enables communication with efficiency, reliability, and range that would have been inconceivable a few generations ago. Ongoing improvements in high-density magnetic and optical storage media have brought about a tremendous reduction in the physical space required to store information, thus amplifying the utility of these recently developed encoding techniques. SEE ALSO BELL LABS; BINARY NUMBER SYSTEM; CODES.

Paul Munro

Bibliography

Lucky, Robert W. *Silicon Dreams.* New York: St. Martin's Press, 1989.

Wells, Richard B. *Applied Coding and Information Theory for Engineers.* Upper Saddle River, NJ: Prentice Hall, 1999.

Communication Devices

The versatility of a computer is enhanced considerably if it can communicate with other computers or a number of users. The very first computers were large machines that occupied an entire room with a control console at the center. The input and output devices for these machines were located at that console and only one user could operate the machine at a time. However, not long after the first computers were made, engineers realized that it would be more efficient if users could access the machine from their desks via a "terminal." This was the beginning of the "mainframe" computer.

The key to a mainframe computer was a communications network that would allow users to link to the machine. The terminals had no computing power themselves, but were connected to the mainframe computer via copper wire, sometimes called **twisted pair**. As computers became larger and faster, developers realized that computing time could be sold to other

twisted pair an inexpensive, medium bandwidth communication channel commonly used in local area networks

companies or offered to other offices of the same company. This necessitated gaining access to the computer via long distance communication. In the beginning, during the late 1950s and 1960s, the only available long distance communications device was the telephone line.

However, telephonic communications were designed for voice transmission, while computers require data transmission. Computer data can not be applied to a telephone line directly but must be transformed into a signal that is compatible with the telephone system. To enable this compatibility, a signal, usually a sine or cosine function, called a carrier, is modulated, or modified in some way. This is done via a modulator—a device that produces a signal that can be handled by the telephone system without undue distortion, and without the modulated signal interfering with the operation of the telephone system.

On the receiving end, the modulated signal must be "demodulated" in order to retrieve the digital data. For two-way communications, the computer must be equipped with a modulator for outgoing data and a demodulator for incoming data. This device is now known as a **modem**, a term that was derived from the combination of MOdulator and DEModulator.

modem the contraction of MOdulator DEModulator; a device which converts digital signals into signals suitable for transmission over analog channels, like telephone lines

The first computer modems modulated the carrier signal by changing the frequency of the sine or cosine function. The frequency of a carrier is the rate at which it repeats. For example, if the function repeats 1,000 times each second, its frequency is 1,000 Hertz or 1,000 Hz. A modem can have two distinct frequencies, called tones, at 1,200 and 2,200 Hz, where 1,200 Hz represents a "mark" and the 2,200 Hz represents a "space." In the early days, the modem would shift between these two frequencies, a method of modulation called frequency shift keying or FSK. This technology was already in place before the invention of computers and was used for teleprinters, better known by their brand name, Teletype machines. It was therefore easy to attach a logic one or zero to the mark and space respectively and use the modem to transmit digital data.

The speed of the modem is expressed in baud, named after Jean-Maurice-Émile Baudot, who invented the fixed-length teleprinter code in 1874. This code was the model on which many computer codes were configured. In modern terminology, baud represents bits per second.

The first computer modems were very slow, at 300 baud. However, the computer input/output devices were Teletype machines, which could not print any faster than 100 baud. When electronic terminals appeared, the 300 baud modem became a major bottleneck, and the speed of the FSK modem was increased to 1200, 2400, 4800 and later 9600 baud. Increasing the speed of modems beyond 9600 baud required a modulation scheme more sophisticated than the simple FSK.

Jean-Maurice-Émile Baudot was famous for his telegraph code, created in 1874, that became more popular than Morse Code by the mid-twentieth century.

Later modulation schemes use much more sophisticated techniques that vary the amplitude, angle, or combinations of both. In addition, improved encoding and error detection techniques are used. With the creation of the Internet, the need for even faster modems increased. The quality of the telephone line, which is the communications "channel," now becomes the limiting factor for increased data rates. The highest data rate available from a commercial product for telephone line use is 56,000 baud, 56 kilobaud, or 56kB. When a communications channel is used at speeds beyond its limits, errors occur. These high-speed telephone modems automatically adjust the data rate downward when the errors increase.

Modems faster than 56kB require a higher capacity channel, which is available on cable television systems. The bandwidth of a telephone channel is about 3.5 kHz. In comparison, the bandwidth of one television channel is 6 MHz. The cable television system is an inherently broadband system, making it possible to add high-speed data signals to the cable television system without interfering with existing television signals. In these cases as well, modems are used to perform exactly the same function they do when connected to a telephone line. Data rates vary but a typical cable modem data rate is more than 1 million baud or 1 MB.

Another high speed modem is the **digital subscriber loop (DSL)**. This system uses telephone wires, but not the telephone channel. Just as the cable modem connects to the cable television system while the normal television service is uninterrupted, DSL connects to the telephone system with no effect on normal telephone service.

Special equipment is required by the subscriber and the telephone company to "multiplex" computer data on the telephone line with normal telephone service. The only difference is that telephone wires being used for the DSL are incapable of being handled by any telephone equipment. Therefore, the digital signals must be separated at the point where the telephone wires enter the telephone network, which is usually a central office.

DSL uses telephone wires that were never intended to handle high speed data. Therefore, the digital signals are quickly reduced in strength, limiting the distance these signals can travel to the central office. Because of this limitation, some telephone customers, who are too distant from the central office, cannot obtain DSL. Other variations on DSL, which allow users to take advantage of the maximum distance and data rate, such as the asymmetric DSL or ADSL, are also available now. This system has a higher speed down-link than up-link.

Wireless modems are also available with data rates up to several MB. These systems are usually privately owned by large companies or other organizations. There have been some installations of public access wireless systems but the most common is the cellular telephone system. New cellular telephone systems, called "third generation" or 3G, will offer extensive data transmission capability.

The highest performing data links are those based on fiber optics. These links offer data rates measured in the hundreds of MB. These systems are used within a company or an industrial complex. Until there is a fiber optic infrastructure capable of delivering fiber to the home, or FTH, this option is not available to many individual subscribers. Fortunately, these FTH systems are being installed at various locations around the world. SEE ALSO BRIDGING DEVICES; NETWORK DESIGN; NETWORK TOPOLOGIES.

Albert D. Helfrick

TRUE VALUE OF COMPUTERS

The Internet is a household word. To most, the Internet is associated with computers and is not regarded as a communications system. But the Internet has more to do with Teletype machines, FAX machines, telephones, and telegraphs than computers. The value of many computers is based more on their ability to communicate than compute.

digital subscriber loop (DSL) the enabling of high-speed digital data transfer over standard telephone cables and systems in conjunction with normal telephone speech data

Bibliography

Black, Uyless D. *Physical Layer Interfaces and Protocols.* Los Alamitos, CA: IEEE Computer Society Press, 1966.

Glossbrenner, Alfred, and Emily Glossbrenner. *The Complete Modem Handbook.* New York: MIS Press, 1995.

Hakala, David. *Modems Made Easy: The Basics and Beyond.* Berkeley, CA: Osborne McGraw-Hill, 1995.

Compatibility (Open Systems Design)

Compatibility is the ability to connect things together and have them work, such as connecting a refrigerator to electrical power, a video recorder to a television, or a computer to a printer. Compatibility is an issue that is important in all branches of engineering, especially computer and software engineering. The standard solution to ensuring compatibility is the use of common, well-understood means of defining how to connect things together. These means are commonly called standards. The standards with which compatibility is concerned are the standards at the connection, or the **interface**. The interface is the place where the two devices join, or communicate or interact.

Within any country (for example, the United States of America) you can move from one house, take all of your electrical appliances, and plug them into the electrical system of another house with confidence that they will work without modification. This is true from city to city, from state to state; you can be assured that the appliances will work. This is because there is a common standard for the electrical interface throughout the United States. The standard requires that the plugs and wall sockets have the same pins of the same shape, that the voltage is 120 volts, and the frequency is 60 Hz.

In fact, within most countries the electrical systems are built to conform to a common standard. Between countries, however, the standards are often different. The consequence is that very few appliances will work when one moves, for example, from the United States to Australia. One may say that the electrical power systems in the United States and Australia are not compatible.

Compatibility has become a big issue in the computing industry. There are a few main suppliers of computer systems (e.g., Microsoft, Intel, Sun, Apple) and many other companies wishing to supply software and hardware that is compatible with these main suppliers of computer systems. The early lack of compatibility between parts, or components, of computer systems led to the development of open systems. The interfaces of open systems are specified by freely available, publicly controlled standards. An example of a non-computer-specific open system is the electrical system within the United States.

Open systems developed because many organizations discovered that it was difficult to build large and complex computer systems economically and effectively during the 1970s and the 1980s. One of the major problems facing large systems was the integration, or joining together, of subsystems to create the whole system. The underlying problem for these early systems was that the desired components were not compatible with each other. The components would not exchange information correctly, and it was difficult to move components from one system to another, in order to reuse components.

TRANSFERRING INFORMATION

For two systems to transfer information or to interact together, they must have some common basis. If they are hardware systems, then the wiring and the signals must be commonly defined.

interface a boundary or border between two or more objects or systems; also a point of access

The birth of open computer-based systems came from the construction of reliable **infrastructures**, based on standards (see Figure A). This stylized representation shows the elements of an open system with the application "sitting" on top of the infrastructure. (To return to the electrical system example, the power network that runs throughout the United States is an infrastructure.) In a computer, the infrastructure is a computer program that manages the interfaces between components to help ensure that they interface, or interact, correctly.

A critical portion of the infrastructure is the network interface. The most well known open system is probably the Internet. Its development has only been possible because of the standards that exist for the network interface, and for the language used to present the pages on the screen of a user's computer.

Standards are critical to compatibility. Without an agreement, shared between two or more component manufacturers, that specifies standards for the interfaces, there would be no possibility of compatibility. The issue that arises is whether computer companies are prepared to allow these interface documents to become public, freely available standards. Computer and software companies are concerned that either they will lose money by not keeping the standard to themselves, or, that the bureaucracy of a public standard will destroy the product due to inertia.

Upgradability and portability are important outcomes of using standard infrastructures and open systems. The aim of upgradability is to allow customers to buy a fast, new computer with the assurance that all of one's software will run on the new computer, or to upgrade a piece of software and have all the surrounding hardware work. That is, if customers upgrade their word processing software, their printers will still work correctly.

The aim of portability is to be able to move software from one computer (e.g., a Windows PC) to another computer (e.g., a Macintosh, or a Linux machine), and have the software work correctly. Standard infrastructures and open systems assist in making upgradability and portability happen because they ensure that the interfaces are managed, and that the manufacturers are aware of the interfaces because they are published as standards.

TYPES OF COMPATIBILITY

Products that effectively interact or transfer information between each other are compatible. A computer and a printer are compatible if information transferred between them results in a correctly printed page. Databases are said to be compatible if they can read each other's files. Products are also said to be compatible if they work within a particular computer system. Software is called Microsoft Windows compatible if it can work within the Microsoft Windows environment. Finally, products are called compatible if they can be substituted for other products—i.e., a personal computer is called IBM-PC compatible if it can run the same software as a brand-name IBM-PC.

infrastructures the foundations or permanent installations necessary for structures or systems to operate

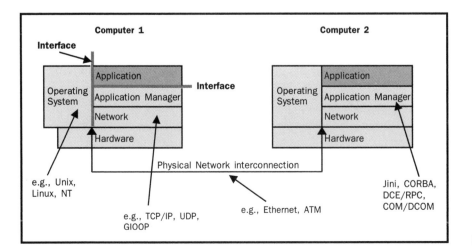

Figure A.

Manufacturers of computers and operating systems (such as Apple, Intel, and Microsoft) have an interest in compatibility, but not necessarily a commitment to public, freely available standards. Microsoft appears principally interested in having other manufacturers make hardware and software that is compatible with their operating systems. Apple appears to be principally interested in having other manufacturers make software (but not hardware) that is compatible with their operating systems. IBM and Compaq appear to have embraced compatibility, and are focused on the construction of infrastructures as their core business. For the most part, traditional computer manufacturers who are now manufacturing infrastructures do not seem to be interested in open systems—as governed by public, freely available standards—but rather in controlled compatibility that allows them to protect their market niches. SEE ALSO Bridging Devices; Communication Devices; Information Technology Standards.

John Leaney

Bibliography

Roark, Chuck, and Bill Kiczuk. "Open Systems—A Process for Achieving Affordability." *IEEE AES*. September 1996, p. 15-20.

Internet Resources

"The Open System Approach at the SEI." The Carnegie Mellon Software Engineering Institute web site. <http://www.sei.cmu.edu/opensystems/welcome.html>

Raymond, K. *Reference Model of Open Distributed Processing (RM-ODP): Introduction.* Distributed Systems Technology Centre web site. <http://www.dstc.edu.au/>

Compilers

The compiler is a program that translates the source language (which takes the form of a written program), into machine code, the language of the machine. There are several portions to the compiler, some of the most prominent being the **lexical analyzer**, the **syntactic analyzer**, the code generation phase, and a code optimizer, which is optional. The generation of an intermediate code is also optional, but often done to facilitate the portability of the compiler to various machines.

The lexical analyzer finds the words of the source language. It is similar to a dictionary in a natural language such as English. It determines what symbols constitute words, and what types of word they are. In English, this includes words such as "cat" (N or Noun), "ran" (V or Verb), or "the" (Determinant). In programming languages these are "words" like "+-sign" (+), identifiers (user-defined identifiers or variables), and keywords (while, for, read, print). The words are used to form sentences in programming language, such as "while (a≤5) do. . . ."

The syntactic analyzer checks the form, or organization, of the sentences in programming languages. In other words, it checks to be sure the programming language's "grammar" is correct. For example, a sentence like "to the store he went" would be considered ungrammatical while "he went to the store" would be considered grammatical. In programming languages, the following statement would be considered grammatical:

```
for(j=0; j<MAXNUM;j++)
    printf("%d",j);
```

lexical analyzer a portion of a compiler that is responsible for checking the program source code produced by a programmer for proper words and symbols

syntactic analyzer a part of a compiler that scans program source code ensuring that the code meets essential language rules with regard to structure or organization

Compare this to the following statement, which is considered ungrammatical in a language such as C:

```
for(j=0; printf("%d", j);
    j<MAXNUM; j++)
```

The syntactic analyzer receives the words and their respective types (number, constant, +-sign, keyword, identifier) from the lexical analyzer and sees that they are organized in the proper way according to the rules of the language. The organization, or syntax, of the language is defined by the grammar for the language.

Together, the lexical analyzer and syntactic analyzer determine whether a program is "well-written." If it is, the code generator generates the code for the program. The code is specific to each type of machine the compiler will run on. An example would be the assignment statement:

```
c = a + b
```

This adds the values of a and b, and places the result in c. This might be translated as:

```
movl a, R6

addl b, R6

movl R6, c
```

This is read as:

"move the value of *a* into register 6"

"add the value of *b* to register 6"

"move the value of register 6 to *c*"

The registers are special locations in the **central processing unit** where the arithmetic is done. The previous code is assembly language code. The compiler might also be written to generate machine code directly. This might look like:

```
70 52,6

72 54,6

70 6,56
```

central processing unit (CPU) the part of a computer that performs computations and controls and coordinates other parts of the computer

Here, the code 70 would stand for "movl," 72 for "addl," and 52, 54, and 56 are the addresses of a, b, and c, respectively. The 6 is register 6. Although the example is hypothetical, it is based on the machine language (**binary code**) and assembly language (symbolic code) of a real machine, the VAX family of Digital Equipment Corporation. It is because the code is machine-dependent, based on the architecture and **mnemonics** (symbols or symbolic language) of the machine, that the compiler must be written differently for different machines in this phase.

binary code a representation of information that permits only two states like one or zero

mnemonics devices or processes that aid one's memory

The lexical and syntactic analyzers are machine-independent. They base their decisions and actions on the grammar of the language being translated, such as C or Pascal. The code generation phase is machine-dependent. The code generated depends on the architecture of the machine.

A fourth phase that is often implemented is the intermediate code generation. This is a machine-independent code that can be used by the compiler writer to generate the machine code. An example might be:

Add A, B

Store C

The first instruction indicates that one should add B to A, and the second indicates that the result should be stored in C. The use of the intermediate code allows for a machine-independent code to be optimized, with the final code being translated into the code of the machine.

The machine-independent phases are sometimes referred to as the front end of the compiler, and the final phase as the back end. The front end is the same for all machines, but the back end is machine-dependent. Thus the front end, which comprises a good portion of the work, can be done once for all machines, while the back end is tailored specifically to the machine at hand. This allows the single compiler for a language, such as C, to be ported, or implemented, to many machines. SEE ALSO BINARY NUMBER SYSTEM; EARLY COMPUTERS; PROCEDURAL LANGUAGES.

Roger R. Flynn

Bibliography

Aho, Alfred V., Ravi Sethi, and Jeffrey D. Ullman. *Compilers: Principles, Techniques and Tools.* Reading, MA: Addison-Wesley, 1986.

Computer System Interfaces

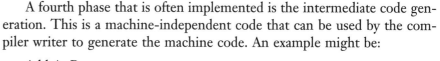

bus a group of related signals that form an interconnecting pathway between two or more electronic devices

input/output (I/O) used to describe devices that can accept input data to a computer and to other devices that can produce output

algorithms rules or procedures used to solve mathematical problems—most often described as sequences of steps

central processing unit (CPU) the part of a computer that performs computations and controls and coordinates other parts of the computer

interfaces boundaries or borders between two or more objects or systems; also points of access

All computer systems must possess certain elements before they can be considered useful to human users. Computers require a processing unit, some memory, perhaps secondary storage, and interconnecting **bus** networks—but computers also need **input/output (I/O)** devices. Computers are programmed to execute **algorithms** on data and then make the results of these computations available. If a user cannot supply data to the computer through input devices and then see how the algorithms operate on it through output devices, then the computer is ineffective.

What makes dealing with input and output devices sometimes problematic is that they differ so much in shape and form, and they tend to operate at speeds that are extremely slow compared to the **central processing unit (CPU)**. Users prefer that the processor not be continually held up as it waits for tardy I/O devices to catch up with commands. A more satisfactory solution is to have the processor command the I/O devices to begin a lengthy operation of some sort and then busy itself with other activities while it waits for the slow I/O devices to complete their tasks. The I/O devices that are so necessary to make a computer system useful are connected to the rest of the computer by what are known as **interfaces**.

Strictly speaking, an interface is just a boundary or border line between two different objects. In the context of a computer system, an I/O interface is the physical dividing line between the computer system and its I/O devices. In order for an interface to connect two pieces of equipment successfully, several requirements must be met. First, the physical intercon-

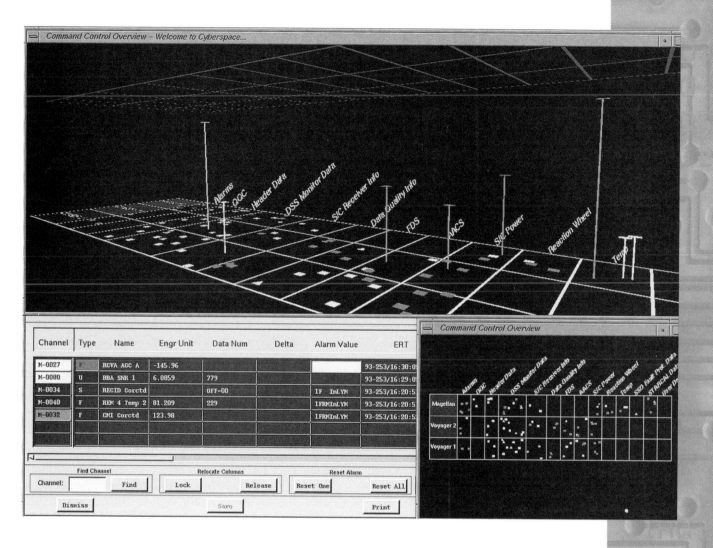

nections must match—there must be compatible plugs, sockets, cables, and connectors. Beyond this, there must be electrical compatibility across the interface—the electrical signals must be of consistent voltage and current levels. These signals must also be traveling in the correct directions. Lastly, they must also obey timing constraints. This last requirement can be quite an obstacle in practice, as specialized measuring instruments like **oscilloscopes** and logic analyzers are the only way to view the time domain characteristics of the electrical signals.

Fortunately, manufacturers of computer systems and input/output devices take care of much of the hard work. The manufacturers of all of the various pieces of equipment select an appropriate standard that is well documented and they build and test their equipment to this standard. The result is a guarantee that their products will inter-operate properly with others that are designed and built to meet the same standards.

Over time, various standards are introduced and adopted to facilitate all sorts of different interconnection schemes. Due to the underlying limitations of the technology, some common characteristics are present across these standards. For example, on a shared communication channel of some sort like a cable or bus, only one device can be permitted to be supplying (or transmitting) information at any one instant. This is because the

Designed for the U.S. Air Force, the Cyberspace Data Monitoring System featured three-dimensional imagery that enabled personnel to monitor satellites and space probes. This computer system interface was built to monitor the Voyager and Magellan spacecraft.

oscilloscopes measuring instruments for electrical circuitry; connected to circuits under test using probes on leads and having small screens that display the signal waveforms

protocol an agreed understanding for the sub-operations that make up a transaction; usually found in the specification of inter-computer communications

resistors electrical components that slow the flow of current

INTERACTION AT A NEW LEVEL

Whereas most users are comfortable with keyboards and mouse pointing devices currently in use, there is evidence to suggest that input devices will become more elaborate in the future. There are some companies that offer specialized input devices like gloves that are directly connected to the computer. The gloves measure the movement of the user's hand and translate these movements into operations that allow the user to "pick up," for example, objects that he or she views on the screen or in a headset/visor.

electrical signals from two or more transmitters will clash, possibly resulting in component damage. Consequently, a standard that documents rules for managing an interface must include a definition of the rules of conversation between devices—otherwise known as a **protocol**. Usually, specialized electrical devices are included within the computer system to guarantee that the protocol is adhered to. These devices are called "arbiters" or "I/O controllers."

One of the most popular standards has been the small computer systems interface (SCSI) standard. This has been used in a variety of personal computers as well as industrial computers. SCSI was originally developed to support the connection of mass storage devices to computer systems—these have traditionally been hard disks and tape drives, but more recently have included CD-ROM (compact disc-read only memory) drives. Each device with a SCSI interface is connected to a flat ribbon cable with fifty conducting wires. Up to eight SCSI interfaces can share the one cable, although they all cannot be using it at the same instant.

One aspect that often catches the unwary when using SCSI devices is that the last SCSI device attached to the cable must have some special **resistors** installed on it. These resistors (often called terminating resistors) are needed to ensure that the electrical signals that pass along the cable are not reflected when they reach the end. If they are permitted to reflect, they can cause problems for the SCSI interfaces that might misinterpret them.

A modern alternative to the SCSI standard is that of the universal serial bus (USB), which permits simultaneous external connection of more than 100 input/output devices. Not just mass storage devices either, but computer mice and even more exotic devices like digital cameras, scanners, and games controllers.

The preceding descriptions involve the connection of input/output devices to the computer system, which primarily are external to the computer itself. Within the computer system though, the term "interfacing" takes on a more specialized meaning. It is also necessary to interface the processor to the various memory devices that it needs to access. In addition to this, the processor must be interfaced to various controller devices that manage bus networks internal to the computer.

The physical nature of the interface is usually less of an issue here, mainly because the devices are expected to be placed on a printed circuit board, and copper tracks and plastic sockets can be laid out to suit the geometry of the components. However the electrical and temporal characteristics must be correctly matched—just as before.

SCSI, USB, and other standards applicable to the connection of external devices are not really appropriate here, because those standards are intended for managing input/output devices that are slower in operation than the processor and usually involve comparatively large amounts of data. Instead, other standards are employed that permit high speed operation (at, or near, the natural operating speed of the processor) and usually smaller amounts of information in each transfer.

When the system designer is deciding how to interface networking devices to a processor, for example, then standards like the peripheral components interconnect (PCI) bus protocol might be used. Conversely, an interfacing standard like the accelerated graphics port (AGP) can be used when connecting a graphics device to a processor. SEE ALSO CENTRAL PROCESSING UNIT; MICROCOMPUTERS.

Stephen Murray

Bibliography

Triebel, Walter A., and Avtar Singh. *The 8088 and 8086 Microprocessors.* Upper Saddle River, NJ: Prentice Hall, 1991.

Internet Resources

"Accelerated Graphics Port (AGP)." *The PC Guide.* <http://www.pcguide.com/ref/mbsys/buses/types/agp-c.html>

"USB Info: Frequently Asked Questions." USB Implementers Forum Inc. <http://www.usb.org/faq.html>

Design Tools

Computer programming is not easy. The programmer has to be able to think logically and know how to break down a big problem into tiny pieces. To accomplish this, some people like to state the problem and the steps necessary for its solution in their natural language before trying to code the program in a computer language. What they are doing is defining the correct **algorithm**—giving the computer the information and process it needs to solve the problem. Writing the program becomes very easy after the algorithm has been spelled out. Since the hard part is defining the problem and the approach needed for its solution, there are several design tools available to help with this planning process. These include flowcharts, pseudocode, and Nassi-Shneiderman diagrams, which are used specifically with structured programs.

algorithm a rule or procedure used to solve a mathematical problem—most often described as a sequence of steps

Flowcharts

A flowchart represents an algorithm using symbols instead of words. The step-by-step process is shown with lines, arrows, and boxes of different shapes demonstrating the flow of the process. Flowcharts are very useful in program development and provide excellent documentation. Because the steps needed for a solution have been defined, a flowchart can easily be translated into any computer language after it has been tested.

Any process can be articulated with these shapes and some connecting lines and arrows. One should note that the only symbol that allows two exits is the diamond-shaped decision symbol. It is used to indicate that the computer can take either of two paths depending on whether the comparison is true or false. All other flow chart symbols have only one exit line.

The symbols are usually read from top to bottom, and from left to right. Straight lines connect the symbols and represent how the algorithm advances from step to step. Their arrows are used to clarify the direction of flow. To complete the picture, brief instructions are written within each symbol to provide a more detailed description of the tasks represented by the symbols.

> **PICTURE THIS!**
>
> Flowcharts are sometimes called block diagrams or logical diagrams. Why were they developed? Because pictures are usually thought to be easier to understand than text.

Figure 1. Some standard flowcharting symbols.

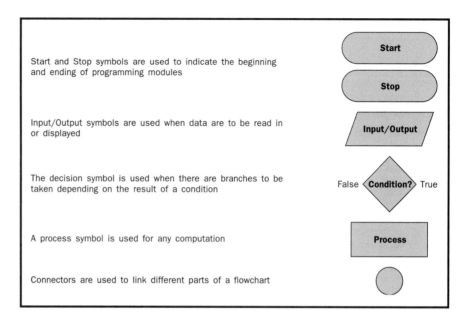

Some standard flowchart symbols and their meaning are shown in Figure 1. Flowcharts can be used to provide an overview of the major components of a program or to detail each of the processing steps within a program. Macro flowcharts outline the general flow of a program and are useful when dividing a complex problem into modules, especially when implementing structured programming techniques. Detail, or micro flowcharts, depict the processing steps required within a particular module and often involve a one-to-one correspondence between flowchart symbols and program state-

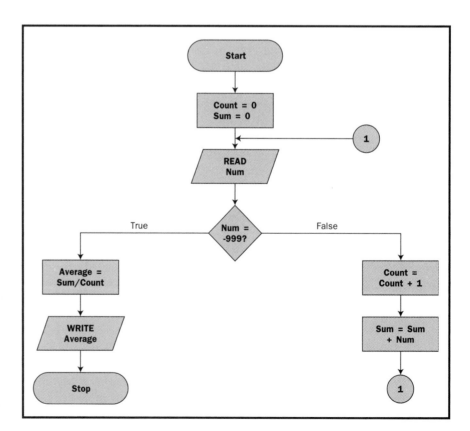

Figure 2. Example of a micro flowchart to compute the average of a list of numbers.

ments. Figure 2 shows a flowchart which computes the average of a list of numbers, in this example an input data value of −999 is used to stop the loop.

Pseudocode

Pseudocode is an English-like description of the processing steps to be performed in a program. The programmer writes these descriptions in the order in which corresponding program statements will appear in the program. Although there are no standards for pseudocode, it usually uses structured programming control structures.

For example, sequence structures are usually written in lowercase, while uppercase START and END are used to denote major blocks of code. In addition, IF, ELSE, ENDIF, DO WHILE and DO UNTIL are always in uppercase, and conditions are indented using lowercase.

The use of pseudocode allows the programmer to focus on the steps needed to perform a specific process without having to worry about how they should be stated in a computer language. Because pseudocode can be easier to update than a flowchart, it is preferred by some programmers. Figure 3 shows an example of a pseudocode used to set up the logic for finding the average of a list of numbers.

Nassi-Shneiderman Diagrams

These charts, an example of which is shown in Figure 4, are also called structured flowcharts or iteration diagrams. They were proposed by Isaac Nassi and Ben Shneiderman as an alternative to flowcharts to help programmers

```
START
set counter to zero
set sum to zero
read first number
DO UNTIL number = -999
    add number to sum
    add one to counter
    read next number
ENDDO
divide sum by counter to get average
write average
END
```

Figure 3. Example of pseudocode to find the average of a list of numbers.

Figure 4. Structured flowcharts.

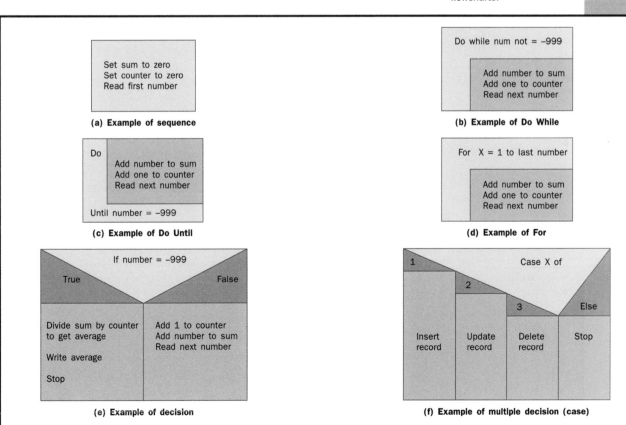

(a) **Example of sequence**

(b) **Example of Do While**

(c) **Example of Do Until**

(d) **Example of For**

(e) **Example of decision**

(f) **Example of multiple decision (case)**

when planning structured programs. Each diagram corresponds to one of the programming control structures: sequence, selection and repetition. For example, a rectangular box is used for sequence, while an "L" or inverted "L" is used for repetition. As shown on page 57, Figure 4 illustrates these and other combinations being used for "if-then-else" and for multiple selections.

The outline of each Nassi-Shneiderman diagram is a rectangle and its subdivision always gives more rectangles that may be subdivided even further. Therefore, these diagrams can be nested within each other, modeling recursion, a feature of structured programming. Programmers like to work with these diagrams because they are easy to follow. They also feel that analyzing an algorithm is made easier because of the simplicity in which the logic is set forth.

All of these design tools can be used in combination to plan and develop accurate and efficient software. Other options may include CASE (computer-aided software engineering) tools, which automate many of the tasks required in developing a system, and structured walkthroughs, which help members of a programming team to review and evaluate the progress of modules in a structured project. SEE ALSO ALGORITHMS; BOOLEAN ALGEBRA; PROGRAMMING.

Ida M. Flynn

Bibliography

Stair, Ralph M., and George W. Reynolds. *Principles of Information Systems*, 5th ed. Boston: Thomson Learning, 2001.

Swirsky, Robert. "The Art of Flowcharting." *Popular Computing* (September, 1982): 75–78.

Welburn, Tyler. *Structured COBOL: Fundamentals and Style*. Palo Alto, CA: Mayfield Publishing, 1981.

Digital Logic Design

Computers, and other digital systems, are designed using elementary electronic circuits called **gates**. In this article, *Inverters, Or gates*, and *And gates* are introduced by logical statements justifying the term "logic design." Then, the design procedure is illustrated, and **integrated circuits** are discussed.

Gates

Gates are used to regulate electronic flow and to construct devices to process data, as well as to build memory devices. There are three fundamental gates—"And," "Or," and "Not"—as well as some "hybrid" gates such as "Nand" (Not-And) and "Nor" (Not-Or).

Not

Consider the logical statement: "The porch light is on ($Z = 1$) when I am *not* home ($A = 0$)." Z is the output; A is the input (I am home). A corresponding **binary** function, of one **variable**, which is also binary, is called "Complement" or "Not." "Not" is represented by "$Z = {\sim}A$" and its behavior is:

gates fundamental building blocks of digital and computer based electric circuits that perform logical operations; for example logical AND, logical OR

integrated circuits circuits with the transistors, resistors, and other circuit elements etched into the surface of single chips of semiconductor material, usually silicon

binary existing in only two states, such as "on" or "off," "one" or "zero"

variable a symbol, such as a string of letters, which may assume any one of a set of values known as the domain

A	Not-A (Z)
0	1
1	0

The electronic implementation of *Not* is the *inverter*, a one-transistor current amplifier with one input and one output. A high (binary-1) input voltage, typically about +5 Volts, forces current into the amplifier's input. So, the amplifier draws current from its output, pulling its output voltage low (binary-0), typically, close to 0 Volts. A 1 or high input gives a 0 output (the complement of the input). Since a low input voltage provides no current to the amplifier's input, the amplifier draws no current from its output, causing a high voltage there. A low or 0 input gives a 1 output. The output is the opposite or complement (Not) of the input.

Or

Consider the logical statement: "I wear a jacket (Z = 1) if it is cold (A = 1) *or* if it rains (B = 1) *or*. . . ." A corresponding binary function, of two or more binary variables, is called "Or." The behavior of "Or" is tabulated for two and three variables:

AB	Or	ABC	Or
00	0	000	0
01	1	001	1
10	1	010	1
11	1	011	1
		100	1
		101	1
		110	1
		111	1

One or the other or both (or "all" three) of the inputs "on" cause the output to be true. A *Nor gate* is like an inverter, but with N input terminals instead of one. A high input voltage on any of the inputs causes a low output voltage and a low voltage on all inputs causes a high output voltage. Since "Nor" is the complement of "Or," "Or" is implemented in electronics by a "Nor-Not" tandem. "Not-Nor" or "OR." But, "Nor" has another application.

Consider a pair of two-input "Nor" gates, and let the output of each gate be one of the other gate's inputs. Label the unused inputs as S and R, and assume both these inputs are low. A positive pulse on S causes the corresponding "Nor" gate's output to go low. Since both inputs to the other gate are low, its output is high. The pair of gates remains in this state even after the pulse on S returns to 0. A positive pulse on R causes the output of R's "Nor" gate to go low. Since both inputs to S's gate are low, its output is high. The pair of gates now remains in this opposite state even after the pulse on R returns to 0. This pair of cross-connected "Nor" gates is called a "Set-Reset Flip-Flop" and it is the basic binary storage element used throughout digital design. The memory element is a 1 if S (Set) is 1, 0 if S is 0, or, what is the same, R (Reset) is 1.

And

Consider the logical statement: "I wear a hat (Z = 1) when it is cold (A = 1) *and* when it is raining (B = 1) *and*. . . ." A corresponding binary function

of two or more binary variables is called "And." The behavior of "And" is tabulated for two and three variables:

AB	And	ABC	And
00	0	000	0
01	0	001	0
10	0	010	0
11	1	011	0
		100	0
		101	0
		110	0
		111	1

All inputs must be on for the output to be on.

Like a "Nor" gate, a "Nand gate" also has N input terminals and one output terminal. But, "Nand" is more complicated than "Nor," because a low output voltage is caused by a high voltage on all the inputs, and the output voltage is high if any of the input voltages is low. "And" is implemented in electronics by a "Nand-Not" tandem. Again, "Not-Nand," or "Not-Not-And," hence, "And."

Design Example

Consider a binary circuit, with output X and three inputs. D and E are separate streams of binary data, and C is a control signal so that X = D when C = 0 and X = E when C = 1. That is, the output is equal to D when C is 0, and equals E when C is 1. C controls the output. This *Binary Multiplexor's* behavior is tabulated:

CDE	X
000	0
001	0
010	1
011	1
100	0
101	1
110	0
111	1

Compare the output to D's value when C is 0; compare the output to E's value when C is 1. In the first four rows of the table, X = D because C = 0. In the last four rows, X = E because C = 1. The device is called a **multiplexor** because it switches ("multiplexes") between the data streams D and E under the control of C. It is a "binary multiplexor" because it switches between or "multiplexes" among two devices, D and E. It takes turns servicing them under the control of C. Consider two approaches for implementing this function.

multiplexor a complex device that acts as a multi-way switch for analog or digital signals

Canonic And-Or Implementation. Any binary function can be implemented in three layers of logic: (1) a layer of inverters that provides the complement of each input if it is needed; (2) a layer with K different N-input "And" gates where the circuit has N inputs and the circuit's output function has K one-points (one outputs); and (3) one K-input *Or* gate. Since the multiplexor's output function, X, has four one-points, the canonic "And-

Or" implementation has four "And" gates, each with three inputs. The different "And" gates' inputs are appropriately inverted so each gate identifies a different one-point (one in the output). For example, an "And" gate whose inputs are ~C, D, and ~E has a 1-output when CDE = 010. A four-input "Or" gate, with an input from each "And" gate, provides the circuit's output. This would be (~C,D,~E) + (or) (~C,D,E) + (or) (C,~D,E) + (or) (C,D,E) for the four one-points (one outputs) given.

Based on the Logical Description. We can design the multiplexor in an ad-hoc manner from its logical description. If the inputs to a two-input "And" gate are ~C and D, this gate's output equals D when C equals 0, and is 0 when C equals 1. If the inputs to another two-input "And" gate are C and E, this gate's output equals E when C equals 1, and equal 0 when C equals 0. The "Or" of these two "And" gates gives X. That is, the output is D (equal to D) when C is off (~C or C = 0), the output equals E when C is on.

Obviously this second implementation, with only two two-input "And"-gates and one two-input "Or"-gate, is less expensive than the first. This is one of the issues in design. Cost, a complex issue, is illustrated next.

Integrated Circuits

Integration is the manufacture of more than one gate, an entire binary circuit, or even a whole system, on the same **silicon** chip. Transistorized gates and flip-flops were made in the 1950s from discrete resistors and transistors. Then, they were integrated onto a single chip, called a "small-scale" integrated circuit (IC). Often, a chip's complexity is limited by the package's pin-outs. The "7400 series" of integrated circuits, introduced in the late 1960s, is still used today. If a part is popular, its per-chip **overhead** is small. Then, its price covers only the cost of materials and manufacturing—about $3 (in quantity). Allowing pins for common battery and ground, a 14-pin package has the following limits:

silicon a chemical element with symbol Si; the most abundant element in the Earth's crust and the most commonly used semiconductor material

overhead the expense or cost involved in carrying out a particular operation

Part#	Description	Pins/gate	Max# (12÷pins/gate) (14 − 2, battery and ground, = 12)	$/gate ($3÷ # of gates)
7404	Inverter	2	Hex (6)	.50
7400	2-input Nand	3	Quad(4)	.75
7410	3-input Nand	4	Triple(3)	1.00
7420	4-input Nand	5	Dual(2)	1.50

As chip manufacturers placed more logic circuits on a single chip of silicon, integration proceeded through three subsequent *scales* of fabrication. Simple binary functions are fabricated on a single chip with up to 100 **transistors** on a chip, in what has come to be called "Medium Scale Integration." For example, the Quad Set-Reset Flip-Flop is a useful digital integrated circuit (IC). But, when fitting four SR-FFs within the pin constraints of a 14-pin DIP (Dual In-Line Package), each SR-FF gets only three pins (14 − 2 (for battery and ground) = 12; 12 / 4 (Quad) FF's = 3 pins per SR flip-flop, 2 inputs, 1 output) and only one of each flip-flop's outputs is connected to a pin (the S or the R but not both).

More complicated digital circuits, such as binary counters and shift registers, are fabricated with many hundreds of transistors on a chip in "Large

transistors the plural of transistor, which is a contraction of TRANSfer resISTOR; semiconductor device, invented by John Bardeen, Walter Brattain, and William Shockley, which have three terminals; can be used for switching and amplifying electrical signals

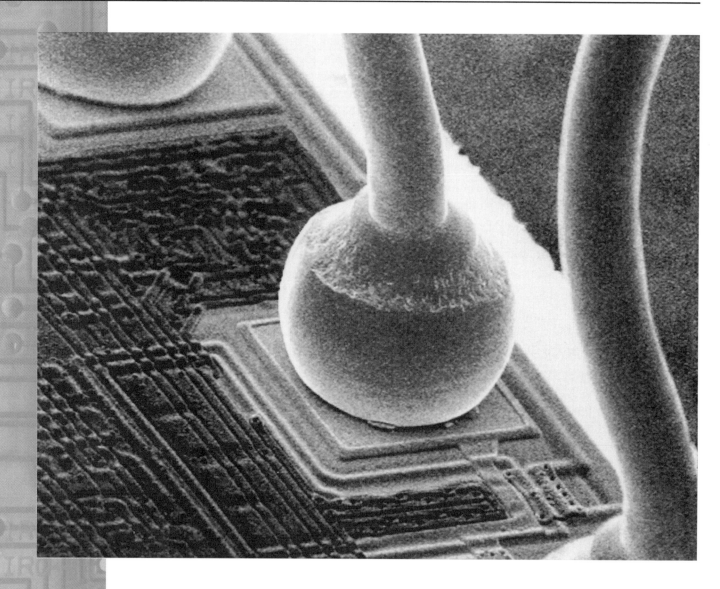

Micro-wires bonded onto the silicon chip of a computer system's hardware facilitate the flow of data through the different channels dictated by the logic systems in place.

Scale Integration." Finally, modern digital circuits—like 16- and 32-bit CPUs and memory chips with vast amounts of binary storage—are fabricated with thousands of transistors on a chip in "Very Large Scale Integration" (VLSI). SEE ALSO BOOLEAN ALGEBRA; INTEGRATED CIRCUITS; TRANSISTORS.

Richard A. Thompson

Bibliography

Booth, Taylor L. *Digital Networks and Computer Systems.* New York: Wiley, 1971.

Hill, Fredrick J., and G. R. Peterson. *Introduction to Switching Theory and Logical Design.* New York: Wiley, 1974.

Display Devices

The first computer display devices were modified typewriters and Teletype machines. These devices were slow, noisy, and expensive, and could only handle text. For graphic output, an X-Y plotter, a device that pulled a pen over a piece of paper, was used. It shared all the problems of the Teletype machine.

It did not take long before these mechanical machines were replaced with electronic counterparts. The replacement was called a terminal. It consisted of a typewriter-like keyboard, which activated switches, and a display screen, which was a modified television receiver. Thus, the first computer display device was a cathode ray tube or CRT.

Cathode Ray Tubes

A cathode ray tube paints an image on a **phosphor** screen using a beam of electrons. The concept of the CRT was formulated before the nature of the electron was known. Cathode rays are not rays at all but high-speed streams of particles called electrons. The CRT is a vacuum tube where the processing of electrons takes place in an evacuated glass envelope. If the electron beam passed through air or another gas, the electrons would collide with the molecules of that gas, making it difficult to manipulate the electron beam.

The CRT generates a source of electrons from an electron gun. The electrons are accelerated in a straight line to a very high velocity using a high voltage and then deflected from the straight line using a magnetic field. The beam can be turned on or off with an electrical signal. The screen of the CRT is coated with a phosphorus compound, which gives off light energy when it is struck with high-speed electrons. When the beam hits the face of the CRT, a spot of light results. The beam is scanned from left to right and from top to bottom. The beam is turned on when a light area is to be generated and it is turned off when an area is to be dark. This scanning is clearly visible on both computer monitors and television screens.

There are two basic methods of scanning a picture. The first is called "progressive." Every line is scanned beginning at the top left corner and finishing at the lower right. Another method is called "interlace." The picture is scanned twice with half of the lines being scanned each time. This is done to refresh the picture at twice the actual scan rate and reduce the flicker of the display.

From Monochrome to Color Displays

The first CRTs were one color, also called monochrome; the display color was usually green. The first display devices were designed to replace a mechanical printer, so a single color was sufficient. However, the CRT is not limited to only printing text but is capable of producing images and complex graphics where full color is highly desirable. Again, technology was adapted from the television industry, and color monitors were quick to follow the early monochrome versions.

The color CRT is effectively three monochrome CRTs, all in the same glass envelope. There are three electron guns but each gun is individually controlled. The three electron beams are deflected together and strike the face of the CRT. The electron beams must pass through a screen with hundreds of thousands of small holes, called a **shadow mask**, before striking the phosphor on the front of the CRT. The holes are arranged in groups of three so that when one electron beam passes through the hole, it strikes

phosphor a coating applied to the back of a glass screen on a cathode ray tube (CRT) that emits light when a beam of electrons strikes its surface

TALKING THE TALK

Computing systems that interface with the human operator have to speak the language. This means aural (audio), tactile (touch), or visual means of communication. Of the three, the visual display is the most powerful for most applications.

shadow mask a metal sheet behind the glass screen of a cathode ray tube (CRT) that ensures the correct color phosphor elements are struck by the electron beams

a small dot of phosphor that gives off red light. Another beam strikes only a dot of phosphor that gives off green light. The third beam falls on a phosphor dot that gives off blue light.

The mechanics of the color CRT are such that each of the three electron beams produces scanning beams of only one color. These three colors—red, green, and blue, or RGB—are the three additive primary colors. Any color may be generated by using a combination of these three. This shadow mask technology was the first to be used for color television and is still used in most CRTs.

Over the years the shadow mask CRT has been refined. Modern tubes have a nearly flat face, have much improved color, and have very high resolution, which is the ability of a display to show very small detail. One improvement is a shadow mask using stripes rather than round holes. This arrangement is easier to align. These improvements are not only found in computer displays but television receivers as well.

Cathode Ray Tube Disadvantages

Since its inception, the CRT has shown a number of disadvantages. First, the tube is large and heavy. CRT sizes are relative to the diagonal measurement and most CRT displays are deeper than their diagonal measurement. Secondly, the electrons in the tube are accelerated using high voltage. The larger the tube, the higher the accelerating voltage, which reaches to the tens of thousands of volts and requires a large power supply. The tube is made of glass, which is not suited for portable equipment or for applications with significant vibration such as aircraft. Finally, the tube requires significant power.

As hard as it is to believe today, the first "portable" computers actually used CRTs for display devices! In a word, these early portable computers were huge and would have remained so if a suitable replacement for the CRT had not been found. What was needed was a low power display device that had the capability of the CRT yet was small, not as fragile, and required low power and low voltage.

From Cathode Ray Tube to Liquid Crystal Display

The liquid crystal display, or LCD, is a low voltage device. It requires very low power but it was not originally a graphics device or capable of color. The LCD is essentially a light gate, which can be opened to allow light to pass, or closed to shut light off. To use the LCD as a full color graphics display, the display is divided up into picture elements called pixels. Each **pixel** represents the color and intensity of a small part of the complete picture. Three LCD light gates are required for each pixel: one for red, green, and blue. Behind each gate is a color filter, which is illuminated by a white light source. Behind one LCD light gate is a red filter, behind another is a green filter, and the third a blue. By adjusting the amounts of the three primaries, as in the CRT, the correct intensity and color can be generated for each pixel.

LCD construction is simple. The liquid crystal material is sandwiched between two flat glass plates. Crystalline materials, which usually are not liquid, have very profound effects on light waves. The liquid crystal can af-

pixel a single picture element on a video screen; one of the individual dots making up a picture on a video screen or digital image

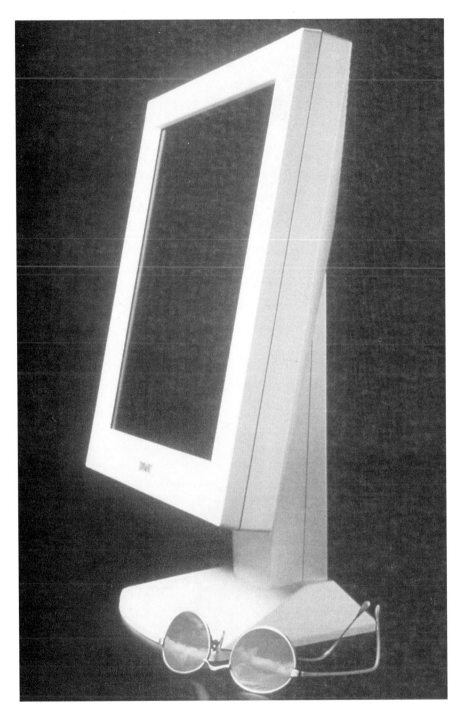

Flat screen monitors are highly sought by individuals looking to free up some space in their offices. Future technological advances are expected to bring even narrower screens.

fect the manner in which light energy passes through the material, and this can be changed by the application of an electric field. A thin metal electrode is placed over the area where the LCD is to change from dark to light. The electrode is so thin that it is completely transparent and cannot be seen. An electric field is created when a voltage is applied to the electrodes on the LCD glass.

Most LCDs use the rotation of polarized light to change the intensity of the light. The light entering the pixel is *plane polarized*, meaning that the light waves are in one plane. This is done with a **polarizer**, which is the same technique used in sunglasses to reduce glare. A simple way to visual-

polarizer a translucent sheet that permits only plane-polarized light to pass through, blocking all other light

ize a polarizer is to think about a venetian blind where the separation of the slats is so close that light waves can only pass through in one plane.

On the front of the LCD there is a second polarizer, which is oriented at a right angle to the first. If these two polarizers were placed together with nothing but vacuum or air between them, no light could pass through. This is because the light is polarized by the first polarizer and is incompatible with the second.

Liquid crystal material has the ability to overcome this by rotating the polarization of light waves, but only when an electric field is placed across the liquid crystal. Therefore, if a voltage is placed across the liquid crystal, the light is rotated by 90 degrees and will pass through the front polarizer. The application of a voltage can permit or shut off the light intensity.

In the color LCD display three "sub pixels" are required because the intensity of light from the three primaries must be independently controlled. If one pixel could provide both brightness and color, the LCD could be simplified. An improved LCD display uses a single light valve where the liquid crystal material generates both the color and brightness. This new LCD material is called *cholesteric* because it was originally derived from animal cholesterol.

Display Device Picture Quality

The number of pixels into which an image is divided will directly affect the quality of the picture. As an example, a conventional television picture is generated with 525 scanning lines (the U.S. standard). Of these, only about 484 lines are visible. The aspect ratio of the television picture is 4:3, which means that the width of the picture is four-thirds the height. If the pixels were square, there would be 484 rows and 660 columns of pixels. Because of the interlace scan, the actual number of rows and columns is half of that, or 242 by 330.

When an image is generated with an insufficient number of pixels, the picture lacks resolution and the pixels are very evident. The individual lines of a television picture are clearly visible, particularly in a large screen television. Common computer displays have resolutions of 340 X 680, 680 X 1760, and so on. Computer monitors can have a better picture than some television receivers.

An improved television standard is set to replace the older 525 line system; this is called high definition television, or HDTV. In addition to the improved resolution or definition, the aspect ratio is 16:9, which is the same as motion pictures. Because HDTV is a digital system and optical disks are used to store video, the relationship between computer monitors and television receivers will grow closer over the years.

Simplifying LCD Display Technology

In the LCD display, each light gate has to be connected to electronic drivers, which activate or deactivate the gate. An LCD graphics display has a very large number of pixels, which poses a serious challenge in running conductors to each LCD light gate. Thin, transparent conductors can hardly be seen but the sheer number of them would make manufacturing LCD displays difficult, at best. One solution is a method of connecting the LCD seg-

PUTTING CHOLESTEROL TO GOOD USE

Cholesteric display is one of several promising display technologies being developed. The phenomenal growth of computer chips has heightened awareness of the limitations of graphics displays. The cholesteric LCD shows the most promise of the low power displays but is not perfect. Most display engineers will readily admit there is no perfect display.

ments by mounting electronic circuits right on the glass plate. This arrangement is called an "active matrix" and it significantly reduces the number of interconnects required. The transistors used for the active matrix are made from thin films that are so small they are virtually invisible. This is called a thin film transistor active matrix LCD, or TFTAM LCD or AMLCD.

Even though the AMLCD has simplified the LCD graphics display, a large number of light gates, transistors, and interconnections remain. In the manufacturing process, if one pixel fails, the display must be scrapped. In an LCD graphics display, the number of LCD light gates numbers more than one million. The chances are good that one of those LCD gates or the thin film transistors would be defective in the manufacturing process.

The percentage of good products from a factory production run is called the yield. A poor yield is reflected in a high price of a product. Increasing the yield of the LCD production was the major challenge to the LCD industry in producing a cost-effective display product. The cholesteric LCD can be made with one-third the number of pixels and therefore, one-third the number of LCD light gates. This means the cholesteric LCD will have three times the manufacturing yield, which makes the technology potentially much more cost effective than other options.

Lighting Sources for Display Devices

The AMLCD requires a white light source to operate. Some of the more common light sources are not suited for backlighting an LCD display. The incandescent lamp and **LEDs** are point sources of light whereas a distributed source is desired. These two sources are also not energy efficient, which is an important characteristic required for battery power.

LEDs the acronym for Light Emitting Diode; a diode that emits light when passing a current and used as an indicating lamp

For notebook computers, an electroluminescent panel is used. This device generates a low light level with good energy efficiency. The panel is thin and can be sandwiched easily behind the LCD and the display case.

Some portable devices such as small "palm" computers, cellular telephones, and watches must perform in bright sunlight. Displays that reflect, rather than emit, light are used in these devices. LCD displays are well suited to applications where the display operates in the "reflective" mode. When the ambient light is low, a backlight provides the necessary illumination. When backlighting is provided, the LCD is now operating in the "transmissive" mode. LCD displays that operate in both modes are called "transflective." As of the year 2001, transflective LCDs were not yet capable of providing full color.

If the light intensity falling on the front of a transmissive display is greater than the emitted light, the display contrast will be lost and the display will "wash out." Usually, displays are shielded from very bright light such as sunlight but in some applications this is not possible, such as an aircraft instrument panel. Displays used for these applications are called "sunlight readable." This means the display is visible in full sunlight. In these high brightness applications, a thin, serpentine, fluorescent lamp is used for backlighting. This technique provides a high light output but also generates considerable heat. Providing a very high level of backlighting for a color LCD display has become very common as the LCD is used for computer projectors.

The new cholesteric LCD material will also allow for an LCD display that operates with reflected light and will be completely sunlight readable. Improved resolution will result because the cholesteric LCD requires only one light gate per pixel.

Improving LCD Technology

The modern AMLCD display is one of the best display technologies but it still suffers from some weaknesses. The resolution of a good quality AMLCD is not as good as the better CRTs. The cost of AMLCDs, although dropping, is still higher than the equivalent CRT. The AMLCD, or LCD in general, is not well suited for use in harsh environments because it is negatively affected by low temperatures. The response time of an LCD display under these conditions is increased significantly. This would cause moving images to drag and blur. In very cold temperatures, such as those in which military equipment is often operated, the LCD will quit operating completely and could be damaged by the extreme conditions.

A new display technology in the later stages of development is called the field emission display, or FED. The FED uses an array of small, pointed electrodes mounted close to a dot of phosphor. Like the color CRT, the pointed electrode causes an emission of an electron beam, which excites the phosphor to emit light. Essentially, the FED is a flat CRT where the electron beam is not deflected. The FED has all the advantages of the CRT, including good resolution, bright display, full color capability, and sunlight readability, without the major disadvantages, such as low temperature problems. It is not yet clear what direction this new technology will take, but it is likely that FEDs will be used for aircraft instruments and other sunlight readable applications. SEE ALSO COMPUTER SYSTEM INTERFACES; DIGITAL LOGIC DESIGN.

Albert D. Helfrick

Bibliography

Robin, Michael, and Michel Poulin. *Digital Television Fundamentals: Design and Installation of Video and Audio Systems.* New York: McGraw-Hill, 2000.

Whitaker, Jerry C. *Electronic Displays: Technology, Design and Applications.* New York: McGraw Hill, 1994.

——. *Video Display Engineering.* New York: McGraw-Hill, 2000.

Document Processing

Documents serve to archive and communicate information. Document processing is the activity of operating on information captured in some form of persistent medium. Traditionally, that medium is paper, and documents are bundles of paper with information captured in print or in writing.

Document processing may serve to coordinate and conduct business transactions. When a customer submits an order to purchase a certain product, the order becomes a document for processing. The manufacturing company coordinates the activities of acquiring the raw materials, making the product, and finally delivering it to the customer with an invoice to collect payment—all by passing documents from one department to another, from one party to another.

Humans, endowed with the capacity to read, write, and think, are the principal actors in document processing. The invention of the modern digital computer, supported by various key technologies, has revolutionized document processing. Because information can be coded in other media that is read and written by the computer—from **punched cards** in the early 1960s to **magnetic tapes**, disks, and optical CDs (compact discs) today—it is not always necessary for documents to be on paper for processing.

Automatic Data Processing

If one can implement decision-making into the logic of a computer program, and have the relevant information in the documents coded in some medium for the computer to read and write, the computer running the program can process the documents automatically. Unless the decisions in processing the documents require the intelligence of a human expert, the computer is much faster and more reliable.

The repository for the information is a database. Since the information in the database is readily accessible by the computer, one can generate the paper documents with the desired information any time it is necessary. Automatic data processing and the database technologies for information maintenance and archival have existed since the 1960s. For decisions that require the judgment of a human expert, document processing must bring in the knowledge workers—human users with the expertise in the relevant field of knowledge.

Typographics and Reprographics

The computer is also a versatile tool for the preparation and reproduction of documents. During the early 1980s, as a result of advances in printing technology, text formatting and typesetting tools were available on the computer. People can use these tools to create document content while at the same time specify the presentation layout, including typesetting details. People can keep all the information in some persistent medium such as a disk file. This is called a source document, since the computer tool can use it as input to generate the printed document as output.

Commonly the source document contains coded information in a mark-up language—tags that specify typesetting and presentation layout information. Mark-up languages may also incorporate the use of images and graphical drawings supported by the printing technologies. Low-cost laser printers became available in the mid-1980s. These tools greatly enhance one's ability to produce documents readily on demand. It is necessary to keep only the source documents in a computer-readable medium.

Interactive Graphics and Multimedia

A document does not need to be printed on paper in order for people to view it. Since the bit-mapped monitor screen was invented in the 1970s, people can also view a document on the monitor screen. This allows people to interact with the document directly on the screen. The printed document is called a hard copy, and a displayed document on the monitor screen is known as a soft copy. Both copies are generated from the source document.

punched cards paper cards with punched holes which give instructions to a computer in order to encode program instructions and data; now obsolete

magnetic tapes a way of storing programs and data from computers; tapes are generally slow and prone to deterioration over time but are inexpensive

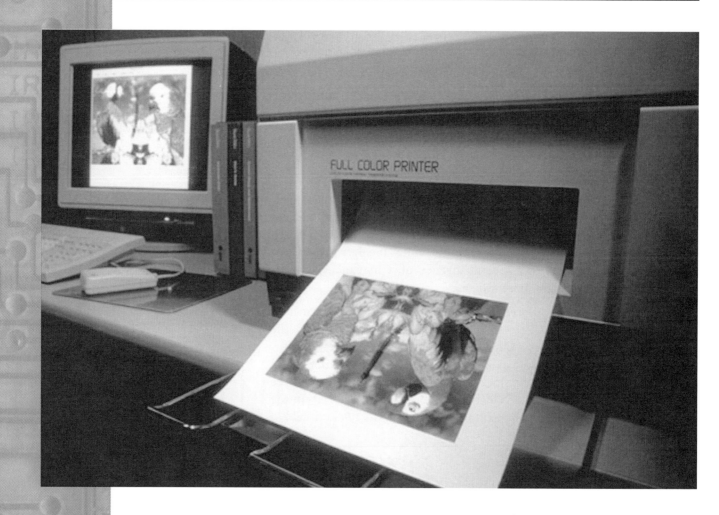

When processing documents, particularly images, the color and contrast can be enhanced. Printing on a color laser will create a clear and crisp image.

Using interactive graphics and window interfaces, users can treat the monitor screen as a desktop and retrieve any document for viewing, or interact with one document to bring up another document. Multiple users can easily share documents and view related documents on the computer at the same time. This also means that someone can use the computer to mediate and coordinate the timing and sequencing of people working on documents. A workflow system can implement the business rules of operation to coordinate multiple parties working together in document processing. It is conceivable that an office may have employees working on documents without ever needing to print out the documents on paper. That is the idea of document processing in a paperless office.

Another worthwhile note is the changing concept of a document. The source document kept in a disk file may incorporate document content with graphical drawing, images, and the typesetting and layout information, as well as audio and video scripts. On a computer equipped with the proper hardware, the soft copy of the document can show a video script or play an audio segment. Such a multimedia document is a new concept of the document: It is no longer a physical bundle of papers.

Telecommunications and E-Commerce

Since people can view a document on a monitor screen to work on it, and they can print out the document on paper only when a hard copy is needed, they can easily share documents by sending them across computer networks. Electronic mail (e-mail) is a document sent from one person to another over a network. The Internet was originally proposed in the early 1980s for the purpose of communication between researchers, connecting the computers in research institutions across the nation. But as the Internet has rapidly grown with documents shared by more and more people, the network has become a channel for publishing. The parties involved, however, need to jointly observe certain standards for the communication **protocol** and the format for source documents.

Servers are the computers that send documents out on request, and **browsers** are the tools that are used to make the requests and view the documents received. Servers and browsers must observe the same standards for communication protocol and document format. Hyper Text Transfer Protocol (HTTP) for communication and Hyper Text Mark-up Language (HTML) were established as the standards for source documents in the 1990s. Computers supporting these standards on the Internet formed the World Wide Web.

The Internet continues to grow, virtually covering the whole world today. Document processing on the web can readily involve anybody in the world. Documents can be published and made available for public access from a web server.

The web has become a marketplace for business. E-commerce is a major application of document processing on the World Wide Web. A company may publish a document on a web server to advertise itself and attract customers. Viewers of the document may then interact with it to go to other documents to seek more information. A viewer may also submit an order to make a purchase, sending the order as a document to the company to initiate trading.

Document Structures and Formats

When there are more and more large, complex documents on the Internet, people want to be able to process most of these documents automatically. They want to mark up the structure of document content, so that computer programs can process the content guided by the markup tags. The generation of a soft copy for viewing is simply one of the functions of processing the document.

HTML is a document format designed primarily for viewing using a web browser. Using HTML, people mark up the content of a document with tags for presentation and layout information. A new document format, called Extensible Markup Language (XML), was drafted in November 1996 and has gone through many revisions. XML is a meta-markup language in the sense that it allows one to design the right tags to mark up the content of a document to indicate the structure of its content. Different areas of application domain apply different sets of vocabulary for markup tags. Although molecular biology researchers may use one set of tags, lawyers may use a different set. The style of presentation can be specified according to content structure, and a computer program will be able to display the document for viewing. XML is now emerging as the standard format for documents on the World Wide Web.

protocol an agreed understanding for the sub-operations that make up a transaction; usually found in the specification of inter-computer communications

servers computers that do not deal directly with human users, but instead handle requests from other computers for services to be performed

browsers programs that permits a user to view and navigate through documents, most often hypertext documents

Intelligent Agents

There is now a vast amount of information on the Internet, and the information changes quickly. It can be difficult to find useful information, to track changes, and monitor certain situations. For example, a user might be interested in collecting information on stock prices and want to pay attention only to those that change quickly, or to a very high or very low price. Even when he can gather the information, it is difficult to watch too many stocks at the same time.

An interesting active research area today is that of intelligent agents. An intelligent agent is like a software robot. It is an active program that processes information from documents on the web. An agent may actively watch changes in stock prices, on behalf of its owner who launched it; or it may determine the right combination of plane tickets and hotel reservations for a travel itinerary specified by its owner. It becomes even more interesting when these intelligent agents interact with one another. An agent may be trying to sell some product while another agent may be looking for the right product to buy. The two agents may make the trade, each serving its particular owner. XML is one of the key technologies that makes this possible, because these agents need to process the contents of documents intelligently.

With the Internet, the amount of information, and therefore the number of documents that people need to deal with, is much larger than ever before. It is often said that the world is in the Information Age. Document processing will continue to be a major activity of people working with information. The possibilities for harnessing the power of information are endless. SEE ALSO Input Devices; Markup Languages.

Peter Y. Wu

Bibliography

Anderson-Freed, Susan. *Weaving a Website.* Upper Saddle River, NJ: Prentice Hall, 2002.

Harold, Elliotte Rusty. *XML: Extensible Markup Language.* Foster City, CA: IDG Books Worldwide, 1998.

Eckert, J. Presper, Jr.
1919–1995

Mauchly, John W.
1907–1980

Computer Designers

The Electronic Numerical Integrator and Computer (ENIAC) fired up its 18,000 vacuum tubes in a large room at the Moore School of Electrical Engineering at the University of Pennsylvania just after the end of World War II. Its youthful designers, (John) Presper Eckert and John Mauchly, looked on with a mixture of pride and anticipation.

Eckert was the chief engineer of the ENIAC. He developed the idea of a reduced electrical load to increase the reliability of the fragile tubes in the

J. Presper Eckert Jr. and John W. Mauchly combined their engineering and scientific talents to produce the ENIAC, which first saw action in U.S. Army ballistics tests in 1947.

machine. Mauchly, effectively the chief scientist, left the hardware problems to Eckert and kept the more fluid software and logic development for himself. Mauchly convinced his younger colleague of the general utility of a perfected model of the machine that they had built for the U.S. Army to calculate tables for firing artillery more accurately and quickly.

Frustrated by the limitations of that machine, these "Wright Brothers of computing" left the university in a patent dispute, and formed what quickly became the Eckert-Mauchly Computer Corporation. Mauchly convinced organizations as diverse as the U.S. Bureau of the Census, Northrop Aircraft, A.C. Neilson, Prudential, and the newly independent U.S. Air Force, to buy a UNIVAC (Universal Automatic Computer), as Eckert and Mauchly called their universal calculator.

Eckert was essentially a prototypical boy genius engineer. He joined the ENIAC project right out of college. He earned both his bachelor's degree (1941) and master's degree (1943) from the Moore School, and started as chief engineer for ENIAC on his twenty-fourth birthday. He stayed close

firing tables precalculated tables that can give an artillery gunner the correct allowances for wind conditions and distance by dictating the elevation and deflection of a gun

to electrical engineering his entire career. He was an expert on vacuum tubes and mercury delay line memories early in his career. After the ENIAC, he was the chief engineer of the Eckert-Mauchly Computer Corporation. When Remington Rand bought the company, Eckert stayed on as director of engineering. Remington Rand merged with Sperry to form Sperry-Rand in 1955. Eckert became a vice president and retained that rank until they ironically retired him and the UNIVAC brand name the same year, 1982.

Mauchly was a physicist. He taught for most of the 1930s at Ursinis College near Philadelphia, Pennsylvania. He was interested in modeling the weather and built some crude digital circuits that would have to be part of a machine to do that. He went to a summer program in 1941, sponsored by the Moore School, to learn more about electronic systems. Mauchly hit it off with the staff and was asked to join the school's faculty. This he did. When the U.S. Army developed bottlenecks getting out its **firing tables**, he suggested an electronic solution. The army funded his suggestion, and he teamed with Eckert to develop the ENIAC.

During the construction of the ENIAC, mathematician John von Neumann (1903–1957) was brought in to advise the project by Herman H. Goldstine, the army liaison. He facilitated some discussions by Eckert, Mauchly, and other young engineers and scientists who realized ENIAC's shortcomings before it was finished. Von Neumann, in the "Draft Report on the EDVAC," which described a new stored program machine, summarized their discussions. Even though it was only a draft summarizing his own and other people's work, nearly everyone erroneously gave von Neumann complete credit for the insights that led to stored program computers. Von Neumann did nothing to dissuade such beliefs, an omission that embittered both Eckert and Mauchly. When the EDVAC was finally finished in 1951, it, ironically, was put to use by von Neumann to predict the weather.

Mauchly stayed with Eckert until 1959, when he left Sperry-Rand and formed his own consulting firm. While at Sperry-Rand and its predecessors, Mauchly designed logic circuits. Sperry-Rand lost a suit brought in 1968 by Honeywell claiming that John Vincent Atanasoff (1903–1995) had developed a computer that influenced Mauchly. This obviated previously granted patents. Both Eckert and Mauchly disagreed with the decision, but did not challenge it. As a result, both of them were put on the sidelines and kept from receiving much of the credit for the significant work they had done.

The pair had built a small stored program computer, the BINAC, to raise some money and keep Northrop as a client in the late 1940s. This was the first operational stored program computer in the United States. Therefore, Eckert and Mauchly considered themselves to have designed or suggested ENIAC, the stored program concept, BINAC, and UNIVAC in a little more than five years—a truly major feat of pioneering.

Some involved at the Moore School may have believed that Eckert and Mauchly claimed too much credit. But the facts are clear—without Eckert and Mauchly's contributions, the field of computing would have taken significantly longer to develop. SEE ALSO Early Computers; Early Pioneers; von Neumann, John.

James E. Tomayko

Bibliography

Lee, J. A. N. *Computer Pioneers.* Los Alamitos, CA: IEEE Computer Society Press, 1995.

Stern, Nancy. *From ENIAC to UNIVAC.* Bedford, MA: Digital Press, 1981.

Fiber Optics

Fiber optics is the set of technologies that enables the point-to-point transmission of signals in the form of light—instead of in the form of electricity. The main component is optical fiber, the thread of glass-like material that carries the optical signal. Two related components are: (1) the **light emitting diode (LED)** and its advanced cousin, the **semiconductor diode laser**, which convert electrical signals to optical signals and couple them into the fiber; and (2) the photodiode, which receives optical signals from the fiber and converts them back to electrical signals.

Although fiber optics has many applications, including its use in **sensors**, its greatest impact has been in telecommunications. For millennia, humans used optical technology to send signals over distance—for example, as smoke puffs, reflected sunlight, or flares. Remember American Revolutionary War hero Paul Revere's ride and the warning signal: "one if by land and two if by sea?" But, these techniques are limited to what can be seen by human beings within a finite line of sight. Wired and wireless electrical technologies allow global, even interplanetary, transmission. But, these technologies have high **attenuation**, high noise susceptibility, and low **bandwidth**. While **coaxial cable** helps alleviate these problems, fiber optics provides a better point-to-point transmission medium than any form of wired electronics.

Description

An optical fiber's diameter is typically only one-eighth of a millimeter (0.005 inches), but one rarely sees a bare fiber. When it is covered by protective plastic, an individual fiber looks like an insulated wire. Or, many fibers are incorporated into a cable that includes an internal plastic spine, for strength and rigidity, and a hard outer jacket that protects the fibers from external damage (including bites from gophers or sharks). Like wires or coaxial cable (co-ax), fibers can be quite long but, unlike wires or co-ax, an 80-kilometer (50-mile) fiber span may not need an intermediate repeater.

Optical fiber is not uniform in its cross-section. A **concentric** cylindrical region, called the "core," lies inside the fiber. The core has a slightly different chemistry from the fiber's outer layer, called the "cladding." Light, launched into the fiber's core, travels the length of the fiber, staying inside the core by ricocheting off its walls.

Operation

When an electrical signal moves along a wire, individual electrons move slowly, shifting from atom to atom. But, optical signals are carried by photons, which are launched into the fiber and carry the signal as they traverse the fiber. Electrical signals move along a wire or co-ax at a bandwidth-dependent rate, typically around 20 percent of the speed of light. While

light emitting diode (LED) a discrete electronic component that emits visible light when permitting current to flow in a certain direction; often used as an indicating lamp

semiconductor diode laser a diode that emits electromagnetic radiation at wavelengths above about 630 nanometers, creating a laser beam for industrial applications

sensors devices that can record and transmit data regarding altitude, flight path, attitude, etc., so that they can enter into the system's calculations

attenuation the reduction in magnitude (size or amplitude) of a signal that makes a signal weaker

bandwidth a measure of the frequency component of a signal or the capacity of a communication channel to carry signals

coaxial cable a cable with an inner conducting core, a dielectric material and an outer sheath that is designed for high frequency signal transmission

concentric describes objects or shapes that have coincident centers; circles that share centers

optical signals, and electrical signals in free space, move at the speed of light, light moves slower in glass than in air. So, optical signals traverse fiber at about two-thirds the speed of light, which is still three times as fast as electrical signals move along wires.

In multi-mode fiber, different ricochet angles (called "modes") have different **velocities**—so, a narrow optical pulse spreads as it moves. In more expensive single-mode fiber, the smaller core diameter (eight microns or 0.0003 inches, instead of 62.5 microns or 0.0025 inches) supports only one mode, which eliminates this modal distortion and allows pulses to be more closely spaced, giving a higher data-rate. Since different wavelengths have slightly different velocities, even single-mode pulses can spread. Using a light source with a narrow range of wavelength reduces this consequence, known as **chromatic dispersion**, which allows pulses to be even more closely spaced, resulting in an even higher data-rate. Many commercial long-distance optical fibers carry 2.5 gigabits per second (Gbps) today, and new transmitters and receivers support ten Gbps—over the same fiber.

Techniques

Since a digitized voice signal requires 64 kilobits per second (Kbps), a single fiber at 2.5 Gbps carries more than 30,000 voice channels. A process called "time-division multiplexing" interleaves the individual signals. Another technology, called "wavelength division multiplexing" (WDM), has recently become practical. WDM allows several channels, each at 2.5 Gbps, to use the same fiber by using different wavelengths. These wavelengths must be far enough apart to be practically separable at the receiver, but close enough together to reside within a fiber's low-attenuation wavelength windows.

Fiber optics is highly **nonlinear**. When **analog** signals (like conventional television channels) are transmitted over fiber, the fiber can not be pushed to its limits. So, state-of-the-art transmission is digital, because digital signals are not as affected by nonlinearities. One such nonlinearity, which causes light to move faster through a lit fiber than through a dark fiber, imposes practical limits on the number of WDM channels on a single fiber. Data rate and WDM are both being intensely researched.

Characteristics

The maximum span of any transmission link is determined by the signal-to-noise ratio (SNR) at the receiver. Increasing a wire's length increases both the received noise power and the signal's attenuation. So, wire's SNR is a strong inverse function of length. The property that keeps an optical signal inside a fiber's core also keeps external interference outside it. Since fiber's received noise power is practically independent of length, fiber's SNR depends on attenuation only, making it a relatively weak function of length. So, fiber spans can be longer than wire spans.

Different wavelengths not only have different velocities, but they also suffer different attenuation. The practical attenuation needed in a short span of optical fiber requires the light source's wavelength to be in the infrared range of 0.7 to 1.6 microns. Fortunately, cheap LEDs operate at 0.8 microns. The very low attenuation needed in a long span occurs over two narrow regions of wavelength: around 1.3 and 1.5 microns, where light sources

velocities vector quantities that have a magnitude or speed and a direction

chromatic dispersion the natural distortion of pulses of light as they move through an optical network; it results in data corruption

nonlinear a system that has relationships between outputs and inputs which cannot be expressed in the form of a straight line

analog a quantity (often an electrical signal) that is continuous in time and amplitude

are expensive. The lowest attenuation occurs at 1.5 microns, but chromatic dispersion is minimized at 1.3 microns. Not surprisingly, long-distance optical transmission occurs around these two wavelengths.

Although low attenuation and low noise immunity are important, fiber's most important characteristic is its huge bandwidth. Comparing information transmission to water flow, bandwidth corresponds to pipe diameter. On a scale where a telephone channel (4 kHz) corresponds to 1-centimeter (3/8-inch) copper tubing, a co-ax carrying 70 television channels (350 MHz) corresponds to a 2 meter (6-foot) sewer pipe. Fiber's long-span attenuation requirement allows about 15 THz (terahertz) in each of the 1.3- and 1.5-micron windows. This 30 THz of ultimate capacity corresponds to a pipe with 1.6-kilometer (one-mile) diameter. Researchers have only begun to figure out how to use it all.

Cost

Carrying 100 Mbps (megabits per second) over a short span, where multi-mode fiber and LEDs are used, fiber optics costs only a little more than wired electronics. For high rates over long spans, where single-mode fiber and semiconductor diode lasers must be used, fiber optics is expensive. But, the huge bandwidth makes it cost-effective. While fiber's material (silica) is cheaper than wire's (copper), fiber is more expensive to manufacture—especially single-mode fiber. However, since new installation cost is typically

METRIC MAGNITUDES	
The metric system prefixes are as follows:	
ato-	10^{-18}
femto-	10^{-15}
pico-	10^{-12}
nano-	10^{-9}
micro-	10^{-6}
milli-	10^{-3}
kilo-	10^{+3}
mega-	10^{+6}
giga-	10^{+9}
tera-	10^{+12}
peta-	10^{+15}

A technician splices fiber optic cables, which are capable of transmitting data, images, and voice recordings.

Table 1.

	Access infrastructure	Backbone network
Broadcast application	I	III
Point-to-point apps	II	IV

dark fiber a fiber optic network that exists but is not actively in service, hence the darkness

much higher than the cost of what is being installed, it is common practice to include **dark fiber** in any wire installation, even if there are no current plans for it.

There are other cost issues, as well. Fiber optics is more difficult to use than wire, and technicians need to be trained. While wire can be soldered or wrapped around a terminal, optical fiber must be carefully spliced. Fiber connectors, especially for single-mode fiber, are more expensive than wire connectors.

Application

Consider Table 1. Users get access (left column) to information signals by several competing media. People access (I) commercial broadcast television signals by local antenna, co-ax, or direct dish, and (II) point-to-point applications, like telephony or connecting to an Internet service provider, by wire or local wireless (cellular). But, the backbone infrastructures (right column), which distribute these signals over wide areas, use an application-dependent medium-of-choice. Commercial television is effectively (III) broadcast using geo-synchronous satellites, and the wide-area networks for point-to-point applications, like long-distance networks for telephony and the Internet for data, typically use fiber optics.

This may all change, of course, as the technology, the industry, the applications, and the economics evolve. Although technically feasible, fiber-to-the-home and fiber-to-the-desktop are economically difficult to justify. If video-conferencing becomes popular, perhaps it will be the so-called "golden service" that makes it happen.

Future

photons the smallest fundamental units of electromagnetic radiation in the visible spectrum—light

photonic switching the technology that is centered on routing and managing optical packets of digital data

optical computing a proposed computing technology which would operate on particles of light, rather than electric currents

Because of the nonlinearity that causes light to go faster through a lit fiber than a dark fiber, the **photons** at the back of a pulse can actually catch up to the photons at the front. A *soliton* is a pulse whose shape is retained because this effect carefully balances the effects that widen pulses—and researchers are trying to make them practical. With all that unused potential bandwidth, fiber optics is the logical technology for making networks that must scale easily, like the Internet. If research efforts in **photonic switching** and **optical computing** are fruitful, there will be wonderful synergies with fiber optic transmission. If researchers learn to master solitons and these other research efforts are fruitful, fiber optics has a "bright" future.
SEE ALSO DIGITAL LOGIC DESIGN; NETWORKS; TELECOMMUNICATIONS; TRANSMISSION MEDIA.

Richard A. Thompson

Bibliography

Green, Paul E. *Fiber Optic Networks*. Upper Saddle River, NJ: Prentice Hall, 1993.

Palais, Joseph C. *Fiber Optic Communications*, 4th ed. Upper Saddle River, NJ: Prentice Hall, 1998.

Game Controllers

Game controllers are intricate hardware devices that allow game players to send instructions to a computer, which can range in size from a desktop computer to a handheld proprietary game machine. The wide variety of game controllers includes such devices as game pads, joysticks, paddles, steering wheels, fishing rods, aircraft yokes, light guns, and rifles.

History of Controllers

When Atari game consoles became popular in the 1970s, the standard game controller had a single button in the corner of the four-inch square base, which held a three-inch joystick. Players could maneuver the screen cursor by moving the joystick with one hand, and pressing the button with the thumb of the other hand. The only feedback was an occasional "blip" or "doink" noise from primitive speakers, and relatively slow, jerky movements on the screen.

Joystick design evolved to include a taller, ergonomically shaped handle with a trigger mechanism and a miniature stick at the end, called a *top hat*. With this device, players could squeeze such triggers with their forefingers and maneuver the top hat using one of their thumbs. These controllers often featured additional buttons on both the stick and the base that performed specific actions dictated by the game's software. Games were made more realistic with livelier sound effects from more powerful speakers.

Two teens use handheld controllers to play video hockey. The devices control the actions of the game, which are displayed on their TV screen.

ONLINE GAMING

Video games for the home computer can be costly, especially for avid players. So many players turn to the Internet to take part in games offered online, particularly those that are made available for free. Some market analysts project online gaming to become a billion dollar business by 2005. But will people pay to play online games that were once offered for free? Market analysts are working to determine what online gamers will pay, if anything.

capacitor a fundamental electrical component used for storing electrical charge

potentiometer an element in an electrical circuit that resists current flow (a resistor) but the value of the resistance can be mechanically adjusted (a variable resistor)

While the one-handed joystick was sufficient for early games, it proved awkward for other sophisticated software. Soon two-handled yokes, simulating a pilot's cockpit, were introduced. Car racing games were made more realistic with the introduction of steering wheel controllers, some of which included brake and gas pedals. Gun fighting games spawned the introduction of light guns and rifles. Even fishing games were enhanced with the introduction of rod-like sticks with buttons to help the player simulate casting and fishing.

Controllers for proprietary games, such as Nintendo's "Game Boy," Sega's "Dreamcast," and Sony's "PlayStation," became special two-handed devices, each with two one-inch joysticks and many multifunction action buttons.

How They Work

Although modern game controllers sport many different features, they operate in essentially the same way as joysticks do. As the stick or indicator is moved from side to side, the position of the handle is converted into a number, known as the "x" coordinate. Likewise, as the stick is moved forward and back, the handle's position is measured with a "y" coordinate. Using these x-y coordinates, the computer can precisely track the stick's direction as it moves. If the stick has a rotational capability, the r-axis is tracked as well.

To calculate the distance the stick is moved, the controller's positioning sensor uses a **capacitor** and **potentiometer**. As electrical current flows through the potentiometer, the current is temporarily collected by the capacitor, which discharges it only when a certain charge is reached, say five volts. When the stick is in the resting position, not pushed from the center, the capacitor collects and discharges the current rapidly. As the joystick is pushed farther from the center, the capacitor collects and discharges current more slowly. By measuring the number of milliseconds required for the capacitor to charge and discharge, the game adapter card tracks the stick's exact distance from center.

In newer joysticks, the capacitor and potentiometer have been replaced with an optical gray-scale position sensor, which measures the amount of light emitted by an LED (light emitting diode) to track the stick's position. When a button is pushed (to simulate jumping a barrel or hitting a ball), a contact switch sends an electrical signal to the computer's game adapter card and the game software uses the signal to start the intended action. When the button is released, another signal ends the action.

Some controllers, such as those for Sony's "PlayStation 2" and Microsoft's "Xbox," measure the amount of pressure used to push a button. When a button is pushed lightly, the button's curved contact barely touches the conductive strip mounted on the controller's circuit board. But when a button is pressed forcefully, more of the button's contact touches the conductive strip. Therefore, the level of conductivity is greater, signaling to the computer that this is a more intense action than that indicated with a lighter touch.

Force Feedback Controllers

Introduced by several manufacturers in 1997, force feedback controllers allow players to experience tactile stimulation to enhance their gaming experience. In the handgrip of each controller is a built-in electric motor with an unbalanced weight attached to its shaft. When power is supplied to the motor, it spins the unbalanced weight. Ordinarily, such an imbalance would cause the motor to wobble, but since the motor is securely attached to the controller, the wobble is translated into a vibration that shakes the entire handgrip and is felt by the game player.

The force and duration of the wobble in dictated by a **waveform**, which is a graph or formula that tells the software when and how to turn on and off the motor. For example, if the game player drives a car that runs into a wall, the wobble will be sudden and will continue for perhaps a second or two. On the other hand, if the game player is a firing machine gun, the resulting wobble will rapidly accelerate and decelerate many times a second for as long as the button, the "machine gun trigger," on the controller is pressed. Likewise, if the game player is driving a tank over rough terrain, the controller will experience a series of wobbles that correspond to the ground's bumps and dips.

As microprocessors have become smaller and cheaper, they have been integrated into game controllers, greatly expanding their capabilities. For example, each Microsoft Sidewinder Force Feedback Pro Joystick has a 25-megahertz microprocessor in the base to interpret software commands that dictate the feedback motion. When the command is received, the microprocessor accesses a **read-only memory (ROM)** chip, which permanently stores 32 movement effects and unleashes the correct movement on demand. Each movement corresponds to a certain waveform. If the software should dictate a waveform that is not already loaded on the ROM chip, the data can be downloaded to a two-kilobyte **random access memory (RAM) chip** for the microprocessor to use. SEE ALSO Games; Input Devices.

Ann McIver McHoes

waveform an abstraction used in the physical sciences to model energy transmission in the form of longitudinal or transverse waves

read-only memory (ROM) a type of memory device that supports permanent storage of programs

random access memory (RAM) chip a type of memory device that supports the nonpermanent storage of programs and data; so called because various locations can be accessed in any order (as if at random), rather than in a sequence (like a tape memory device)

Bibliography

White, Ron. *How Computers Work*, 6th ed. Indianapolis, IN: Que, 2002.

Internet Resources

Xbox Website. Microsoft Corporation. <http://www.xbox.com>

Graphic Devices

Data output through graphic devices on computer systems is made possible through techniques that use video generation modules to display images. This differs from text mode output, for which the computer generates horizontal lines of **alphanumeric** symbols. Although the technical requirements of both systems overlap, graphic devices use an approach that assumes that every dot on the screen is separately accessible. By contrast, in text mode, the smallest screen element is actually a group of points that together all define a character—a letter, a numeral, or a punctuation mark.

A graphic display is composed of a screen or panel that is made up of a large number of small cells or dots that are called **pixels**. These pixels emit light when they are struck by a beam of electrons and switched on. At any one instant, the computer hardware can switch some pixels on fully so that they emit light, skip over others so that they remain dark, and prompt still

alphanumeric a character set which is the union of the set of alphabetic characters and the set of single digit numbers

pixels single picture elements on a video screen; the individual dots making up a picture on a video screen or digital image

others to emit an intermediate measure of light. In this way the representation of a picture can be displayed on a graphic device using every pixel as a separate component in the image.

Graphic devices are output devices, but their physical characteristics restrict them from taking data as represented in the computer's memory and displaying the data directly. Instead, they require the assistance of a special device to translate data into electrical signals that are compatible with the display hardware. These devices are called graphics controllers.

One way that data can be formulated for display by the computer is through a technique known as a **bitmapped display** or "raster-scan display." Using this approach, the computer contains an area of memory that holds all the data that are to be displayed. The central processor writes data into this region of memory and the video controller collects them from there. The bits of data stored in this block of memory are related to the eventual pattern of pixels that will be used to construct an image on the display.

For example, one could get the central processor to fill the entire video memory region with zeros. This might then correspond to a completely black screen. Then, the processor might selectively fill certain memory locations in the video memory with data that are non-zero. This would result in an image appearing on the graphics display—perhaps a straight line, for example.

This flexible scheme has been used in many computers. However, it does suffer from performance problems. The central processor is reasonably good at executing instructions that are arithmetic or logical in nature, but it is not very good at handling large blocks of data in single operations. Although the central processor can display a line on the screen, it is a time-consuming operation that compromises processor performance.

For this reason, special devices known as video co-processors are usually incorporated to optimize these sorts of operations and perform them under command from the central processor. This means that the central processor can get on with doing the operations for which it is better suited and the video co-processor can handle the video output. Often the video co-processor is a very complex device, bordering on the same level of complexity as the central processor, complete with its own instruction execution unit and local memory. These devices can draw lines, rectangles, and other shapes very quickly on the graphics display because they are designed specifically for that purpose.

An alternative to the bitmapped display design approach is the **vector graphics** display. This design was once popular for engineering workstations since the graphics images produced by these systems are consistent with the diagrams and drawings that are common in engineering analysis and design tasks performed by computer-aided design, manufacturing, and architecture programs, for example.

Instead of sectioning off a large region of computer memory and mapping that to the display device, vector display devices use a variable number of lines to create images—hence the term "vector graphics." Since vector display devices can define a line by dealing with just two points (that is, the coordinates of each end of the line), the device can reduce the total amount of data it must deal with by organizing the image in terms of pairs of points

bitmapped display a computer display that uses a table of binary bits in memory to represent the image that is projected onto the screen

vector graphics graphics output systems whereby pairs of coordinates are passed to the graphics controller, which are interpreted as end points of vectors to be drawn on the screen

WEARABLE GRAPHICS DEVICES

A company in Canada, "tekGear," makes available wearable computer graphics devices. Among the possibilities already at hand are binocular and personal viewing devices that are attached as a visor to the user's head. The devices are lightweight, rugged, and consume little power compared to conventional graphics devices like desktop monitors.

that define lines. The vector graphic display accepts these coordinate pairs, along with other attributes of the line, like color and intensity, and draws the lines directly onto the display.

More advanced graphics systems employ extra specialized devices to help produce more complex images. The presentation of three-dimensional objects on two-dimensional computer screens is an example of an application requiring additional processing. The conventional approach is based on producing a model of the three-dimensional object in a form known as "wire frame," where lines are drawn to represent the object in exactly the same way that a real model might be constructed of it by making a skeletal structure out of wire. Then the wire frame can be filled in with flat, **polygonal** panels being attached to the frame.

To represent this on a computer screen, a new step must be introduced in the rendering of the image; this is known as "hidden surface removal," since if the object is solid and opaque, surfaces not directly in the line of sight should not be visible. In addition, the surface of the object can be made to appear smooth if desired, by making the wire frame appear more finely grained and the corresponding polygons smaller. There are also devices available that provide visual effects like shading. Each of these operations can be performed effectively by specialized graphics devices designed for the purpose.

Human beings are much more receptive to high quality graphical displays than any other form of computer output. Consumer-oriented electronic systems including games consoles, conventional computers, hand-held personal digital assistants (PDAs), and mobile computers all produce graphical displays. There will always be a need for sophisticated graphic devices to meet the demand for faster and better processing of these displays. SEE ALSO COMPUTER SYSTEM INTERFACES; GAMES; INPUT DEVICES.

Stephen Murray

polygonal pertaining to a polygon, which is a many-sided, closed, geometrical figure

Bibliography

Ferraro, Richard F. *Programmer's Guide to the EGA, VGA and Super VGA Cards*, 3rd ed. New York: Addison-Wesley Publishing Company, 1994.

Newman, William M., and Robert F. Sproul. *Principles of Interactive Computer Graphics*, 2nd ed. New York: McGraw-Hill, 1979.

Richter, Jake, and Bud Smith. *Graphics Programming for the 8514/A*. Redwood City, CA: M&T Publishing, 1990.

Tischer, Michael. *PC System Programming*. Grand Rapids, MI: Abacus, 1990.

Hypermedia and Multimedia

When someone turns on a computer, puts a CD (compact disc) in its CD drive, and listens to her favorite music while she works on a paper, she is experiencing multimedia. Other examples of multimedia usage include looking at pictures taken from a digital camera. In contrast, surfing the World Wide Web, following links from one site to another, looking for all types of information, is called experiencing hypermedia. The major difference between multimedia and hypermedia is that the user is more actively involved in the hypermedia experience, whereas the multimedia experience is more passive.

Hypermedia is an enhancement of hypertext, the non-sequential access of text documents, using a multimedia environment and providing users the flexibility to select which document they want to view next based on their current interests. The path followed to get from document to document changes from user to user and is very dynamic. This "make your own adventure" type of experience sets hypermedia apart.

Multimedia is defined as the integration of sound, animation, and digitized video with more traditional types of data such as text. It is an application-oriented technology that is used in a variety of ways, for example, to enhance presentations, and is based on the increasing capability of computers to store, transmit, and present many types of information. Some examples of multimedia applications are: business presentations, online newspapers, distance education, and interactive gaming.

Some Examples

Business presentations use presentation graphics software to create and display a series of on-screen slides that serve as a visual aid to enhance presentations. These slides may include photographs, drawings, spreadsheets, or tables. Some presentation graphics programs allow the inclusion of animation and video clips along with still images. Others can automatically convert presentations into World Wide Web pages.

Multimedia presentations—including images, text, and sound—can be an effective business or educational tool.

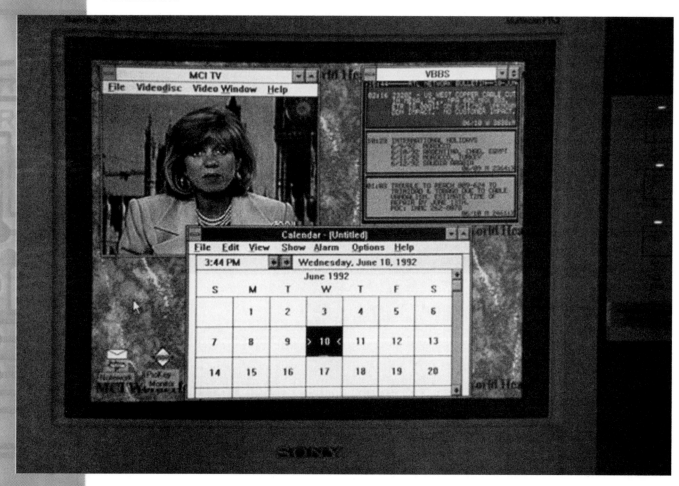

Using a web browser, anyone can browse through pages of online newspapers, read articles, and view pictures or audio/video presentations. In addition, readers can locate a specific article by performing index searches, or by typing detailed requests. In some cases, the user may participate in chat groups and provide feedback to the editors. This type of interactivity requires bringing together images, text, audio, and video elements.

Distance education allows students at remote locations to participate in live instruction through videoconferencing, to collaborate on projects through shared "whiteboards," or to replay instructional material that has been pre-recorded. Using the World Wide Web as the base, a student can browse through a database consisting of course material in various formats: images, audio and video recordings, and textual information. In addition, the student can request more information while reading text, viewing illustrations, or listening to audio presentations.

Interactive games require multimedia delivery systems that can support real-time, three-dimensional imaging as well as interactions among multiple players. Those who have experienced multi-player multimedia games on the World Wide Web know that they can go on for long periods of time and that the number of players is seldom the same. Systems that support interactive gaming applications need to take care of a large number of interacting players for long periods of time.

Technology

Multimedia applications need computers that support multi-sensory **I/O devices**. At this writing, high-performance computer systems with high-resolution monitors and audio output are used as multimedia presentation devices. In these systems, the output devices can present visual material in the form of text, graphics, or video, as well as voice and music components. Multimedia computer systems are providing specialized devices to enter data into the computer system. For example, a scanner can be used to capture still images, voice can be recorded with a microphone and digitizer, and video can be handled with a camera and digitizer. To store multimedia files, which take up a lot of storage, most systems use CD-ROMs (compact disc-read only memory).

In early multimedia systems, interaction between users and the computer was through a mouse and a keyboard. Their limited control of spatial manipulation as required by multimedia applications, especially games, soon made them less than ideal multimedia I/O devices. The new generation of devices includes: multiple-axis joysticks, foot pedals, eye motion tracking systems, and "data gloves"—gloves worn by the user to translate finger and hand position to signals that are then interpreted by the application.

Multimedia systems have to be able to compress data files for transmission and storage, especially those containing motion video and sound. Then, the systems have to decompress such files when the user requests it. Standard video display drivers equipped with software decompression can handle different types of video play-out. However, high-end systems accomplish video decompression with add-on boards that continue to decrease in price. Evolving standards for image and video compression include **JPEG (Joint Photographic Experts Group)** for still image compression, and

I/O devices devices that can accept input data to a computer and to other devices that can produce output

JPEG (Joint Photographic Experts Group) organization that developed a standard for encoding image data in a compressed format to save space

MPEG (Motion Picture Coding Experts Group) an encoding scheme for data files that contain motion pictures—it is lossy in the same way as JPEG (Joint Photographic Experts Group) encoding

bandwidth a measure of the frequency component of a signal or the capacity of a communication channel to carry signals

MPEG (Motion Picture Coding Experts Group) for motion picture image compression.

Requirements for multimedia systems continue to increase. For example, this includes the ability to format the data for display, which includes fonts, panning, and zooming across different systems.

Hypermedia

Hypermedia tools focus on the interactive power of computers, which makes it easy for users to explore a variety of paths through many information sources. As opposed to conventional documents, such as books, that one normally reads one page after the other in the order set by the author, hypermedia documents are very flexible and allow one to explore related documents in any order and navigate through them in any direction.

The hypermedia model is fundamental to the structure of the World Wide Web, which is often based on a relational database organization. In this model, documents are interconnected as in a network, which facilitates extensive cross-referencing of related items. Users can browse effectively through the data by following links connecting associated topics or keywords. Object-oriented and hypermedia models are becoming routine for managing very large multimedia systems such as digital libraries.

Future

Large-scale multimedia applications require significant advances in high-speed networking and storage servers, as well as the production of low-cost presentation devices for the consumer. Trends indicate that processing units will become faster, display devices will become less expensive, memory devices will become larger, and high-**bandwidth** network access will become present everywhere. These changes will probably result in an abundance of multimedia computer technology for our use and enjoyment. SEE ALSO HYPERTEXT; INTERACTIVE SYSTEMS; WORLD WIDE WEB.

Ida M. Flynn

Bibliography

Beekman, George, and Eugene J. Rathswohl. *Computer Confluence: Exploring Tomorrow's Technology.* New York: Addison Wesley Longman, 1999.

Laudon, Kenneth C., Carol Guercio Traver, and Jane Price Laudon. *Information Technology and Society.* Belmont, CA: Wadsworth Publishing Co, 1994.

Information Systems

Before we can understand information systems, we should ask what is information? What is a system? Information can be regarded as that which is happening in our brains: the questions we continuously ask—what, where, when, who—and the answers we get. A second approach is to consider information as something that our minds and hands produce, something we give to others. Information is something tangible that we construct from a state of consciousness. What you are reading here is information. It is a product of the thinking that made it possible. That thinking is also information—it is the process that made the product possible. Information includes what we write about in letters, the subjects we study in school, the things we read in newspapers, or watch on TV or film, and the numbers we find printed on our pay checks. Information is a material product: something that we can acquire, keep, and give to others.

We are all systems. The body we carry around is a system. There are many components, or subsystems, of our bodies—the nervous system, the digestive system, the circulatory system, and others. Almost all things around us are systems: pens and pencils are systems allowing us to write and express ourselves and give ideas and feelings to others. Media entertainment units such as televisions, and computers that help us do many things—all of these are systems. An organization of people, what they do and produce, is a system. The public transportation we use to get to work or school is a system. A system is an environment that includes humans, tools, and ways of doing things for a goal and purpose.

We ourselves are information systems because we use the native capacity of our minds and hands to interact with energy and matter around us, including the air we breathe and the ground on which we stand. We have the capacity to be continuously aware or conscious of what is happening to and around us. This is true from the very moment we are born to the time we die.

We cannot live without information or the ability to process and respond to it. But, we are limited as to what our bodies and minds can see, hear, touch, smell, and, in general, do. So we invent and create tools—technology—that add to our ability and capacity to do things.

The wheel, the carriage, the automobile, and then the airplane are all human-designed technologies—systems—that enable us to move from one place to another, faster and longer, overcoming the physical limits of our bodies. Information technology (IT) is created to extend our biological ability to think, learn, remember, anticipate, and resolve many of the physical and mental tasks we face each day.

Human beings invented paper, chalk, and pens and pencils to help us record and present our thoughts and experiences. Later, in the 1450s, Johannes Gutenberg's invention of the printing press made the sharing of written ideas with multiple people more efficient and affordable. The early Chinese invented the abacus, a kind of primitive accounting and adding machine to help facilitate arithmetic computations. Present-day computers are extensions of this early information technology.

There are many kinds of information technologies, including radars, telephones, FAX machines, computers, and satellites, to list a few. These technologies contribute to many forms of information systems such as systems for information retrieval and systems that help us solve problems or make decisions. Some systems help us avoid or reduce paper work. There are information systems that help manage organizations and there are specialized kinds of information systems such as **artificial intelligence (AI)** and **expert systems**. Basically, information systems are categorized by the specific work they do and the software that enables them to function as they do. Software consists of instructions that tell the computer what to do, how to do it, and when.

artificial intelligence (AI) a branch of computer science dealing with creating computer hardware and software to mimic the way people think and perform practical tasks

expert systems computer systems that use a collection of rules to exhibit behavior which mimics the behavior of a human expert in some area

Information Retrieval Systems

An information retrieval system (IRS) is an environment of people, technologies, and procedures (software) that help find data, information, and knowledge resources that can be located in a particular library or, for that matter, anywhere they exist. Information about available resources is acquired, stored, searched, and retrieved when it is needed. An IRS can help users in general ways, such as obtaining data on a subject of general interest, or in more specific ways, such as retrieving information to help them find a good job. Information retrieval software allows a user to formulate and ask a question, then it searches a database to create an appropriate response. A database is a collection of data on a specific subject organized in such a way that a person can locate and acquire chunks of information for specific purposes. Retrieving information is a skill that requires training and experience. Librarians in general, and reference or special librarians in particular, are the professionals who serve this function.

Decision Support Systems

Information systems are particularly important in adding to our capability to solve problems and make decisions. With the amount of information being generated each day in almost every aspect of our lives, solving problems and making decisions can be complicated. Decision support systems (DSS) are information systems with a specific function to help people with the problem-solving and decision-making process. As with all modern information systems, a DSS consists of a collection of people, procedures, software, and databases with a purpose. The computer is the primary technology in such systems; other information technologies may include electronic displays (e.g. a TV monitor) and teletransmission capabilities (telephone links). DSS systems help identify the factors that are creating the problem, provide ways through which approaches can be established to resolve the problems, and help in the selection of choices that are available to resolve the problem.

Expert Systems

Quite often in solving problems it is wise to benefit from those who know much about a subject—experts in a particular subject area or field. We refer to these information systems as expert systems (ES). An expert system is a specific kind of information system in which computer software serves the same function expected of an expert. The computer, programmed to mimic the thought processes of experts, provides the decision-maker with suggestions as to the best choice of action for a particular problem situation. The hope is that we can design computers (and generally information systems) that extend our ability to think, learn, and act as an expert.

Artificial intelligence (AI) is a familiar expression of this idea. It is exciting to see if a machine can beat a human in playing chess, or vice versa. During the last years of the twentieth century, information processing technologists began using computer-generated images and sounds, rather than real objects, to explore the relationships between human beings and computer-generated environments known as **virtual reality (VR)**. Virtual reality is part of an area in AI where the objective is to explore how the computer can extend the limits of how we see the world and our place in it. Expand-

virtual reality (VR) the use of elaborate input/output devices to create the illusion that the user is in a different environment

ing our understanding of reality can enable us to analyze and design ever better information systems.

Lastly, robots exemplify another perspective on information systems. Robots are machines that are designed to do what humans can do. An important application of this technology has been to create robots to perform certain functions that are dangerous for human beings, or to do tasks that can be more effectively performed by machine than by people. Although it may not have the physical appearance of a human being, a robot may be thought of as a machine acting as a person while being controlled by a computer.

World chess champ Garry Kasparov takes on IBM's Deep Blue in a chess match in 1997. As he began the second game of a six-game match, Kasparov was up 1-0.

Management Information Systems

Information systems can be found in our homes, our schools, our workplaces, and our places of recreation and relaxation. Information systems are part of all sorts of organizations including schools, the local YMCA, worldwide fast food companies, and the governments and military operations of countries around the globe. Within these organizations, resources, both human and technological, require management. A management information system (MIS) is an environment that consists of people, technology (i.e., computers), and procedures that help an organization plan, operate, and control the access and use of resources, both human and material. Resources managed by such systems can include the labor force (executives, line workers, sales people), computer centers, photo and research labs, mailrooms, libraries, and other subsystems of a larger organization. Management information systems help an organization achieve its objectives through the processing and sharing of data and information important to the organization at all levels.

The Internet

Last, but certainly not least, we should include the Internet as an important part of an information system. Since 1950, developments in computer and teletransmission technology (telephone, radio, and FAX, for example) have changed the ways we can communicate with each other. The Internet began as a tool for scientists to discuss their research work over long distances (ARPANET). As this technology evolved and access expanded to business, industry, education, and personal users, the Internet and the World Wide Web (WWW) were born. They have changed the way we work, learn, and stay in touch with others. Now we can find, through the Internet, a friend or relative that we have not seen or communicated with in years; we can send and receive letters electronically and instantly (without a stamp); we can purchase almost anything without physically traveling to a store; and we can quickly locate products and services via the Internet that may not be available in our own geographic neighborhoods. We can even build businesses and create networks of coworkers and customers without the need for office space and daily commuting.

Computer-based information systems have changed the way we gather, process, and share information. They have enhanced our ability to identify and solve problems and to perform tasks that are beyond our physical ability. Information system technology will continue to provide new horizons to us. SEE ALSO ARTIFICIAL INTELLIGENCE; DATABASE MANAGEMENT SOFTWARE; E-COMMERCE; EXPERT SYSTEMS; INTERNET; INTRANET; SQL; VIRTUAL REALITY.

Anthony Debons

Bibliography

Anderson, David. *Managing Information Systems.* Dover, NJ: Prentice Hall, Inc., 2000.

Beniger, James R. *The Control Revolution.* Cambridge, MA: Harvard University Press, 1986.

Debons, Anthony, Esther Horne, and Scott Cronenweth. *Information Science: An Integrated View.* Boston: G. K. Hall & Co., 1988.

Flynn, Roger R. *An Introduction to Information Science.* New York: Marcel Dekker, 1987.

Kobler, Ron, ed. *The Illustrated Book of Terms and Technologies.* Lincoln, NE: Sundhills Publishing, 1998.

Miller, James Grier. *Living Systems.* New York: McGraw-Hill, 1978.

Newell, Allen, and Herbert A. Simon. *Human Problem Solving.* Dover, NJ: Prentice Hall, Inc., 1972.

Stair, Ralph M., and George W. Reynolds. *Principles of Information Systems,* 5th ed. Cambridge, MA: Course Technology, 2001.

Stuart, Rory. *The Design of Virtual Environments.* New York: McGraw-Hill, 1996.

Input Devices

The work of a computer can be characterized by an input-process-output model in which a program receives input from an input device, performs some processing on the input, and produces output to an output device. Users employ a variety of input devices to interact with the computer, but most user interfaces today are based upon a keyboard and a mouse pointing input device.

A keyboard consists of a number of switches and a keyboard controller. The keyboard controller is built into the keyboard itself. When a key is pushed, a signal called a scan code is sent to the controller. A different scan code is sent when the key is released. The use of two scan codes allows keys to be used in combination. The controller is able to tell whether a key is being held down while another key is struck, or to determine when a key causes a repeated action. Keyboard scan codes are sent to the computer via a serial port. New keyboards have been designed for **ergonomic** reasons.

A mouse is a small device that a computer user pushes across a flat surface, points to a place on a display screen, then clicks on icons and menus. The mouse first became a widely used computer tool when Apple Computer made it a standard part of the Macintosh. Today, the mouse is an integral part of the **graphical user interface (GUI)** of any personal computer.

Types of Input Devices

Hundreds of devices can be used as computer input devices, ranging from general-purpose input devices to special-purpose devices used to input specific types of data.

Digital Cameras. A digital camera records and stores photographic images in digital form that can be fed to a computer for viewing and printing. First, the impressions are recorded or stored in the camera. The picture can then be downloaded to a computer by removable disk or by parallel port connection.

Light Pens. A light pen uses a photodetector in the tip of the pen, which can be moved around the screen to move a corresponding cursor.

Magnetic Stripe Readers and Magnetic Tape. Magnetic stripe readers are used to read alphanumeric data from a magnetized stripe on a card, such as a credit card. Magnetic tape can be easily rewritten and stored indefinitely. There are two basic tape mechanisms: reel-to-reel and cartridge. Generally, reel-to-reel tape drives are used with large **mainframe computers**. Smaller computers use tape cartridges. Regardless of type, the tape is removable from the tape drive for offline storage. When the tape is in the tape drive ready for operation, it is said to be mounted. Tape heads store bits across tracks in units called frames, with the most common recording densities being 630 frames per centimeter (1,600 frames per inch) and 2,460 frames per centimeter (6,250 frames) per inch.

Paper Tape. Punching paper tape for storage and data input is an old technique dating back to Sir Charles Wheatstone, who used it in 1857 for the telegraph. Small sprocket holes appear along the length of the tape to feed the tape mechanically. Data are recorded on the paper tape by punching holes in a row across its width. Each row represents one character, and the pattern of holes punched indicates the particular character. Although paper tape is inexpensive, the difficulty of correcting errors and the tape's slow speed have led to its disappearance as a computer input device.

ergonomic being of suitable geometry and structure to permit effective or optimal human user interaction with machines

graphical user interface (GUI) an interface that allows computers to be operated through pictures (icons) and mouse-clicks, rather than through text and typing

mainframe computers large computers used by businesses and government agencies to process massive amounts of data; generally faster and more powerful than desktop computers but usually requiring specialized software

REMEMBERING WHEATSTONE

English physicist Charles Wheatstone (1802–1875) had no formal training in science. He came from a family that made and sold musical instruments. Wheatstone went on to become an inventor of such devices as the stereoscope, in which two images (photographs) are viewed to create the illusion of 3-D.

Government units, such as the Central Intelligence Agency, have used magnetic tape to store extensive collections of information. Called "Happy," the CIA's magnetic tape storage area uses a robotic arm to retrieve tapes.

Punched Cards.   Punched cards, popularly known as IBM cards, were the dominant input device prior to the introduction of personal computers. Punched cards are produced by a keypunch machine offline from the computer, and then read into it with a high-speed card reader. Punched cards use a Hollerith code, named after its inventor, Herman Hollerith (1860–1929). Each card has eighty columns with one character per column; therefore each punched card holds eighty characters or exactly one row of text or characters—a unit record. Punched card readers can operate at speeds from 100 cards per minute to 2,000 cards per minute.

Scanners.   Page and hand-held scanners convert black/white and color images into digital data. A bar code scanner uses a laser scanner to read alphanumeric bar-coded labels. Two types of optical data scanners can be used to scan documents: optical mark recognition (OMR) and optical character recognition (OCR). OMR is used in standardized test scoring and surveys where marks are placed in designated boxes. OCR readers use reflected light to convert typed or handwritten documents into digital data. In magnetic ink character recognition (MICR), data are placed on the bottom of a form using special magnetic ink so that they can be scanned by computers.

Voice Recognition Devices.   Voice recognition devices use microphones and special software to convert a human voice into language that can then be put into digital form. These systems require training the computer to recognize a limited vocabulary of standard words for each user.

Voice input devices may be the input device of the future, but progress has been slow.

Past and Future

Until the advent of stored program computers in the 1950s, punched card machines were the state-of-the-art. Dating back to the U.S. Census of 1890, Hollerith developed a punched card reader that could repeatedly tabulate and sort. The key event that signaled the end of the punched card era was the launch in 1959 of the IBM 1401 computer, which had magnetic tape and disk storage. The keyboard has dominated interactive personal computing and voice input devices have not proven to be reliable. Future hands-free wireless infrared input devices may include a wand with a walk-around button, a ring on the index finger, and a reflective dot that sticks to the user's forehead and signals data by eye movement. SEE ALSO COMPUTER SYSTEM INTERFACES; GAMES; READING TOOLS.

William J. Yurcik

Bibliography

White, Ron. *How Computers Work*, 6th ed. Indianapolis, IN: Que, 2002.

Invasive Programs

Since the late 1990s, outbreaks of malicious computer viruses and worms like LoveLetter have grown increasingly common and have caused billions of dollars in damage and lost productivity. Where do these invasive programs come from? How does the computer industry combat these threats? What are the legal implications of writing or distributing malicious computer software?

Invasive Software Overview

Invasive programs (i.e. viruses, worms, and Trojan horses) are constructed using the same basic computer logic that underlies traditional application programs such as games, word processors, or spreadsheets. Like other programs, invasive software must be written by people, and it must be intentionally designed and programmed to perform specific actions.

Invasive programs act without the computer user's knowledge or permission and may cause a variety of intentional and unintentional damage. Viruses, worms, and Trojan horses that cause intentional damage to computer systems are said to deliver a "payload" when a certain "trigger" condition is met. For example, common payloads include sending files or passwords to the originator of the invasive software or deleting the user's files. Common triggers include a certain date on which files may be deleted, or the user's act of logging on to the Internet (at which point the user's password may be sent to the attacker). A specific consecutive computer action could also trigger a payload—for example, the hard disk may be automatically reformatted upon the tenth system reset after infection, thus losing all saved programs and data.

Although virtually all Trojan horses attempt to cause harm or steal information from a computer system, more than 70 percent of all computer

---

LOVE LETTERS

Most people would agree that it is nice to receive a love letter. Computer hackers, however, took advantage of that feeling by creating the LoveLetter worm that was distributed via e-mail attachments. Many computer users received e-mails with the subject line reading "I LOVE YOU" and curiously opened the attachment, which infected their machines. First appearing in May 2001, the LoveLetter worm tunneled its way into e-mail address books and sent itself to computer users the world over in a matter of days. Since then, more than 80 variations of the worm have been unearthed.

Scan Result: Virus *W32.Sircam.Worm@mm* found. File NOT cleaned.

This file contains a computer worm, a program that spreads very quickly over the Internet to many computers and can delete files, steal sensitive information, or render your machine unusable.

This attachment has a virus that may infect your computer. It cannot be cleaned. We recommend that you DO NOT download this attachment.

Computer viruses and worms are known to wreak havoc on computer systems around the world. Experts recommend scanning all e-mail attachments for viruses and updating virus scan software frequently. Upon scanning for viruses and worms, warning messages like those shown above may appear on a user's monitor.

viruses and worms are designed only to self-replicate. Although they are not intentionally malicious, such invasive programs are still quite dangerous, because they can cause system crashes, clog the Internet and e-mail systems, and generally compromise productivity.

Currently, all invasive software can be categorized into three broad categories: viruses, worms, and Trojan horses.

Viruses

A virus is a computer program that is designed to replicate itself from one file to another (or one disk to another) on a single computer. Viruses spread quickly to many files within a computer, but typically spread slowly between computer systems because they require people to exchange infected files over a network, floppy disk, or in e-mail.

The Pakistani Brain virus, discovered in 1986, is widely believed to be the first computer virus. During the late 1990s, the number of viruses skyrocketed to more than 50,000. Despite the thousands of virus strains, few viruses ever find their way out of research labs and on to end-user computers. Based on industry statistics, less than 1,000 of the more than 50,000 known computer viruses are in circulation at any one time.

Viruses are often classified by the type of file or disk that they infect. The most common types are application viruses, which infect common computer application files, and macro viruses, which infect documents and spreadsheet files.

The average computer virus works as follows:

1. The user runs infected program A.

2. Program A executes the virus logic.

3. The virus locates a new program, B, for infection.

4. The virus checks to see if program B is already infected. If infected, the virus goes back to step 3 to locate another program.

5. If B is not infected, the virus inserts a copy of its logic into program B.

6. The virus then runs program A's original logic (so the user does not suspect any malicious activities).

Viruses have been written in numerous computer programming languages including assembly language, scripting languages (such as Visual Basic or JavaScript), C++, Java, and macro programming languages (such as Microsoft's VBA).

Worms

A worm is a computer program that automatically spreads itself over a computer network from one computer to another. While viruses spread from file to file on a single computer, worms infect as many computers as possible over a network. Virtually all modern computer worms spread through e-mail, sending themselves via Internet e-mail programs.

Usually, a worm infects (or causes its logic to run on) a target system only once. After infecting a computer, the worm attempts to spread to other computers on the network. Because computer worms do not rely on humans to spread themselves between computers, they spread much more rapidly than do computer viruses. The infamous Melissa and LoveLetter threats are both categorized as computer worms.

The first computer worms were written at Xerox Palo Alto Research Center in 1982 to understand how self-replicating logic could be leveraged in a corporation. However, a bug in the worms' logic caused computers on the Xerox network to crash. Xerox researchers had to build the world's first "anti-virus" solution to remove the infections. In 1988 the famous "Internet" worm spread itself to roughly 10 percent of the fledgling Internet (about 6,000 computers).

Like viruses, computer worms can be written in virtually any computer language. While there have been few script language-based virsuses, a high percentage of computer worms have been written in scripting languages like Visual Basic due to the ease of writing self-propagating software with these scripting systems. The stereotypical computer worm works as follows:

1. The user unknowingly runs a worm program.

2. The worm accesses a "directory" source, such as an e-mail address list, to obtain a list of target computers on the network.

3. The worm sends itself to each of the target computers.

4. A user on the target computer unknowingly receives a copy of the worm in e-mail, unintentionally runs the worm e-mail attachment, and repeats the process.

Trojan Horses

Trojan horses are programs disguised as normal computer programs that instead cause damage to the host computer when run. Most commonly, Tro-

jan horses either steal information (such as passwords or files) from the computer or damage the contents of the computer (e.g., delete files).

With the increased popularity of the Internet, the latest generation of Trojan horses has been designed to exploit the Internet. Some of these Internet-enabled Trojan horses can be used to control remotely infected computers or record video/audio from the computer and send it to the attacker. In addition, hackers have used so-called "Zombie" Trojan horse programs to launch large-scale Denial of Service (DoS) attacks against popular Internet web sites.

Trojan horses are not classified as viruses or worms because they do not replicate themselves. However, like viruses and worms, Trojan horses can be written in virtually any language.

Anti-virus Software

Various techniques exist for detecting invasive programs, yet the primary mechanism used by most anti-virus software is called "fingerprint scanning." The anti-virus software maintains a database of thousands of known identification characteristics, or fingerprints, from invasive programs, not unlike a police fingerprint database. When scanning a computer for viruses, the anti-virus program compares the fingerprint of each file on the computer to those in its database. If any of the fingerprints match, the anti-virus program reports the infection and can repair any damage. Since new invasive programs are created daily, anti-virus vendors send fingerprint updates to users as often as once per day.

Legality of Writing Intrusive Programs

Although writing malicious software is not illegal in the United States, willfully spreading such programs is considered a crime punishable by fine or imprisonment. In the United States, some virus authors have argued that writing computer viruses is analogous to exercising free speech. In contrast, countries outside the United States have drafted computer crime laws that are far stricter than those in the United States. For instance, Germany has laws restricting mass exchange of computer viruses for any reason and Finland has recently made writing a computer virus an illegal act. SEE ALSO Privacy; Security; Viruses.

Carey Nachenberg

Bibliography

Atkins, Derek, et al. *Internet Security, Professional Reference.* Indianapolis, IN: New Riders Publishing, 1996.

Cohen, Frederick B. *A Short Course on Computer Viruses,* 2nd ed. New York: John Wiley & Sons, 1994.

JPEG, MPEG

JPEG and MPEG are the abbreviated names of two standards groups that fall under both the International Organization for Standardization and the International Electrotechnical Commission. JPEG is the Joint Photographic Expert Group, which works on the standards for compression of still digital images. MPEG is the Moving Picture Expert Group, which works on the standards for compression of digital movies. JPEG and MPEG are also the names for the standards published by the respective groups.

Digital images or video are compressed primarily for two reasons: to save storage space for archival, and to save **bandwidth** in communication, which saves time required to send the data. A compressed digital image or video can be drastically smaller than its original size and saves a great deal of storage space. Upon retrieval, the data can be decompressed to get back the original image or video. When one needs to transmit the data through a channel of a certain bandwidth, the smaller data size also saves transmission time.

bandwidth a measure of the frequency component of a signal or the capacity of a communication channel to carry signals

There are many different compression **algorithms**, each with its own characteristics and performance. The compressed image or video may be a disk file, or a signal in a transmission channel. People need compression standards for interoperability. As long as the data meet the appropriate compression standards, one can display the image or play the video on any system that would observe the same standards.

algorithms rules or procedures used to solve mathematical problems—most often described as sequences of steps

JPEG

JPEG was proposed in 1991 as a compression standard for digital still images. JPEG compression is **lossy**, which means that some details may be lost when the image is restored from the compressed data. JPEG compression takes advantage of the way the human eyes work, so that people usually do not notice the lost details in the image. With JPEG, one can adjust the amount of loss at compression time by trading image quality for a smaller size of the compressed image.

lossy a nonreversible way of compressing digital images, making images take up less space by permanently removing parts that cannot be easily seen anyway

JPEG is designed for full-color or grayscale images of natural scenes. It works very well with photographic images. JPEG does not work as well on images with sharp edges or artificial scenes such as graphical drawings, text documents, or cartoon pictures.

A few different file formats are used to exchange files with JPEG images. The JPEG File Interchange Format (JFIF) defines a minimum standard necessary to support JPEG, is widely accepted, and is used most often on the personal computer and on the Internet. The conventional file name for JPEG images in this format usually has the extension ~.JPG or ~.JPEG (where ~. represents a file name).

A recent development in the JPEG standard is the JPEG 2000 initiative. JPEG 2000 aims to provide a new image coding system using the latest compression techniques, which are based on the mathematics of wavelets. The effort is expected to find a wide range of applications, from digital cameras to medical imaging.

MPEG

MPEG was first proposed in 1991. It is actually a family of standards for compressed digital movies, and is still evolving. One may think of a digital movie as a sequence of still images displayed one after another at video rate. However, this approach does not take into consideration the extensive redundancy from frame to frame. MPEG takes advantage of that redundancy

Advances in recording capabilities led to the creation of this hard-disc video recorder, released in 2000. It uses MPEG-2 compression to store up to 20 hours of video images.

bit rate the rate at which binary bits can be processed or transferred per unit time, in a system (often a computer communications system)

to achieve even better compression. A movie also has sound channels to play synchronously with the sequence of images.

The MPEG standards actually consist of three main parts: video, audio, and systems. The MPEG systems part coordinates between the video and audio parts, as well as coordinating external synchronization for playing.

The MPEG-1 standard was completed in 1993, and was adopted in video CDs. MP3 audio, which is popular on the Internet, is actually an MPEG-1 standard adopted to handle music in digital audio. It is called MP3 because it is an arrangement for MPEG Audio Layer 3. The MPEG-2 standard was proposed in 1996. It is used as the format for many digital television broadcasting applications, and is the basis for digital versatile disks (DVDs), a much more compact version of the video CD with the capacity for full-length movies. The MPEG-4 standard was completed in 1998, and was adopted in 1999. MPEG-4 is designed for transmission over channels with a low **bit rate**. It is now the popular format for video scripts on the Internet.

These MPEG standards were adopted in a common MPEG format for exchange in disk files. The conventional file name would have the extension

~.MPG or ~.MPEG (where ~ represents a file name). MPEG-7, completed in 2001, is called the Multimedia Content Description Interface. It defines a standard for the textual description of the various multimedia contents, to be arranged in a way that optimizes searching. MPEG-21, called the Multimedia Framework, was started in June 2000. MPEG-21 is intended to integrate the various parts and subsystems into a platform for digital multimedia. SEE ALSO GRAPHIC DEVICES; MUSIC, COMPUTER; WORLD WIDE WEB.

Peter Y. Wu

Bibliography

Ghanbari, Mohammed. *Video Coding: An Introduction to Standard Codecs.* London: Institute of Electrical Engineers, 1999.

Symes, Peter D. *Video Compression Demystified.* New York: McGraw-Hill, 2001.

LISP

LISP, an acronym for LISt Processing, is a programming language developed by John McCarthy in the late 1950s. Although LISP is a general-purpose language, it is often thought of as a language solely for artificial intelligence (AI) programming, for which it is often used. AI programming often deals with symbolic processing that the standard programming languages are ill-prepared to handle. Symbolic processing focuses on the representation of real-world concepts and on the relationships among the objects rather than numeric processing.

At the time that LISP was under development, other AI programming languages were being developed with rather informal approaches. McCarthy, a mathematician, wanted to establish a firm scientific foundation for LISP. That foundation came from formal logic. American logician Alonzo Church (1903–1995) had developed a clear and unambiguous means of describing the inputs and internal computations of functions. The **lambda calculus** notation provided McCarthy, a student of Church's, with a well-defined basis on which to establish this new programming language.

Pure LISP is an example of a functional programming language. In functional programming, functions are applied to arguments and the values that are returned are used as arguments to other functions. Functional programming contrasts with standard or procedural programming, which uses statements that change the program environment in some way, such as assigning a value to a variable. In functional programming, these changes to the environment are minimized by using the values returned by function calls as direct input to other functions without using assignment statements.

As its name implies, the primary data structure in LISP is the list, although it does support a wide variety of data types such as integers, floating point numbers, characters, and strings, as well as user-defined data types. The list is a simple yet flexible data structure. In LISP, a list consists of any number of data elements surrounded by a set of parentheses. For example, a set of integers could be represented by this list: (1 2 3 4 5). But lists can represent more complicated objects. A list representing a record of a person's name, height in inches, and weight in pounds would be expressed as (John 72 180).

American computer scientist John McCarthy (1927–).

lambda calculus important in the development of programming languages, a specialized logic using substitutions that was developed by Alonzo Church (1903–1995)

ABOUT LISP

LISP (LISt Processing) is a programming language developed primarily for symbolic processing in contrast to other programming languages, which were developed primarily for numeric processing. Symbolic processing is needed in some types of problems encountered in artificial intelligence (AI).

syntax a set of rules that a computing language incorporates regarding structure, punctuation, and formatting

artificial intelligence (AI) a branch of computer science dealing with creating computer hardware and software to mimic the way people think and perform practical tasks

algorithmic pertaining to the rules or procedures used to solve mathematical problems —most often described as a sequence of steps

prototypes working models or experimental investigations of proposed systems under development

Lists can contain any type of LISP object, even other lists. Several lists like the one noted earlier, each containing data for one person, could be grouped together in an outer list to represent the height and weight of the members of a sports team, for example. The use of lists in this fashion, along with LISP's list access and retrieval functions, can result in a simple database. Lists can also represent more complicated data structures such as trees and graphs through the use of a more complicated nesting of lists.

The reliance on the list data structure results in a relatively simple **syntax**. With a few exceptions, parentheses are the only punctuation needed. This means that all LISP function definitions are written as lists. Since all LISP programs are written as lists, and since LISP contains a myriad of functions that manipulate lists, LISP programs can serve as data to other LISP programs. This means that LISP programs can use other LISP programs as data to produce new programs.

Not only does the syntax of LISP make it easy to do things that are inherently difficult to do in other programming languages, the LISP programming environment is well suited to the exploratory type of programming that **artificial intelligence** projects demand. These programming problems are often ill-defined at the outset and are not usually developed in the standard **algorithmic** manner. They require an exploratory approach that involves successively refining a series of **prototypes**. The demand for fast prototyping requires an environment that makes it easy for the programmer to develop and revise programs.

Although LISP programs can be compiled in order to speed up program execution, LISP is most often used as an interpreted language. The interpretive environment can considerably shorten development time by allowing programs to be written, debugged, tested, and modified at any time, even while the program itself is running. This avoids the long re-compile time associated with large programs written in other languages and facilitates the development of AI programs.

LISP has long supported facilities that are only recently being incorporated into other programming languages such as a rich object system and function overloading, which is facilitated by run-time type checking. Run-time type checking frees the programmer from declaring a data type for each variable. The type of a variable is one of several pieces of information that LISP maintains about every object in the environment. SEE ALSO ARTIFICIAL INTELLIGENCE; PROCEDURAL LANGUAGES.

Cynthia J. Martincic

Bibliography

Church, Alonzo. "The Calculi of Lambda Conversion." In *Annals of Mathematical Studies*, vol. 6. Princeton, NJ: Princeton University Press, 1941.

McCarthy, John. "Recursive Functions of Symbolic Expressions and Their Computation by Machine, Part I." *Communications of the ACM* 3, no. 4 (1960): 185-195.

Logo

The name of the programming language Logo comes from the Greek for "word." The first version of Logo, a dialect of LISP, was developed in 1966 by several researchers and scholars including Wallace Feurzeig, a researcher at Bolt Beranek and Newman, a Cambridge research firm actively engaged in the study of **artificial intelligence (AI)**, and Seymour Papert, a mathematics and education professor from the Massachusetts Institute of Technology.

Although it was designed originally for MIT's mainframes and minicomputers, within less than a decade, Logo had found a place in elementary school education curricula across the United States. Logo's reach into thousands of elementary school classrooms was made feasible by two technological advances of the 1970s: the creation of computer time-sharing and the development of the first high-level conversational programming language. In 1970 Papert founded the Logo Laboratory at MIT. Logo-based turtles were introduced around 1971, and the use of microcomputers allowed Logo to be used by elementary school students.

The idea of creating a programming language for children grew out of the realization that most existing computer languages were designed to do computation and lacked the ability to handle non-numeric symbols. In addition most languages had complex **syntax** rules and very little support for **debugging** and editing. The Logo creators felt that this new language had to satisfy these requirements:

1. Elementary grade students should be able to use it for simple tasks with very little preparation.

2. Its structure should exemplify mathematically-important concepts with minimal intrusion from programming conventions.

3. It should support the expression of mathematically rich numerical and non-numerical **algorithms** such as changing English into pig Latin, making and breaking secret codes, or determining if words are palindromes.

The plan was to introduce mathematical ideas through experience with familiar problems. The goal was to provide an environment that would encourage mathematical thinking through the completion of concrete projects. Papert and his colleagues felt that this would give students a sense of connectivity between abstract mathematical concepts and everyday practical experiences. For example, when giving directions to someone, a person would likely say: "Go straight for two blocks then turn right," rather than using the words "latitude" and "longitude." In the same way, the commands used in "turtle graphics" are based on right turns and left turns, rather than on absolute coordinates, making them easy to understand.

The "turtle" is a triangular object that appears on the computer screen and moves in response to commands typed on the keyboard. If the pen is activated, the turtle will leave tracks on the screen; if the pen is up, it will not. Papert refers to the turtle as "an object to think with." Users learn to create programs that draw simple geometric figures, such as squares or triangles, which can be combined into bigger programs that draw more complex figures, such as houses. The metaphor of "teaching the computer" new things based on what it already knows is the basis of Logo programming.

In an ideal Logo environment, much of the programming is learned through a series of activities. Students can choose many of their own prob-

artificial intelligence (AI) a branch of computer science dealing with creating computer hardware and software to mimic the way people think and perform practical tasks

syntax a set of rules that a computing language incorporates regarding structure, punctuation, and formatting

debugging trying to trace, identify, and then remove errors in program source code

algorithms rules or procedures used to solve mathematical problems—most often described as sequences of steps

lems and decide how to solve them based on their experience in generating and solving other problems. They teach the computer how to perform a specific action and get immediate feedback. In this environment students learn art, geometry, and computer programming.

Logo Syntax

Logo makes it possible for beginners to learn to program fairly quickly because it starts out with a set of words called *primitives* that are easy to understand and can be used to experiment. For example, FORWARD or FD would make the turtle go forward, and RIGHT or RT would make it turn to the right, while HIDETURTLE or HT would hide it from view.

Using those primitives, a user can write a set of instructions, known as a *procedure*, name it, and use it to build other procedures. A procedure is executed by typing its name. Large problems can be broken down into small chunks that are easy to manage. An example of a procedure that draws a square is shown in Figure 1(a) and 1(b), while one to draw a triangle is shown in Figure 1(c).

These procedures use a constant of 30 for the sides of the square and the triangle, which means that if we wanted to draw squares and triangles of different sizes we would have to modify the procedures. Logo uses **variables** in the title line of a procedure to allow the use of different values every time the procedure is executed, as shown in Figure 2. The variable name is separated from the procedure name by a space and a colon (:). To execute procedures using variables, the name of the procedure must be followed by a space and a numerical value. For example, the command SQUARE 60 would draw a square of 60 units.

A procedure can call other procedures, as shown in Figure 3(a), and can also call itself, as shown in Figure 3(b), making Logo a recursive language.

The example in Figure 3(b) shows the occurrence of an infinite loop because the procedure continues to call itself forever; it has no way of knowing when to stop. All **recursive** procedures need to have a condition that will be used to stop the loop after a certain number of calls have been made, as shown in Figure 4.

variables symbols, such as strings of letters, which may assume any one of a set of values known as the domain

recursive operations expressed and implemented in a way that requires them to invoke themselves

Figure 1. Example of a procedure to draw a square: (a) shows the long version of the procedure; (b) shows the repetition option; and (c) shows a procedure to draw a triangle.

```
    TO SQUARE          TO SQUARE                    TO TRIANGLE
      FD   30            REPEAT 4 [FD 30 RT 90]        REPEAT 3 [FD 30 RT 120]
      RT   90          END                           END
      FD   30
      RT   90                        (b)                         (c)
      FD   30
      RT   90
      FD   30
      RT   90
    END
      (a)
```

Figure 2. Examples of using variables in procedures to allow different values to be given for the sides of the square and triangle.

```
    TO SQUARE :SIDE                 TO TRIANGLE :SIDE
      REPEAT 4 [FD :SIDE RT 90]       REPEAT 3 [FD :SIDE RT 120]
    END                             END
```

```
TO HOUSE :SIDE                TO MANYSQUARES :SIDE
    RT   90                       RT       30
    SQUARE :SIDE                  SQUARE :SIDE
    RT   30                       MANYSQUARES :SIDE
    TRIANGLE :SIDE            END
END
    (a)
```

Figure 3: (a) Example of the SQUARE procedure calling the TRIANGLE procedure to draw a house: a square with a triangle on top. (b) Example of the SQUARE procedure calling itself.

```
TO MANYSQUARES :SIDE
    IF SIDE <5 STOP
    RT   30
    SQUARE :SIDE
    MANYSQUARES :SIDE-5
END
```

Figure 4: Example of a recursive procedure that will reduce the size of the variable SIDE by 5 each time it is called. When this value becomes less than 5, the procedure will stop executing.

LEGO-Logo

LEGO-Logo is a unique member of the Logo family because it allows students to use computers to control the manipulation of special LEGO blocks. Students build LEGO structures that use touch and light sensors, motors, and gears plugged into an interface box, and write Logo programs that give them motion. This expands the computer's reach into the three-dimensional world in a very dynamic way and provides students with the opportunity to learn the behavior of machines, electronics, and motion.

Students learn to break complex problems and machines into simple ones. For example, they can build and operate moving vehicles of different sizes to observe the relationships between speed and weight. While conducting the experiments, students learn about different types of measurement, standard units of measure, rate-distance-time relationships, and the processes of collecting, representing, and analyzing data. Because these experiments combine the manipulation of concrete materials with symbolic representations, such as the names and definitions of Logo procedures, students learn to connect the concrete with the abstract.

Music in Logo

Incorporating music into a program and exploring the development of music can be fun, and one does not need to know music or understand musical notation. In order to program a tune in Logo, one writes a procedure using the PLAY primitive, which requires two lists to designate a musical note. These two lists state its two components, its name, such as "A, B, C" and its duration, such as eighth, quarter, half. The musical program can be broken down into modules, which are then combined to play the tune.

Developments

Much of the development effort in Logo has gone into discovering new application areas, with new sets of primitive procedures and new peripheral hardware. For example, StarLogo explores massive parallelism with thousands of turtles performing their actions at the same time. This environment can be used to explore how large-scale phenomena emerge from simple small-scale behavior. StarLogo can be used to model a variety of systems,

TRY, TRY AGAIN

MicroWorlds, a commercial product, is a Logo interpreter embedded in a painting and animation program. MicroWorlds makes it possible to manage large quantities of data by running experimental trials many times, collecting data and displaying it in graphical or numerical form. MicroWorlds allows one to make small changes to an experiment and try it again without having to start from scratch.

from the foraging behavior of ants in a colony to the formation of traffic jams in a highway, and the interaction between antibodies and antigens in an immune system.

Several versions of Logo have included some form of object-oriented programming, usually with a message-passing syntax in which the first argument is an object and the second is an instruction to be carried out by that object.

A Logo-based object-oriented language for World Wide Web applications, called Bongo, is a current research project designed to be like Java for kids. SEE ALSO EDUCATIONAL SOFTWARE; PROCEDURAL LANGUAGES; PROGRAMMING.

Ida M. Flynn

Bibliography

Flake, Janice L., C. Edwin McClintock, and Sandra Turner. *Fundamentals of Computer Education.* Belmont, CA: Wadsworth Publishing, 1990.

Maddux, Cleborne D., and D. LaMont Johnson, eds. *Logo, a Retrospective.* New York: Haworth Press, Inc, 1997.

Papert, Seymour. *Mindstorms: Children, Computers and Powerful Ideas.* New York: Basic Books, Inc, 1980.

Markup Languages

A markup language is a system for noting the attributes of a document. Historically, the term "markup" has been used to refer to the process of marking manuscript copy for typesetting, usually with directions for the use of type fonts and sizes, spacing, indentation, and other formatting features. In the electronic era, "markup" refers to the sequence of characters or other symbols that are inserted within a text or word processing file to describe the document's logical structure or indicate how the document should appear when it is displayed or printed. (Notation entered with the intention of describing logical properties is usually referred to as descriptive markup, whereas notation concerned with formatting is referred to as procedural markup.)

Unlike programming languages, which are dynamic and process data through various calculations, markup languages are static. In essence, a markup language identifies similar units of information within a document, bringing a form of instructed intelligence to a document so that applications may read and process it more effectively.

Efforts to devise electronic markup languages evolved initially along two distinct lines. **Proprietary** software developers, such as Microsoft, focused largely on procedural markup schemes, expressed in application-specific language and offering functions similar to printers' marks. Their efforts were concerned mainly with the quality and economy of presentation. Interest in descriptive markup languages was motivated by several factors, including the realization that the extent to which electronic documents may be manipulated depends largely on the extent and sophistication of the treatment of logical structures. There was also an awareness that common methods of treatment enhance communication, and the recognition that it will be sim-

proprietary a process or technology developed and owned by an individual or company, and not published openly

```
<!doctype html public "-//W3C//DTD WWW HTML 3.2 Final//EN">
<html>
<head>
<title>Crash Landing in Roswell</title>
<meta name="keywords" content="Roswell, New Mexico, aliens, Air Force">
</head>
<body>
<h1>Space Invaders; Or, Weather Balloon Gone Astray?<h1>
<p>In the summer of 1947, in the desert of central New Mexico, a local rancher found some
unusual debris on his property. After authorities began to investigate the nature of the strange,
metallic material, the U.S. Air Force quickly ruled that the debris was a remnant of a downed
weather balloon. Then and today, many believe the government was trying to hide the
truth<em>that the debris was actually part of a extraterrestrial spacecraft that had crash
landed in the desert, with aliens onboard.<p>
<img src="roswell.jpg" alt="Roswell in 1947" height="350" width="500">
<p><a href="home.html">Home</a></p>
</body>
</html>
```

An example of HTML coding.

pler and less expensive to build backward compatible systems if archived documents have been marked under a standardized system.

This interest grew dramatically, with the advent and rapid expansion of the World Wide Web, a system in which publication and information exchange are based largely on the Hypertext Markup Language (HTML), an open, application-neutral markup language. Application-neutral markup languages have become increasingly important in the design of network-aware applications in recent years. This is in part because proprietary developers have begun to accommodate the interests of users who want to create web documents and take advantage of the other capabilities inherent in application-neutral schemes, and because increasing **bandwidth** has allowed programmers to consider the Internet as a computational environment.

Today, the most important markup languages are the Standard Generalized Markup Language (SGML), the Hypertext Markup Language (HTML), and the Extensible Markup Language (XML).

SGML

The Standard Generalized Markup Language (SGML) is "a set of rules for defining and expressing the logical structure of documents thereby enabling software products to control the searching, retrieval, and structured display of those documents," as noted on the *Encoded Archival Description Official Web Site*. SGML was developed at IBM in the late 1960s by a group of programmers charged with the development of an integrated information system. Led by Charles Goldfarb, the team rejected the idea of application-specific coding, opting instead for an open scheme of descriptive tags capable of accommodating the requirements of different types of documents and different computer platforms. Known first as the Generalized Markup Language (GML), SGML was expanded in its scope and further developed under the auspices of the American National Standards Institute (ANSI) and the International Organization for Standardization (ISO). It was adopted as an international standard (ISO 8879) in 1986.

Originally intended to be a method for creating interchangeable, structured documents, SGML became instead a framework for developing more specific markup languages, based largely on its implementation of the

bandwidth a measure of the frequency component of a signal or the capacity of a communication channel to carry signals

MARKUP LANGUAGE COST CONSIDERATIONS

Economics plays an important role in how and to what extent electronic documents are marked. Although formatting for presentation is relatively inexpensive, until recently formatting documents for both content and presentation represented a significant additional expense in the production of electronic documents. Even now, although the production of "neutrally coded" text, based on the Standard Generalized Markup Language (SGML) and its derivatives, is diminishing in cost, the limited number of suppliers able to produce logical markup of sufficiently high quality for complex text contributes significantly to the interest in presentation-oriented systems, most notably the Portable Document Format (PDF) of Adobe Systems.

concept of a formally defined document type definition (DTD), with an explicit, nested element structure.

HTML

The Hypertext Markup Language is an SGML Document Type Definition (DTD) that was designed specifically for the World Wide Web. In essence, HTML is a set of markup codes inserted in a file that note logical structures and instruct a web browser how to display a web page's words and images.

Under HTML, markup elements are expressed in pairs to indicate when a structure or display effect begins and ends. For example

<p>Now is the time for all good men to come to the aid of their country.</p>

instructs a web browser to treat the sentences as a paragraph. Under the HTML 4.01 version of the Hypertext Markup Language, the paragraph may be formatted through an enhancement known as "inline styling." The expression below

<p STYLE="font:Garmond; font-size:12pt;text-align:justify"> Now is the time for all good men. . . .

renders the paragraph as a line of justified text, using the font and point size specified for display.

The original goal of the World Wide Web was to create an information space in which hypertext links could be made from one document to another without the need to navigate any hierarchical organization of documents. HTML was devised because the web's designers wanted to create a system that would facilitate communication among users, and that would do so whether the user had a **dumb terminal** or a workstation running a **graphical user interface (GUI)**. They concluded that a common and simple descriptive language was needed, deciding early on that the creation of an SGML DTD incorporating a limited and basic **syntax** would be the most effective way to manage documents under their system.

Over the years HTML was expanded and refined, culminating in HTML 4.01, which included enhancements for greater support of forms, tables, and style sheets. But as the World Wide Web has grown in size and in the sophistication of the demands it attempted to support, the limitations of HTML became increasingly evident and problematic.

The main problem is that HTML provides a single way of describing the information in a document. It is not extensible, it cannot be customized, so it cannot be adapted to meet special needs—such as mathematical notation, chemical formulas, or proprietary, vendor-specific tags that would extend capabilities—and it has many formatting limitations. Most important of all, HTML does not deal with content or **semantics**.

Developers concluded that the best way to solve these problems was to abandon the continued improvement of HTML and create a new markup language. The result is the Extensible Markup Language (XML).

XML

The Extensible Markup Language (XML) is a subset of SGML, whose purpose is "to enable generic SGML to be served, received, and processed on

dumb terminal a keyboard and screen connected to a distant computer without any processing capability

graphical user interface (GUI) a technology whereby graphical objects are placed on a computer screen for interaction with the user—examples are icons, menus, and buttons

syntax a set of rules that a computing language incorporates regarding structure, punctuation, and formatting

semantics the study of how words acquire meaning and how those meanings change over time

the web" through a system of notation that is unlimited and self-defining. Although XML has been designed to be compatible with HTML (as well as SGML), it is not another single, predefined markup language. It is a meta-language—a language for describing other languages—for designing markup.

From a functional perspective, the most significant difference between HTML and XML is that although HTML can describe a logical structure within a document by document—<p> is an example—XML permits a notation indicating the content of the structure—<author> is an example—because XML enables authors and editors to create DTDs that conform to the more specific requirements of a document. This capability means that, in addition, an XML document or a portion of its contents can be processed purely as data by a program or stored with similar data on another computer.

Coordinated mainly by the World Wide Web Consortium, XML is under continuing development. Owing to its extensibility, XML has engendered a substantial number of adjunct specifications, including:

- Document Object Model, which is a platform- and language-neutral interface that will allow programs and scripts to dynamically access and update the content, structure, and style of documents;

- XML Query, which is intended to provide flexible query facilities to extract data from real and virtual documents on the web and support full interaction between the web and server-side databases, including databases of XML files;

- XPath, which is a language for addressing parts of an XML document;

- XSL, which is a language for stylesheets intended to support the presentation of XML documents and the specification of formatting semantics.

A number of important XML applications have already been developed. Of them, the most important is XHTML, which is a reformulation of HTML 4.01 in XML that effectively treats HTML as an XML application. Its main purpose is to build a bridge for web designers from HTML to XML. It is also intended to establish a modular standard capable of supporting the provision of "richer web pages" to the increasing wide range of browser platforms that now includes cellular phones, televisions, cars, wireless communicators, and kiosks, as well as desktop computers.

XHTML 1.0 has been formulated in three variant DTDs. *XHMTL Strict* supports strictly structural markup, with formatting available through the use of the World Wide Web Consortium's Cascading Style Sheet (CSS) language to set the font, color, and other layout effects. *XHTML Transitional* enables authors to retain some of HTML's presentation features, so that documents may be successfully addressed by older browsers without support for CSS. *XHTML Framset* replaces HTML Frames for use when an author wants to partition a browser window into two or more frames.

Another important XML application is the Mathematical Markup Language (MathML). MathML, which can be used to encode both mathematical notation and mathematical content, provides a rich vocabulary—30 MathML tags describe abstract notational structures, while another 150 tags

provide the means of specifying the intended meaning of a particular expression—or documents with sophisticated mathematical content. Yet another important XML application is the Synchronized Multimedia Integration Language (SMIL). SMIL defines an XML-based language that allows authors to write interactive multimedia presentations. Using SMIL, an author can describe the temporal behavior of a multimedia presentation, associate hyperlinks with media objects, and describe the layout of the presentation on a screen.

Future Directions

A few things about the future of markup languages are clear. First, extensible languages will be dominant, owing to the extent to which they may be enhanced and customized. Second, in order to accommodate the increasing number of portable devices connected to the web and their more modest computational and display capabilities, markup languages will be necessarily modular. And, third, because XML's data description capabilities affords the opportunity to replace web browsers with more powerful applications, such as the applications that make up Microsoft Office, it seems likely that XML and its successors will shift the principal motif of web-based computing from the browser to productivity suites and other client-based applications. SEE ALSO DOCUMENT PROCESSING; E-COMMERCE; HYPERMEDIA AND MULTIMEDIA; HYPERTEXT; WORLD WIDE WEB.

Christinger Tomer

Bibliography

Aitken, Peter G. *XML: The Microsoft Way*. Boston: Addison-Wesley, 2002.

Bryan, Martin. *SGML and HTML Explained*. Reading, MA: Addison-Wesley Longman, 1997.

Goldfarb, Charles F. *The SGML Handbook*. New York: Oxford University Press, 1990.

Goldfarb, Charles F., and Paul Prescod. *The XML Handbook*, 2nd ed. Upper Saddle River, NJ: Prentice Hall, 2000.

Graham, Ian S., and Liam Quin. *XML Specification Guide*. New York: Wiley, 1999.

St. Laurent, Simon. *XML: A Primer*. Foster City, CA: M&T Books, 1999.

Travis, Brian E., and Dale C. Waldt. *The SGML Implementation Guide: A Blueprint for SGML Migration*. New York: Springer, 1995.

Vint, Danny R. *SGML at Work*. Upper Saddle River, NJ: Prentice Hall, 1999.

Internet Resources

"Extensible Markup Language (XML) 1.0 (Second Edition); W3C Recommendation 6 October 2000." *W3C—World Wide Web Consortium Website*. <http://www.w3.org/TR/REC-xml>

Library of Congress, Network Development & MARC Standards Office. "Development of the Encoded Archival Description Document Type Definition." *Encoded Archival Description Official Web Site*. <http://lcweb.loc.gov/ead/eadback.html>

Memory Devices

Digital computers must convert the information that the user enters into them (e.g., from documents, graphics, videos, or sound) into digital data. These data are really a series of 1s and 0s. Each 1 or 0 is called a binary digit (**bit**). The determination of whether a bit is a 0 (off) or a 1 (on) is

bit a single binary digit, 1 or 0—a contraction of Binary digIT; the smallest unit for storing data in a computer

made by the electronics in the computer hardware. Some computers make this determination by the **polarity** of magnetized material, while others determine the status of a bit by whether or not electricity is flowing along a circuit. Using these binary digits and a coding scheme such as **ASCII** or **EBCDIC**, eight bits are grouped into a **byte** with each byte representing one character (e.g., letter, punctuation mark, or number). These bytes are sent from one area of the computer to another and stored in various areas of the computer.

In order for data to be processed by a computer, they must first be stored in main computer storage. Over the years, different memory devices have been used to store data (as 1s and 0s) in main computer storage. One of the first devices for storing data was the vacuum tube. Vacuum tubes were lightbulb-sized electronic tubes with glowing filaments. Although they worked, vacuum tubes generated a tremendous amount of heat, used a large amount of electric power, and were delicate, bulky, unreliable, and expensive.

In the early 1950s, Jay W. Forrester and his group at Massachusetts Institute of Technology (MIT) developed magnetic core storage, which replaced vacuum tubes and was the most popular device for storing data in main computer storage for two decades. Magnetic cores consisted of small ring-shaped pieces of metal that could be polarized or magnetized in either of two directions to represent a 1 or a 0.

Invented in 1948, transistors become the memory device of choice by the 1960s. Transistors can be thought of as tiny electrically operated switches that can alternate between "on" and "off" many millions of times per second.

Integrated Circuits

Integrated circuits (IC) are entire collections of electrical circuits etched onto very thin slices of silicon. (Silicon is a natural element found in sand that is purified.) A single integrated circuit is less than a quarter-inch square and is often called a "chip" or "microchip." Integrated circuits are housed within ceramic containers of various types including single in-line memory module (SIMM), dual in-line pin (DIP), dual in-line memory module (DIMM), pin-grid array (PGA), or single edge contact (SEC).

At the start of the twenty-first century, integrated circuit-based **semiconductor** memory was the primary memory device used for main computer storage. Semiconductor memory is an integrated circuit made up of millions of tiny transistors printed on small chips of silicon. Data that were stored in magnetic core memory could be accessed in microseconds, but data stored in semiconductor memory are accessed even more quickly, in **nanoseconds**. The use of semiconductor memory devices has increased the speed and decreased the price of main computer storage. The disadvantage to using some semiconductor memory devices is that they are **volatile**; that is, whenever the current no longer flows to the device, the stored data are lost. Magnetic cores did not have this problem.

There are several different categories of semiconductor memory, including: RAM, SRAM, DRAM, ROM, PROM, EPROM, and EAPROM. Each type of memory is characterized by the technology it uses to hold the data and the type of data it stores.

polarity the positive (+) or negative (−) state of an object, which dictates how it will react to forces such as magnetism or electricity

ASCII an acronym that stands for American Standard Code for Information Interchange; assigns a unique 8-bit binary number to every letter of the alphabet, the digits (0 to 9), and most keyboard symbols

EBCDIC the acronym for Extended Binary Coded Decimal Interchange Code, which assigns a unique 8-bit binary number to every letter of the alphabet, the digits (0 to 9), and most keyboard symbols

byte a group of eight binary digits; represents a single character of text

semiconductor solid material that possesses electrical conductivity characteristics that are similar to those of metals under certain conditions, but can also exhibit insulating qualities under other conditions

nanoseconds each is one-thousand-millionth (one billionth, or 10^{-9}) of a second

volatile subject to rapid change

Shown holding an early version of the semiconductor, Robert Noyce is the co-inventor of the integrated circuit and cofounder of the Intel Corporation. His efforts revolutionized the electronics industry and earned him the nickname "Mayor of Silicon Valley."

Random Access Memory (RAM)

Random Access Memory (RAM) is used when program instructions or data are temporarily stored in the computer before and after they are processed. RAM is also called primary storage or main computer storage. RAM is very important to computer systems. When the computer starts, the operating system is loaded from storage into RAM, and when the user opens an application software package, the instructions for it are also loaded into RAM. As someone uses that software to write a letter to his mother, for example, the characters he types are held in RAM until he tells the software to perform some action such as print the document. RAM is the kind of memory referred to when computers are said to be 64 MB (pronounced 64 meg or megabyte) computers. Having enough RAM is important since it affects how quickly the user can perform certain tasks. In some cases, the user will not be able to use certain software programs if he does not have enough RAM.

Random Access Memory can be **static** or **dynamic**. In static random-access memory (SRAM), a small current is used to maintain the stored data values without further manipulation while the power is on. CMOS memory (complementary metal oxide semiconductor), pronounced "SEE moss,"

static without movement; stationary

dynamic changing; possessing volatility

is a type of SRAM that is used to hold data concerning someone's computer configuration. The most common type of device used for main memory is a paired transistor and capacitor, which holds an electric charge. Because capacitors slowly lose their charges, they must be recharged about every 4 milliseconds. This type of memory is called dynamic random access memory (DRAM). DRAM is cheaper, but slower, than SRAM.

One major problem with RAM is that it is volatile. That is, its contents will be lost when the computer's power is lost. Thus, other means of permanently storing data and instructions must be used, including other types of memory such as ROM and external storage devices such as magnetic tapes, magnetic disks, CD-ROMs (compact disc-read only memory), and DVDs (digital versatile discs).

Read-Only Memory (ROM)

ROM, or read-only memory, is a type of semiconductor memory that is permanent and cannot be erased. The Central Processing Unit (CPU) can read data stored in ROM, but cannot write to ROM. With ROM, the data are recorded when the memory is manufactured. The data are activated when the computer is turned on. ROM is normally used to store data and programs, such as language interpreters (BASIC), display controllers, or the storage of manufacturer-specific micro codes such as Basic Input Output System (BIOS). Unlike RAM, ROM is not volatile.

PROM, or programmable read-only memory, is a subclass of ROM. Like ROM, it can be read, but it cannot be altered. PROM differs from ROM in that the stored data are not recorded when the chip is manufactured. Rather, the data to be stored in PROM are recorded by the manufacturer of the computer using special high-current devices to burn fuses on the devices. Thus, PROM is programmed once and the manufacturer of the computer can use this memory device to control a specific product. PROM is non-volatile.

EPROM, or erasable programmable read-only memory, is a special kind of PROM. EPROM allows the user to erase the data stored in this memory device by using special ultraviolet devices and then reprogram it. An example of where EPROM is used is in the field of **robotics**. Because a robot may have to be re-programmed on a routine basis, an EPROM memory device is used.

Another type of PROM is called electrically alterable programmable read-only memory (EAPROM). This type of memory can be changed by the computer using special high-current operations. Programming these devices repeatedly (more than 1,000 times) tends to destroy them, so they are used to hold data that rarely changes.

Managing Memory for Data Retrieval

The type and quantity of memory available in a computer system is important, and so is the user's ability to store and retrieve data. The management of memory is a very significant function of a computer's operating system. A part of the operating system called the Memory Manager controls how programs access memory to store necessary instructions and data before and after processing by the CPU. When a program needs to use RAM, the

IS SILICON FOUND IN SILICON VALLEY?

Yes. In fact, silicon is found in 25 percent of the Earth's crust. First discovered in 1822 by J. J. Berzelius of Sweden, silicon is an element found in many mineral compounds, including mica, quartz, and talc. In its natural state, it appears metallic in luster and has a reddish-brown or black color. It is used mostly in metal alloys such as cast iron and steel, as well as in lubricants and glass. A small amount of silicon is mined each year to be purified and used in the manufacturing of semiconductors and integrated circuits.

robotics the science and engineering of building electromechanical machines that aim to serve as replacements for human laborers

Memory Manager checks for an unused portion and allocates it. The Memory Manager tracks which portions of memory are being used and by whom. One major task of the Memory Manager is to protect the portion of RAM that contains the operating system. It cannot be altered or deleted. The Memory Manager also "deallocates" memory when a program is finished.

There have been many schemes developed to allow the operating system to allocate and manage memory. Early computer systems were single-user and had simple **algorithms**. As computer systems and operating systems have become more sophisticated, the memory management schemes have had to become more sophisticated, too. One of the latest schemes allows programs or data files that are larger than the available memory space to be brought into memory in segments. This is called virtual memory. Using virtual memory is slower than if the entire program was small enough to be stored in RAM in one piece.

algorithms rules or procedures used to solve mathematical problems—most often described as sequences of steps

The cost of memory has decreased rapidly and the speed of memory has increased quickly since the days of the vacuum tube. These trends are expected to continue, partly due to the fact that integrated circuits are packing more and more technology into a very small space. The decrease in memory cost allows programmers to use more and more memory for our favorite application programs while the increasing speed of memory makes these programs run faster and faster. SEE ALSO ASSEMBLY LANGUAGE AND ARCHITECTURE; CENTRAL PROCESSING UNIT; OPERATING SYSTEMS; STORAGE DEVICES.

Charles R. Woratschek and Terri L. Lenox

Bibliography

Baron, Robert J., and Lee Higbie. *Computer Architecture*. Reading, MA: Addison Wesley Publishing Company, 1992.

Flynn, Ida, and Ann McIver McHoes. *Understanding Operating Systems*, 3rd ed. Boston: PWS Publishing Company, 2000.

Parsons, June Jamrich, and Dan Oja. *New Perspectives on Computer Concepts*, 4th ed. Cambridge, MA: Course Technology, Inc., 2000.

Shelly, Gary B., and Thomas J. Cashman. *Introduction to Computers and Data Processing*. Fullerton, CA: Anaheim Publishing Company, 1980.

Morse, Samuel

American Inventor
1791–1872

Samuel Finley Breese Morse was responsible for the creation of the Morse Code, an electronic alphabet that carries messages via electric wires. Morse was born in 1791 in Charlestown, Massachusetts. At a young age, he began to display artistic talent that he developed throughout his life. While attending college lectures in natural philosophy, Morse learned about electricity. Although formal academics did not interest Morse, these lectures were the foundation for his later work and, at the time, inspired him to construct models of batteries.

To supplement his college income, Morse began to paint portraits of fellow students and faculty members. He considered painting professionally

Samuel Morse.

and in 1811 went abroad to study painting, returning home in 1815. During a European trip in 1829 to expand his artistic horizons, he became aware of the French telegraph, a semaphore system. Morse quickly realized that an electric spark could transmit a message more rapidly than the semaphore. His interest again turned toward potential uses for electricity.

As he returned from Europe in 1831, Morse began efforts to develop what would become the American telegraph. In conversations with fellow passengers, Morse learned about sparking properties of an electromagnet and the fact that wires can carry current. These two factors would allow the transmission of coded messages, and Morse started developing a numerical based code.

The digits from one to five were represented by one to five dots, the digits from six to nine by a combination of dots and dashes. The next step was to translate the coded numbers to words. Each group of numbers translates to a word, for example, dots representing 215 would translate to the word "war" and fifteen to "Belgium." Morse started to develop a conversion dictionary for translating the number groups to words. Another problem was how to record the transmissions. Morse's early drawings show an electromagnet causing a pencil to contact a moving paper strip when the electrical circuit closed and another magnet to raise the pencil when the circuit was broken. The pencil marks would record the code dots.

Although he was an art professor, Morse continued working on the telegraph, experimenting with various ways for recording the message and trying various methods to extend the distance over which the message could travel. His art studio doubled as a laboratory where he demonstrated working models of the telegraph to students and visitors. Some changes in the model resulted from discussing ideas and problems with the visitors. He determined that an electronic message could be sent any distance by relaying the signals. There had to be a way to increase the signal distance between relays. Morse needed more than casual advice; he needed partners with expertise.

In 1835 Leonard Gale, a professor of geology and mineralogy, became the first partner. Gale provided the techniques needed to solve the distance/relay problem based on Professor Joseph Henry's scientific articles. The second partner, Alfred Vail, joined in 1837 to design and supervise the production of the instruments. Vail's major contributions were replacing the pencil with a blunt stylus and designing a key for transmitting the message. In 1837 the fourth partner, Maine congressman F. O. J. Smith was enlisted to help with obtaining financial support from Congress and to contact for the services necessary to construct the communications network.

As the telegraph came closer to reality, it became apparent that the number to letter code was too cumbersome. By 1838 the first version of dots and dashes representing letters appeared. The code uses combinations of dots and dashes from one to a set of four. The most frequently occurring letters have the shortest code. For example an E is one dot; the Q is two dots, one dash, one dot. There are two versions of the code: American Morse and International Morse. "What hath God wrought!" was the first inter city telegraph message, which was sent from Washington, D.C., to Baltimore,

Maryland, on May 24, 1844. Telegraphed reports of events and votes at the 1844 Democratic Convention in Baltimore proved the usefulness of the telegraph for transmitting information.

Morse viewed the telegraph as source of financial security and a means to obtain resources to support education. He served as a charter trustee of Vassar College and donated gifts to Yale University, the Cleveland Female Seminary, and other educational institutions. His other ventures included developing improvements in Daguerreotype, an early form of photography using silver and copper plates; running twice for mayor of New York City; and cofounding and serving as first president of the National Academy of Design. At the end of his life, Morse had attained international stature as the inventor of the American telegraph. Today he is also recognized as an important American artist. Morse died in April 1872. SEE ALSO CODES; CODING TECHNIQUES; INTERNET; TELECOMMUNICATIONS.

Bertha Kugelman Morimoto

Bibliography

Mabee, Carleton. *The American Leonardo.* New York: Alfred A. Knopf, 1944.

Music, Computer

The term "computer music" encompasses a wide range of compositional activities, from the generation of conventionally notated scores using data calculated by the computer, to the direct synthesis of sound in a digital form within the computer itself, ready for conversion into audio signals via digital-to-analog converter, amplifier, and loudspeaker.

There are three basic techniques for producing sounds with a computer: sign-bit extraction, the use of hybrid digital-analog systems, and digital-to-analog conversion. Sign-bit extraction has occasionally been used for compositions of serious musical intent. Little interest persists in building hybrid digital-analog facilities because some types of signal processing, such as reverberation and filtering, are time-consuming even in the fastest of computers. Digital-to-analog conversion has become the standard technique for computer sound synthesis because it is the most versatile method of computer sound generation. Since the sound wave is constructed directly, there are almost no restrictions on sound properties.

To use a computer for music production, the composer or performer first "calls up" from the computer memory the appropriate precompiled program, which is written in a programming language such as FORTRAN, ALGOL, PL/1, PASCAL, BASIC, or COBOL. The program includes various "instruments," i.e., digitally stored musical waveforms, and the operator selects the instruments to use before indicating to the computer in detail—note by note, correct in pitch and timbre—the musical composition to be reproduced.

The computer then translates the instrument definitions into a machine language program, and, if necessary, puts the score into the proper format for processing. After that, the program actually "plays" the score on the instruments, thus creating the sound. The processing of a note of the score consists of two stages: initialization and performance. At the initialization

Max Mathews of Bell Labs
was the co-creator of the
first music synthesizer.

of a note, the values that are to remain fixed throughout the duration of the note are set. During the performance of a note, the computer calculates the actual output corresponding to the sound.

The advantage of digital-to-analog conversion is that the computer can be called upon to assemble the individual sounds into a composition so that the composer need only be concerned with the conception of the piece and the preparation of that conception for the computer. Other advantages are that almost any general-purpose computer can be used for sound generation, and the devices of a synthesizer can be simulated by a computer program. A disadvantage is that the music cannot be altered in real time.

As early as 1843, it was suggested that computers might be suitable for the production of music. Referring to Charles Babbage's "Analytical Machine" (a precursor of the modern computer), Ada Byron King, Countess of Lovelace, suggested that the engine could be used for making music if the necessary information could be understood and properly expressed.

It was not until 1957, however, that computer-generated music became a reality when Max Mathews, an engineer at Bell Labs, began working on computer generation of music and speech sounds. Together with John Pierce and Joan Miller, Mathews wrote several computer music programs, the best known of which is MUSIC V. This program was more than just a software system for it included an "orchestration" program that simulated many of

THE VOCODER

Much of today's pop music involves synthesized sounds. Many performers—including Cher, Madonna, and the Beastie Boys—have tried to incorporate this distinct sound into their voices, by using a voice-coding device known as the Vocoder. Although the sound is very high-tech, the Vocoder was originally developed in the 1940s to improve telephone service. Inventor Homer Dudley of Bell Laboratories designed a way to break speech patterns into modules that could be transmitted over a narrow bandwidth. The Vocoder was also used during World War II to enhance poor trans-Atlantic messages between British Prime Minister Winston Churchill and U.S. President Franklin Roosevelt.

the processes employed in the classical electronic music studio. It specified unit generators for the standard waveforms, adders, modulators, filters, and reverberators. It was sufficiently generalized that users could freely define their own generators. Thus, MUSIC V became the software prototype for music production installations all over the world.

One of the most notable successors of MUSIC V was designed by Barry Vercoe at the Massachusetts Institute of Technology during the 1970s. His program, MUSIC XI, ran on a PDP-11 computer and was a tightly designed system that incorporated many new features, including graphic score output and input. MUSIC XI was significant not only for these advances, but also for its direct approach to synthesis, thanks to improvements in the efficient use of memory space. Thus, MUSIC XI became accessible to a family of much smaller machines that many studios were able to afford. Another major advance was discovered in 1973 by John Chowning of Stanford University, who pioneered the use of digital FM (frequency modulation) as a source of musical timbre.

The most advanced digital sound synthesis is conducted in large institutional installations, most of them in American universities, followed by European facilities. Examples of American installations are Columbia University, University of Illinois, Indiana University, University of Michigan, State University of New York at Buffalo, and Queens College, New York. European facilities include the Instituut voor Sonologie in Utrecht, the Netherlands; LIMB (Laboratorio Permanente per l'Informatica Musicale) at the University of Padua, Italy; and IRCAM (Institut de Recherche et de Coordination Acoustique/Musique), part of the Centre Georges Pompidou in Paris, France.

Computer technology has led to a tremendous expansion of music resources by offering composers a spectrum of sounds ranging from pure tones to random noise. Computers have enabled the rhythmic organization of music to a degree of subtlety and complexity never before attainable. They have allowed composers complete control over their work, if they so choose, even to the point of bypassing the performer as an intermediary between the creators of music and their audience. Perhaps computers' greatest contribution to music is that they have brought about the acceptance of the definition of music as "organized sound." SEE ALSO CODES; FILM AND VIDEO EDITING; GRAPHIC DEVICES; MUSIC; MUSIC COMPOSITION.

Joyce H-S Li

Bibliography

Dodge, Charles, and Thomas A. Jerse. *Computer Music: Synthesis, Composition, and Performance*. New York: Schirmer, 1985.

Grout, Donald Jay, and Claude V. Palisca. *A History of Western Music*, 5th ed. New York: W. W. Norton, 1996.

Horn, Delton T. *The Beginner's Book of Electronic Music*. Blue Ridge Summit, PA: Tab Books, 1982.

Manning, Peter. *Electronic and Computer Music*. Oxford: Clarendon, 1985.

Morgan, Robert P. *Twentieth-Century Music: A History of Musical Style in Modern Europe and America*. New York: W. W. Norton, 1991.

Schrader, Barry. *Introduction to Electro-Acoustic Music*. Englewood Cliffs, NJ: Prentice Hall, 1982.

Towers, T. D. *Master Electronics in Music*. Rochelle Park, NJ: Hayden, 1976.

Network Design

Network design is a category of systems design that deals with data transport mechanisms. As with other systems' design disciplines, network design follows an analysis stage, where requirements are generated, and precedes implementation, where the system (or relevant system component) is constructed. The objective of network design is to satisfy data communication requirements while minimizing expense. Requirement scope can vary widely from one network design project to another based on geographic particularities and the nature of the data requiring transport.

Network analysis may be conducted at an inter-organizational, organizational, or departmental level. The requirements generated during the analysis may therefore define an inter-network connecting two or more organizations, an enterprise network that connects the departments of a single organization, or a departmental network to be designed around specific divisional needs. Inter-networks and enterprise networks often span multiple buildings, some of which may be hundreds or thousands of miles apart. The distance between physical connections often dictates the type of technology that must be used to facilitate data transmission.

Components that exist within close physical proximity (usually within the same building) and can be connected to each other directly or through hubs or switches using owned equipment are considered part of a **local area network (LAN)**. It is generally impractical and often impossible to connect the equipment of multiple buildings as a single LAN; so individual LANs are instead interconnected to form a greater network, such as a metropolitan area network (MAN) or wide area network (WAN).

MANs may be constructed where buildings are located close enough to each other to facilitate a reliable high-speed connection (usually less than 50 kilometers or 30 miles). Greater distances generally result in much slower connections, which are often leased from common carriers to create WANs. Due to the close proximity of equipment, LAN connections offer the best performance and control (usually with speeds around 100 Mbps) and WAN connections the worst (with many machines often sharing a single connection of less than 2 Mbps).

Networks connect machines—which may be computers, computer peripherals, digital telephones, or other digital communication equipment—to each other for the purpose of exchanging data. The data carried by a network may represent voice, video, text, numeric values, or computer-readable code. Regardless of its context at the machines that send and receive the data, the data are handled by the physical network as an uninterpreted series of Boolean values or **binary** digits called a **bitstream**. At this lowest logical level, these values of zero and one are represented on the physical network as discrete electronic pulses (baseband) or frequency modulations (broadband) depending on the physical transmission method chosen for a given network segment.

The physical network is responsible for delivering the bitstream to its destination without regard to the high-level meaning of the data. In this sense, all computer networks are responsible for performing the same function. Because the bitstream must include data from many different machines, however, the network needs to define a method for sharing the physical

local area network (LAN) a high-speed computer network that is designed for users who are located near each other

binary existing in only two states, such as "on" or "off," "one" or "zero"

bitstream a serialized collection of bits; usually used in transfer of bits from one system to another

Network design plays a vital role in an organization's effectiveness. At the Central Intelligence Agency (CIA), a computer operator monitors the organization's local area network and routers.

resources. This method, referred to as network architecture, determines the means by which data from competing machines are introduced to the network and delivered to the appropriate destinations.

Common network architectures for LANs and MANs, also called Media Access Control (MAC) protocols, include Ethernet, Token Ring, Fiber Distributed Data Interface (FDDI), and Asynchronous Transfer Mode (ATM). Most network architectures dictate specific physical topologies, including the type of medium to be used and its configuration. Token passing methods, such as FDDI and Token Ring for instance, require physical rings of a specified cable. The various MAC protocols and physical mediums—including copper wire, glass fiber, and radio frequency—all possess relative advantages and limitations in terms of speed, consistency, security, expense, and many other important attributes. The combination of these characteristics means that, although all networks can carry all varieties of data, some network architectures are better suited for certain types of data than others. A primary planning function in network design is the determination of which network architecture best suits the type of data the network is being built to support.

Using inter-networking protocols, such as TCP/IP, MANs, and WANs, one can connect many local area networks incorporating a variety of different LAN architectures. This capability affords the network designer some flexibility to choose MAC protocols that best accommodate the needs of a given network segment without jeopardizing connectivity to the rest of the enterprise or inter-organizational network.

A network planning effort, therefore, may conclude that a segment with requirements focused around multimedia use ATM for its consistent performance, while another segment of the same enterprise network with less demanding performance requirements use Ethernet for its low cost and compatibility with existing hardware. Such network segments are interconnected using **routers**, which strip MAC-specific addressing from data packages, or packets, and rebuild the addresses at the destination segment using the appropriate MAC protocol.

routers network devices that direct packets to the next network device or to the final destination

So although many different MAC configurations can interconnect seamlessly, a common inter-networking protocol must be chosen and adhered to across the network in order to realize data communication between all machines. Increasingly, and especially for organizations wanting to connect to the public Internet, that choice is TCP/IP.

Network design is an ongoing effort at most organizations because new applications and business growth create new requirements, which can be fulfilled with ever improving network technology. Network engineering, of which network design is a component, is a balance between performance and expense. So as communication technology continues to improve, resulting in higher data speeds and lower costs, network analysis and redesign is continually necessary to maintain that balance effectively. SEE ALSO INTERNET; NETWORK PROTOCOLS; NETWORK TOPOLOGIES; SECURITY; TELECOMMUNICATIONS.

Jeffrey C. Wingard

Bibliography

Goldman, James E. *Applied Data Communications: A Business Oriented Approach*. New York: John Wiley & Sons, 1995.

Stamper, David A. *Business Data Communications*. Redwood City, CA: Benjamin/ Cummings Publishing Company, 1989.

Network Protocols

Most modern computers are interconnected with other computers in one way or another, whether by a dialup connection or over a **local area network (LAN)**. For interconnections that cover distances greater than a few meters, *serial* connections are economical. In serial communications, the information bits are sent one at a time over a single communications channel. This stands in contrast to *parallel* communications, where information is sent one byte (or word) at a time over eight or more communications channels between the machines.

local area network (LAN) a high-speed computer network that is designed for users who are located near each other

As in all communications, the problem normally focuses on establishing ways for the receiver (meaning the destination computer) to interpret and decode correctly the transmitted information. Communications **protocols** are designed to facilitate this in serial communications; they are especially important in this case because the receiver must be able to process correctly each bit that it receives.

protocols agreed understanding for the sub-operations that make up a transaction; usually found in the specification of inter-computer communications

Protocol Functions

For serial communications to take place correctly, several functions have to be possible. First, the receiving and sending computers must be able to coordinate their actions, to enable flow control, error control, addressing, and connection management. *Flow control* manages the rate of information flow between machines (note that this may be different than the data rate of the network connecting the machines); *error control* enables transmission errors to be corrected; *addressing* allows information to be routed to the correct destination; and *connection management* is the set of functions associated with setting up and maintaining connections (where needed).

Second, the receiver must be able to determine when a message (or data packet) begins and ends and distinguish control information from the information that the user is transmitting.

Protocol Mechanisms

These functions are implemented through communications protocols. These protocols are a strict set of rules that both the sending and the receiving computers follow when communicating. These rules include the format of information to be sent, as well as rules defining how a machine (sender or receiver) is to behave when an event occurs. An event can be externally created (such as the occurrence of an error) or internally generated (such as a connection request). These behaviors are written into the communications software that runs in both the sender and receiver.

Generally, protocols break the information that the user wishes to send into **packets**. These packets normally consist of a *header*, the user information (message), and often a *trailer*. The trailer is most commonly a **checksum** generated by a *cyclical redundancy check* (CRC) coder and is used for error detection. The header carries information fields that the sender and receiver use to communicate with each other so that they can implement the necessary functions as defined by the protocol. Figure 1 is a graphical illustration of the sequence of bits that would be transmitted in a hypothetical packet.

Network Architectures

Although the general functions of protocols are as stated earlier, it turns out to be convenient and efficient to optimize specific protocols for specific classes of functions, and then to use multiple protocols to get the overall job done rather than designing a "one size fits all" system. To aid in this task, protocol developers created an approach to classify and organize the different functions that have to be performed in data communications. The most common approach to this is called the Open Systems Interconnection Reference Model (OSI Reference Model) that was developed and standardized by the International Organization for Standardization (ISO). The OSI Reference Model is a seven-layer model, with each layer representing a particular set of functions, and for which specific protocols have been developed.

packets collections of digital data elements that are part of a complete message or signal; packets contain their destination addresses to enable reassembly of the message or signal

checksum a number that is derived from adding together parts of an electronic message before it is dispatched; it can be used at the receiver to check against message corruption

Header	Information	Trailer

Figure 1.

Here are the layers and their functions as seen in Figure 2:

- The *physical* layer is concerned with moving bits, and includes physical and electrical connections.

- The *link* layer is concerned with reliable bit transfer, as well as local (as opposed to global) addressing. This involves synchronization, error control, and some flow control.

- The *network* layer is concerned with routing packets through network elements (called nodes) interconnected by reliable links. This layer deals with addresses that are global in scope. Examples of global addresses are a telephone number or a postal address, whereas a local address might be an office telephone extension or mailbox.

- The *transport* layer ensures end-to-end reliability, connection control, and flow control. Its task is to make a network meet the special requirements of end user machines. *End-to-end* means that network elements are not involved in implementing transport layer functionality.

- The *session* layer is concerned with the establishment and maintenance of connections for the communicating end nodes.

- The *presentation* layer is concerned with ensuring that information can be transmitted between different types of computer systems (for example, Apple Macintosh computers and Windows PCs).

- Finally, the *application* layer is concerned with providing the functions needed by networked applications. A networked application may be a mail program (such as Eudora or Microsoft Outlook), and the application layer function would be the mail transport protocols.

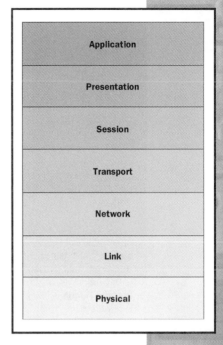

Figure 2.

Quite a number of protocols have been developed under the guidelines of the OSI reference model. Many of these have not met with commercial success, so they are most often used to provide the basis for new protocols today. Still, the OSI reference model serves as a convenient way to organize the necessary functionality of data communications systems.

TCP/IP Protocols

The effort to garner commercial support of OSI protocols has been undermined in large part by the protocols that are used in the Internet, which are called the Transport Control Protocol (TCP) and the Internet Protocol (IP). These protocols were developed outside of the OSI effort, and were designed to provide minimal services. This design strategy moved much of the "intelligence" (i.e., the processing requirements) needed to implement networked applications to the user machines. TCP/IP was developed and debugged before similar OSI protocols got off the ground, so many users adopted them as an interim measure until the OSI protocols were available. They took hold, and users never saw the need to switch protocols, which is a costly procedure that often results in unreliable systems for a time.

Two principal protocols exist in this system. The Internet Protocol (IP) was designed to provide an adaptive (though it is sometimes unreliable) network that could interconnect independently owned and managed sub-networks. It is unreliable because the network makes no assurances that packets are delivered to their destinations, though they do their best to try. Allowing independently owned and managed networks is also important because different organizations have different local requirements, yet they still might want to communicate with other users. IP corresponds fairly closely to the OSI network layer in functionality.

To provide some confidence to end users, the Transport Control Protocol (TCP) was developed to work with IP. TCP provides end-to-end error control as well as flow control. Thus, if IP loses some packets along the way, TCP will recover them transparently to the user, so the network will seem reliable. TCP also performs some session management functions. Thus, it is a mix between OSI's transport and session layers (though it does not contain all session layer functions).

By pushing the processing requirements for services out of the network, TCP/IP has set the stage for rapid innovation in applications and services. Adding a new service means developing the necessary application protocol, constructing a **server**, and advertising the services. What is significant is that no network changes are necessary for new services, which supports the rate of innovation. Thus, TCP/IP networks can carry electronic mail, images, worldwide web traffic, even video images and telephone calls, all without changes to the underlying network systems (with the exception, of course, of the capacity increases needed to handle all of the packets that are generated by these services).

Future Evolution of TCP/IP

Despite its success, TCP/IP faces some challenges. One of the challenges is that the available IP addresses are being exhausted, due to its success. Another is that many of the new services are making demands on the network that would be best served if some additional capabilities existed; for example, telephone calls and interactive video would benefit from "real time" capabilities to minimize network delays.

To address these concerns, a new version of IP was developed, version 6 (called IPv6). When deployed, IPv6 will support a much larger number of addresses and offer a broader range of services to network users, including real-time support and security services. Conversion to IPv6 will eventually require that all network elements and all end-user machines be converted to this new protocol. To ease this pain, a transition strategy exists that calls for parallel (but interconnected) networks to be operated for a number of years. SEE ALSO BRIDGING DEVICES; INTERNET; NETWORK DESIGN; NETWORK TOPOLOGIES; TELECOMMUNICATIONS.

Martin B. Weiss

Bibliography

Blank, Andrew G. *TCP/IP Jumpstart: Internet Protocol Basics*. San Francisco: Sybex, Inc., 2000.

MacKinnon, Dennis, William McCrum, and Donald Sheppard. *An Introduction to Open Systems Interconnection*. New York: Computer Science Press, 1990.

Network Topologies

The topology of a network is the geometric representation of all links and nodes of a network—the structure, consisting of transmission links and processing nodes, that provides communications connectivity between nodes in a network. A link is the physical transmission path that transfers data from one device to another. A node is a network addressable device.

Graph theory describes certain characteristics of a network topology such as the average node degree for robustness (average number of links terminating at a node in a network), network diameter for size (the longest/shortest path between any two nodes in a network), number of paths for complexity (total number of paths between all node pairs), and cutsets for flow (minimum number of removed links to partition a network). However, the most dominant characteristic of a network topology is its shape.

Mesh, Star, Tree, Bus, Ring

The most general shape characteristics are symmetry and regular/irregular shape. There are five basic network topology regular shapes: mesh, star, tree, bus, and ring. The bus is a special case of a tree with only one trunk. The mesh has the highest node degree; the bus has the lowest node degree.

Mesh Topology. In a mesh topology, every node has a dedicated point-to-point link to every other node which requires $n(n-1)/2$ links to connect n nodes. This is the original way the telephone network started in major East Coast U.S. cities. Before long the sky was not visible on certain downtown intersections due to the amount of overhead wire! The mesh topology allows for robustness in presence of faults since the loss of links or nodes can be routed around due to the amount of connectivity. However, this comes at the cost of complex network management due to the number of links and expensive resource usage since each n node must have $n-1$ ports to connect in the mesh.

Star Topology. In a star topology, each node has a dedicated point-to-point link to a central hub. If one node wants to send data to another, it sends to the central hub, which then relays the data to the destination node. A star provides centralized control but also represents a performance bottleneck and single-point-of-failure.

Tree Topology. A tree topology occurs when multiple star topologies are connected together such that not every node is directly connected to a central hub. Thus, a tree extends a star topology, allowing for community clustering around local hubs. The two fundamental trees upon which topologies are built are: the minimum spanning tree, which is the least-cost tree connecting all nodes in a graph; and the Steiner Tree (ST), which is the least-cost tree connecting a subset of member nodes in a graph. (The ST may contain non-member nodes also, which are called Steiner points). Cost is determined by placing weights on links and nodes based on predetermined metrics such as distance, supply/demand, economic cost, delay, or **bandwidth**.

Bus Topology. In a bus topology, a shared medium connects all nodes in the network. This shared medium may be a single wire or radio frequency. The shared medium provides ease-of-installation and flexibility, since it initially consists of a single cable run alongside targeted computers or computers broadcasting on specific frequencies. However, the shared medium also creates two problems: collisions when two nodes broadcast simultaneously, and fault management, since any network problems affect all

---

MORE ABOUT MESH

Mesh topologies can exist in two states: full or partial mesh. Full mesh means that every node has a connection to every other node in the network. Partial mesh is when not all nodes are connected to the others; only some have a full connection. Partial mesh costs less but the results with full mesh are better.

bandwidth a measure of the frequency component of a signal or the capacity of a communication channel to carry signals

connected computers. Isolating the problem requires physically separating the shared medium in a methodological manner.

Ring Topology. The ring topology is a series of unidirectional, dedicated point-to-point links connecting in a physical ring. This topology provides inherent reliability since a signal from a source travels around the ring to the destination and back to the source as an acknowledgement. Least-cost rings may approach the cost of a least-cost tree but are generally more expensive and have more delay. Also a ring is not a flexible topology—adding and deleting links and nodes is disruptive.

Usage Tradeoffs

protocols agreed understanding for the sub-operations that make up transactions; usually found in the specification of inter-computer communications

Protocols are matched to these topologies to enable computer network usage. The bus topology requires a shared medium access protocol based on sensing transmission to avoid collisions with probabilistic retransmission (that is, retransmission after a probabilistically determined time). The ring topology requires a token-passing where a node needs to have a token in order to transmit. At high loads, the bus topology with a shared medium access protocol experiences collisions, and thus offers diminished performance beyond a particular usage threshold. The ring topology with a token-passing protocol has unnecessary overhead at low loads but its performance does not degrade at high loads.

In general, there are two alternatives for operation of a star: (1) the central hub broadcasts all traffic it receives (physically a star but logically a bus), or (2) the central hub selectively switches incoming traffic only to destination nodes. The performance of a star depends on the processing capability of the central hub as well as the capacity of the spoke links, and beyond a threshold connections may be blocked. The tree topology is used for multipoint or group communications and thus depends on the slowest link or node with lowest processing capability in the tree connecting the group.

Examples

Examples of networks matched to these topologies include local area network (LAN) standard ETHERNET, which is a bus topology using a shared media access protocol, and LAN standard TOKEN RING, which is a ring topology using a token-passing protocol. The star is the topology of the local loop, circuit-switched telephone network with the central hub being the local central office. The tree topology is the basis of emerging group communication applications that are not yet standardized. SEE ALSO BRIDGING DEVICES; INTERNET; NETWORK DESIGN; NETWORK PROTOCOLS; OFFICE AUTOMATION SYSTEMS; TELECOMMUNICATIONS.

William J. Yurcik

Bibliography

Stallings, William. *Data and Computer Communications*, 6th ed. Upper Saddle River, NJ: Prentice Hall, 2000.

Object-Oriented Languages

An object-oriented language is a computer programming language that revolves around the concept of an object. Object-oriented languages were developed to make it easier to develop, debug, reuse, and maintain software than is possible with earlier languages. Understanding objects, and object-oriented languages, requires knowledge of the evolution of computer programming languages and data structures.

Evolution of Computer Programming Languages

Computer programming languages have evolved continually over the years. This evolution is detailed in the following examples.

Assembly Language. The first computer programs were written in assembly language. This is a primitive type of language in which each statement corresponds to a single machine instruction; it is the most basic computer operation possible. Accomplishing anything useful takes many machine instructions. Assembly language is specific to a particular type of computer; moving the program to a different type of computer requires writing a whole new program. Assembly language programs are difficult to write, debug, and maintain. Although other languages are now used for most computer applications, assembly language is still used today as the first language when a new chip is developed.

High Order Languages. After assembly language, higher order languages were developed; among the early ones were FORTRAN and BASIC. One statement in a high order language corresponds to a sentence in English. A program called a compiler reads the statements from a source file and generates a file containing machine instructions, which is called an object file. The object file can then be loaded and executed by the computer. A high order language is more portable than an assembly language program; the same source file can be compiled for any computer as long as a suitable compiler exists.

Early high order languages only allowed for simple data types such as integer, floating point number, or string (a sequence of letters). The only data structure available was the array. An array is a list of elements that are all the same data type; for example, a list of numbers or a list of strings. A database was created using a group of arrays. For example, a product database might contain three arrays called Product Number, Product Description, and Product Price. It was up to the programmer to keep the arrays aligned; for example, to make sure the third element of each array corresponded to the same product.

Structured Languages. The next step in the evolution of computer programming languages was the development of structured languages, like C and PASCAL, and the introduction of data structures. A data structure is an assembly of simpler data types into a single record. For example, a product database could be constructed as an array of product records, each record containing Product Number, Product Description, and Product Price fields. Now one record could contain all necessary information about a single item. Structures also became more defined in the procedural part of the language. A function or procedure is a small part of a larger program that could be written to provide some basic operation on a data structure such as a record.

Object Oriented Languages. The next step in the evolution of computer programming languages, object orientation, was introduced in the Smalltalk language. Object orientation takes the concepts of structured programming one step further. Now, instead of data structures and separate program structures, both data and program elements are combined into one structure called an object. The object data elements are called attributes, while the object program elements are called methods. Collectively, attributes and methods are called the object's members. Usually, an object's methods are the only programs able to operate on the object's attributes.

With object orientation, a fundamental change came in the way programs are viewed. The earlier view was that data must be manipulated in some way to achieve a final result, and a program was viewed as a sequential means of performing the manipulations. From an object orientation perspective, a program is viewed as a group of objects that react to messages from the user, other programs, or other objects. This view led to the idea of event-driven programming; i.e. when event A happens, this object performs action B. A message is sent to an object by calling one of its methods.

Characteristics of Object-Oriented Programming

Key characteristics of object-oriented programming include encapsulation and data hiding, inheritance, and polymorphism.

Encapsulation and Data Hiding. The central idea in object-oriented programming (OOP) is that the object attributes and the methods that operate on the attributes are bound together, or encapsulated, in the object. The object's methods provide the only interfaces between the object and other parts of the program. This is different from earlier languages, where any part of a program could operate on any piece of data at any time. Although this seems restrictive, the restrictions result in a more modular program that is easier to develop and less likely to contain errors. It also means it is easier to move an object to a different environment and still have it function correctly.

A software object is somewhat similar to a physical object. For example, an engine can be used to power a car. It has internal components, corresponding to attributes, but one does not have to be concerned with what they are or how they work. The engine must interface with the throttle, fuel system, transmission, intake, and exhaust manifolds, all of which correspond to methods. It is inconceivable that fuel would get into the engine by any means other than by way of the fuel system. As long as the correct interfaces are maintained, the engine will work. So it is with objects. The object attributes are hidden from the outside. The object interacts with its environment through its methods.

Inheritance. Another important concept to object-oriented programming is inheritance. An object class is defined in a hierarchy, and is said to inherit the behavior of its ancestors (those objects above it in the hierarchy). For example, a drawing program might include three object classes: Shape, Rectangle, and Circle. They could be defined so that Rectangle and Circle are both descendents of Shape.

Shape includes attributes common to any shape, such as the location of the shape on a drawing surface. Shape also provides methods for manipulating those attributes. For example, a move method would change the shape's location. Additionally, it would provide a definition for methods to which all shapes must be able to respond, for example, a draw method to

---

AN OBJECT OR A CLASS?

What is the difference between an object and a class? A class is a definition of an object type. For example, say Rectangle is a class. The Rectangle (with a capital "R") class defines what a rectangle (lowercase "r") object is and how it behaves. However, a rectangle *object* does not actually exist until the user instructs the drawing program to create one. Each rectangle object created (or *instantiated*) is said to be an *instance* of the Rectangle class. Because object-oriented languages are frequently case sensitive, class names usually have the first letter capitalized, while instance names and member names have a lowercase first letter.

display the shape on a drawing surface. The draw method in this case is said to be abstract; it does not do anything other than create a requirement that descendent classes must implement it.

Since Rectangle is a descendent of Shape, it inherits attributes (location) and methods (move) from Shape. It provides the additional attributes it needs (width and height) and new methods that manipulate those attributes (setWidth, setHeight). Rectangle must also provide a draw method that paints a rectangle on the drawing surface, because every descendent of Shape must implement a draw method. Likewise, Circle provides a new attribute (radius), methods for manipulating it (setRadius), and a draw method of its own.

With this kind of arrangement, the drawing manager program would have a list of shapes on the drawing surface. To move an object, it would call the object's move method. To draw an object, the manager calls the object's draw method. The manager neither knows nor cares how the object moves or draws itself, as long as the job gets done. In fact, it may not even know what kind of Shape a particular object really is. It could be a Rectangle, a Circle, or any other object descendent from Shape. It only needs to know that it is descendent from Shape, so it can send to it any message that a Shape can receive.

The inheritance capability of an object-oriented language added a whole new dimension to programming. Learning an earlier high order language was mainly involved with learning the language **syntax** (how the language statements are constructed), which is not that difficult. In an object-oriented language, learning the syntax is still necessary, but becoming familiar with the standard class hierarchies—which may include thousands of classes, each class with its own methods—is a much larger task. It is worthwhile, however, because an object inherits the attributes and behavior of its parent. A programmer can avoid unnecessary work by finding an existing object that already does most of what is needed. Then new capability can be added incrementally. The result is lower cost, higher quality software.

syntax a set of rules that a computing language incorporates regarding structure, punctuation, and formatting

This characteristic also led to the inclusion of automatic documentation features in several object-oriented languages. In earlier languages, documentation—if generated at all—was done separately, almost as an afterthought. Now documentation information can be included in the object source code and used to generate a **Hypertext Markup Language (HTML)** document automatically, complete with hyperlinks up and down the class hierarchies, which may be viewed with an Internet browser. This makes it much easier to maintain accurate, up-to-date documentation.

Hypertext Markup Language (HTML) an encoding scheme for text data that uses special tags in the text to signify properties to the viewing program (browser) like links to other documents or document parts

Polymorphism. The next important characteristic of object-oriented language is polymorphism, which means that a descendent object does not have to respond to a message exactly like its ancestor does. A new object can override its parent's methods, which causes the new object to react to a message differently. For example, a common class in a windowing system is a Component, which represents a visible object. A Component is an ancestor class for every visible object on the screen: icons, buttons, menus, slide bars, check boxes, radio buttons, even windows. All of these descendent classes override some of Component's methods to change behavior. For example, an Icon object needs to display itself as a small picture. Icon overrides Component's draw method to show the picture.

Common Object-Oriented Languages

Common object-oriented languages include Smalltalk, C++, Java, and other languages such as BASIC and PASCAL.

Smalltalk. Smalltalk was the original object-oriented language, developed in the early 1970s by Xerox. Since then, several variations have been introduced. It is still being used, but widespread acceptance has been hampered by the lack of a universal standard.

C++. C++ is an extension of the C language that provided OOP capabilities. It is probably the most widespread object-oriented language currently in use. C++ is a hybrid language because it compiles standard C programs; it does not require the use of objects. This enables it to take advantage of existing C software, while using object orientation for new software. C++ is controlled by ANSI standards.

Java. Java is the most widely accepted pure object-oriented language. It was developed by Sun Microsystems originally as a control language for small appliances. However, it proved ideal for use with the Internet. A Java **applet** can be embedded in a web page. When a browser loads the web page, it also loads and displays the applet. Sun still maintains strict control of the language standard.

To facilitate cross-platform operability (working on entirely different computer types without recompiling), Java is implemented in two parts. The compiler produces an object file that can only be executed by a Java Virtual Machine (JVM). A separate JVM is available for each supported operating system (Windows, Unix/Linux, or Solaris). This makes Java programs able to run on any of those systems without recompiling.

Other Languages. Most languages commonly used today allow some form of object orientation. BASIC has evolved into object-oriented Visual BASIC; PASCAL into object-oriented DELPHI. Generally these are hybrid languages, like C++, that support object orientation without requiring it. SEE ALSO COMPILERS; MOUSE; PROCEDURAL LANGUAGES.

Donald M. McIver

applet a program component that requires extra support at run time from a browser or run-time environment in order to execute

Bibliography
Deitel, Harvey M., and Paul J. Deitel. *Java: How to Program*, 2nd ed. Upper Saddle River, NJ: Prentice Hall, 1998.

Voss, Greg. *Object-Oriented Programming, An Introduction*. New York: Osborne McGraw-Hill, 1991.

Operating Systems

The operating system is software that manages every part of a computer system—all hardware and all other software. To be specific, it controls every file, every device, every section of main memory, every **nanosecond** of processing time, and every network connection. It controls who can use the system and how. In short, it is the boss—without it, nothing can happen.

When a computer user sends a command by typing it from the keyboard or clicking with the mouse, the operating system must make sure that the command is executed. If it is not executed, the operating system must arrange for the user to receive a message, usually on the monitor, explain-

nanosecond one-thousand-millionth (one billionth, or 10^{-9}) of a second

Platform	Operating System
Microcomputers	Linux, Macintosh OS, MS-DOS, Windows 98, Windows 2000
Minicomputers	Linux, OpenVMS Alpha, UNIX
Mainframe computers	IBM OS/390, IBM OS/400, UNIX
Supercomputers	IRIX, UNICOS
Workstations	HP-UX, Sun Solaris, UNIX
Networks	Novell NetWare, UNIX, Windows NT, Windows 2000
Handheld computers	Microsoft CE, Palm OS

Popular operating systems associated with various platforms.

ing the error. This does not necessarily mean that the operating system executes the command or sends the error message, but it does control the parts of the system that do.

Every operating system, regardless of its size and complexity, can be represented by a pyramid showing how its five major functions (called managers) work together. The memory manager, the processor manager, the device manager, and the file manager form the pyramid's base; network operating systems add a network manager as well. The user **interface**—the part of the operating system that communicates with the user—is supported by the other four or five managers.

interface a boundary or border between two or more objects or systems; also a point of access

Responsibilities and Relationships

These virtual managers must do more than perform their individual tasks. They must also be able to work harmoniously with every other manager. For example, they must be able to monitor their resources continuously, enforce the policies that determine who gets what, when, and how much, allocate their resources when it is appropriate, and de-allocate their resources—reclaim them—when appropriate.

The *memory manager* is in charge of main memory, also known as **random access memory (RAM)**. It checks the validity of each request for memory space and, if it is a legal request, the memory manager allocates a portion that is not already in use. In a multi-user environment, the memory manager sets up a table to keep track of who is using which section of memory. Finally, when the time comes to reclaim the memory, the memory manager de-allocates the memory space. One of the manager's primary responsibilities is to preserve the part of main memory that is occupied by the operating system itself—it cannot allow any part of it to be altered accidentally or intentionally.

random access memory (RAM) a type of memory device that supports the nonpermanent storage of programs and data; so called because various locations can be accessed in any order (as if at random), rather than in a sequence (like a tape memory device)

The *processor manager* decides how to allocate the **central processing unit (CPU)** and keep track of the status of each executable step of every program (called a process or task). For example, the processor manager monitors whether the CPU is executing a process or waiting for a *READ* or *WRITE* command to finish execution. Later, when the process is finished, or the maximum amount of time has expired, the processor manager reclaims the processor so it can be allocated again.

central processing unit (CPU) the part of a computer that performs computations and controls and coordinates other parts of the computer

The *device manager* chooses the most efficient way to allocate all of the system's devices, including printers, disk drives, CD-ROMs (compact disc-read only memory), keyboard, monitor, and so forth. The device manager makes these decisions based on a scheduling policy chosen by the system's designers. The device manager allocates a device, starts its operation, and, finally, de-allocates it.

The *file manager* keeps track of every piece of software in the system, including application programs, data files, directories, etc. The file manager allocates the file by opening it and de-allocates it by closing it. It is based on predetermined access policies to enforce the correct security for each file so that files can be accessed only by individual or group users that have permission to do so. The file manager also controls the amount of flexibility each user is allowed with that file (such as read-only, read-and-write-only, or the authority to create and/or delete records).

Operating systems with networking capability have a fifth element called the *network manager*, which provides a convenient way for users to share resources. Network resources usually include both hardware (such as CPUs, memory areas, printers, disk drives, modems, and tape drives) and software (such as application programs and data files).

User Interfaces

graphical user interface (GUI) an interface that allows computers to be operated through pictures (icons) and mouse-clicks, rather than through text and typing

Most modern operating systems feature a menu-driven **graphical user interface (GUI)**, which is pronounced "gooey," with menus, icons, and task bars. The Macintosh was the first widely used computer with a GUI, which in turn was based on a desktop created by Xerox. Microsoft introduced Windows version 1.0 in 1985, but it was not a real operating system because it acted merely as an interface between the user and the real operating system. Instead, it was called an "environment" that ran only on computers with the MS-DOS operating system. Microsoft's Windows 95, Windows 98, and Windows 2000 are true operating systems.

Operating systems without GUIs (such as early versions of UNIX and Linux) are called command-driven systems. They accept commands that are typed into the system (menus are not available). Command-driven systems are cumbersome for some new users to learn. Therefore, since the late-1990s, most operating systems (including UNIX and Linux) have been converted from command-driven to menu-driven interfaces, which feature GUIs that allow users to click on menus to make the system run.

Adding GUIs was a popular move for anyone who had trouble working with brief or mysterious-looking command lines. For example, the UNIX command to list all subdirectories (but not files) found in the root directory looks cryptic (ls-l / | grep '^d'). Today, users can achieve a similar result by choosing an option from a menu.

Linux

Linux is an operating system that has been widely adopted in commercial and academic markets around the world. Linux is unique among the most-used operating systems because it is an open-source program, which means the source code is freely available to anyone for improvement.

Programmers from around the world are encouraged to submit improvements to the programming code. If the new code is accepted as a universal improvement to the operating system, it is added to the next version, which is then made available to the computing world for further improvement. This development technique has resulted in a powerful, stable, inexpensive operating system, which is constantly being improved by a variety of people who may never meet in person.

Linux was created in Finland by 21-year-old Linus Torvalds who wanted to build a new operating system for the Intel 80386 microprocessor. Torvalds started with Minix, a miniature version of the well-known UNIX operating system, and rewrote certain parts to add more functionality. The first version of Linux, which was named for Torvalds and UNIX, had much of the basic functionality of the then-popular MS-DOS operating system with UNIX-like power and flexibility. It has been enhanced considerably in the years since.

Although there are similarities between the two systems, Linux is not UNIX. (UNIX is a legal trademark, registered with the federal government. Before a developer can use the term UNIX to describe an operating system, it must demonstrate that it can meet certain certification criteria.)

Policies and Design Considerations

One of the biggest differences among operating systems is the set of policies on which each one is based. These policies, in turn, drive design considerations, which dictate the inner workings of the system, including the following:

- Processor time—the amount of uninterrupted time the processor is allocated to a certain job.
- Memory space—the amount of memory area that a given job is allowed to monopolize at any time.
- Printers—the number of printers that one job is allowed to use.
- User access—the number of users who are allowed to log into the system.
- File access—the identity of the files that a given user can read, write, modify, or delete.
- System resources—the number of system resources that can be allocated to one job before it has to share them.

Before writing an operating system, these issues are examined by system designers who make choices that ideally will optimize the system's day-to-day operations. The goal is to minimize downtime, system crashes, wasted overhead, security breeches, overloaded printers, and other operational problems.

For example, if the designers want to create a simple operating system that would process each job in the order it arrives, without giving a higher priority to any of them, then the team might choose policies that would:

- Assign the processor to one job when it is received;
- Never interrupt processing once the job begins;
- Give it access to all files in the system, just in case they are needed later;
- Give the job all available disk space, printers, and network resources.

This would be a fair, unbiased system, but a very inefficient one. For example, if one big job was printing out thousands of pages for a large report, even if the printing required several days, then all other jobs would sit idle as they waited for it to finish. In the meantime, most of the available

LINUX BEGINNINGS

When Linus Torvalds completed an early version of Linux in 1991, he sent the following message to other programmers in an Internet user group: "Hello everybody out there using minix. I'm doing a (free) operating system (just a hobby, won't be big and professional like gnu) for 386(486)AT clones." Torvalds' message proved only partly correct. His hobby did produce a new operating system, but it turned out to be a very big and highly professional piece of software.

memory space, processor time, disk space, and other resources would also sit idle, waiting for the next job to begin.

Therefore, most modern operating systems feature complex formulas, which allow resources to be allocated wisely. Some systems allow multiple tasks, multiple jobs, multiple users, and even multiple processors, to work together so available resources can be shared without causing the system to crash routinely.

No single operating system can be considered the best for every situation because each one is based on policies that favor certain jobs or certain circumstances. That is why one operating system might be chosen to run an architect's computer and another might be preferred to operate a writer's computer. SEE ALSO COMPATIBILITY (OPEN SYSTEMS DESIGN); MEMORY; NETWORKS; SECURITY.

Ann McIver McHoes

Bibliography

Flynn, Ida M., and Ann M. McHoes. *Understanding Operating Systems*, 3rd ed. Pacific Grove, CA: Brooks/Cole Publishing, 2001.

White, Ron. *How Computers Work*, 6th ed. Indianapolis, IN: Que, 2002.

Optical Character Recognition

Optical Character Recognition (OCR) uses a device that reads pencil marks and converts them into a computer-usable form. OCR technology recognizes characters on a source document using the optical properties of the equipment and media. OCR improves the accuracy of data collection and reduces the time required by human workers to enter the data.

Although OCR is used for high-speed data entry, it did not begin with the computer industry. The beginnings of OCR can be traced back to 1809 when the first patents for devices to aid the blind were awarded. In 1912 Emmanuel Goldberg patented a machine that read characters, converted them into standard telegraph code, and then transmitted telegraphic messages over wires without human intervention. In 1914 Fournier D'Albe invented an OCR device called the **optophone** that produced sounds. Each sound corresponded to a specific letter or character. After learning the character equivalent for various sounds, visually impaired people were able to "read" the printed material. Developments in OCR continued throughout the 1930s, becoming more important with the beginnings of the computer industry in the 1940s. OCR development in the 1950s attempted to address the needs of the business world.

optophone a system that uses artificial intelligence techniques to convert images of text into audible sound

Methods for Recording Data

OCR requires hardware, in the form of a scanning device, and software to convert the images and character data from the source document into a digital form. Three primary methods are used to record data on a source document to be read by an OCR device. These include optically readable marks, bar codes, and optically readable characters, including handwritten characters.

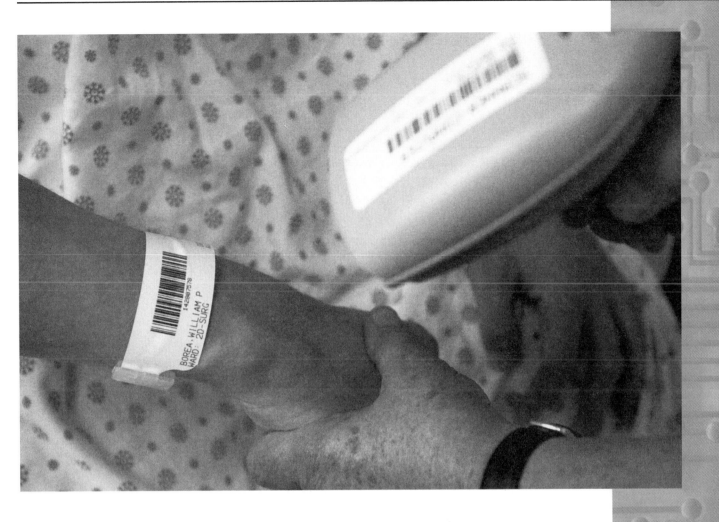

Optical mark recognition (OMR) uses OMR paper, sometimes called a "mark sense form." This paper has a series of rectangular shapes that are filled in using a pencil. The completed form is then fed through a scanning device that reads the filled-in rectangles. The software of the OMR scanning device can perform an elementary statistical analysis of the data. OMR technology is commonly used to score standardized tests, such as the Scholastic Aptitude Test (SAT) and Graduate Management Aptitude Test (GMAT), quickly and accurately.

Bar codes are zebra-striped marks of various widths that appear on, or are attached to, most manufactured retail products. The most common use of the bar code is the 10-digit **Universal Product Code (UPC)**. Other kinds of bar code systems are used in a variety of places—from overnight mail packages to airplane luggage tags. The width and combination of the stripes on the bar code represent data. A bar code reader consists of a scanner and decoder. The scanner emits a beam of light that is swept past the bar code and senses light reflections to distinguish between the bars and spaces. A photo detector converts the spaces into an electrical signal and the bars into the absence of an electrical signal. The decoder analyzes the signal patterns to validate and interpret the corresponding data.

Some OCR readers can convert typed and handwritten documents into digital data. These readers scan the shape of a character on a document, compare the scanned character with a pre-defined shape, and convert the

In the fast-paced health care profession, some medical practitioners are using bar coded bracelets to make sure that patients receive the right medications in hospitals. The bracelets are designed to eliminate medication errors that, over the years, have killed innumerable people.

Universal Product Code (UPC) the first barcode standard developed in 1973 and adopted widely since

bit a single binary digit, 1 or 0—a contraction of Binary digIT; the smallest unit for storing data in a computer

character into its corresponding **bit** pattern for storage in main computer memory. This technology is still in development; handwritten documents do not scan with 100 percent accuracy.

A special type of OCR, magnetic ink character recognition (MICR), is used by several industries, including banks. The enormous amount of paper in the form of checks, loans, and bank statements, combined with the need for accurate and quick processing, prompted the banking industry to seek new ways to manage the flow of paper. In 1956 the American Bankers Association recommended adopting magnetic ink for high-speed automatic character recognition, resulting in MICR. With MICR, data are recorded using a magnetic ink that is readable by either a scanning device or a person. On bank checks, which represent the most common use of MICR, characters in magnetic ink detail the bank's identification number, the individual's account number, and the check number. Checks can be scanned and the data are quickly and accurately read into a computer for further processing.

Another use of OCR allows printed documents—such as text, images, or photographs—to be stored in a computer. Either hand-held scanners or page scanners are used to convert physical documents into computer-readable forms. Page scanners are stationary. The page is typically placed face down on the glass plate of the scanner and then scanned. Hand-held scanners are manually moved over the document. Both types of scanners can convert monochrome or color pictures, forms, text, and other images into machine-readable digital data. The data can then be modified, saved, and distributed over computer networks. SEE ALSO ARTIFICIAL INTELLIGENCE; INPUT DEVICES; PATTERN RECOGNITION; VIRTUAL REALITY; VIRTUAL REALITY IN EDUCATION.

Terri L. Lenox and Charles R. Woratschek

Bibliography

Schantz, Herbert F. *The History of OCR, Optical Character Recognition.* Manchester Center, VT: Recognition Technologies Users Association, 1982.

Shelly, Gary B., and Thomas J. Cashman. *Introduction to Computers and Data Processing.* Brea, CA: Anaheim Publishing Company, 1980.

Stair, Ralph M., and George W. Reynolds. *Principles of Information Systems: A Managerial Approach*, 5th ed. Boston: Course Technology—ITP, 2001.

Parallel Processing

multitasking the ability of a computer system to execute more than one program at the same time; also known as multiprogramming

Parallel processing is information processing that uses more than one computer processor simultaneously to perform work on a problem. This should not be confused with **multitasking**, in which many tasks are performed on a single processor by continuously switching between them, a common practice on serial machines. Computers that are designed for parallel processing are called parallel processors or parallel machines. Many parallel processors can also be described as supercomputers, a more general term applied to the class of computer systems that is most powerful at any given time.

The need to coordinate the work of the individual processors makes parallel processing more complex than processing with a single processor. The processing resources available must be assigned efficiently, and the processors may need to share information as the work progresses. Parallel processors are used for problems that are computationally intensive, that is, they require a very large number of computations. Parallel processing may be appropriate when the problem is very difficult to solve or when it is important to get the results very quickly.

Some examples of problems that may require parallel processing are image processing, molecular modeling, computer animations and simulations, and analysis of models to predict climate and economics. Many problems, such as weather forecasting, can be addressed with increasingly complex models as the computing power is developed to implement them, so there is always an incentive to create newer, more powerful parallel processors. Although early work in parallel processing focused on complex scientific and engineering applications, current uses also include commercial applications such as **data mining** and risk evaluation in investment portfolios. In some situations, the reliability added by additional processors is also important.

Parallel processors are one of the tools used in high-performance computing, a more general term that refers to a group of activities aimed at developing and applying advanced computers and computer networks. In 1991 a U.S. federal program, the HPCC (High Performance Computing and Communications) program, was introduced to support the development of supercomputing, **gigabit networking**, and computation-intensive science and engineering applications. The HPCC program uses the term "Grand Challenges" to identify computationally intensive tasks with broad economic and scientific impact that will only be solved with high performance computing technologies.

As of 2002, most of the world's fastest computers (as cited by the Top 500 Supercomputers list which is published on the Internet) are parallel processors. The number of processors may be from fewer than fifty to many thousands. Companies manufacturing these machines include IBM, SGI, Cray, Hitachi, and Fujitsu.

Parallel Architecture

There are many possible ways of designing a parallel computer, and Michael Flynn in 1966 developed a **taxonomy** for parallel processors, a way of thinking about these alternatives. Flynn categorized them based on two parameters: the stream of instructions (the **algorithm**) and the stream of data (the input). The instructions can be carried out one at a time or concurrently, and the data can be processed one at a time or in multiples. In Flynn's scheme, SISD is "Single Instruction stream, Single Data stream," and refers to a traditional sequential computer in which a single operation can be carried out on a single data item at a time.

The two main categories of parallel processor are SIMD and MIMD. In a SIMD (Single Instruction, Multiple Data) machine, many processors operate simultaneously, carrying out the same operation on many different pieces of data. In a MIMD (Multiple Instruction, Multiple Data) machine, the number of processors may be fewer but they are capable of acting independently on different pieces of data. The remaining category, MISD (Multiple Instruction, Single Data) is rarely used since its meaning is not

data mining a technique of automatically obtaining information from databases that is normally hidden or not obvious

---

WHY PARALLEL?

Parallel processing, in which multiple computers work on a problem simultaneously, is complex because the problem must be broken down into subproblems on which work can be carried out independently. It requires a parallel architecture, through which processors can communicate and share data, a parallel algorithm or method for solving the problem in concurrent steps, and a parallel programming language to implement the algorithm for a specific parallel architecture.

---

gigabit networking the construction and use of a computer network that is capable of transferring information at rates in the gigahertz range

taxonomy the classification of elements or objects based on their characteristics

algorithm a rule or procedure used to solve a mathematical problem—most often described as a sequence of steps

The ASCI White supercomputer in Poughkeepsie, New York, is able to perform 12 trillion calculations per second. Built by IBM, it is large enough to cover two basketball courts.

vector supercomputer
a highly optimized computing machine that provides high performance using a vector processing architecture

synchronously quality of a system that demonstrates synchronized behavior

clearly defined. Since it implies that several instructions are being applied to each piece of data, the term is sometimes used to describe a **vector supercomputer** in which data pass through a pipeline of processors each with a different instruction.

Sometimes Flynn's taxonomy is augmented with the SPMD category, which refers to "Single Program, Multiple Data" to describe a system in which there are many instances of a single type of process, each executing the same code independently. This is equivalent to implementing a SIMD operation in a MIMD machine.

Different parallel architectures have varying strengths and weaknesses depending on the task to be performed. SIMD machines usually have a very large number of simple processors. They are suited to tasks that are massively parallel, in which there are relatively simple operations to be performed on huge amounts of data. Each data stream is assigned to a different processor and the processors operate in lockstep (**synchronously**), each performing the same operation on its data at the same time. Processors communicate to exchange data and results, either through a shared memory and shared variables or through messages passed on an interconnection network between processors, each of which has its own local memory. Array processors such as the ICL DAP (Distributed Array Processor) and the Connection Machine, produced by Thinking Machines Corporation, are well-known examples of SIMD machines.

There is greater variety in the design of MIMD machines, which operate asynchronously with each processor under the control of its own program. In general, MIMD machines have fewer, more powerful processors than SIMD machines. They are divided into two classes: multiprocessors (also called tightly coupled machines) which have a shared memory, and multicomputers (or loosely coupled machines) which operate with an interconnection network. Although many of the earlier, high-performance parallel processors used in government research were very large, highly expensive SIMD machines, MIMD machines can be built more easily and cheaply, often with off-the-shelf components. Many different experimental designs have been created and marketed.

Parallel Algorithms and Languages

In a serial algorithm, each step in the algorithm is completed before the next is begun. A parallel algorithm is a sequence of instructions for solving a problem that identifies the parts of the process that can be carried out simultaneously. To write a program for a parallel processor, the programmer must decide how each sub-task in the algorithm will be assigned to processors and in what order the necessary steps will be performed, and at what points communication is necessary. There can be many algorithms for a particular problem, so the programmer needs to identify and implement the one best suited for a particular parallel architecture.

Sometimes "software inertia," the cost of converting programming applications to parallel form, is cited as a barrier to parallel processing. Some systems automatically adapt a serial process for parallel processing but this may not result in the best performance that can be obtained for that problem. In general, it is difficult to write parallel programs that achieve the kind of high-speed performance of which parallel processors are theoretically capable. Programming languages have been developed specifically for use on parallel processors to handle parallel data structures and functions, scheduling, and memory management. In some cases, these are extensions of existing programming languages, such as parallel versions of C and Lisp; in other cases, they are new languages developed for use on specific parallel architectures.

Performance of Parallel Processors

Designers of parallel processors would like to be able to compare the performance of different machines. The usual measure is the number of **floating point operations** per second, or FLOPS, which is the rate at which a machine can perform single-precision floating point calculations. Many parallel machines are capable of GigaFLOPS (billions of floating point operations per second) performance and newer machines are aimed at performing in the TeraFLOPS range (trillions of floating point operations per second).

floating point operations numerical operations involving real numbers where in achieving a result the number of digits to the left or right of the decimal point can change

As a performance measure, FLOPS refers to the maximum performance of which the machine may be capable. However performance on most problems is dependent on the extent to which they can be parallelized, or broken down into concurrent activities. Another factor is the suitability of the task for a particular parallel architecture. Some problems may be better suited to a SIMD machine, others to some variant of a MIMD machine. A measure of performance relative to the problem to be solved is *speedup*, which

is the ratio of two programs' execution times, usually on a single node and on P nodes of the same computer.

The speedup that can be obtained on a parallel machine depends on the number of processors available, and also on the size of the problem and the way in which it can be broken into parts. Ideally, speedup would be **linear** so that five processors would give a speedup of five, or ten processors a speedup of ten. However, a number of factors contribute to sub-linear speedup, including additional software overhead in the parallel implementation, load balancing to prevent idle processors, and time spent communicating data between processors. A critical limitation is the amount of parallel activity that the problem allows. Gene Amdahl's Law says that the speedup of a parallel algorithm is limited by the fraction of the problem that must be performed sequentially. SEE ALSO ALGORITHMS; PROCEDURAL LANGUAGES; SUPERCOMPUTERS; VIRTUAL MEMORY.

Edie Rasmussen

linear pertaining to a type of system that has a relationship between its outputs and its inputs that can be graphed as a straight line

Bibliography

Flynn, Michael J. *Computer Architecture: Pipelined and Parallel Processor Design.* Boston: Jones & Bartlett, 1995.

Parhami, Behrooz. *Introduction to Parallel Processing: Algorithms and Architectures.* New York: Plenum, 1999.

Roosta, Seyed H. *Parallel Processing and Parallel Algorithms: Theory and Computation.* New York: Springer, 1999.

Pattern Recognition

Pattern recognition is a branch of science that helps develop "classifiers" that can recognize unknown instances of objects. In this context, to recognize an object means to classify it, or to assign it to one of a set of possible classes or labels. This class assignment of objects is based on an analysis of the values of one or more features of the object. Pattern recognition techniques are used in a wide variety of commercial applications. Common examples include character recognition, such as the scanning of a printed page of text into a word processor; natural language recognition, such as using voice commands to relay a set of possible responses to a computer system over the phone; analysis of fingerprint, face, or eye images in order to verify a person's identity; analysis of images taken from airplanes or satellites, perhaps in order to detect and track oil spills in the ocean; or analysis of medical images in order to scan for abnormalities, such as cancer vs. normal tissue.

Humans have a powerful ability to classify objects based on sensory input. They can easily read documents printed in a wide variety of type fonts, including handwritten documents. Such ability is all the more amazing because it often seems to require little conscious effort. Although humans have the ability to read patterns, there are at least two potential advantages to using computer systems for pattern recognition. Even if a person with minimal training could perform a certain task, he or she might not be able to handle the volume of work in a timely fashion, or without becoming bored and error-prone. For example, reading handwritten addresses on pieces of mail is a simple task in principle, but is made difficult by the repetitive

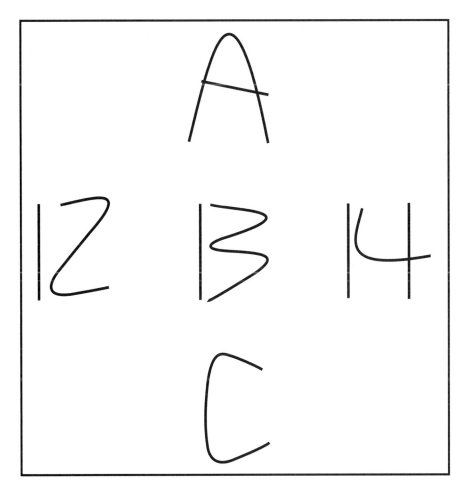

Figure 1. Note how the middle object can be interpreted as a "B" or as the number 13, depending on the context in which it is read. Such ambiguities are key difficulties for pattern recognition.

nature of handling a large number of pieces of mail. In other cases, such as recognizing signs of cancer in x-ray images, the task requires specialized training, and there simply may not be as many human experts as needed.

Another difficulty in pattern recognition is **ambiguity**. That is, a particular pattern may have multiple possible interpretations, each of which is equally reasonable. Sometimes this problem can be resolved by considering the local context of the pattern. A common illustration of ambiguity and context is presented in Figure 1. The interpretation of the middle object is ambiguous. In the context of the column, the object could reasonably be interpreted as a "B," and yet in the context of the row, it could reasonably be interpreted as a "13."

ambiguity the quality of doubtfulness or uncertainty; often subject to multiple interpretations

Construction of a classifier typically requires the use of some examples whose class label is already known by some other means. The examples used in constructing the classifier are referred to as **labeled data** because their classification is already known. They may also be referred to as **training data** because they will be used to train the classifier. Acquiring the appropriate amount and type of training data is one of the secrets to building a successful pattern recognition system.

labeled data a data item whose class assignment is known independent of the classifier being constructed

training data data used in the creation of a classifier

Consider the example of labeling regions in an x-ray image—each region is classified as either cancerous or normal tissue. The following example of an x-ray (mammogram) image shows a cancerous region. Note that many different regions in the image could be identified as possibly

Pattern recognition and image analysis techniques aid in medical diagnosis. The bright region in this x-ray (mammogram) image is cancer. Commercial systems are available to help radiologists detect signs of cancer such as these.

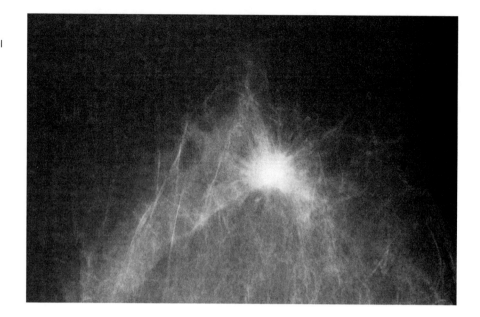

representing an abnormality. The cancerous region is distinguished from the other possible regions by being larger, brighter overall, and having an irregular boundary.

This suggests that useful features for classifying a region might include its size, average brightness, and degree of smoothness of its boundary. To construct the classifier, some example image regions would be identified and their class label determined. The true class label for a region might be determined, for example, by performing a lab test on a tissue sample corresponding to the region. The values of some features of the training samples would be computed. Then the classifier would be constructed by finding some rule for examining the feature values to separate the normal samples from the cancer samples. Then, in use, the classifier would compute the feature values for an unknown region and assign it to either the normal class or the cancer class using the rule "learned" from the training samples. Commercial systems that recognize signs of cancer or other diseases in medical images are more complex than this simple example suggests, but the basic idea is the same.

The essence of constructing a good classifier for a given problem is generally to:

1. Select the pattern recognition approach whose assumptions best match the characteristics of the problem;

2. Use a set of training data that is large enough and representative of the problem;

3. Decide on the "right" features.

Deciding which pattern recognition approach best matches the characteristics of the problem requires an understanding of both the assumptions implicitly made by each approach and a characterization of the problem. Acquiring a set of training data that is large enough, and that is representative of the examples the classifier will see in operation, requires experimental and statistical expertise. Deciding on the right features tends to rely

"BIOMETRICS" FOR HUMAN IDENTIFICATION

In many security applications, it is valuable to recognize a person automatically, or to confirm his/her claimed identity. The field of biometrics uses pattern recognition techniques for this purpose. For example, an image of the eye can be used to obtain features that describe the pattern in someone's iris. One bank has used the technique to confirm customer identity at automated teller machines (ATMs).

on good intuition about the important properties of objects, and also on experimental analysis to select the better-performing features.

At the highest level, pattern recognition techniques can be divided into structural techniques and statistical techniques. A simplified explanation is that structural techniques assume that the parts of an object are known and look at how the parts fit together to form the whole, whereas statistical approaches simply assume that some properties of the whole can be measured and that the values of properties vary between classes. Of the two approaches, statistical pattern recognition techniques are perhaps more widely used. A few of the many possible approaches under the general umbrella of statistical pattern recognition are **Gaussian classifiers**, **k-nearest-neighbors**, and **decision trees**. The approach known as **neural networks** is also sometimes considered as a part of statistical pattern recognition. Neural networks have come to be widely used. The use of the word "neural" tends to invoke the idea that the classifier is working like a human brain. However, the structure and operation of the typical neural network classifier are only very loosely inspired by the structure and operation of neurons in the human brain.

Pattern recognition technology has many important uses beyond those already mentioned. It can be used in the area of "data mining" to sift through large amounts of data and spot important trends. For example, pattern recognition techniques might be used to spot credit card fraud, or to detect attempts to break into computer systems. Pattern recognition techniques can also be used in the area of robotics to help robots interpret visual input and move from one place to another. In summary, it should be clear that pattern recognition technology lies at the core of many applications that involve "intelligent" decisions made by computer. SEE ALSO ARTIFICIAL INTELLIGENCE; COMPUTER VISION; DATA MINING; NEURAL NETWORKS; ROBOTICS; ROBOTS.

Kevin W. Bowyer

Bibliography

Bunke, Horst, and Alberto Sanfeliu. *Syntactic and Structural Pattern Recognition: Theory and Applications.* Teaneck, NJ: World Scientific, 1990.

Duda, Richard O., Peter E. Hart, and David G. Stork. *Pattern Classification.* New York: John Wiley and Sons, 2001.

Fischler, Martin A., and Oscar Firschein. *Intelligence: The Eye, the Brain, and the Computer.* Reading, MA: Addison-Wesley, 1987.

Jain, Anil K., Ruud Bolle, and Sharath Pankanti, eds. *Biometrics: Personal Identification in a Networked Society.* Boston: Kluwer, 1999.

Mitchell, Tom M. *Machine Learning.* Boston: McGraw-Hill, 1997.

Shapiro, Linda G., and George C. Stockman. *Computer Vision.* Upper Saddle River, NJ: Prentice Hall, 2001.

Personal Digital Assistants

Personal digital assistants (PDAs) are small, hand-held computers. They use a form of touch screen technology, using a light pen or stylus as an input device rather than a keyboard. In addition, a detachable keyboard or a voice recorder can be used. PDAs are versatile information processing appliances. They are used frequently as personal information managers (PIMs) to record

Gaussian classifiers classifiers constructed on the assumption that the feature values of data will follow a Gaussian distribution

k-nearest-neighbors a classifier that assigns a class label for an unknown data item by looking at the class labels of the nearest items in the training data

decision trees classifiers in which a sequence of tests are made to decide the class label to assign to an unknown data item; the sequence of tests can be visualized as having a tree structure

neural networks pattern recognition systems whose structure and operation is loosely inspired by analogy to neurons in the human brain

integrated modem a modem device that is built into a computer, rather than being attached as a separate peripheral

random access memory (RAM) a type of memory device that supports the nonpermanent storage of programs and data; so called because various locations can be accessed in any order (as if at random), rather than in a sequence (like a tape memory device)

telephone numbers, addresses, appointments, and to-do lists. Also, PDAs can synchronize with microcomputers to transfer e-mail, text documents, spreadsheets, files, or databases. Other types of PDAs incorporate an **integrated modem** to connect with the Internet or to dial-up another computer in order to transfer data.

Some PDAs use wireless communications technology, providing great mobility. This use of wireless technology allows companies to provide PDAs to their employees in situations where laptops would be unworkable.

Palmtops, which are small computers that fit in the palm of one's hand, are also referred to as PDAs. The difference between a PDA and Palmtop computer is that the PDAs are pen-based, using a stylus rather than a keyboard for input, while the palmtop uses a small, integrated keyboard.

In 1993 Apple Computer introduced the first PDA, which was called the Newton MessagePad. Rather than just storing handwritten words, Newton converted them into typescript. Early versions of Newton had limited success with this difficult process. Three years later, 3Com's Palm Computing introduced the revolutionary PalmPilot. In June 1998, Microsoft began shipping a scaled down Windows operating system for manufacturers of palm-sized PCs. Apple's Newton was later taken off the market.

PDA Features

Several factors should be considered before purchasing a PDA, including what application software the user wishes to run; which types of input devices (keyboard, light pen, touch screen, voice recorder) are available and desired by the user; whether the amount of memory, specifically **random access memory (RAM)**, and the life of the battery are sufficient for the user' needs; what size of the device is desired; and, of course, what price the user wants to pay. In 2001 prices for PDAs ranged from a low of $100 for a simple personal information manager to more than $1,000 for full-screen PDAs with integrated keyboards.

Other features available in PDAs are multimedia and audio capabilities, various screen sizes (starting with a full screen), and modems (integrated or not, wireless, or wired). Which features are most important depends on the tasks that the user wishes to perform. In addition to these standard features, mobile telephones or clip-on cameras can be combined with several PDA models.

Primary PDA Manufacturers

Two of the leading manufacturers of PDAs are Palm, Inc. and Casio, Inc. PDAs made by Palm dominate the market with two popular models: the Palm m100 and the Palm VIIx. Both devices use the Palm OS 3.5 as an operating system, HotSync Manager 2.1.0, Pocket Mirror 2.0.7 as synchronizing software, and a 20-MHz Motorola DragonBall EZ as a processor. The Palm OS is fast, simple, and compatible with both Macintosh and Windows-based computers.

The amount of memory available in these devices is important, especially the amount of RAM. The Palm m100 has 2MB of RAM and 2MB of ROM. The Palm VIIx has more RAM (8MB) and the same amount of read only memory (ROM). Both use a touch screen as their input and have a

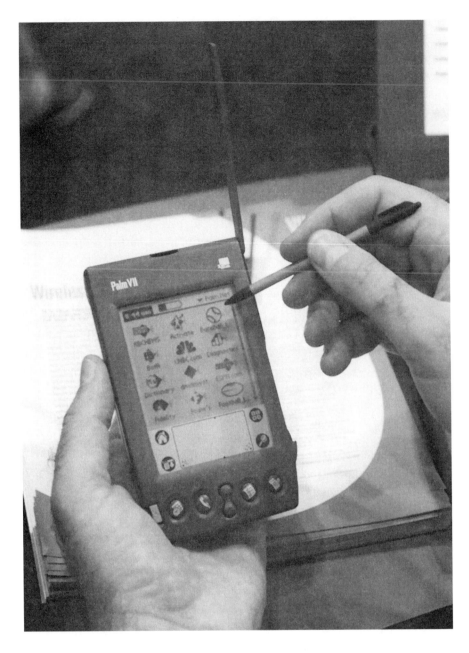

Many business professionals turn to handheld PDAs, like the Palm VII, to organize their lives. The pen helps them input data as they manage appointments, contact names, and other information.

speaker as well as an infrared port. To exchange data between Palm PDAs, users can beam information from one to another using an infrared port. Users also can place the Palm PDA into a docking cradle and synchronize their PDA with their microcomputers. The Palm VIIx has a docking serial cradle for synchronizing with a microcomputer and a built-in modem that can access the Internet or other networks without wires.

The PDA models produced by Casio offered the first 64-bit screens on the market. Casio's PDAs include the Casio Cassiopeia E-125 and the Cassiopeia EM-500. Both have color displays, use Windows CE 3.0 as an operating system and ActiveSync 3.1 as synchronizing software, and use a 150-MHz NEC VR4122 as a processor. Most of these use the Windows CE operating system (WinCE). WinCE is similar to Windows 95/98. It can run set-top TV controllers or small handheld devices that can communicate with each other and synchronize with Windows-based computers.

The Casio E-125 PDA has 32MB RAM while the EM-500 PDA has 16MB RAM. Both use touch screen or voice recorders as input and have a microphone and speaker as well as a stereo headphone jack and an infrared port.

Making PDAs More Useful

PDAs must be trained to recognize their users' handwriting. To do this, the user must write each numeric digit and letter (in uppercase) several times on the screen with the light pen. Even so, recognition is not always 100 percent. For users who really want a keyboard, text can also be entered by tapping the light pen on the appropriate letters from an on-screen virtual keyboard. There are other problems with entering data on the screen with just a light pen. How can users delete an entire word, or bring up an entire document? These problems have been solved in several ingenious ways. For example, deletion of a word occurs by crossing it out on the screen. Tapping the light pen on the name of a stored document brings it up on the screen.

As these problems are being solved, new applications for PDAs are being developed and new technologies are being combined with PDAs. For example, Symbol Technologies, Inc. has combined PDAs with **bar code** scanning equipment. Symbol is supplying the Kmart Corporation with in-store wireless and mobile computing solutions in its entire chain of more than 2,100 stores. Kmart is using Symbol's wireless **local area network (LAN)** and the company's PDT 6840 wireless devices for receiving merchandise, tracking inventory, and printing labels, and on the sales floor for price checking and employee communications. Many market watchers believe that PDAs will gain wide use in a variety of business applications, especially retailing, warehousing, and inventory control. SEE ALSO MICROCOMPUTERS; TELECOMMUNICATIONS; WIRELESS TECHNOLOGY; WORLD WIDE WEB.

Terri L. Lenox and Charles R. Woratschek

bar code a graphical number representation system where alphanumeric characters are represented by vertical black and white lines of varying width

local area network (LAN) a high-speed computer network that is designed for users who are located near each other

Bibliography

Brown, Bruce, and Marge Brown. "Expanding Possibilities." *PC Magazine*, March 6, 2001, pp. 188–200.

Turban, Efraim, R. Kelly Rainer, Jr., and Richard E. Potter. *Introduction to Information Technology*. New York: John Wiley and Sons, Inc., 2001.

Internet Resources

Casio Corporation Web Site. <http://www.casio.com>

Products, Services & Company Information. *Palm, Inc.* <http://www.palm.com>

Symbol Technologies Web Site. <http://www.symbol.com>

Pointing Devices

In the early days of computers, commands and data were input via a keyboard. On early computer monitor screens, the text entry position was denoted by a blinking underscore or vertical bar, called a cursor. At first, users had no control over the location of this cursor; later, directional arrow keys and key commands allowed users to select text entry points. In more recent operating systems that utilize a **graphical user interface (GUI)**, the cursor still indicates the point where text may be entered, but it is also a visible and moving on-screen pointer controlled with an input device, such as a mouse. The computer operator uses the *pointing cursor* to establish where the *position indicator cursor* should be placed, or to select a program to run or file to view. Typically, the pointing cursor appears on the screen as an arrow.

Since early computer use keyboard commands were difficult to learn and cryptic to non-computer specialists, computer manufacturers and software developers quickly embraced the point-and-click **interfaces** first popularized by the Apple Macintosh. However, keyboard arrows were no longer adequate as a way to move a cursor around the screen. The point-and-click concept required the user to move something that would cause a corresponding movement on the screen. This led to the development of input devices such as the mouse, the joystick, and other tools for controlling on-screen movement of the cursor. Although the mouse and its descendants are not replacements for the keyboard, they do supplement the keyboard in tasks for which it is ill suited.

Common Pointing Devices

Common pointing devices used to control on-screen movement include computer mice, touchpads, touch screens, joysticks, graphics tablets, and trackballs. Some of these devices, including the mouse and the joystick, can be added to a computer system according to the needs of a user. Other devices, such as touch screens, are integrated into specialized computer systems designed for particular purposes.

Computer Mouse. A computer mouse is a small, hand-held, interactive input pointing device that, when rolled over a flat surface, controls placement of the cursor on a computer display. A computer mouse is **analogous** to a live mouse in that it is palm-size and mouse-shaped, with rounded corners. Originally, all mice were connected to computers with a wire suggestive of a tail; however, cordless mice are also available now.

A mouse can be a one-, two-, or three-button device. After a user positions the cursor on the computer display by moving the mouse, screen action can be controlled by single or multiple clicks of the mouse buttons. Screen icons can be activated with one click, or dragged across the computer display by a single click that is held as the mouse is moved from one location to another.

Traditional computer mice are electromechanical devices. A rubber-coated steel ball that protrudes from the bottom is detected by two **orthogonal** rollers, which also touch the ball, inside the plastic housing. These rollers act as **transducers** to convert the speed and direction of the rolling ball to electrical signals that are sent to a software **driver** to move the screen cursor. To provide better traction for the rolling ball, a mouse is generally operated on a flat, cushioned pad of foam.

There are also two other kinds of mice: optical mice and optomechanical mice. An optical mouse has no wheels or balls but instead depends on a **light emitting diode (LED)** and a photodetector. As the mouse moves across a grid of closely spaced lines on a specially designed mouse pad, the

graphical user interface (GUI) an interface that allows computers to be operated through pictures (icons) and mouse-clicks, rather than through text and typing

interfaces boundaries or borders between two or more objects or systems; also points of access

analogous a relationship of logical similarity between two or more objects

orthogonal elements or objects that are perpendicular to one another; in a logical sense this means that changes in one have no effect on the other

transducers devices that sense a physical quantity, such as temperature or pressure, and convert that measurement into an electrical signal

driver a special program that manages the sequential execution of several other programs; a part of an operating system that handles input/output devices

light emitting diode (LED) a discrete electronic component that emits visible light when permitting current to flow in a certain direction; often used as an indicating lamp

INVENTION OF THE MOUSE

The creation of the earliest mouse is attributed to Douglas Englebart and his colleagues at the Stanford Research Institute in 1965. The idea was further developed at Xerox Corporation's Palo Alto Research Center (PARC). Englebart's first "mouse"—so named because of its "tail" of wire attaching it to the computer—was a wooden, box-like housing with wheels placed at right angles along the top. The user moved the wheels to regulate cursor movement.

byte a group of eight binary digits; represents a single character of text

dielectric a material that exhibits insulating properties, as opposed to conducting properties

photodetector senses line crossings by changes in reflected light. An optomechanical mouse combines characteristics of the optical mouse and the standard electromechanical mouse: it is built with a moving ball and shafts with slits through which light can pass. As the mouse moves, the shafts rotate and light pulses strike the photodetector through the slits. The amount of cursor motion is proportional to the number of light pulses detected. No special mouse pad is required with optomechanical mice, and they are less vulnerable to dust and dirt-related failure than are mechanical mice.

Common to all types of mice are the serial communications sent back to the computer every time the mouse moves a certain distance (e.g., 0.25 millimeters or 0.01 inch or a *mickey*)—one **byte** for x-movement, one byte for y-movement, and one or two bytes for button status. Low-level software in the computer converts the relative mouse movements to absolute cursor position on the display.

Touchpads. Where using a mouse would be awkward, such as in a laptop computer configuration, or cursor movement is more important than characters, touchpads have become popular. These are generally built into a computer unit, and they often include clickable buttons that correspond to the buttons of a mouse. Beneath the top layer of the touchpad are two or more layers separated by a non-conducting **dielectric**; each layer contains a grid of electrode rows and columns. The different layers create a capacitance (electric field) between them that may be drastically changed by the electric field of a human finger either touching or moving near the touchpad. Changes in capacitance are measured 100 times a second and translated into cursor movement.

Touch Screens. A touch screen is a computer display screen that is sensitive to human touch, allowing the screen to function as an input pointing device. The user touches the screen itself to cause some action to take place.

There are three types of touch screen technology. A *resistive touch screen panel* is coated with a thin, metallic, electrically conductive and resistive layer that causes a change in the electrical current that is registered as a touch event and sent to the controller for processing. A *surface wave touch screen* uses ultrasonic waves that pass over the touch screen panel. When the panel is touched, a portion of the wave is absorbed and this change in the ultrasonic waves registers the position of the touch event and sends this information to the controller for processing. A *capacitive touch screen panel* is coated with a material that stores electrical charges. When the panel is touched, a small amount of charge is drawn to the point of contact. Circuits located at each corner of the panel measure the charge and send the information to the controller for processing.

Resistive touch screen panels are generally the most affordable but they offer only 75 percent clarity and the layer can be damaged by sharp objects. Resistive touch screen panels are not affected by outside elements such as dust or water. Surface wave touch screen panels are the most advanced of the three types, but they can be damaged by outside elements. Touch screens are especially popular in very small computers to eliminate the requirement of a keyboard space. They are also commonly used in retail situations such as gas stations, ATM bank machines, restaurants, and information kiosks.

Joysticks. Joysticks are similar to mice in that they transmit X-Y hand coordinates to the computer to position a cursor on the screen. A joystick

Pointing devices come in various shapes and sizes. This pointing device—a light pen—allows a designer to write on a graphics tablet, displaying the markings on the computer screen behind it.

is connected to a yoke that pivots freely in all directions. **Sensors** detect movement and generate corresponding electric currents that are interpreted by a microcontroller as movement of the cursor. Later model joysticks also have a "tophat button" or contact switch that can be pressed to trigger screen activity. Joysticks are most commonly used in computer games and simulations to provide users with flexibility and quick response time when interacting with on-screen events.

Sensors devices that can record and transmit data regarding altitude, flight path, attitude, etc., so that they can enter into the system's calculations

Graphics Tablets. Digitizing graphics tablets give artists the flexibility to translate precise pen movements into lines on a display. They can also "read" a user's handwriting through the use of specialized software. Graphics tablets use a variety of technologies, including pressure-sensitive sensors, optical

sensors, magnetic sensors, and capacitive sensors, to determine the location of a pen on the pad. Some tablets require the use of a special pen that is attached to the tablet while others allow the use of any pointed object, including a wooden pencil. The resolution and accuracy of a graphics tablet depends on the technology employed. Graphics tablets can be used as mouse replacements but they are particularly suited for drawing.

Trackballs. A trackball is a computer cursor control device usually built into the front of the keyboard, close to the user. Essentially, the trackball is an upside-down mouse that rotates in place within a socket. The user first rolls the ball to direct the cursor to the desired place on the screen and then clicks one of two buttons (identical to mouse buttons) near the trackball to select desktop objects or position the cursor for text entry. Like a touchpad, this pointing device is used in laptop computers and other applications where a mouse would be inconvenient or awkward to use.

Other Pointing Devices

Less commonly used pointing devices include eraser-like pointer sticks built into some laptop keyboards, as well as hand-held units such as light pens, which were among the earliest input units, and pen input devices. Pointing sticks, or eraserhead pointing devices, are so called because they look like a pencil eraser stuck somewhere between the G and K keys on the computer keyboard. When a user's finger puts pressure on the eraserhead, the pressure is passed to contacts underneath the keyboard which varies electric current; a microcontroller translates the variable electric current to cursor movement on the computer display.

Pen input devices and light pens allow users to bypass a keyboard and instead use the familiar hand movements of writing or drawing to control action on a computer screen or input graphics or text information. A photodetector in the tip of a light pen responds to points of light on the screen so when a point of light on the screen is lit, the light pen notifies the program that the current location is correct. By moving a pen around the screen, a cursor can be made to follow the pen. Pen input devices and light pens make it possible to activate a command, execute a task, or draw. Handwriting recognition software is also being developed to convert on-screen handwriting into text. SEE ALSO Game Controllers; Games; Input Devices; Mouse.

William Yurcik

Bibliography

Kolle, Iril C. *Graphics Tablet Solutions.* Cincinnati, OH: Muska & Lipman Publishing, 2001.

White, Ron. *How Computers Work*, 6th ed. Indianapolis, IN: Que, 2002.

Internet Resources

MouseSite. <http://sloan.stanford.edu/mousesite/MouseSitePg1.html>

Printing Devices

The prediction that the computer would create a paperless office could not have been further from reality. More paper is being consumed as computer printing has become available to the masses. In fact, computers have created a new category of computing—desktop publishing—that produces printed paper of near-publication quality.

Printers provide a permanent paper record of computer output data, graphics, or text and are available in a wide variety of different speeds, features, and capabilities. Printers can also be used with different types of paper forms to print labels, stamps, bank checks, and a wide range of business forms. All printers have some level of variable recurring cost in toner cartridges that must be replaced when the toner is completely used. Printers have both a built-in character set and can download new character set fonts. The output of many printers takes the form of graphical **bit maps** that represent image dots exactly. Some printers have built-in processing capability to accept data in the form of a page description language, usually Adobe Postscript or Adobe Portable Document Format. The controller in the printer then processes the page description language to a bit map image within the printer itself. Memory is provided within the printer to store temporarily the bit-mapped image while it is being printed.

The performance of a printer is measured in speed and quality. The speed of a printer is measured by the number of pages printed per minute (ppm). Like a display screen, the quality or resolution of a printer's output is measured by the number of dots printed per inch (dpi). There are, however, two major differences between the dots used in printers and the **pixels** used in computer displays. The number of dots per inch in a printer is generally much higher (300–1200 dpi) than the number of pixels per inch in a monitor (70–100 dpi). While some printers can slightly vary the size of dots, in general the dots created by a printer are fixed in intensity, as opposed to pixels in a display, which can take an infinite range of intensities. To create an intermediate intensity, referred to as a half-tone, printers cluster groups of dots together in close proximity so that the human eye will perceive a gray or intermediate color.

Types of Printers

Regardless of the size of the system, quantity of printing, or capacity of the printer, modern printers use one of three technologies to print dots: dot matrix, inkjet, or laser.

Dot matrix technology results from physical impact of the print head onto paper. The print head on a dot matrix printer consists of a number of printing pins, usually between seven and twenty-four, whose positions can be controlled by individual electromagnets. When a current is applied, the corresponding pin is forced to strike the paper through an inked ribbon to form a dot. Using more pins and overlapping dots by multiple passes over the same line can increase print quality. Most dot matrix printers can operate in several modes offering different tradeoffs between print quality and speed.

In recent years, better print heads and more intelligent controllers have improved the size and accuracy of the dots so that dot matrix printers, originally only intended for character printing, can now print high-quality graphics with resolutions that rival laser printers. Multiple inked ribbons can be used to produce color. However, dot matrix color is not considered acceptable for most purposes. Dot matrix printers are inexpensive in terms

---

A PAPERLESS SOCIETY?

Many industry experts believed that paper sales would decrease as more and more people and businesses turned to electronic documents, networked filing systems, and e-mail. However, the paper industry is not suffering lost sales. Industry forecasts show that the demand for home paper use is on the rise.

bit maps images comprised of bit descriptions of the image, in black and white or color, such that the colors can be represented by the two values of a binary bit

pixels single picture elements on a video screen; the individual dots making up a picture on a video screen or digital image

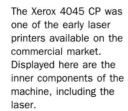

The Xerox 4045 CP was one of the early laser printers available on the commercial market. Displayed here are the inner components of the machine, including the laser.

piezo-crystal an electronic component that when subjected to a current will produce a waveform signal at a precise rate, which can then be used as a clock signal in a computer

of ink ribbon and are reliable, but they are slow, noisy, and poor at graphics. Dot matrix printers have three major uses: printing on large preprinted forms; printing on small pieces of paper (such as cash register receipts, ATM machine receipts, credit card transactions, and airline tickets); and multi-part, continuous forms with carbon paper in between.

Inkjet printers use nonimpact printing by spraying heated ink from a tiny nozzle onto paper. The tiny nozzle is smaller than the width of a human hair and the volume of each sprayed droplet is about one-millionth the volume of an eye-drop. Inside each nozzle, an ink droplet is electrically heated to its boiling point until it explodes so that the only place the ink can go is out the front of the nozzle. The nozzle is then cooled and the resulting vacuum sucks in another droplet of ink. The speed of the printer is thus limited by the length of the boil/cool cycle.

Inkjets have resolutions ranging from 300 dpi to 1440 dpi. Some inkjet printers use a vibrating **piezo-crystal** instead of heat to produce ink droplets. In ink jet printers, the electric current causes a deformation of the crystal that squeezes out the drop of ink. Mechanically the inkjet printer works similarly to a dot matrix printer. It moves across a page to print a row, and mechanical rollers move the paper downward to print successive rows. Multiple reservoirs of ink may be available to print multiple colors. Inkjet printers are popular for low-cost home printing because they are small and economical. However, they are slow and produce ink-soaked output that can be messy.

Laser printing is derived from **xerography** with the difference that the image is produced electronically from the computer using a laser or light-emitting diode rather than scanned with a bright light. There are four steps in the operation of a laser printer. First, a laser illuminates the dots to be printed on a photosensitive drum that becomes electrically charged wherever a dot is to be printed. Second, the photosensitive drum rotates the charged dots into a tank of black toner where the toner sticks to the drum wherever a charge is present. Third, a sheet of paper is fed toward the drum, coated with electrical charges, and contacts the drum, picking up the toner image from the drum. Finally, the toner image on the paper is heated in a fusing system that melts the toner into the paper while the drum has its charge erased by the corona wire in preparation for the next page.

xerography a printing process that uses electrostatic elements derived from a photographic image to deposit the ink

Other Printing Devices

The complete set of colors that a printer can produce is called its gamut. No printer has a gamut that matches the real world. It is limited by colors, discrete intensities, imperfections, non-uniform spacing across the color spectrum, and human perception. Transferring a color image that looks perfect on a computer display to an identical printed page is difficult for the following reasons:

- Display monitors use transmitted light, while color printers use reflected light;

- Display monitors produce 256 intensities per color, while color printers use **half-tones**;

- Display monitors have a dark background, paper has a light background;

- Display monitors have a RGB (red, green, blue) gamut and printers have a CYMK (cyan, yellow, magenta, black) gamut.

half-tones black and white dots of certain sizes, which provide a perception of shades of gray

Common ways to print color images include the use of special inks and paper. Inkjet printers can use dye-based inks or pigment-based inks. Dye-based inks consist of colored dyes dissolved in a fluid carrier. They provide bright colors and flow easily. Pigment-based inks contain solid particles of pigment suspended in a fluid carrier that evaporates from the paper leaving the pigment behind. They do not fade in time like dye-based inks, but they are also not as bright, and the pigment particles tend to clog nozzles requiring periodic cleaning. Coated or glossy paper, specially designed to hold ink droplets and not let them spread, is required for printing photographs.

Solid ink printers are slightly higher quality than inkjet printers. These printers accept solid blocks of special waxy ink that is then melted in hot ink reservoirs. Startup times of these printers are long (typically ten minutes) while the ink blocks are melting. The hot ink is sprayed onto the paper, where it solidifies and is fused with the paper by forcing it between two hard rollers.

A step up from solid ink printers is a color laser printer. A color laser printer works exactly like a black and white laser printer, except an image is transferred to the roller using four different toners (the CYMK gamut). Because the full bit map of an image is generally produced in advance, the memory requirements make this type of printer expensive, but printing is fast, high quality, and images are stable over time. A 1200 by 1200 dpi image for a page containing 516 square centimeters or 80 square inches needs 115 million pixels. At 4 bits per pixel, the printer needs 55 MB just for the bit map, exclusive of memory for the internal processors and fonts.

For highest-quality color images, more specialized methods such as thermal wax transfer or dye sublimation are required. Sublimation is the scientific name for a solid changing into a gas without passing through a liquid state. The mechanisms for both methods are similar. The paper is fed into the printer and clamped against a drum with a print head providing a row of dot-sized heating elements. Between the paper and the print head, a roll of impregnated film is exposed. The heat from the print head melts the wax or dye onto the paper. The film is impregnated with either colored wax or dye in page-sized sections of cyan, yellow, magenta, and black.

For thermal wax transfer, the input paper is pre-coated with clear wax to compensate for slight paper imperfections and so that the wax may be applied more uniformly. For dye sublimation, the dyes diffuse and actually blend in the paper. Although dye sublimation can print continuous color tones without half toning, it also requires high temperatures and expensive specialized paper. The colors fade when exposed to ultraviolet light, such as that contained in sunlight. Small snapshot printers often use the dye sublimation process to produce highly realistic photographic images.

Organizations that produce and store significant copies of paper documents often use computer output microfilm (COM) devices to place data from a computer directly onto microfilm, thus eliminating the need for photographic conversion.

Evolution of Printing and Plotters

Early printers were derived from typewriters using daisywheel printers—form characters that were mounted at the ends of arms attached to wheels shaped like a daisy. Like typewriters, printing resulted from the wheel rotating to the proper position and an energized magnet forcing the wheel through an inked ribbon onto paper. These printers were difficult to maintain and incapable of generating any graphical images or foreign words that could not be formed by the given set of formed characters. Most formed-character impact printers have disappeared from use. Nearly all modern computer printers produce their output as a combination of dots.

Plotters are hard-copy printing devices consisting of one or multiple independently maneuverable ink pens that are used for general design work such as blueprints, schematics, drawings, and plotting mathematical functions. Standard plot widths are 61 centimeters by 91.5 centimeters or 24 inches by 36 inches, but the attractive feature of plotters is limitless size when necessary for uses such as graphic arts. SEE ALSO INPUT DEVICES; POINTING DEVICES; SERIAL AND PARALLEL TRANSMISSION.

William J. Yurcik

Bibliography

Chambers, Mark L. *Printer Handbook*, 2nd ed. Foster City, CA: IDG Books Worldwide, 2000.

Procedural Languages

Procedural languages are computer languages used to define the actions that a computer has to follow to solve a problem. Although it would be convenient for people to give computers instructions in a natural language, such as English, French, or Chinese, they cannot because computers are just too inflexible to understand the subtleties of human communication. Human intelligence can work out the ambiguities of a natural language, but a computer requires a rigid, mathematically precise communication system: each symbol, or group of symbols, must mean exactly the same thing every time.

Computer scientists have created artificial languages that enable programmers to assemble a set of commands for the machine without dealing directly with strings of binary digits. The high-level form of a procedural language frees a programmer from the time-consuming chore of expressing **algorithms** in lower-level languages such as assembly and machine language. Additionally, procedural language instructions are expressed in a machine-independent form that facilitate portability, thus increasing the lifetime and usefulness of a program.

algorithms rules or procedures used to solve mathematical problems—most often described as sequences of steps

Higher-level languages work for people because they are closer to natural language, but a computer cannot carry out instructions until that communication has been translated into zeros and ones. This translation may be done by compilers or interpreters, which are special programs custommade to fit both the language and the machine being used. A compiler reads the entire program, makes a translation, and produces a complete binary code version, which is then loaded into the computer and executed. Once the program is compiled, neither the original program nor the compiler is needed. On the other hand, an interpreter translates and executes the program one instruction at a time, so a program written in an interpreted language must be interpreted each time it is run. Compiled programs execute faster, but interpreted programs are easier to correct or modify.

A procedural language is either compiled or interpreted, depending on the use for which it was created. FORTRAN, for example, is usually implemented with a compiler because it was created to handle large programs for scientific and mathematical applications where speed of execution is very important. On the other hand, BASIC is typically implemented with an interpreter because it was intended for use by novice programmers.

Each programming language has a special vocabulary of keywords, which correspond to specific operations or sequences of operations to be performed by the computer. Some of them act as verbs, or commands, others act as nouns, modifiers, or punctuation marks. By using them to form sentences, a programmer tells a computer exactly what to do with each item of information being processed. Typical commands include: input and output, conditions, and repetition. Because they are indispensable to programmers, these commands are common to all computer languages, but they are written differently in each language because the sentences must follow the **syntax** of the language.

Many of the hundreds of programming languages also have dialects. A dialect is a variation of the main language. While people can understand one another even if they speak different dialects of their language, a computer cannot understand a program written in a different dialect from its own. Dialects present problems when a program using the same data set gives different answers when run on two different machines. This means that the program cannot be ported from one machine to the other. Asking several programmers to name the best computer language will most likely give you several different answers, because there is no best computer language, any more than one natural language is better than all the rest. Theoretically, most programming tasks could be accomplished with any language, but writing a program for a given job is actually considerably easier in some languages than in others.✳ None can claim all-around utility.

✳**A language designed for scientific applications does not readily lend itself to the writing of a program for managing a payroll database.**

This essay covers, in some historical order, procedural languages that were popular or significant during the period of their development: FORTRAN, ALGOL, COBOL, BASIC, Pascal, C, and Ada.

FORTRAN

We can safely say that FORTRAN (FORmula TRANslator) was the first true high-level language. A factor that influenced the development of FORTRAN was the amount of money spent on programming in 1954. The cost of programming heavily impacted on the cost of operating a computer, and as computers got cheaper, the situation got worse. American computer scientist John Backus was able to convince IBM's directors that a language could be developed with a compiler that would produce very efficient object code. He was put in charge of the group—which included Irving Ziller, Roy Nutt, David Sayre and Peter Sheridan—that developed FORTRAN. One of their goals was to design a language that would make it possible for engineers and scientists to write programs on their own for the IBM 704.

The first FORTRAN compiler took about twenty-five person-years to complete and proved to be as efficient as the then-current assemblers, making it a striking achievement in the history of programming languages. FORTRAN I was released in 1957 and was followed in the spring of 1958 by FORTRAN II. It included function statements and better diagnostic messages. A more advanced version, FORTRAN III, depended heavily on the architecture of the IBM 704, and was not made into a commercial product. However, many of its features were incorporated into FORTRAN IV, which was released in 1962 and had a life of almost fifteen years. It added COMMON storage, double-precision and logical data types, and relational expressions as well as the DATA statements, which provided a simple facility to initialize variables. Programs written using versions subsequent to FORTRAN III were machine independent, which meant that they could be run on any scientific machine. For the first time one single language was used by many manufacturers for many different machines.

By the mid-1970s FORTRAN IV was no longer a modern language, and although the investment in FORTRAN programs was immense it was time to bring it up to speed. In 1967 work began on what was later called FORTRAN 77, which became the official standard in April of 1978. By

1981 the demand for FORTRAN 77 compilers was very high, making it clear that it was a success. However, it did not have all the features needed to implement modern control structures, so work on its successor began in 1978. It was to include if-then-else control structures, case selection, do-enddo structure, and recursion, among other things. Work on this project ended in 1990 and FORTRAN 90 was published in 1991. FORTRAN 95, an extension of FORTRAN 90, was published in December 1997, and work on FORTRAN 200x was underway in 2001. It is an upward compatible extension of FORTRAN 95 adding support for exception handling, object-oriented programming, and improved interoperability with C.

ALGOL

Because many languages and dialects were developed between 1956 and 1959 creating portability problems, various computer groups petitioned the Association for Computing Machinery (ACM) to recommend action for the creation of a universal programming language. Representatives from industry and universities were appointed to a committee that met three times, starting in January 1958, and agreed that the new language would be an algebraic language similar to FORTRAN. However, FORTRAN could not be used as a universal language because, in those days, it was a creation of IBM and closely tied to IBM hardware. Some members of the group, including John Backus and Alan Perlis, were chosen to represent the American viewpoint at the meetings that would shape this international language.✶

ALGOL 58 was really a group effort. It was the first formal attempt to address issues of portability, and integrated the best features of programming languages available at the time. It introduced new terms such as: type, formal versus actual parameter, for statement, the *begin end* **delimiters**, and three levels of language description. This effort was considered as a draft and was not commercially implemented. However, many recommendations for its improvement were considered at a Paris meeting in June 1959.

In January 1960 seven representatives of European countries, including Peter Naur and Fritz Bauer, and six from the United States, including Backus and Perlis, met in Paris to develop ALGOL 60, which was expected to become a universal tool with the addition of the following features: block, call by value and call by name, dynamic arrays, *own* variables, global and local variables, *until, while, if then else*, and recursion. ALGOL was used more in Europe than in the United States by computer scientists conducing research. ALGOL 60 became the standard for the publication of algorithms and was a great influence on future language developments.

In 1962 a new international committee of computer scientists was formed to develop an enhanced version of ALGOL 60. The meetings began in 1965 and lasted until 1968 when ALGOL 68 was released. Although it allowed non-English-speaking programmers to write programs in their own language, it proved to be too cumbersome to be readily accepted. Proficient programmers had trouble understanding the document that defined it and very few institutions had an actual ALGOL 68 compiler in use.

However, out of this effort arose a new language, Pascal, developed by Niklaus Wirth who began work on it in 1968.

✶**The ALGOL meetings were conducted from May to June 1958 in Zurich, Switzerland. The name ALGOL (ALGOrithmic Language) was suggested at that time.**

delimiters special symbols that mark the beginnings and/or endings of other groups of symbols (for example to mark out comments in program source code)

COBOL

In April of 1959, two years after the introduction of FORTRAN, a group of academics, computer manufacturers, and computer users, including American programming pioneer Grace Hopper (1906–1992), met to discuss the feasibility of designing a programming language that would satisfy the needs of the business community and would become a standard. FORTRAN did not suit their needs because business programs deal with large quantities of data but do not perform complicated calculations. Existing programming languages were not portable—they could only function in one type of computer, scientific or business. Since large organizations sometimes had different types of computers, their programmers had to know several languages, thus increasing the cost of software. For example, the U.S. Department of Defense had more than 1,000 computers and it was costing the DoD close to $500 million a year to program them and keep them operating smoothly.

A meeting of forty representatives from the government, users, consultants, and manufacturers met at the Pentagon on May 1959 to discuss the need of a common business language. They formed three committees and proceeded to analyze existing business programming languages: FLOW-MATIC, AIMACO, and Commercial Translator. They sought to learn if the best features of each could be merged into one. By December of 1959 the group had completed the specifications for COBOL, which were made public in 1960.

**COBOL is short for COmmon Business Oriented Language.

COBOL programs are composed of four divisions, each one serving a specific purpose.* The IDENTIFICATION division serves to identify the program and programmer. The ENVIRONMENT division is used to identify the actual computer, compiler, and peripheral devices that will be used by the program and it is the most machine dependent. The DATA division describes the files, records, and fields used by the program, and the PROCEDURE division contains the instructions that will process the data. COBOL commands are written using English words and syntax, and its variable names can be up to 30 characters long, making them very descriptive. These features make programs easy to read and understand for nonprogrammers, and it also makes them easier to debug and maintain. COBOL programs are highly portable, therefore COBOL was readily accepted by the American business community.

The 1961 revision of COBOL included the Report Writer and Sort features, and was the first to be widely implemented. COBOL was revised again in 1965 and 1968, the latter was the first American National Standards Institute (ANSI) standard compiler.

COBOL 74 improved indexed file handling, specifically, ISAM (Indexed Sequential Access Method). During the growth of the microcomputer market, several versions of microcomputer COBOL became available and were used in the business community as well as in universities and colleges. COBOL 85 reflected the efforts of making it more compatible with structured programming by providing END IF, END PERFORM, a direct case structure, and an in-line PERFORM. Publication of the next revision was expected in 2002 and was to include object-oriented features.

BASIC

In the early 1960s there were no personal computers. If you wanted to compute, you had to punch your program on cards, carry them to the nearest computer center, and then wait hours for the results. John G. Kemeny and Thomas E. Kurtz, professors at Dartmouth College, believed that computer programming was too important to be relegated exclusively to engineering students and professional programmers. So in 1963 they designed and built a time-sharing system and developed the Beginners All-purpose Symbolic Instruction Code (BASIC). Their goals included ease of learning for the beginner, hardware and operating system independence, the ability to accommodate large programs, and sensible error messages in English. BASIC became available in 1964. Although Kemeny and Kurtz implemented it to run with a compiler, current versions run under interpreters.

BASIC can be classified as a general-purpose language because it can handle business applications as well as scientific and educational applications. Unfortunately the language has been widely modified and extended by computer manufacturers and software companies. Numerous dialects of BASIC, each with its own syntax and special features, make it difficult to port programs from one computer to another.

The original version was revised and expanded by Kemeny and Kurtz to include graphic statements in 1975. The following year, in order to comply with the requirements of structured programming, they dropped the GOTO statement; this version was called SBASIC and was taught to Dartmouth undergraduates. In 1983 they developed "true BASIC," a more powerful and versatile form that follows the proposed ANSI standards. Some of its features were optional line numbers, long variable names, array-handling statements, Do loops, a SELECT case structure, and independent subprograms. BASIC was widely accepted in the educational community because it was an easy language to teach and learn.

Pascal

Pascal was developed by Niklaus Wirth, a Swiss computer scientist who was part of the ALGOL 68 committee. He felt that ALGOL was too complex and wanted to design a computer language that could easily be taught to college students. The new language, which is a derivative of ALGOL, was published in 1971 and was later called Pascal.

Pascal✳ incorporates the ideas of structured programming that started to appear in the 1960s, redefining ALGOL's concept of breaking down a program into modules, procedures, and functions, and also expanding on some of ALGOL's features by adding new data types and control structures. Its structure makes programs easier to read and maintain by people other than the original programmer. Although there are variations among Pascal compilers, the language has a fairly standard form, so programs are portable between different computers.

Wirth's idea found its most important audience at the University of California at San Diego, where in late 1974 Kenneth Bowles worked out a Pascal operating system and compiler to be used on mini- and microcomputers. He went on to develop an entire system containing a compiler, text editor, an assembler, a linker, a file-handling utility, and a set of utility programs.

BASICALLY SPEAKING

It is estimated that by the mid-1980s several million school children in the United States and abroad had learned BASIC. Currently the most popular version is Visual BASIC. It uses data typing and structuring and was first introduced in 1991.

✳**Pascal is named for Blaise Pascal (1623-1662), a seventeenth-century French mathematician.**

PASCAL computer language developer Niklaus Wirth (1934–) is a native of Switzerland who spent time studying in Canada and the United States.

This package, ready for distribution by 1977, was known as UCSD Pascal. By 1978 it began to receive national attention. The growth of personal computers helped it achieve wide acceptance in the educational community, and for almost two decades it was the language of choice for most introductory computer science courses.

Because Pascal was meant to be used as a teaching tool, its input and output functions were limited making it impractical for writing commercial applications. However, several languages including Modula-2 and Ada were based on it.

C

C is one of the descendants of ALGOL 60. It was developed in 1972 by Ken Thompson and Dennis Ritchie, both of Bell Laboratories. Their goal was to create a language that would combine high-level structured language features with those that control low-level programming. This makes C well suited for writing operating systems, compilers, and also business applications. C compilers can basically run on all machines, and since a standard for C was defined in 1988, most C programs are portable. Conversely, C has been defined as a programming language written by a programmer, which means that novices find it difficult to learn.

C supports structured programming and provides for several data types. For example, pointer arithmetic is an integral part of C, as is the use of functions that may be called recursively. Although input and output statements are not part of the language, they are functions found in a "library" ready to be used when needed. Some of the functions found in a standard UNIX C library include string manipulation, character functions, and memory allocation. In addition to external, automatic and static variables, C provides register variables, which shorten execution time because they use registers.

C makes it possible to work on bit data using the bit operators for AND, OR, Exclusive OR, One's complement, SHIFT LEFT, and SHIFT RIGHT, giving programmers great control over data manipulation.

When compared to other programming languages such as FORTRAN or Pascal, C has remained quite stable. Its success in the early 1980s was due in part to its close ties with UNIX and its availability on personal computers. Additionally it satisfied the needs of both system and application programmers alike. Several languages such as C++, Perl, and Javascript are based on C's syntax.

Ada

Development of Ada started in 1975 under the auspices of the U.S. Department of Defense (DoD) for use in its military computer systems. This action was necessary because the expense of developing and maintaining DoD programs was becoming very high due to the variety of programming languages being used. In the early 1970s, the DoD used at least 450 different computer languages and dialects.

The DoD uses most of its programming efforts to guide military equipment, such as tanks, airplanes, and nuclear bombs. Those programs execute in *real time*, at the same time as a tank is moving or an airplane is flying. For example, to perform its mission, a fighter pilot cannot wait for the computer to send back the results later in the day. Although real-time systems can operate outside of the device they are controlling, they can also be embedded within a larger system, for example a robot.

Usually real-time systems are large and multifaceted, so that the task of coordinating the programming effort is key to the success of the system. These systems have to respond to outside events, which happen in the real world, within a specific amount of time. They must be able to communicate with typical computer peripherals, such as printers and modems, as well as non-typical input and output devices like patient monitoring devices. Most importantly, real-time systems have to be reliable because in certain cases an error in the program could result in a loss of human lives. These conditions dictate that programming languages for real-time systems must be robust. That means that the compiler must detect programming errors automatically before any damage is done, and the language must provide for recovery from undetected errors.

In 1975 the High Order Language Working Group (HOLWG) was formed to find the exact language for DoD's needs. After careful study, the committee decided that none of the existing languages would be appropriate and a new one had to be developed. The foundations for the definition and design of this language were: PL/I, ALGOL 68, and Pascal. It came to be called Ada. Its development was carefully monitored; it took five years before the first reference manual was published in 1980. A revision came out in 1982, and in 1995 ANSI adopted a new standard for Ada.

Ada was developed to reduce the cost of software development and maintenance, especially for large, constantly changing programs that will be used for a long period of time. A fundamental idea of this language is the "package," which is used to divide a program into modules that can be compiled, tested separately, and stored in a library until needed. This makes large programs easier to write, debug, and maintain by teams of programmers. Another feature of Ada is that it supports **parallel processing**, including concurrently executable code segments called "tasks," which can execute independently of each other or can be synchronized to relay information between themselves.

Although Ada is not very difficult to learn at the basic level, using it to its full capacity requires programming knowledge and experience. Therefore, Ada is considered a language for advanced programmers, especially suited for large projects, real-time systems, and systems programming.

Because it is a very good language for large critical systems, Ada has achieved a high level of acceptance and is used by many organizations worldwide. Not only is most DoD code written in Ada, but the language has been used to write important non-military applications such as international air traffic control, railways, and commercial satellites. For example, programs for the French TGV rail system, Channel Tunnel, and many Global Positioning System projects are mostly written in Ada. SEE ALSO ALGOL-60 REPORT; ALGORITHMS; COMPILERS; PROGRAMMING.

Ida M. Flynn

ADA'S NAMESAKE

The Ada programming language was named after Ada Byron King, Countess of Lovelace (1815–1852), The daughter of English poet Lord George Gordon Byron, Lovelace is considered to be the first computer programmer. Lovelace worked closely with British mathematician Charles Babbage (1791–1871) in the programming of his hypothetical Analytical Engine.

parallel processing the presence of more than one central processing unit in a computer, which enables the true execution of more than one program

Bibliography

Baron, Naomi S. *Computer Languages.* Garden City, NY: Anchor Books, 1986.

Hsu, Jeffrey. *Microcomputer Languages.* Hasbrouck Heights, NJ: Hayden Book Co., 1986.

Wexelblat, Richard, ed. *History of Programming Languages.* New York: Academic Press, 1981.

Programming

Award-winning computer designer and engineer W. Daniel Hillis captured the essence of programming when he said: "The magic of a computer lies in its ability to become almost anything you can imagine, as long as you can explain exactly what that is. The hitch is in explaining exactly what you want. With the right programming a computer can become a theater, a musical instrument, a reference book, a chess opponent. No other entity in the world except a human being has such an adaptable, universal nature."

Computer programming has many facets: It is like engineering because computer programs must be carefully designed to be reliable and inexpensive to maintain. It is an art because good programs require that the programmer use intuition and a personal sense of style. It is a literary effort because programs must be understood by computers, and this requires mastery of a programming language. That is not all—programs must be analyzed to understand how they work and usually must be modified periodically to accommodate changing requirements. Therefore, as programs are written, programmers should care about how elegant they are, and they should understand how they arrived at the solution of a problem.

Techniques

Telling a computer what to do is not as easy as it sounds. Every detail of the computer's desired operation must be precisely described, and plans must be made for all possible occurrences. For example, if a store has a billing program set up to send monthly bills to all customers, then the computer will send out a bill for $0 to those who owe nothing. If one tells a computer to send a threatening letter to customers who have not paid, then those who owe nothing will receive menacing letters until they send in payments of $0! Avoiding this kind of mix-up is one aspect of computer programming. The programmer's art is stating exactly what is desired. In this example, it means making a distinction between customers who have not sent any money because they do not owe anything, and those who actually still owe money.

A combination of thorough problem definition and straightforward programming techniques lead to precise and effective programs. Therefore, programmers should observe the following steps:

- Define the problem exactly, because this constitutes about 80 percent of the difficulty of programming;

- Design the program simply because simple programs are easier to develop and maintain, and they result in more reliable, secure, robust, and efficient code;

- Execute the program with different sets of data. If possible, test the program by hand with just one input; this is a great way to find bugs, and is easy to use and understand.

The task of writing a computer program requires great attention to detail. Computers demand absolute completeness and precision in their instructions: they do only what they are told and their instructions cannot contain any **ambiguity**. This is true of all software. It applies equally to a simple program that makes a computer play a tune and to a huge program that monitors traffic at an airport.

In programming, nothing can be left to chance. Non-programmers tend to forget that actions they take for granted must be spelled out in great detail for the machine. Every action must be broken down into its most elementary parts to produce an **algorithm**. No detail, however self-evident to the human mind, can be omitted or taken for granted in a computer program. A good programmer must be capable of thinking about the big-picture that generates useful algorithms, and paying attention to the details that convert those algorithms into unambiguous computer code.

In its simplest form, an algorithm is like a recipe, but a computer programmer must specify extra steps that a cook would usually skip over. For example, a recipe might call for two eggs, without specifying that the eggs must be fresh, uncooked, and added to the mixture without the shell. If such criteria were assumed and not detailed precisely in a computer program, the recipe would fail. When hundreds or thousands of instructions covering every contingency have to be spelled out for the computer, expense naturally rises and **bugs** creep in.

Programming a computer is not something that everyone can do. It takes an analytical mind and the ability to spell out every step that a computer needs to do to complete the task at hand.

ambiguity the quality of doubtfulness or uncertainty; often subject to multiple interpretations

algorithm a rule or procedure used to solve a mathematical problem—most often described as a sequence of steps

bugs errors in program source code

flowcharts techniques for graphically describing the sequencing and structure of program source code

pseudocode a language-neutral, structural description of the algorithms that are to be used in a program

modules a generic term that is applied to small elements or components that can be used in combination to build an operational system

debug the act of trying to trace, identify, and then remove errors in program source code

There are several ways programmers can approach the problem systematically. Two of them are **flowcharts** and **pseudocode**. A flowchart is a graphic representation of the algorithm using standard symbols that can then be translated into computer language instructions. Pseudocode involves refining the problem in several stages starting with English sentences, which are then restated in subsequent steps with more computer-like words and statements.

Structured Programming

Structured programming, championed in 1968 by Dutch computer scientist Edsger W. Dijkstra, has exerted a major influence on the development of software ranging from small personal computer programs to multimillion-dollar defense projects. Only three control structures are required to turn out useful structured programs:

- Simple sequencing or instructing the computer to do one thing after another;

- Looping, or telling the computer to perform the same set of instructions while a condition holds or until a condition is met;

- Decision making, or enabling the computer's ability to branch in one of two directions depending on the outcome of a condition.

In addition, structured programs are typically divided into **modules**, which each perform one function, and do it well. The algorithms are easy to follow because there is only one logic entry into each module and one logic exit from it. Since the modules are small, usually not exceeding one page of code, they are easy to **debug**.

Programmers

A programmer's goal is not to solve a problem but to map out instructions that will let the computer find the solution. Performing rapid calculations is a job tailor-made for a computer, but designing the step-by-step algorithm that tells the computer exactly how to proceed with a given assignment is better left to human intelligence. To make the algorithm as clear as possible, a programmer always starts by assembling the known facts and setting out a clear statement of the problem. Then the programmer begins devising a logical progression of steps for the computer to follow en route to the solution. Often the programmer will use an extreme version of the problem just to see if the logic of the algorithm holds up. This test often discovers missing steps or inaccurate instructions that would cause the computer to flash error messages.

Finally, the programmer has to consider the types of data the computer will be handling and decide on the best method for storing and retrieving the data for processing. By making the right decision regarding language, logic, and programming techniques, programmers can harness the power of the computer with maximum effectiveness.

The computer programmer is the link between a problem and its computer solution. Good programmers write well-structured and clear programs that others can read and modify. Writing good programs requires creativity, but it must be tempered with great patience and intense discipline so that the resulting programs will be correct and efficient. SEE ALSO ALGO-RITHMS; COMPILERS; DESIGN TOOLS; LOGO; PROCEDURAL LANGUAGES.

Ida M. Flynn

Bibliography

Bentley, Jon. *Programming Pearls*, 2nd ed. Reading, MA: Addison-Wesley, 2000.

Hillis, W. Daniel. *The Pattern on the Stone*. New York: Basic Books, 1998.

Time-Life Books. *Understanding Computers: Software*. Alexandria, VA: Time-Life Books, 1986.

Reading Tools

Systems for recognizing printed text and images originated in the late 1950s and have been in widespread use on desktop computers since the early 1990s. Examples of such reading tools include bar code technology, optical character recognition, optical mark readers, and "smart card" technology.

Bar Code Technology

A bar code is a printed series of black parallel bars or lines of varying width on a white background that is used for entering data into a computer system. The bars represent the binary digits 0 and 1, sequences of which, in turn, can represent numbers from 0 to 9. The numbers presented by a bar code are also printed out at its base. Bar code information is read by an optical scanner such as a handheld "wand" or a bar code pen that is moved across the code or vice versa. The computer then stores or immediately processes the data in the bar code.

History of the Bar Code. As a graduate student at Drexel Institute of Technology, Bernard Silver overheard the president of a local food chain asking one of the deans to develop a system that would automatically read product information during checkout. The problem intrigued Silver so much that he and another Drexel student, Joseph Woodland, invented the "bull's eye" symbol, the **prototype** of the bar code, which was patented on October 7, 1952.

Bar code technology was first used commercially in 1966. Soon afterward, consumers and industry leaders realized that bar code standardization was needed. Thus, by 1970, Logicon, Inc. introduced the Universal Grocery Products Identification Code (UGPIC). The first company to produce bar code equipment for the retail sector using UGPIC was Monarch Marking, and for the industrial sector, Plessey Telecommunications. In 1973 UGPIC gave way to the Universal Product Code (UPC), which has been used in the United States ever since. The first UPC scanner (made by National Cash Register Co., now NCR Corp.) was installed at a Marsh's supermarket in Troy, Ohio, in June 1974. The first product to bear a bar code was a pack of Wrigley's Juicy Fruit chewing gum, which is now on display at the Smithsonian Institution's National Museum of American History.

Uses of Bar Codes. In retail, bar codes are used to obtain price information and other data about goods at the point of purchase by customers. At ski resorts, tags with codes are affixed to skiers' jackets and scanned as

---

BAR CODES AND THE MAIL

The United States Postal Service (USPS) delivers millions of pieces of mail each day. Much of the sorting and distribution process is done quickly and efficiently through the use of bar codes. As each piece of mail arrives at the processing center, it is passed through an optical character reader (OCR), which translates and prints the ZIP Code as a bar code onto the lower right corner of the envelope. Bar code sorters (BCS) then read the code and direct the mail to its destination.

prototype a working model or experimental investigation of proposed systems under development

people enter ski lifts in order to monitor patterns of slope use. In industry, bar codes are used to track products as they are manufactured, distributed, stored, sold, and serviced.

Optical Character Recognition (OCR)

Optical character recognition is the method for the machine-reading of type-set, type, and hand-printed letters, numbers, and symbols using an optical scanner and optical character software. The light reflected by a printed text or image is recorded as patterns of light and dark areas by photoelectric cells in the scanner. A computer program then analyzes the patterns and identifies the characters they represent. OCR is also used to produce text files from computer files that contain images of alphanumeric characters such as those produced by fax transmissions.

History of OCR.　Engineering attempts at automated recognition of printed characters began before World War II. However, it was not until the early 1950s that a commercial venture justified funding for research and development of such technology. The American Bankers Association and the financial services industry challenged major equipment manufacturers to develop a "common language" to process checks automatically. Although the banking industry eventually favored Magnetic Ink Character Recognition (MICR)—a branch of character recognition involving the sensing of characters containing magnetic particles to determine the character's most probable identity—some vendors had proposed the use of OCR technology.

Uses of OCR.　Any standard form or document with repetitive variable data is suitable for OCR—for example, credit card sales drafts and invoices. Perhaps the most innovative use of OCR can be found in the Kurzwell scanners that read for the blind by scanning pages and converting the text into spoken words.

Optical Mark Reader (OMR)

An Optical Mark Reader (OMR) unit scans for either the presence or absence of a mark in a particular location on a page, as specified by the user. The technology is also known as "mark sense," and it is familiar to students and teachers at all levels because it is widely used for standardized and classroom testing purposes.

OMR technology was pioneered in the United States and was first used for student assessments in the 1950s. Its introduction was related to advances in behavioral and child psychology as well as to the development of tests designed to measure various aspects of human performance. Since that time, OMR has become commonplace throughout the American education system. Although OMR has a variety of administrative applications, its major use is to score multiple-choice tests such as the SAT and GRE. Other uses include the recording of responses for surveys and questionnaires.

Smart Card Technology

Unlike the magnetic swipe card (a plastic card with a magnetic strip containing encoded data), a smart card is a plastic card containing a chip that

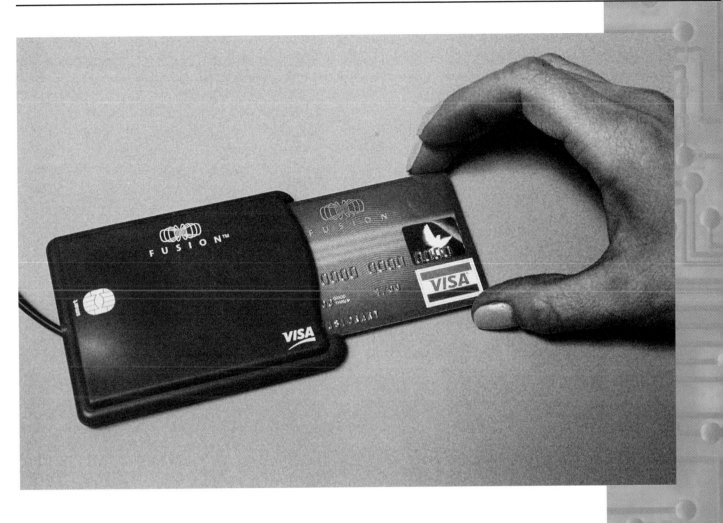

holds a microprocessor and data storage unit. Such cards have standardized electrical contacts for drawing power and for communicating with external devices.

History of Smart Cards. The first smart card-related research began in 1968 when Jürgen Dethloff and Helmut Grötrupp patented their idea of using plastic cards as a carrier for microchips. In 1973 Roland Marino developed and patented the first smart card. The first commercial field trial did not occur until 1981 when a banking chip card was tested in several French cities. In 1984 France Télécom introduced the first phone chip card. This led to widespread use in that country, followed by adoption in Germany, where patients have health records stored on such cards. In the United States, field trials were conducted for identification cards, and a pilot for an electronic purse (a.k.a. "stored value cards") took place in Atlanta, Georgia, in conjunction with the 1996 Summer Olympics.

Uses of Smart Cards. Smart card technology is used in a variety of applications, including building access systems, electronic payment schemes, and public transportation. Smart cards are also used to provide conditional access for satellite television users, and to store and retrieve information about customers and their purchases through grocery or retail "loyalty" cards. SEE ALSO INPUT DEVICES; OPTICAL CHARACTER RECOGNITION; VIDEO DEVICES.

Joyce H-S Li

Major credit card companies have invested in smart cards and readers. The card contains an imbedded computer chip that is programmable.

Bibliography

Nelson, Benjamin. *Punched Cards to Bar Codes.* Petersborough, NH: Helmers, 1997.

Rankl, Wolfgang, and Wolfgang Effing. *Smart Card Handbook*, 2nd ed., trans. Kenneth Cox. New York: John Wiley & Sons, 2000.

Schantz, Herbert F. *The History of OCR, Optical Character Recognition.* Manchester Center, VT: Recognition Technologies Users Association, 1982.

Internet Resources

History of Bar Codes. LASCO Fittings, Inc. web site. <http://www.lascofittings.com/BarCode-EDI/bc-history.htm>

Robots

The traditional romantic portrayal of the robot is as an **anthropomorphic**, **autonomous** entity that possesses intelligence and walks and talks in a way that mimics human behavior. The truth is not quite so glamorous. Robots are electromechanical machines that rarely resemble the human form. Instead, the overwhelming majority of robots are often anchored to one point and consist of a single flexible arm.

The purpose of robotics technology is essentially to carry out repetitive, physically demanding and potentially dangerous manual activities so that humans are relieved from these tasks. Examples of these chores include working on a factory production line assembly, handling hazardous materials, and dealing with hostile environments like underground mines, underwater construction sites, and explosives plants. Industrial robots can also be scheduled to work twenty-four hours a day to maximize productivity in manufacturing environments—something that human workers have never been able to do.

Conventional robots possess a base which is usually anchored to the floor, but may also be attached to a rail or gantry (platform) that permits sliding movement. An arm called a manipulator, which is flexible and is one of the main features of the robot, is connected to the base. On the tip of the arm is an attachment called the **end-effector**—this is the mounting point for interchangeable grippers or tools. The arm is moved about by using either **hydraulic** or **pneumatic** actuators, or by gears, linkages, and cables driven by electric motors. The motors used are usually of the servo or stepper type. Servo motors rotate at a required speed under command, whereas stepper motors rotate through a given angular displacement (in steps of a certain number of degrees) before stopping. In this way, controlled movement of the arm can be affected within a region known as the workspace or workcell.

Depending on the number of limbs and the type and number of joints that the arm possesses, the robot will be described as having a certain number of degrees of freedom of movement. This indicates the dexterity with which the robot can work using tools and workpieces. A typical robot of moderate complexity will have three degrees of freedom including translational movement and a rotating wrist at the end-effector. The term "payload" is used to refer to the mass that the robot is capable of lifting at the end-effector—a payload of more than 100 kilograms (220.5 pounds) is not uncommon, and loads that would be beyond the capabilities of most human

anthropomorphic having human form, or generally resembling human appearance

autonomous self governing, or being able to exist independently

end-effector the end piece of a robotic arm that can receive various types of grippers and tools

hydraulic motion being powered by a pressurized liquid (such as water or oil), supplied through tubes or pipes

pneumatic motion being powered by pressurized air, supplied through tubes or pipes

Robots are instrumental in obtaining data where humans have yet to travel. Here, NASA's Sojourner robot cuts a path across the Mermaid Dune on Mars during the Mars Pathfinder Mission.

laborers are no trouble for a suitably structured robot. In addition to handling massive payloads, some specialized robots are able to work with a high degree of precision—many guarantee accuracy of placement to within a fraction of a millimeter.

Another type of robot is the mobile robot. These offer features that are uncommon to standard industrial robots used on production lines. Instead, mobile robots often propel themselves on wheels or tracks and carry **telemetry** equipment like video cameras, microphones, and sensors of other types. The information they collect is then encoded and transmitted to a remote receiving station where human operators interpret the information and guide the mobile robot. Mobile robots are often used to handle dangerous goods like explosives, but perhaps the finest example of this type of robot was the Sojourner rover from the Mars Pathfinder Mission of 1997. This small robot demonstrated that it was possible to guide

telemetry the science of taking measurements of something and transmitting the data to a distant receiver

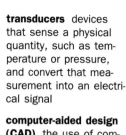

transducers devices that sense a physical quantity, such as temperature or pressure, and convert that measurement into an electrical signal

computer-aided design (CAD) the use of computers to replace traditional drawing instruments and tools for engineering or architectural design

nanotechnology the design and construction of machines at the atomic or molecular level

ROBOTIC SURGERY

Throughout the world, computer scientists are working to perfect robots to assist in and ultimately perform surgery. With the help of such robots, surgeons have more control and precision in performing operations. Plus, small robotic tools can reach places that human hands cannot. The first robotic surgical system was approved for use by the U.S. Food and Drug Administration in 2000. Called the da Vinci Surgical System, it was developed by Intuitive Surgical in California.

reliably and accurately a small robotic vehicle over the vast distance between Earth and Mars.

Beyond the source of power that is needed to animate the robot, a computer system of some sort is generally employed to control its actions. This system acts in real-time to both command the robot's movements and to monitor its actions to ensure that it is complying with instructions. Command signals are sent to the motors to initiate a movement, and special sensing devices called **transducers** are used to measure the amount of actual movement. If the actual movement does not correspond to the requested movement, then the computer system is notified and can make further adjustments. This continual measurement of the robot's activities is called feedback and is of the utmost importance in guaranteeing precise control over its movements. Three-dimensional geometry is the primary mathematical approach that is used to specify the dynamics of robots. Matrix representations of rotational and translational motion are the favored way of programming the required movements of the manipulator and the end-effector.

Frequently, one reasonably small computer is responsible for managing the movements of one robot. However, in large installations that contain many robots, it is also necessary to coordinate their collective operations effectively. This means that other computers need to be used in a supervisory role. The supervisory computer system works at a more abstract level, ensuring that overall production processes can be carried out efficiently. It passes down commands to the individual computers linked to the robots, leaving them to carry out the details of each allotted job. As an example, the supervisory computer might take a **computer-aided design (CAD)** drawing of a complex assembly and separate out various parts from the drawing, for fabrication by a collection of individual robots. The robots can be retooled for these new tasks and then the supervisory computer can dispatch to their computers coordinates and commands for grasping, moving, cutting, milling or whatever else is required—directly from the CAD drawings.

The future offers a great deal for robotics technology. Established areas of research are slowly making significant strides toward becoming mainstream. Artificial intelligence and robot vision become closer to being standard features each year. It is also proposed that microscopic robots could be developed using the results of advances in **nanotechnology**, expanding their current role in medical science, where they already assist in performing surgery. SEE ALSO ARTIFICIAL INTELLIGENCE; DIGITAL LOGIC DESIGN; NANOCOMPUTING; ROBOTICS.

Stephen Murray

Bibliography

Malcolm, Douglas R. Jr. *Robotics—An Introduction.* Belmont, CA: Wadsworth, 1985.

Shahinpoor, Mohsen. *A Robot Engineering Textbook.* New York: Harper and Row, 1987.

Snyder, Wesley E. *Industrial Robots: Computer Interfacing and Control.* Englewood Cliffs, NJ: Prentice Hall, 1985.

Internet Resources

Mars Pathfinder. National Aeronautics and Space Administration Jet Propulsion Laboratory. <http://www.jpl.nasa.gov/>

Satellite Technology

The world changed on October 4, 1957, when the Soviet Union launched the Earth's first artificial **satellite** (the Moon is a natural satellite). Sputnik, a Russian word meaning "fellow traveler," was an 83 kilogram (183-pound) satellite the size and shape of a basketball. It did little except orbit the Earth every 98 minutes and emit a simple radio signal, a recording of which can be downloaded from a National Aeronautics and Space Administration (NASA) web site (http://www.hq.nasa.gov/office/pao/History/sputnik/). Yet, this simple event started what was to be known as "The Space Race" that eventually led to the lunar landings as well as space shuttle missions, and weather and direct broadcast television satellites.

Although the satellite concept is theoretically simple—an object placed high enough above Earth's atmosphere to be moving at a speed of eight km/sec (17,280 miles/hour)—the successful launch, orbital insertion, and control of any satellite is extremely complex. This is evidenced by the many failures that occurred before Sputnik (and since). However, as of 2002 there are more than 2,670 artificial satellites orbiting Earth. In addition to these, the U.S. Space Command is also tracking 6,186 pieces of space debris. This demonstrates that humans have not only mastered satellite technology but also succeeded in extending well-developed littering capabilities into space.

A satellite's orbit is described in one or more of three dimensions: the *perigee*, its closest distance from the Earth; the *apogee*, its furthest distance from the Earth; and, its *inclination*, the angle the orbit makes with the equa-

satellite an object that orbits a planet

In 1957 the basketball-sized Sputnik (pictured) weighed 83 kilograms or 183 pounds. In contrast, NASA's Extreme Ultraviolet Explorer, which was launched in 1992 and re-entered the Earth's atmosphere in early 2002, weighed 3,175 kilograms or 7,000 pounds.

protocols agreed understanding for the sub-operations that make up transactions; usually found in the specification of inter-computer communications

ubiquitous to be commonly available everywhere

tor. Satellites are put into particular types of orbit depending on their mission. In a geostationary orbit, the satellite speed is synchronized with the Earth's rotation so that the satellite stays in the same relative position. A polar orbit is characterized by its 90-degree inclination to Earth's equator. When a satellite is in low Earth orbit, the apogee and perigee are each only about 483 kilometers or 300 miles.

Types of Satellites

Most satellites today are in place for communication, environmental monitoring, or navigational purposes. There are both government and commercial satellites in space.

Communication. Of all satellite technologies, communication technology has probably had the greatest impact on our world. It has been called one of the greatest forces for the "super-tribalization" of the human species. Communication satellites have also proven to be one of the most successful commercial applications of space technology. In 2002 there are about 200 communication satellites orbiting above Earth.

The first telephone communication satellites, ECHO and Telstar, were launched in 1960 and 1962, respectively. These and many subsequent satellites carried analog signals to all parts of the world. Because the computer resources in such satellites were minimal, in computer terms they could be called "dumb," since they were, for the most part, simple passive transceivers.

However, the demands of the Internet and personal communication devices such as pagers and wireless phones have resulted in radically changed communication satellite technologies. Present satellites not only utilize digital signals and processing but also, in some systems, provide satellite-to-satellite communications. Perhaps this was nowhere more evident than in the Iridium system, a constellation of 66 Low Earth Orbit (LEO) communication satellites that featured sophisticated computer resources and **protocols** for inter-satellite communication.

Television broadcast or, more precisely, relay, from satellite also began in 1962 with the launch of the Relay satellite. This technology has similarly improved, as is evidenced by the shrinking sizes of the **ubiquitous** home satellite "dishes" that, owing to greater satellite transmission power and other advances in technology, are now almost unnoticeable.

Environmental Monitoring. The view from a geostationary environmental satellite is often shown during televised weather broadcasts. The Geostationary Operational Environmental Satellites (GOES) orbit simultaneously with the Earth's rotation at an altitude of just under 37,115 kilometers or 23,000 miles. Typically, there are two such satellites in orbit stationed to offer views of both the eastern and western parts of the United States. The GOES are true environmental satellites; in addition to images of the clouds, they also provide information on water vapor, land and sea temperatures, winds, and estimates of precipitation.

Landsat is also an environmental as well as a natural resource satellite. Over the last 30 years, seven Landsat satellites have been launched and two are currently in polar, sun-synchronous orbits. A sun-synchronous orbit is one in which the satellite passes over points on the ground at the same local time. Landsat's multi-spectral scanner (MSS) and thematic mapper imag-

A researcher at NASA Ames Research Center in California tests out a softball-sized personal satellite assistant (PSA), which includes environmental sensors, video conferencing cameras, propulsion components, and navigation sensors.

ing systems provide digital imagery over discrete sections of the visible and infrared portions of the electromagnetic spectrum. Such multi-spectral imagery and its analyses are routinely used in environmental studies such as deforestation, water pollution, tracking oil spills, and monitoring forest fires and droughts. It is also utilized in natural resource studies such as land use classification, vegetation and soil mapping, and geological, hydrological, and coastal resource studies.

Navigation. Lines of latitude and longitude have been noted on maps since ancient times. Yet, the accurate determination of one's exact position on the Earth has always been a vexing problem. Perhaps at no time was this more evident than during the eighteenth century when scholars and inventors vied to solve the problem of accurately determining longitude at sea. Such a determination required a highly accurate (and stable) clock,

since it was necessary to know simultaneously the time on the ship and at a land-based point of known longitude. It is interesting to note that the problem of determining accurate time was the basis of accurate position determination then, as it is also the basis of today's most accurate world-wide satellite navigation or position system. Indeed the navigation satellites of the twenty-first century have precise clocks that are accurate to within three nanoseconds, or three billionths of a second.

The navigational system known as the Global Positioning System (GPS) is a constellation of 24 NAVSTAR (NAVigation Satellite Timing And Ranging) satellites orbiting at 20,278 kilometers or 12,600 miles altitude in six orbital planes. Each orbital plane is at an inclination of 55 degrees with four satellites spaced so that a minimum of five satellites is visible from any location on the planet. Each satellite broadcasts time and orbit information. Receivers on the ground also contain internal clocks. The difference in time between when a signal was sent and when it was received from each observable satellite is used to solve a spherical **trigonometry** problem to determine the exact location of the observer. With certain receiver systems, this satellite technology means that someone's exact position on the surface of the Earth can be determined to within one centimeter or four-tenths of an inch! SEE ALSO COMMUNICATION DEVICES; TELECOMMUNICATIONS; WIRELESS TECHNOLOGY.

Robert D. Regan

trigonometry a branch of mathematics founded upon the geometry of triangles

Bibliography

Sobel, Dava. *Longitude.* New York: Walker and Company, 1995.

Internet Resources

"GOES Next at a Glance." *USA Today.* 6 January 1999. <http://www.usatoday.com/weather/wds10.htm>

Edelson, Burton I., Joseph N. Pelton, and Neil R. Helm. *NASA/NSF Panel Report: Satellite Communication Systems and Technology* (1993 Study). <http://itri.loyola.edu/ar93_94/scst.htm>

Security Hardware

The use of hardware to provide or enhance security dates from the early days of shared or multi-user computing systems. The Multics system (Multiplexed Information and Computing Service), developed in the 1960s and 1970s, was one of the first to use hardware mechanisms to isolate user processes from each other and from the operating system core and utility functions, and to permit sharing of information according to a well-defined security policy. In 1985 Multics was given a highly coveted B2 "Orange Book" security rating by the **National Computer Security Center (NCSC)**, the first such designation granted by the government to a computer security system. The Multics system was in operation in many organizations and institutions from the mid-1960s until the last Multics installation was decommissioned in 2000.

The history of Multics and subsequent systems has demonstrated that it is difficult to design and implement software to provide security, even with adequate hardware support in the **central processing unit (CPU)**. The LOCK by Secure Computing Corporation used a security coprocessor, a sec-

National Computer Security Center (NCSC) a branch of the National Security Agency responsible for evaluating secure computing systems; the *Trusted Computer Systems Evaluation Criteria* (TCSEC) were developed by the NCSC

central processing unit (CPU) the part of a computer that performs computations and controls and coordinates other parts of the computer

ondary CPU with its own address space, which controlled the memory and device accesses of user processes that run in the primary CPU. This isolated the security enforcement mechanism from potentially hostile user code. Most present day hardware processors support memory management systems and multiple CPU privilege modes that can be used to provide process isolation. However, few operating systems take full advantage of them.

Hardware **authentication** "tokens" are frequently used to reduce the risks associated with transmitting passwords over lines that might be subject to interception. These tokens establish security systems that are a combination of "Something you have (the token), plus something you know (a password or PIN)." The first such system, Polonius, was developed in the mid-1980s by Ray Wong, Tom Berson, and Rich Feiertag of Sytek, Inc.

In the Polonius system, each token contains a keypad, an encryption device with a key, and a display. The key is protected with a **PIN (personal identification number)** known only to the user. Authentication is done as follows: When the user is identified to the remote computer with a user ID or account name, this information is used by the computer to look up its copy of the key shared with the Polonius device. The computer then generates a random number, which is sent to the user as a challenge, and encrypts the number with its copy of the user's key. The user enters both a PIN and the challenge number into the Polonius device. The Polonius device uses its copy of the key, modified if an incorrect PIN is given, to encrypt the challenge and display the result. The user sends the result to the remote computer, which compares it with its own result. The user is granted access only if the results agree. Because the challenge is a large, randomly generated number, an observer who captures both the challenge and the response is unlikely to be able to use them again.

A number of similar devices exist. Some simply display a password that changes every minute or so, based on a key associated with the token and an internal clock that must be synchronized with the remote computer. In this case, the PIN is transmitted along with the token, placing the user at risk should the token be stolen after the PIN has been intercepted. On other tokens, the user enters the PIN into the token where it is combined with a time-dependent value before encryption, giving a password that is valid for a minute or so.

Authentication tokens represent a simple example of a cryptographic processor. Specialized cryptographic hardware can be combined with general purpose computers to enhance security in a number of ways. It is increasingly common to provide encryption as a part of communications devices, such as wireless cards or wired network links. Encryption hardware can also be incorporated into disk controllers or disk drives. Although encryption **algorithms** can be implemented in software, they are computationally intensive. In addition, the encryption keys used are likely to appear in the computer's memory and can often be recovered from the **swap files** maintained on disk by the operating system.

Certain cryptographic coprocessors such as Dallas Semiconductor's Crypto iButton can be used to generate and maintain cryptographic keys that are extremely difficult for unauthorized users to extract. These devices also contain general purpose processors that can be used with the crypto-

THE "ORANGE BOOK"

Called the "Orange Book," the TCSEC (or *Trusted Computer Systems Evaluation Criteria*) contained the basic criteria for evaluating computer systems intended to handle sensitive or classified material. It divided the systems into four classes: D (no security features), C (user-based access controls), B (mandatory access controls based on information classification and user clearance), and A (the same as B, with formal assurance arguments). Class B2 systems enforce security based on a clearly defined and documented formal security policy model. The security enforcement must be carefully structured into protection-critical and non-protection-critical elements. Multics' hardware isolation mechanisms played a key role in meeting these requirements.

authentication the act of ensuring that an object or entity is what it is intended to be

PIN (personal identification number) a password, usually numeric, used in conjunction with a cryptographic token, smart card, or bank card, to ensure that only an authorized user can activate an account

algorithms rules or procedures used to solve a mathematical problem— most often described as sequences of steps

swap files files used by an operating system to support a virtual memory system, in which the user appears to have access to more memory than is physically available

PUBLIC KEY INFRASTRUCTURE (PKI)

A public key infrastructure (PKI) is a system designed to facilitate the use of public/ private keys in encryption. The public keys are published but a private one is held securely by each individual in the network. A message can be sent to individuals using the public key to encrypt it, but only the holder of the private key can decipher it.

graphic hardware. The iButton is about the size and shape of a watch battery and is extremely durable and tamper-resistant. The processor contains a Java virtual machine that complies with recent Java **smart card** standards. The iButton has been used to develop a variety of security-related applications such as secure postage meters for the issuance of postage from a home computer and the management of certificates for a public key infrastructure (PKI). SEE ALSO Privacy; Security; Security Software.

John McHugh

Bibliography

Organick, Elliot I. *The Multics System: An Examination of its Structure.* Cambridge, MA: MIT Press, 1972.

Saydjari, O. Sami, Joseph M. Beckman, and Jeffrey R. Leaman. "LOCK Trek: Navigating Uncharted Space." *Proceedings of the 1989 IEEE Symposium on Security and Privacy*, Oakland, CA, May, 1989, pp. 167-175.

Wong, Raymond M., Thomas A. Berson, and Richard J. Feiertag. "Polonius: An Identity Authentication System." *Proceedings of the 1985 IEEE Symposium on Security and Privacy*, Oakland, CA, April 1985, pp. 101-107.

Internet Resources

Multics. <http://www.multicians.org/>

Security Software

Security involves making sure the good guys get in and the bad guys stay out. Throughout the development of the computer, security has been an increasingly important consideration. Software has evolved to include security functions, and with the advent of the Internet and large networks, security has become a daily issue. In fact, security software is considered by many in the computer industry to be a "necessary evil."

At the core of any security software process is the fundamental proposition that the level of risk associated with electronic data (often called an information asset) is the product of the data's value, threats, and vulnerabilities. Understanding this risk and being able to determine its relative rating are key components of security. As the significance of any of these factors increases, the risk also increases. Conversely, reducing any of these factors will significantly reduce the relevant risk. All three factors must be understood before it is possible to assess risk in a reliable manner.

- *Asset Value* is measured in terms of importance of data to the organization's business, operations, or ongoing support.
- *Threats* are measured in terms of events or actions that could have a negative impact on the availability, integrity, or confidentiality of an information asset. Threats are typically evaluated in terms of the source (internal or external), nature (structured or unstructured), and agents (hostile or non-hostile).
- *Vulnerabilities* are measured in terms of the absence, inadequacy, or inconsistency of facilities and processes that are deployed to protect the asset's value from the identified threats.

Basic Structure

Security software has been incorporated into large computer systems for many years. The basic proposition is to lock up and protect computing re-

U.S. President Bill Clinton met with leaders from the computer and technology industries to discuss Internet security measures after hackers broke into e-commerce sites. Among those with Clinton are attorney general Janet Reno and Douglas Bush of Intel Corporation.

sources (data and programs) from unauthorized use and access. Large computing systems typically use the following three-part scheme: (1) Identification; (2) Authentication; (3) Authorization.

Identification is usually done with a user identification (userid) indicator. The userid can be similar to the person's name or it can be a totally arbitrary indicator (i.e., JOHN1 or WX99RCA).

Authentication is the process of proving that you are really who you say you are. It is typically accomplished using a password or secret phrase. The password is known only to the user and allows the security software to ensure (with a limited degree of comfort) that users are, in fact, who they purport to be.

Authorization, the last step, assigns the userid the appropriate privileges within the system once identification and authentication have been completed.

While these steps sound easy enough, it can be difficult to provide assurance that the person attempting to gain access is actually an authorized user. Userids tend to be publicly known or easily guessed. Passwords are often guessed or not changed with sufficient frequency. And creative people can come up with new ways to circumvent the process. As a result, security software has become more sophisticated.

A Brief History

Before networks and the Internet, security software was much easier to create, manage, and even understand. Individual machines and their software could be protected from unauthorized use through the use of protection programs that ensured that only one authorized user could gain entry to the machine's capabilities. In most cases, this involved a userid tied to the individual machine. Some software systems also allowed the user to restrict access to the data and software housed in the individual machine.

Once **local area networks (LANs)** and other connection capabilities (i.e., the Internet) appeared, security software became a top priority. From the smallest to the largest network, it was necessary to make sure that the system was secure from attack, theft, or other malicious use. This required security software functionality to increase. In addition, the number of system components to be protected multiplied as people added capabilities to their networks. The advent of business transactions over the Internet (e-commerce) has led to great advances in security software.

Summary

Security software has evolved as the systems it protects have grown in complexity and capabilities. There are basic activities that any security software performs. Specialized needs can be accommodated with more complex software programs.

Selecting the appropriate security software requires a careful analysis of several criteria including degrees of risk and vulnerability; types of assets to be protected; budget considerations; the security policy underlying the system; implementation resources; and auditing processes to test system security. As computing technology grows, security software will continue to develop in sophistication and function. SEE ALSO Invasive Programs; Privacy; Security; Security Hardware; Viruses.

Richard Archer

Bibliography

Allen, Julia H. *The CERT Guide to System and Network Security Practices.* Boston: Addison-Wesley, 2001.

Goncalves, Marcus. *Firewalls: A Complete Guide.* New York: McGraw-Hill, 2000.

Internet Resources

Symantec. <http://www.symantec.com/>

Information Systems Security Association. <http://www.issa.org/>

The Information Systems Audit and Control Association and Foundation. <http://www.isaca.org/>

local area networks (LANs) high-speed computer networks designed for users who are located near each other

buses groups of related signals that form interconnecting pathways between two or more electronic devices

Serial and Parallel Transmission

Digital data transmission can occur in two basic modes: serial or parallel. Data within a computer system is transmitted via parallel mode on **buses** with the width of the parallel bus matched to the word size of the computer system. Data between computer systems is usually transmitted in **bit serial mode**. Consequently, it is necessary to make a parallel-to-serial conversion at a computer **interface** when sending data from a computer system into a network and a serial-to-parallel conversion at a computer interface when receiving information from a network. The type of transmission mode used may also depend upon distance and required data rate.

Parallel Transmission

In parallel transmission, multiple **bits** (usually 8 bits or a byte/character) are sent simultaneously on different channels (wires, frequency channels) within the same cable, or radio path, and **synchronized** to a clock. Parallel devices have a wider data bus than serial devices and can therefore transfer data in words of one or more bytes at a time. As a result, there is a speedup in parallel transmission bit rate over serial transmission bit rate. However, this speedup is a tradeoff versus cost since multiple wires cost more than a single wire, and as a parallel cable gets longer, the synchronization timing between multiple channels becomes more sensitive to distance. The timing for parallel transmission is provided by a constant clocking signal sent over a separate wire within the parallel cable; thus parallel transmission is considered **synchronous**.

Serial Transmission

In serial transmission, bits are sent **sequentially** on the same channel (wire) which reduces costs for wire but also slows the speed of transmission. Also, for serial transmission, some overhead time is needed since bits must be assembled and sent as a unit and then disassembled at the receiver.

Serial transmission can be either synchronous or **asynchronous**. In synchronous transmission, groups of bits are combined into frames and frames are sent continuously with or without data to be transmitted. In asynchronous transmission, groups of bits are sent as independent units with start/stop flags and no data link synchronization, to allow for arbitrary size gaps between frames. However, start/stop bits maintain physical bit level synchronization once detected.

Applications

Serial transmission is between two computers or from a computer to an external device located some distance away. Parallel transmission either takes place within a computer system (on a computer bus) or to an external device located a close distance away.

A special computer chip known as a universal asynchronous receiver transmitter (UART) acts as the interface between the parallel transmission of the computer bus and the serial transmission of the serial port. UARTs differ in performance capabilities based on the amount of on-chip memory they possess.

Examples

Examples of parallel mode transmission include connections between a computer and a printer (parallel printer port and cable). Most printers are within

bit serial mode a method of transferring binary bits one after another in a sequence or serial stream

interface a boundary or border between two or more objects or systems; also a point of access

bits plural of bit, a single binary digit, 1 or 0—a contraction of Binary digIT; the smallest unit for storing data in a computer

synchronized events occurring at specific points in time with respect to one another

synchronous synchronized behavior

sequentially operations occurring in order, one after another

asynchronous events that have no systematic relationship to one another in time

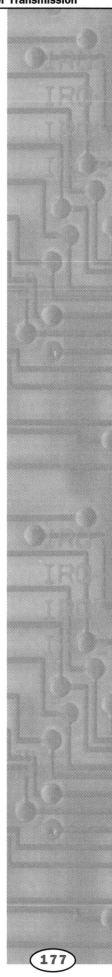

6 meters or 20 feet of the transmitting computer and the slight cost for extra wires is offset by the added speed gained through parallel transmission of data.

Examples of serial mode transmission include connections between a computer and a modem using the RS-232 **protocol**. Although an RS-232 cable can theoretically accommodate 25 wires, all but two of these wires are for overhead control signaling and not data transmission; the two data wires perform simple serial transmission in either direction. In this case, a computer may not be close to a modem, making the cost of parallel transmission prohibitive—thus speed of transmission may be considered less important than the economical advantage of serial transmission.

Tradeoffs

Serial transmission via RS-232 is officially limited to 20 **Kbps** for a distance of 15 meters or 50 feet. Depending on the type of media used and the amount of external interference present, RS-232 can be transmitted at higher speeds, or over greater distances, or both. Parallel transmission has similar distance-versus-speed tradeoffs, as well as a clocking threshold distance. Techniques to increase the performance of serial and parallel transmission (longer distance for same speed or higher speed for same distance) include using better transmission media, such as **fiber optics** or conditioned cables, implementing repeaters, or using shielded/multiple wires for noise immunity.

Technology

To resolve the speed and distance limitations of serial transmission via RS-232, several other serial transmission standards have been developed including RS-449, V.35, Universal Serial Bus (USB), and IEEE-1394 (Firewire). Each of these standards has different electrical, mechanical, functional, and procedural characteristics. The electrical characteristics define voltage levels and timing of voltage level changes. Mechanical characteristics define the actual connector shape and number of wires. Common mechanical interface standards associated with parallel transmission are the DB-25 and Centronics connectors. The Centronics connector is a 36-pin parallel interface that also defines electrical signaling. Functional characteristics specify the operations performed by each pin in a connector; these can be classified into the broad categories of data, control, timing, and electrical ground. The procedural characteristics or protocol define the sequence of operations performed by pins in the connector. SEE ALSO ASYNCHRONOUS AND SYNCHRONOUS TRANSMISSION; ATM TRANSMISSION; INTERNET; TELECOMMUNICATIONS.

William J. Yurcik

Bibliography

Stallings, William. *Data and Computer Communications*, 6th ed. Upper Saddle River, NJ: Prentice Hall, 2000.

Simulators

One area experiencing rapid growth in the use of computers in recent years is simulation. Simulations are used for training in procedures that would be

---

protocol an agreed understanding for the sub-operations that make up a transaction; usually found in the specification of inter-computer communications

Kbps a measure of digital data transfer per unit time—one thousand (kilo, K) bits per second

fiber optics transmission technology using long, thin strands of glass fiber; internal reflections in the fibers assure that light entering one end is transmitted to the other end with only small losses in intensity; used widely in transmitting digital information

too dangerous or expensive to perform in real life. Some simulations are even used for routine and repetitive tasks. As computers become more powerful, the variety of things that they can imitate becomes larger, and the accuracy of the simulations is better.

Aviation was among the first fields to use simulation. Today, military and airline pilots spend much of their time interacting with the computers that are flying the airplane. Computers have taken over both the mundane and the most difficult piloting tasks. The mundane tasks are automated because in many cases they are more distracting than they are worth. The difficult tasks are automated to increase efficiency and safety. The pilot of an aircraft approaching a busy terminal area with a low, thick cloud cover need not hand-fly the instrument landing procedure when a computer is on board carrying all the information necessary for the task and programmed to follow all the steps in order without making a mistake.

Even with good autopilots and computers, human pilots must still monitor the systems and be ready to recognize failures and take over the controls. Pilots of highly automated aircraft have training that involves all of the computer systems. They must be put into situations where events occur that might not happen in years of routine flight so that they can see how they and their systems react. Most of these situations are dangerous: engine fires, hail storms, and electrical failures, for example.

Two airline captains view a virtual version of Boston's Logan Airport from a Boeing 737-300 flight simulator. The pilots gain familiarity with the international airport through the simulator located at the United Flight Center in Denver, Colorado.

interface a boundary or border between two or more objects or systems; also a point of access

It is not sensible or possible to put pilots and multi-million dollar aircraft at risk for training purposes. Fortunately, for every computer advance that makes the cockpit more automated, there is an advance that makes it easier to create an artificial environment for training that is closer to reality. Simulations of real airplanes are now of such high fidelity that a pilot training on them can legally log actual flying time.

Simulators of aircraft are of two types: fixed-base and motion-base. The main purpose of a fixed-base simulator is to enable a student to practice complex procedures in a specialized environment. Many part-task trainers exist for the trainee to concentrate on one set of events or components, such as the **interface** to the computer systems. At the high end of the scale of fixed-base simulators is a stationary version of the forward area of an airliner cockpit.

As desktop computers become more powerful and graphics capability increases, procedures trainers can be created out of one computer system. The simulator can configure itself to be a different airplane in a few seconds. In contrast, current simulators, both fixed- and motion-base, would have to be rebuilt to represent a different airplane. There is research underway to take advantage of improved hardware and software by enabling a larger simulator to simulate several cockpits using very big displays to show instruments graphically.

Motion-base simulators are much different. The hallmark of the very best motion-base simulators is the complete cockpit. Every instrument, lever, and control in the cockpit is exactly the same as on the aircraft. In most cases, the equipment is on the same maintenance and replacement schedule as that in real airplanes. This means that when an airline pilot comes to his airline's simulator center for transition or recurrent training, there is complete carryover back to operations.

From the outside, a motion-base simulator looks like a box on stilts. The box contains the cockpit and the instructor's stations. The stilts are hydraulically actuated pistons that can move the box in response to control inputs by the pilot. In the earlier days of these simulators, they only operated on three axes. So, the feel was close, but not quite right. Currently, most motion-base simulators move with six degrees of freedom. They can mix roll and yaw, pitch and roll, and so on, in order to give the pilots a more realistic feel. This improvement is due to advances in computer technology.

On top of the front of the cockpit are image generators connected to computers in an adjacent machine room. The image generators place scenes on the windows of the cockpit. Full-color, daylight imaging is available, but very expensive. Many airlines opt for dusk/dark imaging. The outside scene appears to be well after sunset. Buildings are in ghostly light, cars have their lights on, forests are shades of greys. Aside from making the simulator less costly, it also forces pilots to practice in what is the most common time of day for accidents: twilight.

Inside the cockpit, the flight deck from the forward bulkhead (where the door to the cabin would be in a real airplane) to the nose is a precise copy of the actual aircraft. Just off the flight deck is a rectangular room containing a workstation for the instructor and a maintenance terminal for the software and hardware technicians. These technicians work in three shifts.

The simulators are in use twenty-four hours a day. Time not used by the owner airline can be rented out to another airline's crews and instructors.

A typical motion-base simulator has several different computer systems to create artificial reality. The main computer is often a 32-bit word-size machine, like the average desktop. FORTRAN programs reside in this computer to analyze control inputs and send commands to the hydraulics and the instruments. The commands travel on an ARINC 429 serial data **bus**—the standard bus in actual commercial aircraft. Another system drives displays and handles input and output to the instructor's station. Three large cabinets of image generation hardware—one for the front generators, one for each side—complete the system.

bus a group of related signals that form an interconnecting pathway between two or more electronic devices

The best thing about the simulator is that it can do some things that would be impossible in real life. It can return the simulation to a marked point for repetitive practice, say at 2,438 kilometers (8,000 feet) and 24 kilometers (15 miles) from the runway. After a few keystrokes, the entire airplane is transported from the landing point back up into the air. The movement of the simulation can be frozen at any point and then resumed at that point. An approach to landing in instrument conditions can be run a few feet at a time for teaching purposes.

The pilots who do the training emphasize to their students that they should treat the simulator just like a real airplane. That way they can get the maximum benefit from the training. In fact, the simulator makes it easy to maintain the illusion. Sitting on the simulated ramp in Indianapolis, for example, pilots can see the terminal building and the lights of cars going by on Interstate 70 in the distance. Beginning to taxi to the active runway, the building moves out of view and the taxiway lights pass by the windows. The runway is a dark ribbon bordered by its rows of lights.

Pilots are not the only ones trained for complex tasks using simulation. Nuclear reactor operators, air traffic controllers, and astronauts are all able to take advantage of computer power to create a virtual world that allows them to practice their occupation safely and cheaply. SEE ALSO ARTIFICIAL INTELLIGENCE; ROBOTICS; SIMULATION; VIRTUAL REALITY; VIRTUAL REALITY IN EDUCATION.

James E. Tomayko

Bibliography

Campbell-Kelly, Martin, and William Aspray. *Computer: A History of the Information Machine.* New York: Basic Books, 1996.

Ceruzzi, Paul E. "Advances in Simulation, Testing, and Control." In *Beyond the Limits: Flight Enters the Computer Age.* Boston: MIT Press, 1989.

Sound Devices

Sound devices are computer peripherals that produce, manipulate, or record sound or electronic signals representing sound. Virtually all modern music and movie sound production is done digitally using computer sound devices.

Speakers and Signals

Whether it is in a computer, a pair of headphones, or a stereo system, a speaker produces sound by causing the cone (external surface) to vibrate.

The cone, often made of paper, is attached to the voice coil, an electromagnet. Behind the voice coil is a second magnet. By sending a positive or negative electrical signal to the voice coil, it is alternatively attracted to and repelled from the second magnet. By continuously alternating the signal between positive and negative, the voice coil, and therefore the cone, can be made to vibrate. The faster the material vibrates, the higher the frequency of the sound; the larger the vibration, the louder the sound.

Figure 1. An electronic (analog) sound signal.

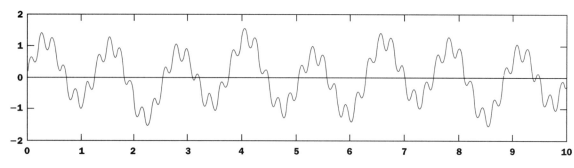

Digital Sound

Instead of directly recording or manipulating a continuous, continuously varying (analog) signal, sound devices record a digital signal, which is a series of whole numbers, represented in binary notation, at regular intervals. For example, a compact disc records a number between 0 and 65,535 at a rate of 44,100 times per second. In order to move from the analog world of speakers and microphones to the digital one, a device must sample (measure), quantize (divide), and compand (renumber) the signal.

First, the analog signal is sampled once in each interval (in this example, every 1/44,100 of a second). Any changes that happen between samples are lost. Second, the entire range of the signal, from zero volume to full volume, is quantized into sections (in this example, 65,535 of them) and the value of each sample is moved to the closest quantization level (dividing line). Third, each dividing line is renumbered, or companded, to be a whole number (in this example, between 0 and 65,535).

Figures 2 & 3. (Top) An analog sound signal with sample points. (Bottom) A sampled analog sound signal.

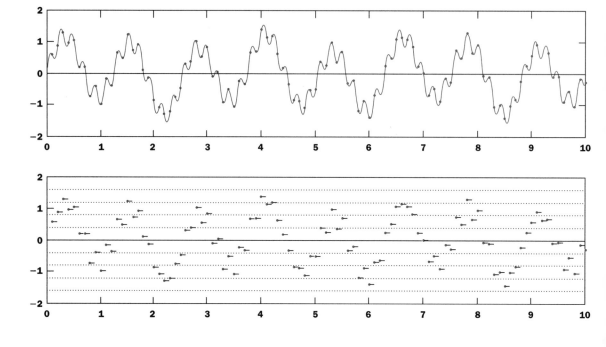

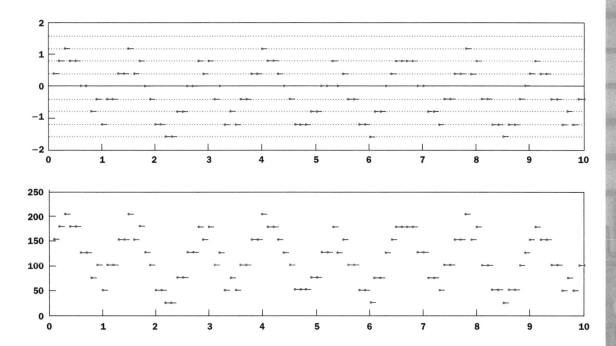

Figures 4 & 5. (Top) A quantized sound signal. (Bottom) A companded sound signal.

These samples can now be easily converted into binary data (in this example, 16 bits per sample) and recorded to a digital medium such as a hard drive, floppy drive, or compact disc. In order to reconstruct (play back) the sound, the binary data are read from the media, companded back to the original range (no volume to full volume), and each sample is played until a new sample is found (in this example, every 1/44,100 of a second).

Encoding and Compression

Converting an analog signal to a digital one is called "encoding." The encoding method described earlier is Linear Pulse Coding Modulation. This means that the quantization levels are equally spaced (linear), the signal is sampled regularly (pulse), the signal is encoded (coding), and the signal is being converted from an analog signal (modulation). The human ear, however, is better at detecting changes in quiet sounds than those in loud sounds. In linear encoding, then, the ear often cannot distinguish between two adjacent levels in loud sound.

Most encoding methods take advantage of this by placing the levels very close together at low volumes and further apart for high volumes. Every sound format (e.g., WAVE from Microsoft and IBM, AIFF from Apple, μ-Law from NeXT and Sun Microsystems) has its own method of nonlinear quantization, though most space the levels logarithmically.

With carefully chosen quantization levels, sound can take roughly four fewer bits per sample than a linearly encoded sound of the same quality. In general, if the digital signal is changed to contain less information (e.g., fewer bits per sample), then the signal has been "compressed."

Compression is important because it takes an extraordinary amount of binary code to represent high-quality digital sound. A three-minute song, recorded accurately enough for the human ear, requires 30 megabytes of storage. A compact disc, though it can store more than 700 megabytes of data, can only hold 74 minutes of music.

lossy a nonreversible way of compressing digital images, making images take up less space by permanently removing parts that cannot be easily seen anyway

sound card a plug-in card for a computer that contains hardware devices for sound processing, conversion, and generation

Many encoding techniques compress the data after they have been digitized (sampled) and companded. Though these techniques are "**lossy**" (they degrade the quality of the recording), like non-linear encoding, they take advantage of characteristics of human hearing to minimize the audible effect of those losses. No matter what method is used, however, there is always a trade off between the quality of the sound and the amount of compression.

Like companding, there are many methods of compression. The MPEG-2 Layer III (MP3) format is particularly popular because it can compress sound by a factor of ten while reliably reproducing popular music. It also allows the user to trade off compression for quality by explicitly specifying the number of bits per second of music.

There are many other methods of encoding and compression, both public (e.g., differential pulse code modulation, adaptive differential pulse code modulation) and proprietary (e.g., RealAudio from RealNetworks, Advanced Streaming Format from Microsoft). The Musical Instrument Digital Interface (MIDI) is a method for electronic instruments to communicate and is also a form of encoding. Instead of encoding analog signals, it encodes the length, pitch, volume, and instrument of each note.

Sound Cards

In a computer, digital sound data are read from a medium and decoded or uncompressed by the central processing unit, but the **sound card** performs the signal processing (companding, quantization, mixing, etc.). It is the sound card that digitizes the signal from the microphone or other input device or converts it to analog for the speakers.

In the case of MIDI encoding, the digital data only includes qualitative data about notes, but no actual recorded sound. For MIDI, sound cards have methods for emulating specific instruments. In "wave table synthesis," the sound card itself contains a short recording of each instrument, and is very accurate because it is based upon recordings of real instruments. In "frequency modulation synthesis" (FM synthesis), the sound card contains information about how to simulate each instrument. This method is less realistic because the simulation is not exact. In either case, by shifting the frequency of samples and combining them according to the MIDI data, the sound card can reproduce an entire piece of music. By using polyphony (imitating more than one instrument at the same time), the sound card can simulate entire groups of instruments.

Sound cards have other techniques for enhancing sound or making it more realistic. "Head-related transfer functions" allow the device to warp the music in order to make the sound seem to originate from somewhere other than the speakers. Digital filters can boost or change components of the sound (e.g., boost the bass) in ways that are difficult and expensive on analog equipment. Digital devices also rarely lose accuracy over time as all analog devices do.

Social Issues

Music, like any artistic work, is copyrighted under U.S. law. Like patents, copyrights were created so that people could make their work public without losing the right to protect and profit from their work. Copyright law dictates that the copyright holder has control over the distribution of the work, for profit or otherwise.

Though making audiotape "mixes" for other people is illegal, the labor-intensive quality of making them and the degradation of quality associated with copying from one tape to another has limited its popularity. Digital technology created new ways for users to "share" music widely without the sound quality problems associated with tape recordings. During the late 1990s, the speed of modern computers, the availability of high-speed Internet connections for private use, the low price of computer compact disc players and recorders, and the wide availability of compression techniques like MP3, turned computers into tools for obtaining and storing enormous amounts of music. These collections, like taped mixes, are only legal if their owner purchased the original tape or compact disc as well.

By the end of the twentieth century, the illegal copying and distribution of music became so widespread that the music industry feared such actions were substantially infringing on the rights of the copyright holders. The music industry began experimenting with cryptographic methods for ensuring that music is not copied. Industry watchers know that any solutions are likely to be temporary, since digital security is always vulnerable to the efforts of technologically savvy programmers who seek ways to break through new digital boundaries. SEE ALSO Codes; Coding Techniques; Music, Computer.

Salvatore Domenick Desiano

Bibliography

Berg, Richard E., and David G. Stork. *The Physics of Sound*, 2nd ed. Upper Saddle River, NJ: Prentice Hall, 1995.

Haring, Bruce. *Beyond the Charts: MP3 and the Digital Music Revolution*. Los Angeles, CA: JM Northern Media, LLC, 2000.

Kientzle, Tim. *A Programmer's Guide to Sound*. Reading, MA: Addison-Wesley, 1998.

Pohlmann, Ken. *Principles of Digital Audio*, 4th ed. New York: McGraw-Hill Professional Publishing, 2000.

SQL

Databases are designed, built, and populated with data for a specific purpose and for an intended group of users. Databases are built for many different users, including banks, hospitals, high schools, government agencies, and manufacturing companies. The data contained in databases vary and can include account, patient, student, employee, planning, or product data. Users of a database can add new records, insert or change data in existing records, retrieve data from existing records, or delete records from the database.

Databases are designed, built, maintained, and queried using a set of tools called a database management system (DBMS). Often, the DBMS is considered the user interface to the database system because everything else is invisible to the user. The DBMS defines the data in a database using the Data Definition Language (DDL) and handles requests to retrieve, update, or delete existing data or add new data to the database using the Data

---

MP3 AND NAPSTER

The popularity of MP3 as a format gave rise to audio file-sharing services on the Internet such as Napster and mp3.com. Some of these services ran afoul of the music and entertainment industries in the late 1990s and early 2000s because they allegedly facilitated unauthorized sharing of copyrighted music. Settlements of the copyright claims were expensive and caused major changes in the file-sharing services, but listeners continued to seek sources of music files while the music industry developed secure ways of selling music to audio consumers.

concurrency control the management and coordination of several actions that occur simultaneously; for example, several computer programs running at once

client a program or computer often managed by a human user, that makes requests to another computer for information

server a computer that does not deal directly with human users, but instead handles requests from other computers for services to be performed

Manipulation Language (DML). In addition, the DBMS must monitor user requests and reject any attempts to violate integrity or security constraints defined for the data. The DBMS must be able to recover the data in case of problems. The DBMS also performs a function called **concurrency control**. Finally, the DBMS provides a tool called the data dictionary that stores data about the data. One language used with the DBMS to provide this functionality is called SQL. It is the industry standard adopted by many database vendors for relational databases.

Database architecture can be configured in one of three basic ways:

- Host-based, where users are connected directly to the same computer on which the database resides;

- Client/server, where a user accesses the data from a microcomputer (**client**) via a network and the database sits on a separate computer (**server**);

- Distributed processing, where users access a database that resides on more than one computer. The database is distributed across these computers in various ways.

In the client/server architecture, the server supports all basic DBMS functions (data definition, data manipulation, data security, and integrity). The clients are the various applications that run on top of the DBMS. These applications are provided by the DBMS vendor or a third party to query the database, write reports, produce graphics and spreadsheets, and many other functions. The server machine in a client/server architecture can be tailored to the DBMS function and thus provide better performance. Typically, several clients share the same server.

When more than one person can access a database, several SQL commands can be given at the same time. Each of these commands is called a transaction. A transaction is simply a logical unit of work. Since many transactions can access the same database at the same time, some means of controlling them is necessary. This is called concurrency control. One way to understand the need for concurrency control is to consider what would happen if Emily and Christopher both wish to modify a particular record for Jon Vogler from the SCHOOL table at the same time. Emily wishes to change the grade point average (GPA) for Jon, and Christopher wishes to change Jon's address, as the two SQL commands that follow show.

UPDATE STUDENT **SET** GPA = 3.9 **WHERE** LNAME = 'Vogler' **AND** FNAME = 'Jon'; **UPDATE** STUDENT **SET** ADDRESS = '3 Soccer Lane' **WHERE** LNAME = 'Vogler' **AND** FNAME = 'Jon';

If both retrieve the record at approximately the same time but Emily updates the record before Christopher does, Emily's modifications are lost and only Christopher's changes are made to the record, so Jon's address changes, but his GPA does not. This situation is called the lost update problem and it can reduce the quality of the data in a database.

Locking is the most common method of concurrency control. When a transaction needs to access a part of the database (typically a database record), the DBMS locks other transactions out of that part. The first transaction can perform its processing without being affected by any other changes that might be made to the record. In our SCHOOL example, if Emily is the first to request Jon's record, Christopher is prevented from requesting that record until Emily finishes. This is a type of locking called exclusive locking. However, if another type of locking called shared locking is used for concurrency control, Christopher would be permitted to see Jon's record, but not change it. SEE ALSO DATABASE MANAGEMENT SOFTWARE; INFORMATION SYSTEMS; STORAGE DEVICES.

Terri L. Lenox and Charles R. Woratschek

Bibliography

Abbey, Michael, and Michael J. Corey. *Oracle: A Beginner's Guide*. Berkeley, CA: Osborne McGraw-Hill, 1995.

Date, Chris J. *An Introduction to Database Systems*. Reading, MA: Addison-Wesley, 2000.

Elmasri, Ramez A., and Shamkant B. Navathe. *Fundamentals of Database Systems*, 3rd ed. Reading, MA: Addison-Wesley, 2000.

Storage Devices

Data and programs are stored in main memory, as **random access memory (RAM)**, before and after processing by the **central processing unit (CPU)**. However, RAM is **volatile**—its contents disappear when a computer's power is turned off. So what does one do with data that will be reused, stored on a long-term basis, or is simply too large to fit into the main memory of a computer? Mechanical storage devices, called secondary storage or external storage, are used to store data externally. Secondary storage is non-volatile—that is, data and programs are permanent.

Types of Storage Devices

There are many secondary storage devices, including magnetic drums, magnetic tapes, magnetic disks, and optical disks. These devices vary with respect to their versatility, durability, capacity, and speed.

Magnetic Drums. These are very early high-speed, direct access storage devices used in the 1950s and 1960s. The magnetic drum is a metal cylinder coated with a sensitive magnetic material. The cylinder has tracks around its circumference. Each track has its own read/write head, and data are stored as magnetic spots on the tracks. Like the magnetic disk, which was introduced later, the read/write head can move quickly to any track, providing direct access to the data stored on the drum.

Magnetic Tape. This is one of the oldest secondary storage devices. It was first used for storing data in the early 1950s. At that time, the tape was made of a flexible metal and was stored on reels. The metal tape was plated with a thin film of iron, which allowed data to be stored as a series of small, magnetized spots. Although the tape provided a compact form of storage, it was extremely heavy and not universally accepted. It was not until a very thin, flexible material called **mylar** was developed that tape processing gained wide acceptance. This plastic mylar was coated with an iron oxide that could be magnetized to store data. In the 1950s and 1960s, magnetic tape was the primary means for storing large amounts of data.

Data are stored on magnetic tape in columns. Each **byte** of data (eight **bits**) utilizes one column across the width of the tape. Data are stored on

random access memory (RAM) a type of memory device that supports the nonpermanent storage of programs and data; so called because various locations can be accessed in any order (as if at random), rather than in a sequence (like a tape memory device)

central processing unit (CPU) the part of a computer that performs computations and controls and coordinates other parts of the computer

volatile subject to rapid change

mylar a synthetic film, invented by the DuPont corporation, used in photographic printing and production processes, as well as disks and tapes

byte a group of eight binary digits; represents a single character of text

bits plural of bit, a single binary digit, 1 or 0—a contraction of Binary digIT; the smallest unit for storing data in a computer

One type of computer memory storage device was the magnetic drum, popular in the 1950s and 1960s. As it quickly rotates, the drum records bits of electronic signal information.

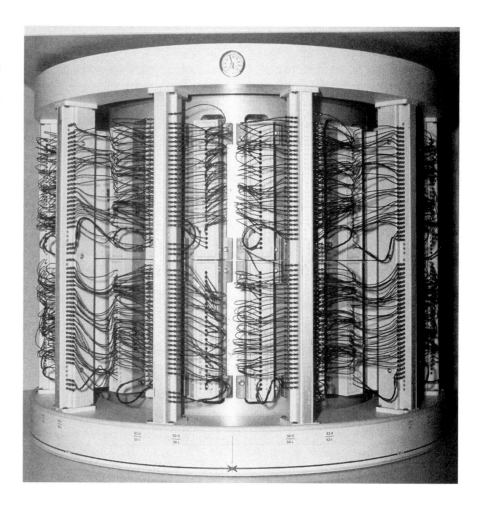

densities measures of the density of a material; defined as the mass of a sample of material, divided by its volume

the magnetic tape at different **densities**. Low density is 1,600 bytes per inch (bpi). Densities of 6,250 bpi and greater were common in the 1980s.

The old reel-to-reel magnetic tapes are being replaced by tape cartridges, which are used to back up or archive data. A tape backup is a copy of the data used to restore lost data. If one loses the data on a hard disk, he can copy the data from the tape backup. Tape cartridges used on microcomputers are similar to audiocassettes and can hold up to 35 gigabytes (GB) of data. There are several different types of tape cartridges, including quarter-inch cartridge (QIC), digital audio tape (DAT), digital linear tape (DLT), Travan, and advanced digital recording (ADR).

Magnetic tapes are an inexpensive and relatively stable way to store large volumes of data. Tapes can be used repeatedly, although time and environmental factors such as heat and humidity do affect them. The principle disadvantage of magnetic tape is that it stores data sequentially—that is, one record is stored right after another. Retrieving data from the tape is slow since the tape must be read from the beginning up to the location of the desired record. Thus, magnetic tapes are not a good choice when one needs to find information rapidly.

Magnetic Disk. Currently, the most widely used secondary storage device is the magnetic disk. There are two kinds of magnetic disks: hard disks and floppy disks. Hard disks are thin, metallic platters developed in the 1950s. Each hard disk contains one or, more commonly, a series of platters that rotate on a shaft at a high rate of speed. The platters have a top and bottom surface where data can be recorded as magnetic spots. The platters have **concentric** circles called tracks where the data are actually stored. Access arms containing read/write heads move across the spinning platters to read or write data on the tracks. There is a read/write head for each platter surface. These read/write heads float on a cushion of air and do not actually touch the surface of the disk. When reading data from the disk, the read head senses the magnetic spots on the surface and transfers the data to main memory. When writing, the data are transferred from main memory and are stored as magnetic spots on the recording surface.

The speed of access to data on a disk is based on both the rotational speed of the disk and the speed of the access arm. The read/write heads must position themselves over the platter at the proper address and the disk pack must rotate until the proper data are located. The time it takes the read/write heads to position themselves to the correct address is referred to as access motion time. Rotational delay time is the time needed for the disk to rotate the data under the read/write head.

The read/write heads move horizontally (from left to right) to any of 200 positions, called cylinders, on the platter surface. The cylinder represents the circular tracks on the same vertical line within the disk pack. To find data on the disk, an address is used. This address consists of a cylinder number, the recording surface number, and the data record number. The computer's operating system figures out how to fit data into the fixed spaces on the disk.

The microcomputer utilizes a hard disk, but it also uses floppy disks, also called floppy diskettes. Floppy disks are the second kind of magnetic disk and are removable. The two common standard sizes of floppy disks are 8.9 centimeters (3.5 inches) and 13.3 centimeters (5.25 inches). It is difficult today to find a microcomputer that uses the 5.25-inch floppy disk. Floppy disks are made up of one platter constructed from polyester film rather than metal. This polyester film is covered with a magnetic coating. Data are stored on the floppy disk in much the same manner as on a hard disk—in the form of magnetic spots on tracks. However, floppy disks use sectors to store data rather than cylinders. In this method of storing data, the disk is divided into pie-shaped pieces called sectors. Each sector is assigned a unique address to locate data. Sectors are created on a floppy disk by formatting it. Floppy disks have a much lower data storage capacity (usually 1.44MB for a 3.5-inch floppy disk) and a much slower data access rate than hard disks.

As software packages such as Microsoft Office became popular, the need for larger data capacity for items such as text and graphics in a portable form became necessary. The zip drive and zip disk were introduced in the 1990s as a relatively inexpensive large-storage-capacity floppy disk. The zip disk is 8.9 centimeters (3.5 inches), removable, and provides about 100 megabytes (MB) of data storage. In late 1998, a 250 MB version of the zip disk was introduced. While this zip disk has double the storage capacity of its predecessor, it is still only 8.9 centimeters (3.5 inches) in size!

The main advantages of using a magnetic disk as a secondary storage device are its speed and direct access capability. Data can be easily and rapidly

concentric objects or shapes that have coincident centers; circles that share centers

MYLAR

Data storage devices—compact disks, floppy disks, and magnetic tapes—come in all shapes and sizes. The first magnetic tapes were made of thin strips of metal. In the early 1950s the DuPont corporation patented a thin, polyester film that revolutionized the magnetic tape market. Called Mylar, this plastic material is chemically stable and is virtually as strong as metal, yet heat-resistant and lightweight. Mylar has a myriad of uses and is used in the manufacturing of numerous plastic products, including photo negative sleeves, food wraps, and magnetic tape.

read, written, or accessed. Floppy disks provide the added advantage of portability. Disadvantages of using a magnetic disk as a secondary storage device include cost, environmental factors, user misuse and abuse, head crashes, and update problems.

The magnetic disk is more expensive than magnetic tape (DAT). The February 1998 CompUSA catalog reported that DAT cost $49.95 and stored 10,000 MB. This is a $.005 cost per megabyte. An 18 GB hard drive cost $230.00 or $.08 per megabyte. A 3.5 inch diskette cost $.50 and stored 1.4MB. This is a cost of $.35 per megabyte. A Zip Plus Drive cost $100.00 and stored 100MG to 250MG. This is a cost of $1.00 per megabyte. It was reported by Dataquest, a research firm, that the average cost of data storage across various media was 15 cents per megabyte in the year 2000. This cost decreased to 3 cents per megabyte in 2002, as noted by Effy Oz in *Management Information Systems.*

Magnetic disks, both hard and floppy, are also susceptible to environmental factors such as dust, dirt, and smoke. Any of these factors will cause a hard disk to fail. Because of this, hard disks are sealed. Floppy disks are also vulnerable to environmental factors. Also, because of their portability, the floppy disk is vulnerable to misuse or abuse by users.

Head crashes can occur with any magnetic disk technology. This is when the read/write head touches the surface of the disk platter, destroying it and all of the stored data. Head crashes are normally caused by misalignment of the platter and the read/write head. A head crash renders a magnetic disk unusable. Another disadvantage of any magnetic disk is that when updating data, the old data are written over, destroying them instantly and permanently. Unless proper precautions are taken, data may be written over by mistake.

Optical Disks.   These are the newest secondary storage devices. Originally optical disks were called optical disk-read-only memory (OD-ROM) and are now called compact disk-read only memory (CD-ROM). Data are not recorded on optical disks magnetically, but with a laser device that burns microscopic holes on the surface of the disk. Binary information (0s and 1s) is encoded by the length of these bumps and the space between them. Optical disks can store much more data than floppy disks. Data can be stored in the form of text as well as pictures, sound, and full-motion video. The disks are not as sensitive to dust, dirt, and smoke as magnetic disks are, and they are portable.

CD-ROM is read-only storage. No new data can be written to it. Once recorded, the CD can be read an indefinite number of times. This is commonly referred to as write once/read many (WORM). CD-ROM has been used for storage of large financial, legal, educational, or demographic databases, and by the music industry. Encyclopedias and multimedia applications are also stored using CD-ROM technology.

Individuals and organizations can now record their own CD-ROMs using compact disk-recordable (CD-R) technology. CD-ReWritable (CD-RW) is a newer technology that has been developed to allow users to create rewritable optical disks. Currently CD-RW has slower access speeds and is more expensive than magnetic storage devices.

Another optical storage medium is the digital video disk or digital versatile disk (DVD). This optical disk is the same size as a CD-ROM, but has

THE DVD

Watching your favorite films on VHS may become as antiquated as listening to your favorite songs on vinyl albums. DVD technology is fast becoming popular, especially in the movie rental market. In addition to providing a clearer picture, films on DVD are enhanced with many extras, which can include director commentaries, deleted scenes, cast bios and interviews, and games.

much higher storage capacity. DVDs can store large amounts of data, video, graphics, digitized text, and audio, and are portable. It is likely that DVD will eventually replace the CD-ROM. SEE ALSO Codes; Computer System Interfaces; Memory.

Charles R. Woratschek and Terri L. Lenox

Bibliography

Laudon, Kenneth C., and Jane P. Laudon. *Essentials of Management Information Systems: Organization and Technology.* Englewood Cliffs, NJ: Prentice Hall Inc., 1995.

———. *Essentials of Management Information Systems: Organization and Technology in the Networked Enterprise,* 4th ed. Upper Saddle River, NJ: Prentice Hall Inc., 2001.

Oz, Effy. *Management Information Systems,* 3rd ed. Boston: Course Technology, 2002.

Parsons, June Jamrich, and Dan Oja. *New Perspectives on Computer Concepts,* 4th ed. Cambridge, MA: Course Technology, 2000.

Shelly, Gary B., and Thomas J. Cashman. *Introduction to Computers and Data Processing.* Brea, CA: Anaheim Publishing Company, 1980.

Spencer, David D. *Data Processing: An Introduction.* Columbus, OH: Charles E. Merrill Publishing Company, 1978.

Stair, Ralph M., and George W. Reynolds. *Principles of Information Systems: A Managerial Approach,* 5th ed. Boston: Course Technology-ITP, 2001.

System Analysis

System analysis is a broad, technical area focused on the creation, enhancement, and trouble-shooting of systems for users. These can be data, information, or knowledge systems. The purpose of these systems is to provide an understanding of what is going on in a particular environment. Sensors, including **radar**, **sonar**, and **satellites**, for example, are components of systems that provide specific knowledge about the physical world. Sensors in the home can warn residents that someone is breaking in. Telephones are part of a system that brings police assistance when one dials 911. People have computers they use to perform a number of tasks—from writing term papers or diaries to communicating with people they have never met via "messaging" software programs. There are decision support systems that help people use computers to solve problems, and communication systems that tell people what is happening around them. System analysis is used to design, enhance, and fix problems in all of these systems.

System Analysis Methods

System analysis is creative work. The systems analyst can be considered an artist, an information scientist, and an engineer, all in one. The work begins with thinking about how to accomplish something. System analysis can be considered to have three primary functions, each of which is related to the others. First, system analysis is done to fix something that has gone wrong and to help one understand why there is a problem. Second, analysis is used to figure out how to do something more easily and less expensively as new technologies become available. Third, system analysis is done to help design a system that can accommodate future circumstances, such as anticipated events that are not being experienced now, but that might need to be dealt with in the future.

radar the acronym for RAdio Direction And Ranging; a technique developed in the 1930s that uses frequency shifts in reflected radio waves to measure distance and speed of a target

sonar the science and engineering of sound propagation in water

satellites objects that orbit planets

Trouble-Shooting Systems. Each system has components that perform certain functions and, when put together, do a particular job, or serve a specific purpose. System analysts are trained to ensure that each component or function of a system—whether people, tools (technology), or procedures—is acting properly. If a system fails, the system analyst tries to find out how and why. The systems analyst then communicates with the designer about the factors found to be related to the failures in order to find a solution and avoid future problems. One way to consider system analysis is that it is a process that first identifies the factors that influence and lead to system breakdown, and then identifies ways to repair or avoid breakdowns.

Retrofitting Systems. Systems have a life cycle. They become operational, they age, and they become obsolete. Typewriters have given way to computers. People still use telephone booths but cell phones are replacing them because they allow people to make phone calls and do many other things better and faster. As new tools and technologies become available, people want to use them. The system analyst examines and studies how technology and people can be placed and used in current systems, and figures out how existing systems could benefit from all the new ideas and inventions that are coming to market. System analysis is a process for updating or retrofitting systems, replacing old technology with new, and installing new ways of doing things.

Creating Systems. System analysis also considers situations or events where no existing system may yet be available to deal with them, such as biological warfare, or global warming, and analysts work to find ways to better address other large-scale events that affect the fabric of human life. Systems do exist that can respond to events such as hurricanes, tornadoes, floods, and health epidemics. Yet the need to anticipate unpredictable global circumstances—economic, political, medical, or environmental—demands new, creative approaches to minimize the potential damage to lives and property. System analysis is a way to explore how new situations or challenges can be met.

The Relationship Between Analysis and Design

A system analyst investigates; a system design specifies. The analyst asks questions such as who, what, when, where, why, and how. The system designer finds the best procedures, tools, and human skills to meet the needs and requirements of people and organizations. System analysis and system design work best when analyst and designer work together. The analysis component helps reduce the likelihood that design and technology will drive and influence the problem-solving process. If design precedes and directs analysis, there is a good chance that a given system may not be what the user needs or requires. Basements are full of technologically interesting gadgets that people buy and rarely use because they never needed them in the first place—no matter how intriguing the design, they were not designed specifically to meet the identified needs or requirements of the user!

Needs and Requirements

People are born with needs and requirements. A need is a state of being. Requirements are the things that meet these needs. People are hungry or

thirsty; they need to feel well; they need shelter from environmental conditions and circumstances. They need to make a living; they need to feel as if their actions have some meaning. To address these varied needs, they require food, water, air, shelter, and other resources. But the resources, or requirements, applied to address these needs in a tropical environment, for example, would be inappropriate in an arctic climate. Individual human characteristics such as personality or physical limitations can also influence the appropriateness of certain resources being applied to meet these needs. Requirements to meet needs vary from situation to situation. The same logic applies to system analysts. They must learn how to match up needs and requirements so that a system will actually function effectively in its particular environment.

Human needs may be physical, psychological, intellectual, emotional, or social. They can generally be identified only through a careful process of examination and investigation. Needs and requirements can be difficult to sort out and obtain from users because dictionaries and people's language habits lead them to ignore the distinctions. But the success of any system depends on the skills of a system analyst to recognize these distinctions and gather the correct needs and requirements information before trying to engineer a system.

System analysis is used to study the causes and impact of global warming. Scientists study computer-enhanced images of the Earth viewed from space to determine changes in polar ice caps and land masses.

conceptualization a creative process that is directed at envisaging a structure or collection of relationships within components of a complex system

The System Development Cycle

The system development cycle consists of the steps taken for the **conceptualization** and engineering of a system. There are several ways to represent or describe the system development cycle. One is to show the analysis process in a series of blocks in hierarchical (top-down) or horizontal line (timeline) form. Another way is to show the system analysis process as a circle of operations, namely, requirement analysis, specifications, design, implementation, testing, and maintenance. Another approach is to regard the process as representing a waterfall cycle—one step flowing into another in a continuous stream. All share a common property of sequencing. System analysis is a step-by-step procedure: each step follows or interacts with the others, and all are directed toward meeting the objectives stated by the intended user of the system.

The Conceptual Stage

Once the initial information gathering stage is completed—that is, user needs and requirements have been identified, and the parties involved in a system design process have agreed on certain parameters of time, money investment, and expected outcomes—the system analyst begins conceptualizing the problems to be solved and the possible solutions to be applied.

One of the first steps is known as event analysis. The system analyst will engage in a detective-like process of investigating the properties and attributes of an event, or of a series of events that make up the problem to be solved. For each event, the system analyst creates a model, which is a tool in the analytical process. A model provides a view, a mental and physical picture, of the total system, explaining how the various parts of the system are structured and how they work together.

A prevailing model for system analysis is to consider three functions: namely, input, throughput, and output. What goes into the system? What happens to it? What is the outcome? These three dimensions of the analysis are applied to each component or event within the system and to the total system, as well, in its final configuration.

Input refers to the data that are acquired, through human or machine means, as part of an event in which the system is engaged. At the *throughput* stage, these data are transmitted to a processor, which can again be human, machine, or both. The data may then be modified, organized, stored for retrieval, or used in problem-solving and decision-making activities; whatever happens to it during processing is part of the throughput function. The *output* of a system, or of an event within the system, is the result of the processing steps being applied to the data originally entered into the system. The system analyst's model should account for everything that happens from the time data enters the system to the point at which the end results are achieved.

Throughout the system analysis process, analysts test the ideas and conclusions that arise. Often the model of the system provides the basis for creating a **prototype** of what is being studied. Although prototyping is a common exercise of designers, who use prototypes to test system configurations and hardware-software specifications, it is also a method for the system analyst to refine the conclusions of the analysis before design decisions are made.

prototype a working model or experimental investigation of proposed systems under development

Documentation

Documentation is a necessary part of system analysis. Documentation means that all actions taken in the process of analyzing a system are recorded. This provides an enduring record of everything that has taken place and all the thoughts or ideas generated throughout the process. This includes both the individual work and testing done by a particular system analyst, and the group work, such as brain-storming, that is usually part of the overall process of analyzing and designing a system. Documentation objectifies the system analysis process. Thorough documentation can help reduce the amount of guessing that goes into solving certain system problems. It helps analysts keep track of what has been tried, and when, and under what specific circumstances. It can be useful in future work on a particular system, and it is a practice through which the process and outcomes of system analysis can be improved and validated. SEE ALSO DECISION SUPPORT SYSTEMS; DESIGN TOOLS; INFORMATION SYSTEMS; OFFICE AUTOMATION SYSTEMS; SYSTEMS DESIGN.

Anthony Debons

documentation literature in a human readable form that is referred to in support of using a computer or computer system

Bibliography

Coad, Peter, and Edward Yourdon. *Object-oriented Analysis*, 2nd ed. Englewood Cliffs, NJ: Yourdon Press, 1991.

Debons, Anthony. *Information Science: Forty Years of Teaching*. Philadelphia: Foundation for Information Technology Education, 2000.

Miller, James Grier. *Living Systems*. New York: McGraw-Hill, 1978.

Osborne, Larry N., and Margaret Nakamura. *Systems Analysis for Librarians and Information Professionals*, 2nd ed. Englewood, CO: Libraries Unlimited, 2000.

Sage, Andrew P., and William B. Rouse, eds. *Handbook of Systems Engineering and Management*. New York: John Wiley and Sons, 1999.

Satzinger, John W., Robert B. Jackson, and Stephen D. Burd. *Systems Analysis and Design in a Changing World*. Cambridge, MA: Course Technology, 2000.

Systems Design

Systems design is a component of the systems engineering process. Typically, it follows systems analysis, precedes implementation, and is driven by the requirements generated during the earlier phases of the project. Within the context of computer sciences, systems design includes the specification of hardware and software architecture granulated to the necessary components, modules, and interfaces.

The systems design process may include such subcategories as network design, software design, and data design. The scope of the project is a primary determinant of the degree to which any of these and potentially other sub-processes factor into the overall system design effort. Organizational standards and budgetary constraints may also limit design activity.

The sequence of design events relative to other processes in a system's life cycle is largely determined by the systems methodology chosen for the project. This is often based upon the nature of the system being considered. The traditional systems engineering methodology, often referred to as the waterfall **paradigm**, assumes that all planning, business analysis, risk assessment, and requirements definition occur before any of the design activity

paradigm an example, pattern, or way of thinking

begins. All systems design activity must then be completed and verified against requirements before any implementation can begin. Implementation may include constructing a network, developing software, or a combination of such activities, depending on the scope of the system. When implementation is complete, the system is evaluated and ultimately introduced to the operational environment.

Often, such a strict serial methodology is impractical. Increasingly, and especially for the development of software, an **iterative** approach is chosen. The most evolutionary of the iterative models, often preferred for object-oriented software construction, is the spiral methodology. Under this paradigm, a **prototype** is rapidly constructed through much shorter phases of analysis, design, development, and testing. The cycle is then repeated many times until the original prototype is adequately refined and ready for operation.

While the waterfall paradigm is structurally confining, the spiral approach has the potential for lack of structure and initial planning. For this reason, a compromise is often chosen between the two models. For instance, project managers may choose an approach that is predominately sequential, but with review and refinement iterations planned between each phase. Or they may choose an incremental model, which is closer to the spiral methodology but defines a limited number of structured iterations.

Regardless of the scope or chosen methodology, systems engineering activities occur in the same functional sequence: Analysis is followed by design, which is followed by implementation. The scope of design activities changes on a per-project basis, but effective design practices apply to all engineering projects regardless of scope or chosen methodology.

The design phase deals with decisions regarding the specific architecture of the system so that it meets all of the stated requirements when constructed. During the first round of an iterative project, requirements may be few and vague. A large-scale waterfall-based project, by contrast, may present many specific requirements. Regardless of scope or methodology, stated requirements must be addressed and verified before the design can be considered complete.

A well-designed system will operate efficiently, providing maximum value given its use of resources. Surplus resources sometimes permit the designer to incorporate features or performance in excess of basic requirements. Such decisions must be carefully evaluated because improving one aspect generally diminishes another. Most systems design decisions involve some degree of compromise, so effective evaluation methods are an important part of the design process.

Decision models, often constructed as tables or trees, may be incorporated to assist designers in quantifying alternatives. Decision tables assist in translating actions and conditions into a tabular format, while tree models generally break a high-level decision into alternatives, each of which is further aggregated into individual consequences and further alternatives. Decision models may extend into several layers of conditions and actions. If systems and their associated decisions are complex enough to justify it, decision support systems may be implemented to assist the decision process. Decision support systems are often computer-based and built specifically to help evaluate both objective and subjective considerations of much larger

iterative describes a procedure that involves repetitive operations before being completed

prototype a working model or experimental investigation of proposed systems under development

independent systems. Decision models may be used to help the designer evaluate high-level decisions about the system's construct as well as to demonstrate the internal decision processes that occur within a system.

Other models that assist designers in visualizing system processes include flowcharts and data flow diagrams (DFDs). Both models graphically depict process flows through a system using shapes to represent processes or entities. The shapes are connected by arrows that direct flow.

Flowcharts primarily depict the sequence of decisions internal to a system, based on logical conditions. By convention, boxes indicate processing steps and diamonds depict conditions. This simple set of constructs was originally proposed in the late 1960s and is most effective for designing procedural programs. Object-oriented software development projects may benefit from a program design language such as the Unified Modeling Language (UML), which defines a robust set of notational conventions.

Data flow diagrams provide a means to depict the movement of data through a system or organization. They were introduced in 1979 in the book *Structured Analysis and System Specification* by Tom DeMarco. The DFD depicts data flow between processes, external agents, and data stores. DFD convention defines an oval to be a process, a rectangle to be an external agent, and two horizontal lines to represent a data store. Other tools for modeling data include entity-relationship diagrams and state-transition diagrams.

Systems design that is complete, based upon solid decisions, and well-documented produces a valuable blueprint for the remaining phases of the engineering project. This is especially important under the waterfall approach, since all subsequent activity is reliant on the product of the design effort, and previous project phases are not easily revisited. An effective design product provides measurable deliverables and verifies that, in concept, the finished system will satisfy all requirements. SEE ALSO DESIGN TOOLS; OFFICE AUTOMATION SYSTEMS; SYSTEM ANALYSIS.

Jeffrey C. Wingard

MORE ABOUT FLOWCHARTS

A flowchart represents an algorithm—which is a rule or procedure used to solve a mathematical problem. However, the flowchart uses symbols rather than words. In addition to their use in program development, flowcharts are also used to enhance documentation.

Bibliography

Harmon, Paul, and Mark Watson. *Understanding UML: The Developer's Guide*. San Francisco: Morgan Kaufmann Publishers, 1998.

McDaniel, George. *IBM Dictionary of Computing*, 10th ed. New York: McGraw-Hill, 1994.

Pressman, Roger S. *Software Engineering: A Practitioner's Approach*, 4th ed. New York: McGraw-Hill, 1997.

Ruble, David A. *Practical Analysis and Design for Client/Server and GUI Systems*. Upper Saddle River, NJ: Prentice Hall, 1997.

Touch Screens

Touch screens are devices that allow a user to provide input to a computer or electronic system by making physical contact or near-contact with the system's display. Most often seen in Automated Teller Machines (ATMs), information kiosks, and other public computers, touch screens are also widely used in computer graphics and animation. They also play a role in assistive technology for users with special needs.

Applications

Public computer systems are often designed around a touch screen, which is often the only visible component. Automated Teller Machines (ATMs) are the most common application, but falling prices for touch screen technology are making it available for other applications such as museum exhibits, ticket sales in airports and movie theaters, and public information kiosks. Touch screens are ideal for these applications because they provide input and output capabilities. They are often the only part of the system contacted by the user and are sturdier than many other input devices because they have no moving parts. These qualities make touch screen-based systems easy and inexpensive to maintain and repair.

Touch screens are used, like mice, as pointing devices. Instead of moving a mouse to activate and relocate the cursor, the user touches the screen to position the cursor. For specifying precise location, a touch screen often works with a stylus—a device like a pencil that has a rubber or plastic point. The user modifies what is seen on the screen by touching it, rather than by manipulating a cursor or other on-screen component with a mouse, keyboard, or joystick. Touch screens are invaluable to artists who have been trained to use pencils, brushes, and other implements that effect change wherever they touch the canvas.

Touch screens have revolutionized **personal digital assistants (PDAs)**. Older PDAs required the user to enter data using an extremely small keyboard. Modern PDAs consist almost entirely of a touch screen, which makes them substantially smaller and easier to use because the user can "write" information directly into the device.

In the late twentieth century, companies began to integrate touch screen technology with dry-erase boards (wall-mounted surfaces that allow the user to write with markers and erase the markings with a cloth). With these devices, whatever a user writes on the board can be simultaneously recorded and saved in a computer file.

Development

The touch screen was derived from the digitizing tablet, which is still in use as a **computer peripheral**. The digitizing tablet, developed by Dr. G. Sam Hurst in 1971 at the University of Kentucky, was designed to allow scientists to record data from graphs by placing the graph on the tablet and pressing the paper against the tablet with a stylus. In 1977 Elographics (now EloTouch Systems), the first commercial producer of digitizing tablets, paired with Siemens Corporation to develop a transparent version of the tablet on curved glass so that it could fit over a CRT (cathode ray tube) screen, which was then the predominant display technology. The first touch screens were built by hand, but advances soon allowed all of the layers to be produced by machine.

Touch Screen Technologies

Touch screens consist of a display component, typically a **liquid crystal display (LCD)** or CRT covered or surrounded with a transparent sensor device that allows the screen to detect the contact or proximity of an object. There is a wide variety of sensor devices. Some devices are not entirely trans-

personal digital assistants (PDAs) small scale hand-held computers that can be used in place of diaries and appointment books

computer peripheral a device that is connected to a computer to support its operation; for example, a keyboard or a disk drive unit

liquid crystal display (LCD) a type of crystal that changes its level of transparency when subjected to an electric current; used as an output device on a computer

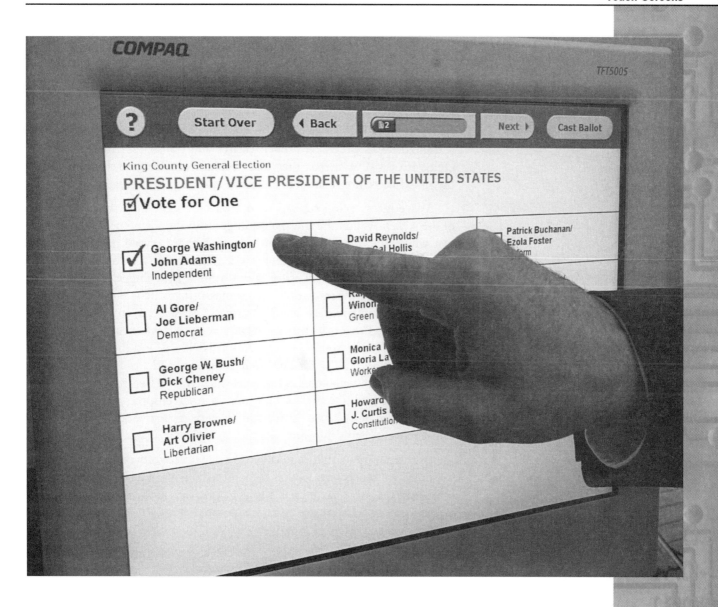

parent or create glare that makes the screen behind the device hard to see. The amount of pressure or types of contact needed to detect a touch varies from device to device. Devices also vary widely in accuracy (determining exactly where the touch occurred), durability (reliability with repeated use or in inclement circumstances), expected lifetime (time before failure of the device or parts of it), and response time (how long it takes the screen to detect a touch).

A 4-wire resistive (pressure sensitive) screen is made of two thin sheets separated by a grid of plastic dots. Each sheet, though clear, conducts electricity. When the user touches the screen, the sheets contact each other only at the spot where the user touched it. The screen measures the amount of electricity flowing between the two sheets to determine where the user touched. The term "4-wire" comes from the four wires used to provide and measure the currents on the screen. These are the cheapest and most common touch screens. A 5-wire screen increases durability by adding a sheet so that the surface touched by the user is not one carrying the currents. An 8-wire screen is the same as 4-wire screens except that it uses an extra set of wires to measure the currents and has increased durability.

Many punched-card ballots could not be counted during the 2000 U.S. Presidential election because the holes were not adequately punched. As lawmakers looked into voting reforms, some recommended touch-screen voting machines, which allow voters simply to touch the candidate's name.

oscillators electronic components that produce a precise waveform of a fixed known frequency; they can be used as time base (clock) signals to other devices

Capacitive screens use a single thin sheet. The screen is connected to electric **oscillators**. A signal of a specific frequency is broadcast through the sheet creating an oscillating electric field around it. When the user comes near the screen with a conductive object, such as a finger, the electric field is changed, which changes the signal in the sheet. The screen can determine the location of the conductive object by measuring the signal in the sheet. Although these screens are much clearer and transparent than those covered with resistive sheets, they lose accuracy over time and do not detect the presence of non-conductive objects, such as gloved fingers.

Wave interruption screens send a wave of some kind over the surface of the screen. When the user puts a finger into the wave, the screen can detect where the interference occurred. An infrared screen has a row of infrared lights along two adjacent sides. The opposite sides have infrared detectors. When the light wave is interrupted by a finger, the screen can determine where the interruption is by measuring which detectors went into the shadows. With surface acoustic wave (SAW) screens, an inaudible sound wave is "played" over the surface of the screen. A finger near the screen will absorb some of the sound wave, even if it is gloved, and the screen can determine the location by the change in frequency and strength of the sound wave. With near-field imaging, an object changes the frequency and strength of an electric (radio) wave. As with capacitive screens, the object interfering with the wave must be capacitive. Unlike with capacitive screens, the object can be covered with thin non-conductive covering, like a glove.

For applications that require more accuracy in terms of screen sensitivity, there are touch screens that respond to a stylus. The stylus triggers the sensors in the same manner as a finger does, but allows the user to specify a more precise location for software action. SEE ALSO ANIMATION; INFORMATION RETRIEVAL; PERSONAL DIGITAL ASSISTANTS.

Salvatore Domenick Desiano

Internet Resources

"History of Elo TouchSystems." Elo TouchSystems web site. <http://www.elotouch.com/about/history.asp>

"Touch Screens for Window of Computer Monitor." AbilityHub Assistive Technology Solutions. <http://www.abilityhub.com/mouse/touchscreen.htm>

Touch Screens Inc. <http://www.touchwindow.com/>

Transmission Media

random access memory (RAM) a type of memory device that supports the nonpermanent storage of programs and data; so called because various locations can be accessed in any order (as if at random), rather than in a sequence (like a tape memory device)

Communication is one of the most important functions performed by computers. It is easy to understand that a computer must calculate, compare, and store data. It is also easy to see that the computer must input and output data used to communicate with the input and output devices. Also, within the computer, data must be transferred from one location—for example, from read only memory to **random access memory (RAM)**, or from permanent storage such as a compact disc to temporary memory, etc. Transferring data, therefore, is just another way of referring to communication.

Communicating from one device to another within the computer is usually done through a bus, which is essentially a set of printed circuit board traces or wires within the computer. Buses are usually local to the device. Very special wire arrangements, called transmission lines, must be used when the required communications travel a significant distance or are executed at a very high speed. For high-speed computers, these transmission line techniques are even used for the internal computer buses.

To understand transmission lines, it is helpful to appreciate what makes a very poor transmission line. When Guglielmo Marconi (1874–1937) first spanned the Atlantic Ocean with radio waves in 1901, he erected a very long wire as an antenna at both the transmitter site and the receiver site. It was Marconi's goal to radiate energy in the form of radio waves and receive the energy on the other side of the Atlantic. When one desires to transmit signals *through long wires*, one does not want the radiation and reception of radio waves. A transmission line is the opposite of an antenna; it transmits data from one place to another with no loss of energy by radiating radio waves, called **egress**, and receives no energy from external radio waves, called **ingress**.

A very simple transmission line consists of a pair of wires that are kept precisely side by side. Since the wires are often twisted to keep them together, they have earned the title "twisted pair." The twisted pair was one of the first transmission lines originally used, and remains in use for telephone systems. The twisted pair is inexpensive to manufacture and is also used extensively for computer communications.

Twisted pairs are used in many **local area networks (LANs)**. There is a large selection of standard cable for use in LANs. Some twisted pairs include a shield, which reduces the amount of egress and ingress. The two basic types of twisted pairs are unshielded twisted pair (or UTP) and shielded twisted pair (or STP).

Although twisted pairs can have very little ingress and egress, they are not perfect, particularly at higher frequencies and data rates. The imperfections in transmission lines become more pronounced when the data rates are very high. One transmission line topology that reduces the amount of egress and ingress for very high data rates, extending to the gigabit per second range, is the coaxial transmission line, commonly called **coaxial cable** or co-ax. In this transmission line design, one conductor is actually a hollow cylinder and the other conductor is placed in the center of the cylinder. Egress and ingress can be reduced to very low levels but coaxial cable is much more expensive than unshielded twisted pairs. Coaxial cable is used for television distribution despite the increased cost because of the very broad frequency range of television signals.

The loss of energy due to radiation and from other losses within the transmission line subtracts from the signal energy in the line. This means that the signal has to be amplified or restored if the transmission line is long. Since there are more losses at higher frequencies, more amplification is required for the higher frequencies. Very high-speed data communications systems will require more amplifiers or repeaters for the same length of cable.

The best transmission line for very high-speed data or wide bandwidth is a glass fiber. It is often difficult to view the glass fiber as a transmission line because the signals within the fiber are not electrical but light waves.

egress to move out of an object, system, or environment

ingress the act of entering a system or object

local area networks (LANs) high-speed computer networks designed for users who are located near each other

coaxial cable a cable with an inner conducting core, a dielectric material and an outer sheath that is designed for high frequency signal transmission

PERPLEXING SITUATION

Signals for communicating must travel through some medium. The idea that energy could travel through total emptiness, a total vacuum, perplexed scientists for centuries. To satisfy their theories, scientists invented a medium called "aether." Modern science knows there is no aether and signals can pass through a vacuum as well as wires, and fiber optics.

But, light waves are electromagnetic waves just like radio. The glass fiber has characteristics exactly like a wire transmission line. However, the transmission rate is generally higher.

Many computer communications applications require a "wireless" communications medium. Of course, in modern terminology it must be understood that wireless also implies "fiber optic-less." Clearly this is the only communications solution for portable and vehicle-mounted devices. Wireless transmission is accomplished through electromagnetic waves, radio, and light. These electromagnetic waves require no physical medium because they are able to flourish through a vacuum better than through any substance. In fact, wireless signals can be partially blocked by common building materials causing difficulties with wireless systems used indoors.

For transmission through short distances, "wireless modems" are used. These **modems** are low powered radio transmitters and receivers that require no government license. Long distance data communications using radio waves include terrestrial microwave links and satellite data links. These applications involve much higher power transmitters and require government licensing to insure that users do not interfere with other users. Microwave links propagate in straight lines. Depending on the height of the transmitting and receiving antennas, the microwave links are seldom more than 100 kilometers (or approximately 62 miles) apart because of the curvature of the Earth. As with wired communications, repeaters are required to extend microwave communications.

There are two basic types of satellite links, LEO for low earth orbiting and GEO for geostationary orbit. LEO satellites orbit the Earth in less than two hours and are visible to the user for only 20 minutes or so. To provide continuous communications, a number of satellites called a "constellation" is required. Thus when one satellite "sets" or is no longer in view, another satellite can be used for communications. Because the satellites are close to the Earth, typically only 800 kilometers (497 miles) or so, a modest antenna and transmitter power will provide reliable communications. On the other hand, because the user must switch from one satellite to another, a complex system must be employed to switch the communications channel between satellites much like a cellular telephone system in space.

The GEO satellite is always in view and the antenna is pointed at the satellite. Since the satellite never sets, only one satellite is used. Most GEO satellite systems are used by large organizations. This is because the uplink transmitter must use a rather large antenna and needs to be licensed by the government. For small users and individuals, satellite systems are available where the uplink is provided via a conventional telephone line and the downlink is via the satellite. Generally, the uplink data rate required by the individual user is much less than the downlink and this arrangement is acceptable.

For short distance communications, such as from a large room of computers to a LAN, infrared radiation may be used. Low-powered infrared radiation from a light emitting diode (LED) provides the transmitter while the receiver is a phototransistor or diode. This type of infrared technology has been used for many years for remote control devices for consumer en-

modems the contraction of MOdulator DEModulator; devices which convert digital signals into signals suitable for transmission over analog channels, like telephone lines

Microwave relay towers, seen along major highways and in many cities, enable cellular telephone users to stay in communication with friends, family, and business colleagues while on the road.

tertainment equipment such as television. The range of these systems can be as much as 30 meters (98.5 feet), but the light energy can be blocked easily. SEE ALSO BRIDGING DEVICES; SATELLITE TECHNOLOGY; TELECOMMUNICATIONS; WIRELESS TECHNOLOGY.

Albert D. Helfrick

Bibliography

Jamalipour, Abbas. *Low Earth Orbital Satellites for Personal Communication Networks.* Boston: Artech House, 1998.

Sloan, John P., ed. *Local Area Network Handbook.* Boca Raton, FL: Auerbach, 2000.

Video Devices

Video devices are peripherals added to a computer to allow it to work with video. A video capture card provides a way to input video to the computer from conventional sources such as a camera, a VCR, or a TV cable or antenna. A video output card allows video to be output from the computer to a monitor. It is also possible to get video output cards that output video via a cable that can be connected directly to a television, allowing video to be played from a computer and watched on a television.

All information stored on a computer is stored in digital form as a sequence of numbers. When video is received from a source outside the computer, such as a VCR, it is usually in analog format and must be converted into digital form that can be stored in the computer. This is one of the key functions of a video capture card. To record a video sequence in digital form with the quality of a standard TV program would require approximately ninety gigabytes for one hour, equivalent to the capacity of approximately 140 CDs. A significant reduction in the required disc space, without a noticeable loss of quality, can be achieved by compressing the video. Instead of ninety gigabytes to store one hour of TV-quality video, the same information can be compressed to approximately two gigabytes. Because video is almost always stored on a computer in compressed form, most video capture cards also include hardware to perform video compression.

In the same way that the video capture card converts the incoming video to digital form, the video output card must do the opposite conversion, taking the digital video from the computer and outputting analog video for display on a monitor or television. Often the video output card will include hardware for decompression of the video as well as the conversion from digital to analog. Software running on the computer can also perform the decompression, but if the computer is not fast enough, the video will not play back smoothly.

It is also possible to get digital, as opposed to analog, video cameras. Many commercially available camcorders record compressed digital video onto tape. Such a camcorder can be connected directly to a computer without the need to use a video capture card because the video is already in a compressed digital video form. Digital video cameras are also available for connection directly to a computer. Again, because they output video in a digital format, a video capture card is not needed.

One reason to transfer video to a computer is to allow for editing. Once the video is stored on the computer, sophisticated editing software can be used to manipulate the video. For example, holiday camcorder recordings typically contain much unwanted material. After transferring the video from the camcorder to a computer, the video can be edited to remove the unwanted parts. When the editing is finished, the holiday video can be transferred back to the camcorder tapes or to a standard VCR. Or, the edited video can be kept on the computer and played from the computer to a monitor or television.

If a computer is equipped with both a camera and a video output card, it can be used for video conferencing. In video conferencing, two or more people in different locations communicate with each other using both sound and video through their computers. The camera captures a digital video signal of the person, and the computer transmits it through a network to the other participants. Similarly, the other participants have cameras so that video is transmitted to them also. Each person also needs a video output card to display the video received from the other video conference participants. Video conferencing allows people to both see and hear each other while in remote locations.

When a computer is equipped to handle video, it can be used to perform functions normally done by consumer electronics devices. If a computer includes a digital versatile disc read-only memory (DVD-ROM) drive and a

suitable video output card, it is possible to play DVD videos on the computer. Or, the output from the video card can be connected to a television and the DVDs can be watched on the television instead of the computer monitor. SEE ALSO ANIMATION; GAMES; INTERACTIVE SYSTEMS; VIRTUAL REALITY.

Declan P. Kelly

DVDs (digital versatile discs), resembling CDs (compact discs), are replacing videotapes as the preferred storage medium.

Bibliography

Fischetti, Mark, ed. "The Future of Digital Entertainment." *Scientific American* 283, no. 5 (2000): 31–64.

Fox, Barry. "Big Squeeze for Video." *New Scientist* 139, no. 1888 (1993): 21–23.

Johnson, Dave. *How to Use Digital Video*. Indianapolis, IN: Sams, 2000.

Taylor, Jim. *DVD Demystified: The Guidebook for DVD-Video and DVD-ROM*. New York: McGraw-Hill, 1997.

Virtual Memory

Virtual memory is a model—one of many possible models—for managing the resource of physical memory, or main memory. Such management is necessary because a microprocessor, the heart of a computer, has direct access only to main memory, while all programs and data are stored on permanent media such as hard disks.

Reading or writing main memory is as simple as executing a single computer instruction. In contrast, any access to hard disks, digital versatile discs

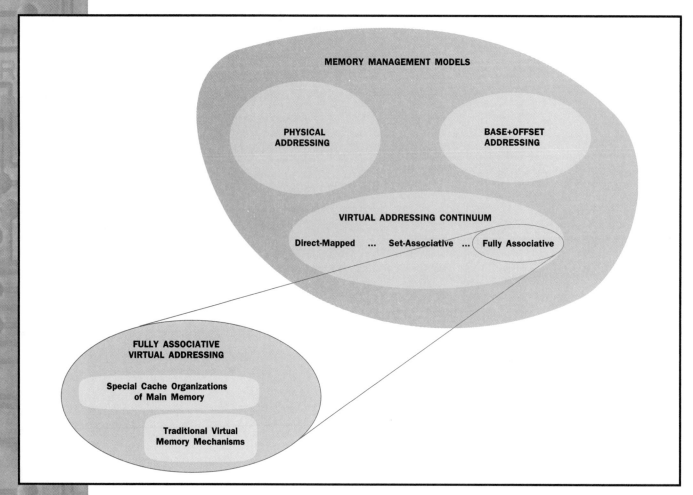

MEMORY MANAGEMENT MODELS

PHYSICAL ADDRESSING

BASE+OFFSET ADDRESSING

VIRTUAL ADDRESSING CONTINUUM

Direct-Mapped ... Set-Associative ... Fully Associative

FULLY ASSOCIATIVE VIRTUAL ADDRESSING

Special Cache Organizations of Main Memory

Traditional Virtual Memory Mechanisms

Figure 1: Memory management models. There are at least three ways to manage physical memory. The first, *physical addressing,* uses physical addresses in the program itself. The second, *base+offset addressing,* uses relative offsets in the program and adds the physical base address at runtime. The third, *virtual addressing,* uses any appropriate naming scheme in the program (usually relative offsets) and relies upon the operating system and hardware to translate the references to physical addresses at runtime. Tradition virtual memory is therefore a small subset of the virtual addressing model of memory management.

protocols agreed understanding for the sub-operations that make up transactions; usually found in the specification of inter-computer communications

(DVDs), compact discs-read only memory (CD-ROMs), or floppy disks is indirect and requires relatively complex communication **protocols** involving dozens to thousands of computer instructions. Therefore, accessing a file or running a program requires that the data on disk first be moved into main memory. Virtual memory is one method for handling this management of data. To illustrate what it is and how it differs from other possibilities, we will compare it to several alternatives.

Memory-Management Alternatives

In the simplest model of program creation and execution, physical addressing, a programmer determines what physical memory is available, reserves it so that no one else uses it, and writes a program to use the reserved memory locations. This allows the program to execute without any runtime support required from the operating system. However, because a program is not likely to use the same physical location on every invocation, this requires a rewrite of the program every time it runs—a tedious task, but one that could be left to the operating system. At process start-up, the

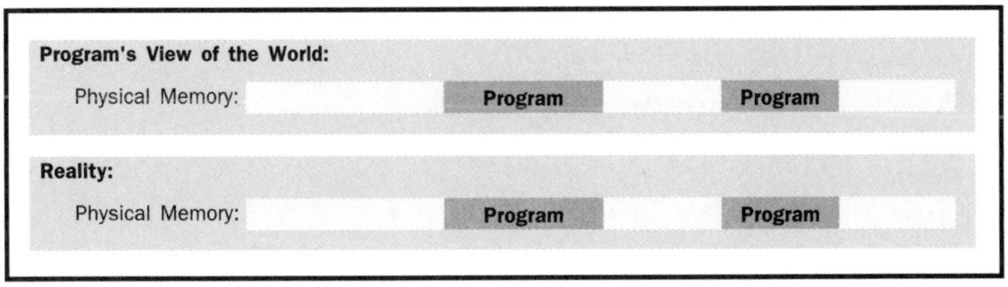

Figure 2: The Physical Addressing model of program creation and execution. In this model, a program's view of itself in its environment (physical memory) is equivalent to reality; a program contains knowledge of the structure of the hardware. A program can be entirely contiguous in memory, or it can be split into multiple pieces, but the locations of all parts of the program are known to the program's code and data.

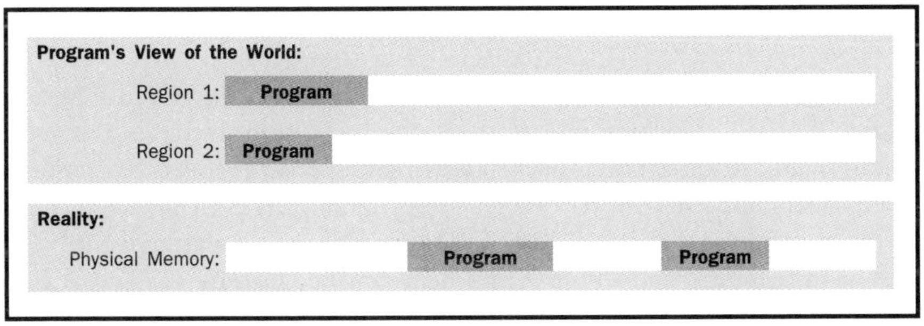

Figure 3: The Base+Offset Addressing model of program creation and execution. In this model, a program's view of itself in its environment is not equivalent to reality, but it does see itself as a set of contiguous regions. It does not know where in physical memory these regions are located, but the regions must be contiguous; they cannot be fragmented.

operating system could modify every pointer reference in the application (including loads, stores, and absolute jumps such as function calls) to reflect the physical address at which the program is loaded. The program as it resides in main memory references itself directly and so contains implicit knowledge about the structure and organization of the physical memory. This model is depicted in Figure 2. A program sees itself exactly as it resides in main memory.

A second model, base+offset addressing, involves writing the program once using pointer addresses that are not absolute but are instead relative offsets from the beginning of the program. If the location of the program in physical memory is a variable stored in a known hardware register, at runtime one can load the program wherever it fits in physical memory and place this location information in the known register so that all memory references first incorporate this base address and are then redirected to the correct physical location. This model is depicted in Figure 3. The process sees itself as a contiguous region or set of contiguous regions, each with its physical location stored in a known hardware register. The advantage is that, as opposed to the previous scheme, knowledge of the memory-system organization is not exposed to the program. The disadvantage is that the program must be divided into a relatively small number of contiguous segments, and each segment must fit entirely in main memory if it is to be used.

A third model, virtual addressing, involves writing the program as if it is loaded at physical memory location zero, loading the program wherever it fits (not necessarily location zero), and using some as-yet-undefined

Program's View of the World:

"Virtual" Memory: Program   Program

Reality:

Physical Memory:

Figure 4: The Virtual Addressing model of program creation and execution. In this model, a program's view of itself in its environment has virtually nothing to do with reality; a program can consider itself a collection of contiguous regions or a set of fragments, or one large monolithic program. The operating system considers the program nothing more than a set of uniform virtual pages and loads them as necessary into physical memory. The entire program need not be resident in memory, and it need not be contiguous.

granularity a description of the level of precision that can be achieved in making measurements of a quantity; for example coarse granularity means inexpensive but imprecise measurements

mechanism to translate the program's addresses to the equivalent physical addresses while it is running. If the translation **granularity** is relatively small (that is, the program is broken down into smaller pieces that are translated independently of each other), the program can even be fragmented in main memory. Bits and pieces of the program can lie scattered throughout main memory, and the program need not be entirely resident to execute. This model is depicted in Figure 4. The advantage of this scheme is that one never needs to rewrite the program. The disadvantage is the potential overhead of the translation mechanism.

Physical addressing can be implemented on any hardware architecture; base+offset addressing can be implemented on any architecture that has the appropriate addressing mode or address-translation hardware; and virtual addressing is typically implemented on microprocessors with memory-management units (MMUs). The following paragraphs discuss the relative merits of the three models.

Physical Addressing.   In physical addressing, program execution behaves differently every time the program is executed on a machine with a different memory organization, and it is likely to behave differently every time it is executed on the same machine with the same organization, because the program is likely to be loaded at a different location every time. Physical addressing systems outnumber virtual addressing systems. An example of a physical addressing system is the operating system for the original Macintosh, which did not have the benefit of a memory-management unit. Though later Macintosh systems added an optional virtual memory implementation, many applications require that the option be disabled during their execution for performance reasons. The newest version of the Macintosh operating system, Mac OS X, is based on a UNIX core and has true high-performance virtual memory at its heart.

amortized phasing out something until it is gradually extinguished, like a mortgage loan

The advantages of the physically addressed scheme are its simplicity and performance. The disadvantages include slow program start-up and decreased flexibility. At start-up, the program must be edited to reflect its location in main memory. While this is easily **amortized** over the run-time of a long-running program, it is not clear whether the speed advantages outweigh this initial cost for short-running programs. Decreased flexibility can also lead to performance loss. Since the program cannot be fragmented or partially loaded, the entire program file must be read into main memory to execute. This can create problems for systems with too little memory to hold all the running programs.

Base+Offset Addressing. In base+offset addressing, like physical addressing, program execution behaves differently every time the program is executed. However, unlike physical addressing, base+offset addressing does not require a rewrite of the program every time it is executed. Base+offset systems far outweigh all other systems combined: an example is the DOS/Windows system running on the Intel x86. The Intel processor architecture has a combined memory management unit that places a base+offset design on top of a virtual addressing design. The architecture provides several registers that hold "segment" offsets, so a program can be composed of multiple regions, each of which must be complete and contiguous, but which need not touch each other.

The advantages of this scheme are that the code needs no editing at process start-up, and the performance is equal to that of the physical addressing model. The disadvantages of the scheme are similar to physical addressing: A region must not be fragmented in main memory because this can be problematic when a system has many running programs scattered about main memory.

Virtual Addressing. In virtual addressing, program execution behaves identically every time the program is executed, even if the machine's organization changes, and even if the program is run on different machines with wildly different memory organizations. Virtual addressing systems include nearly all academic systems, most UNIX-based systems such as Mac OS X, and many UNIX-influenced systems such as Windows NT and Windows 2000. The advantages of virtual memory are that a program needs no rewrite on start-up, one can run programs on systems with very little memory, and one can easily juggle many programs in physical memory because fragmentation of a program's code and data regions is allowed. In contrast, systems that require program regions to remain contiguous in physical memory might be unable to execute a program because no single unused space in main memory is large enough to hold the program, even if many scattered unused areas together would be large enough. The disadvantage of the virtual addressing scheme is the increased space required to hold the translation information and the performance overhead of translating addresses. These overheads have traditionally been no more than a few percent.

Now that the cost of physical memory, **DRAM**, has decreased significantly, the schemes that use memory for better performance—physical and base+offset addressing—have become better choices. Because memory is cheap, perhaps the best design is now one that simply loads every program entirely into memory and assumes that any memory shortage will be fixed by the addition of more DRAM. However, the general consensus is that virtual addressing is more flexible than the other schemes, and its overhead is accepted as reasonable. Moreover, it seems to provide a more intuitive and bug-free **paradigm** for program design and development than the other schemes.

How Are Virtual Addresses Translated?

In the virtual addressing model, programs execute in imaginary address spaces that are mapped onto physical memory by the operating system and

---

MANAGING MEMORY

Virtual memory is a technique for managing memory resources in which one uses physical memory as a cache for program code and data stored on disk. Because it provides such an intuitive model, all modern systems support virtual memory, even though the problem for which is was originally invented—running a program on memory systems smaller than the program itself—is no longer an issue.

DRAM the acronym for Dynamic Random Access Memory; high density, low cost and low speed memory devices used in most computer systems

paradigm an example, pattern, or way of thinking

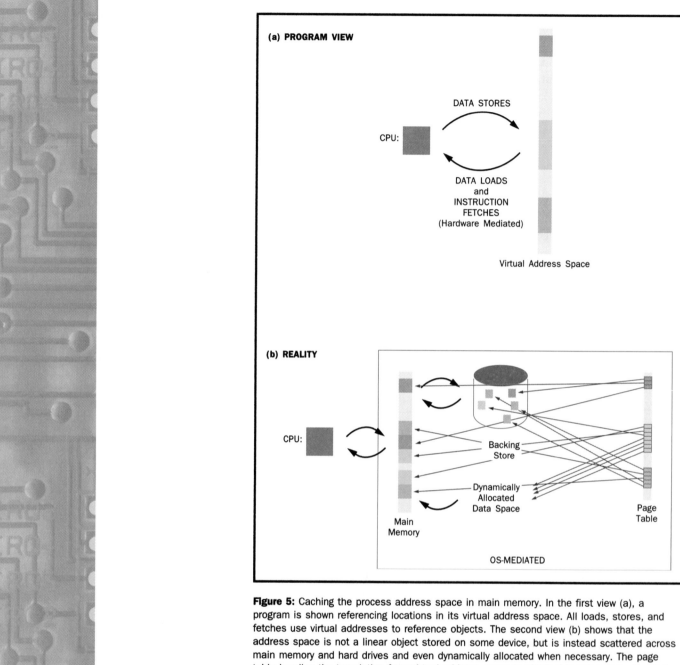

Figure 5: Caching the process address space in main memory. In the first view (a), a program is shown referencing locations in its virtual address space. All loads, stores, and fetches use virtual addresses to reference objects. The second view (b) shows that the address space is not a linear object stored on some device, but is instead scattered across main memory and hard drives and even dynamically allocated when necessary. The page table handles the translation from virtual address space to physical location. Note that it has the same shape as the address space in figure (a), indicating that for every chunk of data in the virtual address space (each chunk is called a "virtual page"), there is exactly one translation entry in the page table.

hardware. Executing programs generate instruction fetches, loads, and stores using imaginary or "virtual" addresses for their instructions and data. The ultimate home for the program's address space is backing store, usually a disk drive. This is where the program's instructions and data originate and where all of its permanent changes go. Every hardware memory structure between the central processing unit (CPU) and the backing store is a cache—temporary storage—for the instructions and data in the program's address space. This includes main memory. Main memory is nothing more than a cache for a program's virtual address space. Everything in the address space initially comes from the program file stored on disk or is created on demand and defined to be zero. Figure 5 illustrates this.

In Figure 5(a), the program view is shown. A program simply makes data loads stores, and implicit instruction fetches to its virtual address space. The address space, as far as the program is concerned, is contiguous and held completely in main memory, and any unused holes between objects in the space are simply wasted space.

Figure 5(b) shows a more realistic picture. There is no linear storage structure that contains a program's address space, especially since every address space is at least several gigabytes when one includes the unused holes. The address space is actually a collection of fixed-sized "pages" that are stored piecemeal on disk or conjured up out of thin air. The instructions and initialized data can be found in the program file, and when the running program needs extra workspace, the operating system can dynamically allocate new pages in main memory. The enabling mechanism is the page table. This is a database managed by the operating system that indicates whether a given page in a program's address space is found on disk, needs to be created from scratch, or can be found in physical memory at some location. Every virtual address generated by the program is translated according to the page table before the request is sent to the memory system. To speed access to the page table, parts of it are held temporarily in hardware. This is one of the functions of a memory-management unit.

Virtual memory is but one of many models of program creation and execution and one of many techniques to manage one's physical memory resources. Other models include base+offset addressing and physical addressing, each of which offers performance advantages over virtual addressing but at a cost in terms of flexibility. The widespread use of virtual memory in contemporary operating systems is testimony to the fact that flexibility is regarded as a valuable system characteristic, outweighing any small amount of performance loss. SEE ALSO GENERATIONS, COMPUTERS; MEMORY; OPERATING SYSTEMS.

Bruce Jacob

Bibliography

Apple Computer, Inc. *Technical Introduction to the Macintosh Family*, 2nd ed. Reading, MA: Addison-Wesley, 1992.

———. *Inside Mac OS X: System Overview*. Cupertino, CA: Apple Computer, Inc., 2000.

Custer, Helen. *Inside Windows NT*. Redmond, WA: Microsoft Press, 1993.

Duncan, Ray, et al. *Extending DOS—A Programmer's Guide to Protected-Mode DOS*, 2nd ed. Reading, MA: Addison-Wesley, 1994.

Jacob, Bruce, and Trevor Mudge. "Virtual Memory: Issues of Implementation." *IEEE Computer* 31, no. 6 (1998): 33–43.

———. "Virtual Memory in Contemporary Microprocessors." *IEEE Micro* 18, no. 4 (1998): 60–75.

Virtual Private Network

Corporations have traditionally leased transmission capacity or contracted **bandwidth** services from common carriers to create their own private

bandwidth a measure of the frequency component of a signal or the capacity of a communication channel to carry signals

wide area network (WAN) interconnected network of computers that spans upward from several buildings to whole cities or entire countries and across countries

TCP/IP protocol suite Transmission Control Protocol/Internet Protocol; a range of functions that can be used to facilitate applications working on the Internet

At a medical facility in New York, a patient from Colombia uses the hospital's private Internet page to communicate with family and friends back home. Such private networks help loved ones learn how a patient is progressing.

wide area network (WAN). However, a WAN is expensive to create and maintain. The economics and technology justifying a WAN drastically changed in the 1990s due to the following factors:

- Decreasing costs for Internet connectivity;
- Increasingly higher bandwidth connections to the Internet; and
- Mature encryption technology for secure Internet communications.

These changes made feasible a new type of network called a Virtual Private Network (VPN) which provides all the features of a private WAN for a fraction of the cost.

A Virtual Private Network is simply a secure system of connectivity over a public network—a private network on a public network infrastructure (the Internet). A VPN is "virtual" in the sense that it has no corresponding physical network but rather shares physical circuits with other traffic. A VPN is "private" in the sense that it isolates and secures Internet traffic using routing and encryption respectively.

How Does It Work?

There are different types of VPNs corresponding to the different layers within the **TCP/IP protocol suite**: Data Link, Network, Transport, and

Application Layers. The most common VPN in use provides secure dial-up (data link) access. Here, a remote user connects to the Internet through an **Internet Service Provider (ISP)**. Software on the user's computer creates a secure, virtual circuit or tunnel to the company's VPN gateway. The benefits include lower costs through the elimination of long distance telephone charges, improved security through the integration of the latest security technology, and unparalleled flexibility, since any Internet connection from dial-up can be used as a VPN connection.

The key to a VPN is **tunneling**. VPN traffic is logically routed separately from other traffic by tunneling mechanisms which repackage data from one network to another. Tunneling at the network layer between a source and a destination wraps (encapsulates) packets with a new header and forwards them into a tunnel with a destination address of the tunnel endpoint. When the packet reaches the tunnel endpoint, the header is unwrapped (unencapsulated) and the packet is forwarded to its original destination. A VPN can thus be created by a collection of tunnels.

Tunneling does not ensure privacy since even encapsulated IP packets are typically transported in plain text. This is clearly a problem if a corporation wants to use the Internet to transmit important business information. Privacy is ensured by **cryptography**. "End-to-end" encryption to individual end systems provides for the highest level of security. "Tunnel mode" encryption is performed between intermediate routers leaving traffic between the end system and the first hop router in plain text. Any corruption of operation or interception of traffic at tunnel endpoints will compromise the entire VPN. Hackers foiled in attempts to crack network traffic may instead target client machines. To help maintain security and privacy, a Certificate Authority (CA) is needed to issue and manage **digital certificates** to VPN devices and users.

Applications

VPNs have been implemented for both data and voice. The idea of using a public network to create the illusion of a private network devoted exclusively to VPN subscribers is not new. The first packet network VPN was created in 1975 when BBN delivered the first Private Line Interface (PLI) packet encryption devices to protect classified data for transmission over the U.S. Department of Defense's ARPANET. Another example is CENTREX service, which has been offered for many years by local telephone companies as a central office switch service providing private data and voice networks. In 1985 AT&T began offering **software-defined networks (SDNs)** for private voice networks based on dedicated and later switched connections; users were billed differently for on-net and off-net calls.

There are several strong motivations for building VPNs: (1) to make a standard corporate computing environment "transparent" to users; (2) to secure communications; and (3) to take advantage of the cost efficiencies of a common public infrastructure versus building and operating a private WAN. A VPN also increases flexibility since global Internet connections can be established and released on-demand. Internet connectivity is also a VPN's major disadvantage: it is difficult to guarantee **quality-of-service (QoS)** over the Internet since **aggregate** traffic flows can be unpredictable. Service Level Agreements (SLAs) between Internet Service Providers (ISPs)

GLOBAL VPN

In 2002 the U.S. State Department was developing a Virtual Private Network (VPN) to coordinate the government's thirty agencies with overseas offices. This network will allow Internet access to e-mail and other communications between agencies, as well as the distribution of information—unclassified, of course.

Internet Service Provider (ISP) a commercial enterprise which offers paying subscribers access to the Internet (usually via modem) for a fee

tunneling a way of handling different communication protocols, by taking packets of a foreign protocol and changing them so that they appear to be a locally known type

cryptography the science of understanding codes and ciphers and their application

digital certificates certificates used in authentication that contain encrypted digital identification information

software-defined networks (SDNs) the same as virtual private networks (VPNs), where the subscriber can set up and maintain a communications system using management software, on a public network

quality-of-service (QoS) a set of performance criteria that a system is designed to guarantee and support as a minimum

aggregate a numerical summation of multiple individual scores

and corporations are an evolving contractual solution designed to guarantee QoS based upon throughput, availability, and response time thresholds. One example of a large VPN is the U.S. State Department, which is implementing a VPN to connect all its embassies around the world. SEE ALSO E-COMMERCE; NETWORK DESIGN; NETWORKS; TELECOMMUNICATIONS; SECURITY; WORLD WIDE WEB.

William J. Yurcik

Bibliography

Comer, Douglas E. *The Internet Book: Everything You Need to Know About Computer Networking and How the Internet Works*, 3rd ed. Upper Saddle River, NJ: Prentice Hall, 2000.

Virtual Reality

The terms virtual reality (VR) and virtual environment (VE) refer to an artificial reality created by computer technology that provides the user with a first-person, interactive view into the virtual world that has been created. It is this interactive capability that distinguishes VR from other systems based on computer graphics such as the extremely realistic computer animations that are increasingly being used by the filmmaking industry. Actors do not actually interact with the computer animations that will ultimately appear in a film. Instead, they interact with an "imaginary" scene or animation that is then added later to provide realism for the moviegoer. This provides the audience with a third-person view of a virtual world. Such a view is in sharp contrast to VR, in which the environment is centered around the perspective of the user who will also typically have the ability to interact dynamically with it.

Although its origins date back to the 1950s, the phrase "virtual reality" first became widely known in the mid-1980s, when mainstream computer technology finally become powerful enough to perform the calculations necessary to create a minimally realistic virtual environment. However, in spite of earlier technological limitations, VR ideas were envisioned long before the 1980s. In 1957 Mort Heilig filed a patent for a head-mounted "stereoscopic television apparatus for personal use." Thus, the head-mounted display (HMD) was born, though at the time, applying this technology to view a virtual world created by a computer was not considered or envisioned.

In 1965 Ivan Sutherland published an article called "The Ultimate Display," which described how a computer could someday be used to provide a window into virtual worlds. Then in 1968, Sutherland combined these ideas together with head tracking and built a head-mounted display providing a stereoscopic view into a simple 3D world that remained stationary despite viewer head movements! Virtual reality was born.

Today VR consists of much more than just head-mounted displays. Gloves containing strain gauges or **fiber optics** can be used to allow a user to interact with a virtual world through hand gestures. Force feedback information, such as the weight of a virtual object, can be provided via **haptic** devices, and a virtual reality modeling language, called VRML, has even been developed to allow Internet browsers to interact with 3D environments.

fiber optics transmission technology using long, thin strands of glass fiber; internal reflections in the fiber ensure that light entering one end is transmitted to the other end with only small losses in intensity; used widely in transmitting digital information

haptic pertaining to the sense of touch

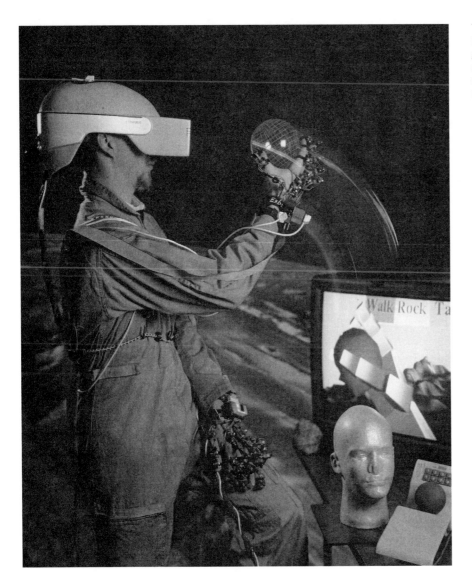

Typical VR equipment includes a helmet and gloves. In this VR simulation, a man attempts to lift a rock on Mars.

The Theory Behind VR

Philosophically speaking, the objective of VR is to create an environment that is believable to the user, but which does not exist in the physical world. The understanding of our world, our reality, is ultimately derived from our senses. Humans have five major senses: sight, hearing, touch, smell, and taste. These senses provide our brains with information that enables us to understand the world around us—our "reality." The most important sense for understanding the physical world is sight, followed by sound and touch.

At the present time, computer technology has enabled the development of sophisticated means to stimulate our senses of sight and hearing. To a lesser degree, the technology for stimulating touch has also been developed. A virtual environment which the brain can easily interpret as being real is created when these technologies are integrated into a system where the sensory data that are produced are consistent with (i.e., conforms to) what we have observed in the physical world.

Anyone who has experienced "motion sickness" while sitting perfectly still and watching a plane fly in a 360-degree theater will attest to the fact

that the brain can be decisively tricked through visual stimulus alone. Recognizing that a large part of our understanding of reality is based on visual stimulus has led significant effort in VR research to be devoted to visual-based stimulus such as image generation and animation.

Concepts such as perspective, reflection of light, texturing, and rotation of 3D images form the basis of constructing stationary images and provide us with a way to navigate through such images. These concepts are well understood and have been precisely defined by mathematical equations. Manipulating these mathematical equations has allowed computers to generate images that are exceedingly real. However, generating such ultra-realistic images involves tremendous mathematical calculations and even the fastest computers yet made cannot support real-time animation of such images. This is why the computer animations used in movies are so much more realistic than present-day VR systems.

The next piece of the visual puzzle is animation, that is, making objects in the virtual world move. Animation is based on **kinetics** and **kinematics**. These fields of study are essentially concerned with how things move and react to forces. Although the advances in this area have been significant, there is much work that remains to be done in order for computers to be able to generate animations that are truly consistent with our understanding of the physical world. For example, we all know how people and animals walk or run, and we are very good at distinguishing "natural" motion from the motion that computer animations are presently capable of generating. We have never actually seen a dinosaur run, but when we see it in a movie, we know that its motion is close, but not quite right.

A complementary technique that can be used to amplify the realism of a virtual word is called immersion. A user can be immersed in a virtual world by removing the conflicting stimulus associated with the physical world. In other words, it is easier for someone to imagine she is in a virtual world if she is only allowed to see that virtual world and nothing else. Immersion is what makes 360-degree theaters so realistic.

Applications

As with all technologies, the use of virtual reality is often limited only by the imagination of the user. In movies like *The Lawnmower Man* and *The Matrix*, Hollywood shows a more sinister look at how VR might someday be abused. However, the ability to create realistic virtual environments has the potential to benefit society significantly. This stems from the fact that a virtual environment is a model of reality. Models typically do not contain every aspect of the thing they are modeling. What this means in the context of VR is that in a virtual environment, the rules of the physical world can be broken or bent!

For example, a pilot can learn to fly a commercial airliner in a virtual environment, without having to worry about experiencing the consequences associated with an actual crash. Fly-by-wire systems or new airplane designs can be tested without the cost or worry of crashing an aircraft. Surgeons can master complex operations without having to worry about accidentally killing a patient. The effects of a nuclear reactor meltdown can be studied without any risk to the environment. New designs for supertankers that min-

kinetics a branch of physics or chemistry concerned with the rate of change in chemical or physical systems

kinematics a branch of physics and mechanical engineering that involves the study of moving bodies and particles

imize oil spillage in the event of a collision can be studied without the cost associated with physically testing. The list of interesting and useful applications of VR is long and growing rapidly. SEE ALSO INTERACTIVE SYSTEMS; OPTICAL TECHNOLOGY; SIMULATION; SIMULATORS; VIRTUAL REALITY IN EDUCATION.

Victor Winter

Bibliography

Hollands, Robin. *The Virtual Reality Homebrewer's Handbook.* New York: John Wiley & Sons, 1996.

Vince, John. *Essential Virtual Reality Fast: How to Understand the Techniques and Potential of Virtual Reality.* New York: Springer-Verlag, 1998.

von Neumann, John

Hungarian Computer Scientist and Mathematician
1903–1957

John Louis von Neumann was one of the great pioneers of computer science and mathematics during the twentieth century. Known for his concept of the stored computer program, he performed work that paved the way for the powerful and **ubiquitous** electronic computers of the early twenty-first century. His work on the Institute for Advanced Studies (IAS) computers built the foundation for what is now known as the "von Neumann Architecture." This architecture resulted in the development of powerful **supercomputers** employed by government, universities, and other institutions.

Von Neumann was born December 28, 1903, in Budapest, Hungary, and died February 8, 1957, in Washington D.C. During his youth, he was often referred to as a prodigy, having published his first technical paper at the age of eighteen. He began attending the University of Budapest in 1921, where he studied chemistry, receiving his diploma in chemical engineering in 1925.

In 1930 von Neumann was invited to Princeton University in the United States, and he was one of the original professors when the university established the Institute for Advanced Studies in 1933. He recognized the importance of computers in the field of applied mathematics and other disciplines and was involved in several strategic government research projects during World War II. Indeed, one of the cornerstones of von Neumann's philosophy was to apply computers to fields of study that interested him. His work in the fields of statistics, ballistics, meteorology, hydrodynamics, and game theory was invaluable during World War II.

He contributed his scientific expertise to the Manhattan Project, the first attempt to develop an atomic bomb for military purposes. At the time, it was feared that Nazi Germany would be the first to develop and deploy the atomic bomb and thus win the war. Von Neumann played an important role as an adviser to the U.S. government, and his talent for finding solutions to complex problems proved invaluable on the projects with which he was involved. He also played an important part as a trusted conduit between groups of scientists working on separate projects that were sequestered from one another due to wartime needs of security. Thus, he brought together

John von Neumann.

ubiquitous to be commonly available everywhere

supercomputers very high performance computers, usually comprised of many processors and used for modeling and simulation of complex phenomena, like meteorology

the talents of scientists working at Los Alamos National Laboratory, the scientists working on the Manhattan Project, and the scientists and engineers working on the first digital computer, Electronic Numerical Integrator and Computer (ENIAC).

After World War II, von Neumann continued to work on government research projects with military applications. His work with supercomputers helped perform the calculations necessary for developing the next generation hydrogen bomb. His ongoing research also led to increasingly capable supercomputers used by the U.S. national laboratories. These proved important for both military and peacetime scientific applications. Hired as a consultant by the IBM Corporation in the 1950s, von Neumann performed duties that involved reviewing proposed and ongoing projects for the company.

Von Neumann is also considered the father of "self replicating systems," systems that could reproduce themselves in a manner not greatly dissimilar from biological life. Von Neumann's concept consisted of two central components: a universal computer and a universal constructor. The universal computer contained the software that directed the universal constructor, and was essentially the central brain of the system. Guided by the universal computer, the constructor was a machine that was fully capable of creating copies of the universal computer and of itself. Once the constructor built another copy of itself, the control software was copied from the original universal computer.

The newly created constructors would then begin to execute the control software, and the process would repeat. The system as a whole is thus self-replicating. The self-replicating concept has been extended to constructors capable of building other objects, depending on the control software employed by the universal computer. The self-replicating machine concept has been explored by scientists at the National Aeronautics and Space Administration (NASA) for building inexpensive and self replicating probes for future space exploration.

One of von Neumann's most famous quotes illustrates the brilliance and depth of his intelligence and personality: "If people do not believe that mathematics is simple, it is only because they do not realize how complicated life is." SEE ALSO BABBAGE, CHARLES; EARLY COMPUTERS; EARLY PIONEERS; GOVERNMENT FUNDING, RESEARCH; HOLLERITH, HERMAN; TURING, ALAN M.

Joseph J. Lazzaro

Bibliography

Goldstine, Herman H. *The Computer from Pascal to von Neumann*. Princeton, NJ: Princeton University Press, 1972.

von Neumann, Nicholas A. *John von Neumann: As Seen by His Brother*. Meadowbrook, PA: Private Printing, 1988.

Wireless Technology

Wireless technology provides the ability to communicate between two or more entities over distances without the use of wires or cables of any sort. This includes communications using radio frequency (RF) as well as **infrared (IR) waves.**

The birth of wireless technology started with the discovery of electromagnetic waves by Heinrich Hertz (1857–1894). Guglielmo Marconi (1874–1937) established the very first commercial RF communications, the wireless telegraph, in the late 1890s—more than fifty years after the first commercial wired telegraph service that was demonstrated in 1832 by Samuel F. B. Morse (1791–1872). Marconi was also the first to transmit radio signals to a mobile receiver on ships in the early 1900s. Wireless technology has always been preceded by wired technology and is usually more expensive, but it has provided the additional advantage of mobility, allowing the user to receive and transmit information while on the move.

Another major thrust of wireless technology has been in the area of broadcast communications like radio, television, and direct broadcast satellite. A single wireless transmitter can send signals to several hundreds of thousands of receivers as long as they all receive the same information. Today, wireless technology encompasses such diverse communication devices as garage-door openers, baby monitors, walkie-talkies, and cellular telephones, as well as transmission systems such as point-to-point microwave links, wireless Internet service, and satellite communications.

Wireless technology involves transmitting electromagnetic signals over the air. Interference and obstacles that block RF signals are common problems with wireless technology. Wireless technology allows users to communicate simultaneously over the same medium without their signals

An early form of wireless technology, the radio receiver opened the door for more advanced capabilities such as cellular and digital communications.

infrared (IR) waves radiation in a band of the electromagnetic spectrum within the infrared range

interfering with one another. This is made possible because of two physical phenomena—the weakening of electromagnetic signals with distance, and the **electromagnetic spectrum**. While listening to a radio station as one drives along a highway, one can observe how an RF or IR signal rapidly loses its strength as it travels away from the transmitter. Thus, two people can transmit at the same time if they are sufficiently far apart. If there are no obstacles, signals fall as the square of the distance. This is called free-space loss.

RF and IR signals can also be generated at different frequencies that do not interfere with each other. The range of frequencies is from a few cycles per second—called **hertz (Hz)** in honor of the scientist who discovered electromagnetic waves—to trillions of hertz, and is called the electromagnetic spectrum. Visible light is included on this spectrum. The 3 **kilohertz (kHz)** to 300 **gigahertz (GHz)** frequency range is the RF spectrum. The IR spectrum corresponds to frequencies beyond 300 GHz. There are strict government regulations on the usage of chunks of the RF spectrum (called **frequency bands**) in all nations of the world. In the United States, the Federal Communications Commission (FCC) decides who uses what frequency bands and for what purpose. They also set limitations on transmit power and on how much interference can be caused between frequency bands.

Frequency bands are either licensed or unlicensed. Licensed bands are owned by certain companies or facilities for specific purposes and cannot be used by anyone else. Unlicensed bands are free and anyone can use them, subject to certain etiquettes. Licensed bands are usually free from interference and more reliable, since there is control over who can transmit in them.

Numerous applications of wireless technology continue to appear on the horizon. Wireless keyboards and mice for computers, wireless speakers and headphones, and wireless smart sensors are now available on the market. In addition to point-to-point microwave links and broadcast radio, wireless appliances and devices are becoming increasingly common. Wireless technology is often employed to provide communications in places where it is difficult to run cables, for mobile communications, as extensions to wired communications, and for emergency deployment. Bluetooth is a new cable replacement wireless technology that can connect almost any appliance that can be networked to any other appliance—a digital camera to a laptop, or a coffee machine to the Internet, for example. Bluetooth applications include cordless telephones, laptops, and other devices.

Wireless technology can also be classified based on voice or data applications or based on mobility—fixed, stationary, portable, and mobile. Cordless and cellular telephones are common examples of voice applications. Cordless telephones operate in unlicensed bands, and cell phones in licensed bands, at frequencies around 1,000 **megahertz (MHz)**. Satellites have been used for a long time to provide voice communications. Pagers are examples of data applications.

Today, it is also possible to access the Internet using wireless technology. Cellular digital packet data (CDPD) service is available for accessing the Internet in the same licensed frequency bands as cell phones. It is possible to buy a CDPD modem for handheld computers and palmtops and to browse the web and send e-mail without connecting via a cable to the Internet. **Wireless local area networks (WLANs)** in unlicensed bands are also very popular, both in companies and for residential networking, for shared access to the Internet.

Modern fixed wireless technology applications include wireless local loops (WLLs) that provide local telephone service using rooftop antennas, and local multipoint distribution service (LMDS), a digital wireless transmission at 28 GHz that can provide several megabits per second of data for access to the Internet. Stationary wireless technology includes desktop computers that connect to the Internet using WLANs. Cordless phones, laptops, and palmtop computers with wireless connectivity fall into the portable category, while cell phones are the most common example of mobile wireless technology.

Wireless access to the Internet is expected to exceed wired access in the next few years, and the prospects for the future are exciting. SEE ALSO NETWORK TOPOLOGIES; NETWORKS; WORLD WIDE WEB.

Prashant Krishnamurthy

wireless local area networks (WLANs) interconnected networks of computers that use radio and/or infrared communication channels, rather than cables

Bibliography

Carr, Joseph J. *Microwave and Wireless Communications Technology*. Boston: Butterworth-Heinemann, 1997.

Gralla, Preston. *How Wireless Works*. Indianapolis, IN: Que, 2002.

Zuse, Konrad

German Engineer
1910–1995

Konrad Zuse was a German engineer who designed and built a binary computer during the 1930s. He is thought to have created the first functioning program-controlled computer, however his earliest efforts were destroyed during World War II. By the end of his life, Zuse had received many honors for his contributions to the development of the computer, and he was recognized as one of the pioneers of electromechanical computing.

Zuse was born in Berlin, Germany, in 1910. During his youth he showed talent in art and engineering. As an artist, he created block prints, drawings, and cartoons; as an engineer, he built mechanical devices such as grab cranes and model train rail networks. He graduated from high school at the age of sixteen and entered the Technical University of Berlin, having made the decision to study civil engineering. While he was a university student, he built a vending machine that delivered selected items, accepted money, and returned change.

Zuse completed his degree in 1935 and worked for a brief time as a structural engineer for the Henschel Aircraft Company. He left this position to work independently on building a computer. His parents' living room served as his laboratory, his assistants were unpaid college friends, and his funding was raised from friends and family members. His goal was to create a mechanical calculating machine based on a binary system rather than on the decimal system used in calculators. The machine would consist of a memory unit and an arithmetic unit, and it would be programmable.

Konrad Zuse.

WORKING INDEPENDENTLY

When Konrad Zuse began his experiments developing computer technology, he was unaware of the work done by Charles Babbage more than 100 years earlier. Babbage envisioned the Analytical Engine, an early calculating machine. Zuse ultimately carried on that work.

vacuum tubes electronic devices constructed of sealed glass tubes containing metal elements in a vacuum; used to control electrical signals

electromagnetic relays switches that have a high current carrying capacity, which are opened and closed by an electromagnet

punched cards paper cards with punched holes which give instructions to a computer in order to encode program instructions and data

algorithmic pertaining to the rules or procedures used to solve mathematical problems—most often described as a sequence of steps

prototype a working model or experimental investigation of proposed systems under development

Zuse's Z1 computer was operational by 1938. Helmut Schreyer, a friend and electronic engineer, suggested replacing the mechanical relay system with **vacuum tubes** and telephone relay switches to shorten the processing time. Zuse rejected the vacuum tube idea but considered using the telephone relay switches. The design of the Z2 incorporated this idea.

In 1939 Adolf Hitler and the Nazis invaded Poland, beginning World War II. The war interrupted Zuse's work and he was soon drafted into the German army. To no avail, both Zuse and Schreyer tried to interest the German military in the computer project. However, Zuse was transferred from active duty to work as a structural engineer for Henschel Aircraft. His assignment was related to the development of unmanned flying bombs, or cruise missiles. This transfer allowed him time to complete construction of the Z2, which used telephone relays for the arithmetic unit. In 1940 Zuse successfully demonstrated the Z2 to the German Aeronautics Research Institute or DLV.

As a result, he received partial funding for the next generation model, the Z3, which was constructed from recycled materials. Once again he relied on the support of family and friends. The telephone relays were used equipment rescued by associates who worked for the state telephone and postal system. The Z3 used **electromagnetic relays** for the memory and arithmetic units, was based on a binary number system, and was programmable. Discarded film strips were used in place of **punched cards** for input. The Z3 was destroyed during a bombing raid over Berlin.

Construction of the Z4 began in 1942. This model was moved from Berlin to southern Germany when the Allied bombing became intense. At the end of the war in 1945, Zuse, his family, and the Z4 were refugees in Hinterstein, a small alpine village in southern Germany. For the next two years Zuse worked on theoretical problems, developing Plankalkül, an **algorithmic** language, and formalizing the game of chess. To support his family, he painted and sold alpine scenes to vacationing American troops.

In 1947 Zuse and Harro Stucken, an engineer from the Henschel Aircraft Company, founded Zuse Engineering Company to build computers for science and industry. Later the company became ZUSE KG. The company contracted with Remington Rand to build punched card devices. In 1950 the company leased the Z4 to the Swiss Federal Institute of Technology, where it remained in use until 1955. The company's first German contract was with Leitz Camera to build computers to determine lens specifications.

As the company grew, Zuse began to receive honorary degrees and awards for his work. In 1962 Howard H. Aiken, who designed the MARK I computer (the first American-built programmable computing system) acknowledged Zuse's claim to being one of the first to build a program-controlled computer. During this time a copy of model Z3 was built for display in the German Museum. By the late 1960s the company had been sold to Seimans, and Zuse turned his attention to other areas. He continued to work on problems related to computers and developed a **prototype** for a CAD, or computer-aided design, machine.

The claim that Zuse built the first computer will remain unresolved, due in part to the destruction of both the Z1 and the Z3 computers in wartime bombings. What is clear, however, is that he developed his machines without knowledge of or interaction with others in the field, without proper funding, and using scavenged materials while always in danger from the war. At the time of his death in 1995, he had gained recognition for his contribution to computer science. SEE ALSO EARLY COMPUTERS; EARLY PIONEERS.

Bertha Kugelman Morimoto

Bibliography

Zuse, Konrad. *The Computer: My Life*. Berlin and Heidelberg: Springer-Verlag, 1993.

Photo and Illustration Credits

The illustrations and tables featured in Computer Sciences *were created by GGS Information Services. The photographs appearing in the text were reproduced by permission of the following sources:*

Volume 1

Gale Research: **1**; AP/Wide World Photos, Inc.: **4, 35, 39, 44, 60, 82, 91, 136, 148, 190, 209, 219**; Courtesy of the Library of Congress: **6, 25, 52, 58, 83, 98, 103, 126, 150, 193, 211**; Kobal Collection/Warner Bros.: **9**; Kobal Collection: **11**; Archive Photos/Reuters/Sell: **16**; National Audubon Society Collection/Photo Researchers, Inc.: **19**; CORBIS/Bettmann: **22, 41, 73, 86, 165, 201, 221**; AT&T Archives: **28**; U.S. Census Bureau: **33**; Elena Rooraid/Photo Edit: **48**; Photo Edit: **66**; IBM Corporate Archives: **70, 163**; Colin Braley/Reuters/Getty Images: **94**; Adam Hart-Davis/National Audubon Society Collection/Photo Researchers, Inc.: **105**; Michael S. Yamashita/CORBIS: **110**; Reuters NewMedia Inc./CORBIS: **116**; UPI/CORBIS-Bettmann: **118, 176**; Associated Press/AP: **121**; Doris Langley Moore Collection: **122**; Astrid & Hanns-Frieder Michler/Photo Researchers, Inc.: **133**; Microsoft Corporation: **139**; Ted Spiegel/CORBIS: **140**; Prestige/Getty Images: **143**; Richard T. Nowitz/CORBIS: **146**; U.S. National Aeronautics and Space Administration (NASA): **152**; Robert Cattan/Index Stock Imagery/PictureQuest: **156**; Dave Bartruff/Stock, Boston Inc./PictureQuest: **159**; Courtesy Carnegie Mellon University Field Robotics Center/NASA: **172**; Roger Ressmeyer/CORBIS: **179, 184**; Hulton-Deutsch Collection/CORBIS: **187**; Granger Collection, Ltd.: **197**; Larry Chan/Reuters/Getty Images: **204**; Microsoft programs: **213, 214, 215, 216, 217**.

Volume 2

Thomas E. Kurtz: **2**; Courtesy of the Library of Congress: **4, 18, 99, 112**; CORBIS/Bettmann: **13**; U.S. National Aeronautics and Space Administration (NASA): **16**; Roger Ressmeyer/CORBIS: **25, 92, 115, 118, 150, 179, 215**; A/P Wide World Photos, Inc.: **31, 36, 40, 65, 73, 89, 110, 133, 136, 143, 161, 165, 167, 171, 199, 205, 212, 221**; UPI/CORBIS-Bettmann: **34, 169, 217, 219**; Courtesy of BT Archives: **46**; CORBIS: **53**; Andrew Syred/National Audubon Society Collection/Photo Researchers, Inc.: **62**; Richard Pasley/Stock, Boston Inc./PictureQuest: **70**; Bob Krist/CORBIS: **77**; Patrik Giardino/CORBIS: **79**; Rob Crandall/Stock, Boston Inc./PictureQuest: **84**; Mario Tama/Getty Images: **94**; AFP/CORBIS: **98**; Custom Medical Stock Photo: **140**; William McCoy/Rainbow/PictureQuest: **147**; Courtesy of Niklaus Wirth: **157**; Reuters NewMedia Inc./CORBIS: **175**; Paul Almasy/CORBIS: **188**; Detlev Van Ravenswaay/Picture Press/CORBIS-Bettmann: **193**; James Marshall/CORBIS: **203**.

Volume 3

Bill Lai/Rainbow/PictureQuest: **2**; Agricultural Research Service/USDA: **5**; Carlos Lopez-Barillas/Getty Images: **8**; A/P Wide World Photos, Inc.: **11, 19, 28, 39, 89, 102, 106, 111, 118, 131**; Laima Druskis/Stock, Boston Inc./PictureQuest: **13**; Bojan Brecelj/CORBIS: **17**; JLM Visuals: **23**; Mediafocus: **24**; Ed Kashi/Phototake NYC: **30**; Reuters NewMedia Inc./CORBIS: **34**; Royalty Free/CORBIS: **42**; Srulik Haramaty/Phototake NYC: **46**; Mark

Antman/Phototake, NYC: **52**;
CORBIS/Bettmann: **55, 206, 211**; Hulton-
Deutsch Collection/CORBIS: **56**; Walter A.
Lyons: **60, 210**; Smith & Santori/Gale
Group: **62**; Darren McCollester/Getty
Images: **69**; Richard Palsey/Stock, Boston
Inc./PictureQuest: **73**; Ed Kashi/CORBIS:
79; Index Stock Imagery: **81**; AFP/CORBIS:
85; Montes De Oca & Associates: **92**; Millard
Berry: **95**; Courtesy of
NASA/JPL/NIMA/Visible Earth: **100**;
Courtesy of the Library of Congress: **108,
124**; Nehau Kulyk/Photo Researchers, Inc.:
116; CORBIS: **122**; U.S. Department of
Education/National Audubon Society
Collection/Photo Researchers, Inc.: **125**; Bob
Rowan/Progressive Image/CORBIS: **133**; Bill
Ross/CORBIS: **137**; Geoff
Tompkincon/National Audubon Society
Collection/Photo Researchers, Inc.: **141**;
Clive Freeman/Photo Researchers, Inc.: **143**;
Roger Ressmeyer/CORBIS: **150**; Free
Software Foundation: **157**; Kenneth
Eward/BioGrafx/National Audubon Society
Collection/Photo Researchers, Inc.: **163**;
Steven McBride/Picturesque/PictureQuest:
168; Michael S. Yamashita/CORBIS: **175**;
Photo Researchers, Inc.: **178**; Chris
Hondros/Getty Images: **181**; David
Silverman/Getty Images: **183**; U.S. National
Aeronautics and Space Administration
(NASA): **188**; Jim Sugar
Photography/CORBIS: **200**; Leif
Skoogfors/CORBIS: **205**.

Volume 4

A/P Wide World Photos, Inc.: **2, 15, 23, 29,
33, 41, 44, 59, 75, 100, 147, 151, 162, 168,
177, 180, 184, 186, 190, 195, 197, 201,**
203; Gene M. Amdahl: **4**; Vittoriano
Rastelli/CORBIS: **7**; Jim Sugar
Photography/CORBIS: **10**; NNS: **22**; John
Maher/Stock, Boston Inc./PictureQuest: **26**;
Kenneth Eward/Photo Researchers, Inc.: **35**;
Steve Chenn/CORBIS: **47**; Christopher
Morris/Black Star Publishing/PictureQuest:
50; Jonathan Elderfield/Getty Images: **54**;
Courtesy of the Library of Congress: **56, 103,
163**; Amy Ritterbush/Stock, Boston
Inc./PictureQuest: **64**; AFP/CORBIS: **66,
113, 125, 131, 134**; Reuters NewMedia
Inc./CORBIS: **70, 89, 108, 120, 194**; Shahn
Kermani/Getty Images: **76**; Associated
Press/AP: **78, 93, 95**; Patricia Nagle/Center
for Instructional Development and Distance
Education/University of Pittsburgh: **85**; Alec
Sarkas/Center for Instructional Development
and Distance Education/University of
Pittsburgh: **87**; Kobal Collection/MGM/UA:
106; Space Imaging: **115**; Courtesy of USGS
Landsat 7 Team at the Eros Data Center and
NASA's Visible Earth: **116**; Reuters/News
and Observer-Jim/Archive Photos, Inc.: **122**;
Reuters/Getty Images: **128**; Oleg
Nikishin/Getty Images: **139**; Netscape
Communicator browser window (c) 1999
Netscape Communications Corporation—
used with permission (Netscape
Communications has not authorized,
sponsored, endorsed, or approved this
publication and is not responsible for its
content): **155, 156, 157, 159**;
YBSHY/CORBIS: **165**; James King-
Holmes/Science Photo Library/The National
Audubon Society Collection/Photo
Researchers, Inc.: **171**; Carnegie Mellon
University: **173**; Microsoft Visual Basic
program: **209, 210, 211**.

Glossary

abacus: an ancient counting device that probably originated in Babylon around 2,400 B.C.E.

acuity: sharpness or keenness, especially when used to describe vision

address bus: a collection of electrical signals used to transmit the address of a memory location or input/output port in a computer

aerodynamics: the science and engineering of systems that are capable of flight

agents: systems (software programs and/or computing machines) that can act on behalf of another, or on behalf of a human

aggregate: a numerical summation of multiple individual scores

ailerons: control surfaces on the trailing edges of the wings of an aircraft—used to manage roll control

ALGOL: a language developed by the ALGOL committee for scientific applications—acronym for ALGOrithmic Language

algorithm: a rule or procedure used to solve a mathematical problem—most often described as a sequence of steps

all-points-addressable mode: a technique for organizing graphics devices where all points (pixels) on the screen are individually accessible to a running program

alpha beta pruning: a technique that under certain conditions offers an optimal way to search through data structures called "trees"

alphanumeric: a character set which is the union of the set of alphabetic characters and the set of single digit numbers

ambient: pertaining to the surrounding atmosphere or environment

ambiguity: the quality of doubtfulness or uncertainty; often subject to multiple interpretations

amortized: phasing out something in until it is gradually extinguished, like a mortgage loan

amplitude: the size or magnitude of an electrical signal

analog: a quantity (often an electrical signal) that is continuous in time and amplitude

analogous: a relationship of logical similarity between two or more objects

analytic simulation: modeling of systems by using mathematical equations (often differential equations) and programming a computer with them to simulate the behavior of the real system

Analytical Engine: Charles Babbage's vision of a programmable mechanical computer

animatronics: the animation (movement) of something by the use of electronic motors, drives, and controls

anthropomorphic: having human form, or generally resembling human appearance

anti-aliasing: introducing shades of gray or other intermediate shades around an image to make the edge appear to be smoother

applet: a program component that requires extra support at run time from a browser or run-time environment in order to execute

approximation: an estimate

arc tangent: the circular trigonometric function that is the inverse of the tangent function; values range from $-\Pi/2$ to $\Pi/2$

artificial intelligence (AI): a branch of computer science dealing with creating computer hardware and software to mimic the way people think and perform practical tasks

ASCII: an acronym that stands for American Standard Code for Information Interchange; assigns a unique 8-bit binary number to every letter of the alphabet, the digits (0 to 9), and most keyboard symbols

assembler: a program that translates human-readable assembly language programs to machine-readable instructions

assembly language: the natural language of a central processing unit (CPU); often classed as a low-level language

asynchronous: events that have no systematic relationship to one another in time

attenuation: the reduction in magnitude (size or amplitude) of a signal that makes a signal weaker

authentication: the act of ensuring that an object or entity is what it is intended to be

automata theory: the analytical (mathematical) treatment and study of automated systems

automaton: an object or being that has a behavior that can be modeled or explained completely by using automata theory

autonomous: self governing, or being able to exist independently

autonomy: the capability of acting in a self-governing manner; being able to exist independently or with some degree of independence

axioms: statements that are taken to be true, the foundation of a theory

Bakelite: an insulating material used in synthetic goods, including plastics and resins

ballistics: the science and engineering of the motion of projectiles of various types, including bullets, bombs, and rockets

bandwidth: a measure of the frequency component of a signal or the capacity of a communication channel to carry signals

bar code: a graphical number representation system where alphanumeric characters are represented by vertical black and white lines of varying width

base-2: a number system in which each place represents a power of 2 larger than the place to its right (binary)

base-8: a number system in which each place represents a power of 8 larger than the place to its right (octal)

base-10: a number system in which each place represents a power of 10 larger than the place to its right (decimal)

base-16: a number system in which each place represents a power of 16 larger than the place to its right (hexadecimal)

batch processing: an approach to computer utilization that queues non-interactive programs and runs them one after another

Bayesian networks: structures that describe systems in which there is a degree of uncertainty; used in automated decision making

Bernoulli numbers: the sums of powers of consecutive integers; named after Swiss mathematician Jacques Bernoulli (1654-1705)

binary: existing in only two states, such as "on" or "off," "one" or "zero"

binary code: a representation of information that permits only two states, such as "on" or "off," "one" or "zero"

binary coded decimal (BCD): an ANSI/ISO standard encoding of the digits 0 to 9 using 4 binary bits; the encoding only uses 10 of the available 16 4-bit combinations

binary digit: a single bit, 1 or 0

binary number system: a number system in which each place represents a power of 2 larger than the place on its right (base-2)

binary system: a machine or abstraction that uses binary codes

binomial theorem: a theorem giving the procedure by which a binomial expression may be raised to any power without using successive multiplications

bit: a single binary digit, 1 or 0—a contraction of Binary digIT; the smallest unit for storing data in a computer

bit mapped display: a computer display that uses a table of binary bits in memory to represent the image that is projected onto the screen

bit maps: images comprised of bit descriptions of the image, in black and white or color, such that the colors can be represented by the two values of a binary bit

bit rate: the rate at which binary bits can be processed or transferred per unit time, in a system (often a computer communications system)

bit serial mode: a method of transferring binary bits one after another in a sequence or serial stream

bitstream: a serialized collection of bits; usually used in transfer of bits from one system to another

Boolean algebra: a system developed by George Boole that deals with the theorems of undefined symbols and axioms concerning those symbols

Boolean logic: a system, developed by George Boole, which treats abstract objects (such as sets or classes) as algebraic quantities; Boole applied his mathematical system to the study of classical logic

Boolean operators: fundamental logical operations (for example "and" and "or") expressed in a mathematical form

broadband access: a term given to denote high bandwidth services

browsers: programs that permits a user to view and navigate through documents, most often hypertext documents

bugs: errors in program source code

bus: a group of related signals that form an interconnecting pathway between two or more electronic devices

bus topology: a particular arrangement of buses that constitutes a designed set of pathways for information transfer within a computer

byte: a group of eight binary digits; represents a single character of text

C: a programming language developed for the UNIX operating system; it is designed to run on most machines and with most operating systems

cache: a small sample of a larger set of objects, stored in a way that makes them accessible

calculus: a method of dealing mathematically with variables that may be changing continuously with respect to each other

Callback modems: security techniques that collect telephone numbers from authorized users on calls and then dial the users to establish the connections

capacitates: fundamental electrical components used for storing electrical charges

capacitor: a fundamental electrical component used for storing an electrical charge

carpal tunnel syndrome: a repetitive stress injury that can lead to pain, numbness, tingling, and loss of muscle control in the hands and wrists

cartography: map making

cathode ray tube (CRT): a glass enclosure that projects images by directing a beam of electrons onto the back of a screen

cellular automata: a collection or array of objects that are programmed identically to interact with one another

cellular neural networks (CNN): a neural network topology that uses multidimensional array structures comprised of cells that work together in localized groups

central processing unit (CPU): the part of a computer that performs computations and controls and coordinates other parts of the computer

certificate: a unique electronic document that is used to assist authentication

chaos theory: a branch of mathematics dealing with differential equations having solutions which are very sensitive to initial conditions

checksum: a number that is derived from adding together parts of an electronic message before it is dispatched; it can be used at the receiver to check against message corruption

chromatic dispersion: the natural distortion of pulses of light as they move through an optical network; it results in data corruption

cipher: a code or encryption method

client: a program or computer often managed by a human user, that makes requests to another computer for information

client/server technology: computer systems that are structured using clients (usually human driven computers) to access information stored (often remotely) on other computers known as servers

coaxial cable: a cable with an inner conducting core, a dielectric material and an outer sheath that is designed for high frequency signal transmission

cognitive: pertaining to the concepts of knowing or perceiving

collocation: the act of placing elements or objects in a specific order

commodity: raw material or service marketed prior to being used

compiled: a program that is translated from human-readable code to binary code that a central processing unit (CPU) can understand

compiled executable code: the binary code that a central processing unit (CPU) can understand; the product of the compilation process

compilers: programs that translate human-readable high-level computer languages to machine-readable code

computer-aided design (CAD): the use of computers to replace traditional drawing instruments and tools for engineering or architectural design

computer-assisted tomography: the use of computers in assisting with the management of X-ray images

computer peripheral: a device that is connected to a computer to support its operation; for example, a keyboard or a disk drive unit

concatenates: the joining together of two elements or objects; for example, words are formed by concatenating letters

concentric circles: circles that have coincident centers

conceptualization: a creative process that is directed at envisaging a structure or collection of relationships within components of a complex system

concurrency control: the management and coordination of several actions that occur simultaneously; for example, several computer programs running at once

concurrent: pertaining to simultaneous activities, for example simultaneous execution of many computer programs

configuration files: special disk files containing information that can be used to tell running programs about system settings

cookie: a small text file that a web site can place on a computer's hard drive to collect information about a user's browsing activities or to activate an online shopping cart to keep track of purchases

copyrights: the legal rules and regulations concerning the copying and redistribution of documents

cosine: a trigonometric function of an angle, defined as the ratio of the length of the adjacent side of a right-angled triangle divided by the length of its hypotenuse

counterfeiting: the act of knowingly producing non-genuine objects, especially in relation to currency

crawls: severe weather warnings that are broadcast on the bottom of TV screens

cross-platform: pertaining to a program that can run on many different computer types (often called hardware platforms)

CRT: the acronym for cathode ray tube, which is a glass enclosure that projects images by directing a beam of electrons onto the back of a screen

cryptanalysis: the act of attempting to discover the algorithm used to encrypt a message

cryptanalyst: a person or agent who attempts to discover the algorithm used to encrypt a message

cryptography: the science of understanding codes and ciphers and their application

cryptosystem: a system or mechanism that is used to automate the processes of encryption and decryption

cuneiform: in the shape of a wedge

cybercafe: a shop, cafe, or meeting place where users can rent a computer for a short time to access the Internet

cybernetics: a unified approach to understanding the behavior of machines and animals developed by Norbert Wiener (1894-1964)

cycloids: pertaining to circles, in either a static way or in a way that involves movement

dark fiber: a fiber optic network that exists but is not actively in service, hence the darkness

data mining: a technique of automatically obtaining information from databases that is normally hidden or not obvious

data partitioning: a technique applied to databases (but not restricted to them) which organizes data objects into related groups

data reduction technique: an approach to simplifying data, e.g. summarization

data warehousing: to implement an informational database used to store shared data

de facto: as is

de jure: strictly according to the law

debug: the act of trying to trace, identify, and then remove errors in program source code

decimal system: a number system in which each place represents a power of 10 larger than the place to its right (base-10)

decision trees: classifiers in which a sequence of tests are made to decide the class label to assign to an unknown data item; the sequence of tests can be visualized as having a tree structure

deformations: mechanical systems where a structure is physically misshapen, e.g., dented

degrade: to reduce quality or performance of a system

delimiters: special symbols that mark the beginnings and/or endings of other groups of symbols (for example to mark out comments in program source code)

demographics: the study of the statistical data pertaining to a population

densities: measures of the density of a material; defined as the mass of a sample of material, divided by its volume

deregulation: the lowering of restrictions, rules, or regulations pertaining to an activity or operation (often commercial)

die: the silicon chip that is the heart of integrated circuit fabrication; the die is encased in a ceramic or plastic package to make the completed integrated circuit (IC)

dielectric: a material that exhibits insulating properties, as opposed to conducting properties

Difference Engine: a mechanical calculator designed by Charles Babbage that automated the production of mathematical tables by using the method of differences

differential analyzer: a computer constructed in the early 1930s by Vannevar Bush at Massachusetts Institute of Technology (MIT); it solved differential equations by mechanical integration

digital: a quantity that can exist only at distinct levels, not having values in between these levels (for example, binary)

digital certificates: certificates used in authentication that contain encrypted digital identification information

digital divide: imaginary line separating those who can access digital information from those who cannot

digital library: distributed access to collections of digital information

digital signature: identifier used to authenticate the sender of an electronic message or the signer of an electronic document

digital subscriber line (DSL): a technology that permits high-speed voice and data communications over public telephone networks; it requires the use of a DSL modem

digital subscriber loop (DSL): the enabling of high-speed digital data transfer over standard telephone cables and systems in conjunction with normal telephone speech data

digital watermarks: special data structures permanently embedded into a program or other file type, which contain information about the author and the program

digitizes: converts analog information into a digital form for processing by a computer

diode: a semiconductor device that forces current flow in a conductor to be in one direction only, also known as a rectifier

diode tube: an obsolete form of diode that was made of metal elements in a sealed and evacuated glass tube

direction buttons: buttons on a program with a graphical user interface that provide a way of navigating through information or documents

discrete: composed of distinct elements

disintermediation: a change in business practice whereby consumers elect to cut out intermediary agencies and deal directly with a provider or vendor

distance learning: the form of education where the instructor and students are separated by either location or time (or both), usually mediated by some electronic communication mechanism

distributed denial of service (DDoS): an attack in which large numbers of messages are directed to send network traffic to a target computer, overloading it or its network connection; typically, the attacking computers have been subverted

distributed systems: computer systems comprised of many individual computers that are interconnected and act in concert to complete operations

documentation: literature in a human-readable form that is referred to in support of using a computer or computer system

domain: a region in which a particular element or object exists or has influence; (math) the inputs to a function or relation

doping: a step used in the production of semiconductor materials where charged particles are embedded into the device so as to tailor its operational characteristics

dot.com: a common term used to describe an Internet-based commercial company or organization

dragged: to have been moved by the application of an external pulling force; quite often occurring in graphical user interfaces when objects are moved with a mouse

DRAM: the acronym for Dynamic Random Access Memory; high density, low cost and low speed memory devices used in most computer systems

driver: a special program that manages the sequential execution of several other programs; a part of an operating system that handles input/output devices

drop-down menu: a menu on a program with a graphical user interface that produces a vertical list of items when activated

dumb terminal: a keyboard and screen connected to a distant computer without any processing capability

duplex: simultaneous two-directional communication over a single communication channel

dynamic: changing; possessing volatility

dynamic links: logical connections between two objects that can be modified if the objects themselves move or change state

e-books: short for electronic books; books available for downloading onto an e-book reader

EBCDIC: the acronym for Extended Binary Coded Decimal Interchange Code, which assigns a unique 8-bit binary number to every letter of the alphabet, the digits (0-9), and most keyboard symbols

egress: to move out of an object, system, or environment

electromagnetic: a piece of metal that becomes magnetic only when electricity is applied to it; in general, the more electricity applied to metal, the stronger its magnetism

electromagnetic relays: switches that have a high current carrying capacity, which are opened and closed by an electromagnet

electromagnetic spectrum: a range of frequencies over which electromagnetic radiation can be generated, transmitted, and received

embedded computers: computers that do not have human user orientated I/O devices; they are directly contained within other machines

embedded systems: another term for "embedded computers"; computers that do not have human user orientated input/output devices; they are directly contained within other machines

emoticons: symbols or key combinations used in electronic correspondence to convey emotions

enciphered: encrypted or encoded; a mathematical process that disguises the content of messages transmitted

encryption: also known as encoding; a mathematical process that disguises the content of messages transmitted

end-effector: the end piece of a robotic arm that can receive various types of grippers and tools

end users: computer users

enterprise information system: a system of client and server computers that can be used to manage all of the tasks required to manage and run a large organization

entropy: a measure of the state of disorder or randomness in a system

ephemeris: a record showing positions of astronomical objects and artificial satellites in a time-ordered sequence

ergonomic: being of suitable geometry and structure to permit effective or optimal human user interaction with machines

esoteric: relating to a specialized field of endeavor that is characterized by its restricted size

ether: a highly volatile liquid solvent; also, the far regions of outer space

ethernets: a networking technology for mini and microcomputer systems consisting of network interface cards and interconnecting coaxial cables; invented in the 1970s by Xerox Corporation

Euclidean geometry: the study of points, lines, angles, polygons, and curves confined to a plane

expert system: a computer system that uses a collection of rules to exhibit behavior which mimics the behavior of a human expert in some area

fiber optics: transmission technology using long, thin strands of glass fiber; internal reflections in the fiber assure that light entering one end is transmitted to the other end with only small losses in intensity; used widely in transmitting digital information

field searching: a strategy in which a search is limited to a particular field; in a search engine, a search may be limited to a particular domain name or date, narrowing the scope of searchable items and helping to eliminate the chance of retrieving irrelevant data

file transfer protocol (FTP): a communications protocol used to transfer files

filter queries: queries used to select subsets from a data collection, e.g., all documents with a creation date later than 01/01/2000

firewall: a special purpose network computer or software that is used to ensure that no access is permitted to a sub-network unless authenticated and authorized

firing tables: precalculated tables that can give an artillery gunner the correct allowances for wind conditions and distance by dictating the elevation and deflection of a gun

floating point operations: numerical operations involving real numbers where in achieving a result, the number of digits to the left or right of the decimal point can change

flowcharts: techniques for graphically describing the sequencing and structure of program source code

fluid dynamics: the science and engineering of the motion of gases and liquids

Freedom of Information Act (FOIA): permits individuals to gain access to records and documents that are in the possession of the government

freon: hydrocarbon-based gases used as refrigerants and as pressurants in aerosols

frequency bands: ranges of signal frequencies that are of particular interest in a given application

frequency modulation: a technique whereby a signal is transformed so that it is represented by another signal with a frequency that varies in a way related to the original signal

full-text indexing: a search engine feature in which every word in a document, significant or insignificant, is indexed and retrievable through a search

fuzzy logic: models human reasoning by permitting elements to have partial membership to a set; derived from fuzzy set theory

gallium arsenide: a chemical used in the production of semiconductor devices; chemical symbol GaAs

gates: fundamental building blocks of digital and computer-based electric circuits that perform logical operations; for example logical AND, logical OR

Gaussian classifiers: classifiers constructed on the assumption that the feature values of data will follow a Gaussian distribution

gbps: acronym for gigabits per second; a binary data transfer rate that corresponds to a thousand million (billion, or 10⁹) bits per second

geometric: relating to the principles of geometry, a branch of mathematics related to the properties and relationships of points, lines, angles, surfaces, planes, and solids

germanium: a chemical often used as a high performance semiconductor material; chemical symbol Ge

GIF animation: a technique using Graphic Interchange Format where many images are overlaid on one another and cycled through a sequence to produce an animation

GIF image: the acronym for Graphic Interchange Format where a static image is represented by binary bits in a data file

gigabit networking: the construction and use of a computer network that is capable of transferring information at rates in the gigahertz range

gigabytes: units of measure equivalent to a thousand million (billion, or 109) bytes

gigahertz (GHz): a unit or measure of frequency, equivalent to a thousand million (billion, or 109) hertz, or cycles per second

Global Positioning System (GPS): a method of locating a point on the Earth's surface that uses received signals transmitted from satellites to calculate position accurately

granularity: a description of the level of precision that can be achieved in making measurements of a quantity; for example coarse granularity means inexpensive but imprecise measurements

graphical user interface (GUI): an interface that allows computers to be operated through pictures (icons) and mouse-clicks, rather than through text and typing

groupware: a software technology common in client/server systems whereby many users can access and process data at the same time

gyros: a contraction of gyroscopes; a mechanical device that uses one or more spinning discs which resist changes to their position in space

half tones: black and white dots of certain sizes, which provide a perception of shades of gray

ham radio: a legal (or licensed) amateur radio

haptic: pertaining to the sense of touch

Harvard Cyclotron: a specialized machine (cyclotron) developed in 1948 at Harvard University; it is used to carry out experiments in sub-atomic physics and medicine

head-mounted displays (HMD): helmets worn by a virtual reality (VR) participant that include speakers and screens for each eye, which display three-dimensional images

hertz (Hz): a unit of measurement of frequency, equal to one cycle per second; named in honor of German physicist Heinrich Hertz (1857-1894)

heuristic: a procedure that serves to guide investigation but that has not been proven

hexadecimal: a number system in which each place represents a power of 16 larger than the place to its right (base-16)

high-bandwidth: a communication channel that permits many signals of differing frequencies to be transmitted simultaneously

high precision/high recall: a phenomenon that occurs during a search when all the relevant documents are retrieved with no unwanted ones

high precision/low recall: a phenomenon that occurs when a search yields a small set of hits; although each one may be highly relevant to the search topic, some relevant documents are missed

high-speed data links: digital communications systems that permit digital data to be reliably transferred at high speed

hoaxes: false claims or assertions, sometimes made unlawfully in order to extort money

holistic: looking at the entire system, rather than just its parts

hydraulic: motion being powered by a pressurized liquid (such as water or oil), supplied through tubes or pipes

hydrologic: relating to water

hyperlinks: connections between electronic documents that permit automatic browsing transfer at the point of the link

Hypertext Markup Language (HTML): an encoding scheme for text data that uses special tags in the text to signify properties to the viewing program (browser) like links to other documents or document parts

Hypertext Transfer Protocol (HTTP): a simple connectionless communications protocol developed for the electronic transfer (serving) of HTML documents

I/O: the acronym for input/output; used to describe devices that can accept input data to a computer and to other devices that can produce output

I/O devices: devices that can accept "input" data to a computer and to other devices that can produce "output"

icon: a small image that is used to signify a program or operation to a user

illiquid: lacking in liquid assets; or something that is not easily transferable into currency

ImmersaDesks: large 4 x 5 foot screens that allow for stereoscopic visualization; the 3-D computer graphics create the illusion of a virtual environment

ImmersaWalls: large-scale, flat screen visualization environments that include passive and active multi-projector displays of 3-D images

immersive: involved in something totally

in-band: pertaining to elements or objects that are within the limits of a certain local area network (LAN)

inference: a suggestion or implication of something based on other known related facts and conclusions

information theory: a branch of mathematics and engineering that deals with the encoding, transmission, reception, and decoding of information

infrared (IR) waves: radiation in a band of the electromagnetic spectrum within the infrared range

infrastructure: the foundation or permanent installation necessary for a structure or system to operate

ingot: a formed block of metal (often cast) used to facilitate bulk handling and transportation

ingress: the act of entering a system or object

init method: a special function in an object oriented program that is automatically called to initialize the elements of an object when it is created

input/output (I/O): used to describe devices that can accept input data to a computer and to other devices that can produce output

intangible: a concept to which it is difficult to apply any form of analysis; something which is not perceived by the sense of touch

integrated circuit: a circuit with the transistors, resistors, and other circuit elements etched into the surface of a single chip of semiconducting material, usually silicon

integrated modem: a modem device that is built into a computer, rather than being attached as a separate peripheral

intellectual property: the acknowledgement that an individual's creativity and innovation can be owned in the same way as physical property

interconnectivity: the ability of more than one physical computer to operate with one or more other physical computers; interconnectivity is usually accomplished by means of network wiring, cable, or telephone lines

interface: a boundary or border between two or more objects or systems; also a point of access

Internet Protocol (IP): a method of organizing information transfer between computers; the IP was specifically designed to offer low-level support to Transmission Control Protocol (TCP)

Internet Service Provider (ISP): a commercial enterprise which offers paying subscribers access to the Internet (usually via modem) for a fee

interpolation: estimating data values between known points but the values in between are not and are therefore estimated

intranet: an interconnected network of computers that operates like the Internet, but is restricted in size to a company or organization

ionosphere: a region of the upper atmosphere (above about 60,000 meters or 196,850 feet) where the air molecules are affected by the sun's radiation and influence electromagnetic wave propagation

isosceles triangle: a triangle that has two sides of equivalent length (and therefore two angles of the same size)

iterative: a procedure that involves repetitive operations before being completed

Jacquard's Loom: a weaving loom, developed by Joseph-Marie Jacquard (1752-1834), controlled by punched cards; identified as one of the earliest examples of programming automation

Java applets: applets written in the Java programming language and executed with the support of a Java Virtual Machine (JVM) or a Java enabled browser

joysticks: the main controlling levers of small aircraft; models of these can be connected to computers to facilitate playing interactive games

JPEG (Joint Photographic Experts Group): organization that developed a standard for encoding image data in a compressed format to save space

k-nearest neighbors: a classifier that assigns a class label for an unknown data item by looking at the class labels of the nearest items in the training data

Kbps: a measure of digital data transfer per unit time—one thousand (kilo, K) bits per second

keywords: words that are significant in some context or topic (often used in searching)

kilohertz (kHz): a unit or measure of frequency, equivalent to a thousand (or 103) hertz, or cycles per second

kinematics: a branch of physics and mechanical engineering that involves the study of moving bodies and particles

kinetics: a branch of physics or chemistry concerned with the rate of change in chemical or physical systems

labeled data: a data item whose class assignment is known independent of the classifier being constructed

lambda calculus: important in the development of programming languages, a specialized logic using substitutions that was developed by Alonzo Church (1903-1995)

LEDs: the acronym for Light Emitting Diode; a diode that emits light when passing a current and used as an indicating lamp

lexical analyzer: a portion of a compiler that is responsible for checking the program source code produced by a programmer for proper words and symbols

Library of Congress Classification: the scheme by which the Library of Congress organizes classes of books and documents

light emitting diode (LED): a discrete electronic component that emits visible light when permitting current to flow in a certain direction; often used as an indicating lamp

linear: pertaining to a type of system that has a relationship between its outputs and its inputs that can be graphed as a straight line

Linux operating system: an open source UNIX operating system that was originally created by Linus Torvalds in the early 1990s

liquid crystal display (LCD): a type of crystal that changes its level of transparency when subjected to an electric current; used as an output device on a computer

local area network (LAN): a high-speed computer network that is designed for users who are located near each other

logarithm: the power to which a certain number called the base is to be raised to produce a particular number

logic: a branch of philosophy and mathematics that uses provable rules to apply deductive reasoning

lossy: a nonreversible way of compressing digital images; making images take up less space by permanently removing parts that cannot be easily seen anyway

low precision/high recall: a phenomenon that occurs during a search when a large set of results are retrieved, including many relevant and irrelevant documents

lumens: a unit of measure of light intensity

magnetic tape: a way of storing programs and data from computers; tapes are generally slow and prone to deterioration over time but are inexpensive

mainframe: large computer used by businesses and government agencies to process massive amounts of data; generally faster and more powerful than desktop computers but usually requiring specialized software

malicious code: program instructions that are intended to carry out malicious or hostile actions; e.g., deleting a user's files

mammogram: an X-ray image of the breast, used to detect signs of possible cancer

Manhattan Project: the U.S. project designed to create the world's first atomic bomb

mass spectrometers: instruments that can identify elemental particles in a sample by examining the frequencies of the particles that comprise the sample

mass spectrometry: the process of identifying the compounds or elemental particles within a substance

megahertz (MHz): a unit or measure of frequency, equivalent to a million (or 106) hertz, or cycles per second

memex: a device that can be used to store personal information, notes, and records that permits managed access at high speed; a hypothetical creation of Vannevar Bush

menu label: the text or icon on a menu item in a program with a graphical user interface

metadata: data about data, such as the date and time created

meteorologists: people who have studied the science of weather and weather forecasting

metropolitan area network (MAN): a high-speed interconnected network of computers spanning entire cities

microampere: a unit of measure of electrical current that is one-millionth (10-6) amperes

microchip: a common term for a semiconductor integrated circuit device

microcomputer: a computer that is small enough to be used and managed by one person alone; often called a personal computer

microprocessor: the principle element in a computer; the component that understands how to carry out operations under the direction of the running program (CPU)

millisecond: a time measurement indicating one-thousandth (or 10-3) of a second

milliwatt: a power measurement indicating one-thousandth (or 10-3) of a watt

minicomputers: computers midway in size between a desktop computer and a mainframe computer; most modern desktops are much more powerful than the older minicomputers

minimax algorithm: an approach to developing an optimal solution to a game or contest where two opposing systems are aiming at mutually exclusive goals

Minitel: network used in France that preceded the Internet, connecting most French homes, businesses, cultural organizations, and government offices

mnemonic: a device or process that aids one's memory

modalities: classifications of the truth of a logical proposition or statement, or characteristics of an object or entity

modem: the contraction of MOdulator DEModulator; a device which converts digital signals into signals suitable for transmission over analog channels, like telephone lines

modulation: a technique whereby signals are translated to analog so that the resultant signal can be more easily transmitted and received by other elements in a communication system

modules: a generic term that is applied to small elements or components that can be used in combination to build an operational system

molecular modeling: a technique that uses high performance computer graphics to represent the structure of chemical compounds

motherboard: the part of the computer that holds vital hardware, such as the processors, memory, expansion slots, and circuitry

MPEG (Motion Picture Coding Experts Group): an encoding scheme for data files that contain motion pictures—it is lossy in the same way as JPEG (Joint Photographic Experts Group) encoding

multiplexes: operations in ATM communications whereby data cells are blended into one continuous stream at the transmitter and then separated again at the receiver

multiplexor: a complex device that acts as a multi-way switch for analog or digital signals

multitasking: the ability of a computer system to execute more than one program at the same time; also known as multiprogramming

mylar: a synthetic film, invented by the DuPont corporation, used in photographic printing and production processes, as well as disks and tapes

nanocomputing: the science and engineering of building mechanical machines at the atomic level

nanometers: one-thousand-millionth (one billionth, or 10-9) of a meter

nanosecond: one-thousand-millionth (one billionth, or 10-9) of a second

nanotechnology: the design and construction of machines at the atomic or molecular level

narrowband: a general term in communication systems pertaining to a signal that has a small collection of differing frequency components (as opposed to broadband which has many frequency components)

National Computer Security Center (NCSC): a branch of the National Security Agency responsible for evaluating secure computing systems; the Trusted Computer Systems Evaluation Criteria (TCSEC) were developed by the NCSC

Network Control Protocol (NCP): a host-to-host protocol originally developed in the early 1970s to support the Internet, which was then a research project

network packet switching: the act of routing and transferring packets (or small sections) of a carrier signal that conveys digital information

neural modeling: the mathematical study and the construction of elements that mimic the behavior of the brain cell (neuron)

neural networks: pattern recognition systems whose structure and operation are loosely inspired by analogy to neurons in the human brain

Newtonian view: an approach to the study of mechanics that obeys the rules of Newtonian physics, as opposed to relativistic mechanics; named after Sir Isaac Newton (1642-1727)

nonlinear: a system that has relationships between outputs and inputs which cannot be expressed in the form of a straight line

O-rings: 37-foot rubber circles (rings) that seal the joints between the space shuttle's rocket booster segments

OEM: the acronym for Original Equipment Manufacturer; a manufacturer of computer components

offline: the mode of operation of a computer that applies when it is completely disconnected from other computers and peripherals (like printers)

Open Systems Interconnections (OSI): a communications standard developed by the International Organization for Standardization (ISO) to facilitate compatible network systems

operands: when a computer is executing instructions in a program, the elements on which it performs the instructions are known as the operands

operating system: a set of programs which control all the hardware of a computer and provide user and device input/output functions

optical character recognition: the science and engineering of creating programs that can recognize and interpret printed characters

optical computing: a proposed computing technology which would operate on particles of light, rather than electric currents

optophone: a system that uses artificial intelligence techniques to convert images of text into audible sound

orthogonal: elements or objects that are perpendicular to one another; in a logical sense this means that changes in one have no effect on the other

oscillator: an electronic component that produces a precise waveform of a fixed known frequency; this can be used as a time base (clock) signal to other devices

oscilloscopes: measuring instruments for electrical circuitry; connected to circuits under test using probes on leads and having small screens that display the signal waveforms

out-of-band: pertaining to elements or objects that are external to the limits of a certain local area network (LAN)

overhead: the expense or cost involved in carrying out a particular operation

packet-switched network: a network based on digital communications systems whereby packets of data are dispatched to receivers based on addresses that they contain

packet-switching: an operation used in digital communications systems whereby packets (collections) of data are dispatched to receivers based on addresses contained in the packets

packets: collections of digital data elements that are part of a complete message or signal; packets contain their destination addresses to enable reassembly of the message or signal

paradigm: an example, pattern, or way of thinking

parallel debugging: specialized approaches to locating and correcting errors in computer programs that are to be executed on parallel computing machine architectures

parallel processing: the presence of more than one central processing unit (CPU) in a computer, which enables the true execution of more than one program

parametric: modeling a system using variables or parameters that can be observed to change as the system operates

parity: a method of introducing error checking on binary data by adding a redundant bit and using that to enable consistency checks

pattern recognition: a process used by some artificial-intelligence systems to identify a variety of patterns, including visual patterns, information patterns buried in a noisy signal, and word patterns imbedded in text

PDF: the acronym for Portable Document Format, developed by Adobe Corporation to facilitate the storage and transfer of electronic documents

peer-to-peer services: the ways in which computers on the same logical level can interoperate in a structured network hierarchy

permutations: significant changes or rearrangement

personal area networking: the interconnectivity of personal productivity devices like computers, mobile telephones, and personal organizers

personal digital assistants (PDA): small-scale hand-held computers that can be used in place of diaries and appointment books

phosphor: a coating applied to the back of a glass screen on a cathode ray tube (CRT) that emits light when a beam of electrons strikes its surface

photolithography: the process of transferring an image from a film to a metal surface for etching, often used in the production of printed circuit boards

photonic switching: the technology that is centered on routing and managing optical packets of digital data

photons: the smallest fundamental units of electromagnetic radiation in the visible spectrum—light

photosensitive: describes any material that will change its properties in some way if subjected to visible light, such as photographic film

picoseconds: one-millionth of a millionth of a second (one-trillionth, or 10-12)

piezoelectric crystal: an electronic component that when subjected to a current will produce a waveform signal at a precise rate, which can then be used as a clock signal in a computer

PIN (personal identification number): a password, usually numeric, used in conjunction with a cryptographic token, smart card, or bank card, to ensure that only an authorized user can activate an account governed by the token or card

ping sweeps: technique that identifies properties belonging to a server computer, by sending it collections of "ping" packets and examining the responses from the server

piracy: the unlawful copying and redistribution of computer software, ignoring the copyright and ownership rights of the publisher

pixel: a single picture element on a video screen; one of the individual dots making up a picture on a video screen or digital image

pixilation: the process of generating animation, frame by frame

plug-in: a term used to describe the way that hardware and software modules can be added to a computer system, if they possess interfaces that have been built to a documented standard

pneumatic: powered by pressurized air, supplied through tubes or pipes

polarity: the positive (+) or negative (−) state of an object, which dictates how it will react to forces such as magnetism or electricity

polarizer: a translucent sheet that permits only plane-polarized light to pass through, blocking all other light

polygon: a many-sided, closed, geometrical figure

polynomial: an expression with more than one term

polypeptide: the product of many amino acid molecules bonded together

population inversion: used in quantum mechanics to describe when the number of atoms at higher energy levels is greater than the number at lower energy levels—a condition needed for photons (light) to be emitted

port: logical input/output points on computers that exist in a network

port scans: operations whereby ports are probed so that information about their status can be collected

potentiometer: an element in an electrical circuit that resists current flow (a resistor) but the value of the resistance can be mechanically adjusted (a variable resistor)

predicate calculus: a branch of logic that uses individuals and predicates, or elements and classes, and the existential and universal quantifiers, all and some, to represent statements

privatized: to convert a service traditionally offered by a government or public agency into a service provided by a private corporation or other private entity

progenitor: the direct parent of something or someone

propositional calculus: a branch of logic that uses expressions such as "If ... then ..." to make statements and deductions

proprietary: a process or technology developed and owned by an individual or company, and not published openly

proprietary software: software created by an individual or company that is sold under a license that dictates use and distribution

protocol: an agreed understanding for the sub-operations that make up a transaction, usually found in the specification of inter-computer communications

prototype: a working model or experimental investigation of proposed systems under development

pseudocode: a language-neutral, structural description of the algorithms that are to be used in a program

public key information: certain status and identification information that pertains to a particular public key (i.e., a key available for public use in encryption)

public key infrastructure (PKI): the supporting programs and protocols that act together to enable public key encryption/decryption

punched card: a paper card with punched holes which give instructions to a computer in order to encode program instructions and data

quadtrees: data structures resembling trees, which have four branches at every node (rather than two as with a binary tree); used in the construction of complex databases

quality-of-service (QoS): a set of performance criteria that a system is designed to guarantee and support as a minimum

quantification: to quantify (or measure) something

quantum-dot cellular automata (QCA): the theory of automata as applied to quantum dot architectures, which are a proposed approach for the development of computers at nanotechnology scales

quantum mechanical: something influenced by the set of rules that govern the energy and wave behavior of subatomic particles on the scale of sizes that are comparable to the particles themselves

queue: the ordering of elements or objects such that they are processed in turn; first-in, first-out

radar: the acronym for RAdio Direction And Ranging; a technique developed in the 1930s that uses frequency shifts in reflected radio waves to measure distance and speed of a target

radio telescopes: telescopes used for astronomical observation that operate on collecting electromagnetic radiation in frequency bands above the visible spectrum

random access memory (RAM): a type of memory device that supports the nonpermanent storage of programs and data; so called because various locations can be accessed in any order (as if at random), rather than in a sequence (like a tape memory device)

raster: a line traced out by a beam of electrons as they strike a cathode ray tube (CRT)

raster scan pattern: a sequence of raster lines drawn on a cathode ray tube such that an image or text can be made to appear

read only memory (ROM): a type of memory device that supports permanent storage of programs

real-time: a system, often computer based, that ensures the rates at which it inputs, processes, and outputs information meet the timing requirements of another system

recursive: operations expressed and implemented in a way that requires them to invoke themselves

relational database: a collection of records that permits logical and business relationships to be developed between themselves and their contents

relay contact systems: systems constructed to carry out logic functions, implemented in relays (electromechanical switches) rather than semiconductor devices

resistors: electrical components that slow the flow of current

retinal scan: a scan of the retina of the eye, which contains a unique pattern for each individual, in order to identify (or authenticate) someone

robotics: the science and engineering of building electromechanical machines that aim to serve as replacements for human laborers

routers: network devices that direct packets to the next network device or to the final destination

routing: the operation that involves collecting and forwarding packets of information by way of address

satellite: an object that orbits a planet

scalar: a quantity that has magnitude (size) only; there is no associated direction or bearing

scalar processor: a processor designed for high-speed computation of scalar values

schematic: a diagrammatic representation of a system, showing logical structure without regard to physical constraints

scripting languages: modern high-level programming languages that are interpreted rather than compiled; they are usually cross-platform and support rapid application development

Secure Sockets Layer (SSL): a technology that supports encryption, authentication, and other facilities and is built into standard UNIX communication protocols (sockets over TCP/IP)

semantics: the study of how words acquire meaning and how those meanings change over time

semiconductor: solid material that possesses electrical conductivity characteristics that are similar to those of metals under certain conditions, but can also exhibit insulating qualities under other conditions

semiconductor diode laser: a diode that emits electromagnetic radiation at wavelengths above about 630 nanometers, creating a laser beam for industrial applications

sensors: devices that can record and transmit data regarding the altitude, flight path, attitude, etc., so that they can enter into the system's calculations

sequentially: operations occurring in order, one after another

server: a computer that does not deal directly with human users, but instead handles requests from other computers for services to be performed

SGML: the acronym for Standard Generalized Markup Language, an international standard for structuring electronic documents

shadow mask: a metal sheet behind the glass screen of a cathode ray tube (CRT) that ensures the correct color phosphor elements are struck by the electron beams

shareware: a software distribution technique, whereby the author shares copies of his programs at no cost, in the expectation that users will later pay a fee of some sort

Sherman Antitrust Act: the act of the U.S. Congress in 1890 that is the foundation for all American anti-monopoly laws

signaling protocols: protocols used in the management of integrated data networks that convey a mix of audio, video, and data packets

SIGs: short for "Special Interest Group," SIGs concentrate their energies on specific categories of computer science, such as programming languages or computer architecture

silica: silicon oxide; found in sand and some forms of rock

silicon: a chemical element with symbol Si; the most abundant element in the Earth's crust and the most commonly used semiconductor material

silicon chip: a common term for a semiconductor integrated circuit device

Silicon Valley: an area in California near San Francisco, which has been the home location of many of the most significant information technology orientated companies and universities

silver halide: a photosensitive product that has been used in traditional cameras to record an image

simplex: uni-directional communication over a single communication channel

simputers: simple to use computers that take on the functionality of personal computers, but are mobile and act as personal assistants and information organizers

sine wave: a wave traced by a point on the circumference of a circle when the point starts at height zero (amplitude zero) and goes through one full revolution

single-chip: a computer system that is constructed so that it contains just one integrated circuit device

slide rule: invented by Scotsman John Napier (1550-1617), it permits the mechanical automation of calculations using logarithms

smart card: a credit-card style card that has a microcomputer embedded within it; it carries more information to assist the owner or user

smart devices: devices and appliances that host an embedded computer system that offers greater control and flexibility

smart matter: materials, machines, and systems whose physical properties depend on the computing that is embedded within them

social informatics: a field of study that centers on the social aspects of computing technology

softlifting: the act of stealing software, usually for personal use (piracy)

software-defined networks (SDNs): the same as virtual private networks (VPNs), where the subscriber can set up and maintain a communications system using management software, on a public network

sonar: the science and engineering of sound propagation in water

SONET: the acronym for Synchronous Optical NETwork, a published standard for networks based on fiber optic communications technology

sound card: a plug-in card for a computer that contains hardware devices for sound processing, conversion, and generation

source code: the human-readable programs that are compiled or interpreted so that they can be executed by a computing machine

speech recognition: the science and engineering of decoding and interpreting audible speech, usually using a computer system

spider: a computer program that travels the Internet to locate web documents and FTP resources, then indexes the documents in a database, which are then searched using software that the search engine provides

spreadsheet: an accounting or business tool that details numerical data in columns for tabulation purposes

static: without movement; stationary

stellar: pertaining to the stars

subnet: a logical section of a large network that simplifies the management of machine addresses

supercomputer: a very high performance computer, usually comprised of many processors and used for modeling and simulation of complex phenomena, like meteorology

superconductivity: the property of a material to pass an electric current with almost no losses; most metals are superconductive only at temperatures near absolute zero

swap files: files used by an operating system to support a virtual memory system, in which the user appears to have access to more memory than is physically available

syllogistic statements: the essential tenets of western philosophical thought, based on hypotheses and categories

synchronization: the time domain ordering of events; often applied when events repeatedly occur simultaneously

synchronized: events occurring at specific points in time with respect to one another

synchronous: synchronized behavior

synergistic: relating to synergism, which is the phenomenon whereby the action of a group of elements is greater than their individual actions

syntactic analyzer: a part of a compiler that scans program source code ensuring that the code meets essential language rules with regard to structure or organization

syntax: a set of rules that a computing language incorporates regarding structure, punctuation, and formatting

tangible: of a nature that is real, as opposed to something that is imaginary or abstract

task partitioning: the act of dividing up work to be done so that it can be separated into distinct tasks, processes, or phases

taxonomy: the classification of elements or objects based on their characteristics

TCP: the acronym for Transmission Control Protocol; a fundamental protocol used in the networks that support the Internet (ARPANET)

TCP/IP networks: interconnected computer networks that use Transmission Control Protocol/Internet Protocol

TCP/IP protocol suite: Transmission Control Protocol/Internet Protocol; a range of functions that can be used to facilitate applications working on the Internet

telegraph: a communication channel that uses cables to convey encoded low bandwidth electrical signals

telemedicine: the technology that permits remote diagnosis and treatment of patients by a medical practitioner; usually interactive bi-directional audio and video signals

telemetry: the science of taking measurements of something and transmitting the data to a distant receiver

teleoperation: any operation that can be carried out remotely by a communications system that enables interactive audio and video signals

teletype: a machine that sends and receives telephonic signals

terabyte: one million million (one trillion, or 10^{12}) bytes

thermal ignition: the combustion of a substance caused by heating it to the point that its particles have enough energy to commence burning without an externally applied flame

thermodynamic: relating to heat energy

three-body problem: an intractable problem in mechanics that involves the attempts to predict the behavior of three bodies under gravitational effects

thumbnail: an image which is a scaled down copy of a much larger image; used to assist in the management of a large catalog of images

time lapse mode: to show a sequence of events occurring at a higher than natural speed so it looks like it is happening rapidly rather than in real time

title bar: the top horizontal border of a rectangular region owned by a program running in a graphical user interface (GUI); it usually contains the program name and can be used to move the region around

tomography: the process of capturing and analyzing X-ray images

T1 digital circuitry: a type of digital network technology that can handle separate voice and/or digital communications lines

topographic: pertaining to the features of a terrain or surface

topology: a method of describing the structure of a system that emphasizes its logical nature rather than its physical characteristics

trademark rights: a trademark is a name, symbol, or phrase that identifies a trading organization and is owned by that organization

trafficking: transporting and selling; especially with regard to illegal merchandise

training data: data used in the creation of a classifier

transaction processing: operations between client and server computers that are made up of many small exchanges that must all be completed for the transaction to proceed

transducers: devices that sense a physical quantity, such as temperature or pressure, and convert that measurement into an electrical signal

transistor: a contraction of TRANSfer resISTOR; a semiconductor device, invented by John Bardeen, Walter Brattain, and William Shockley, which has three terminals; can be used for switching and amplifying electrical signals

translational bridges: special network devices that convert low-level protocols from one type to another

Transmission Control Protocol (TCP): a stream-orientated protocol that uses Internet Protocol (IP); it is responsible for splitting data into packets, transferring it, and reassembling it at the receiver

transmutation: the act of converting one thing into another

trigonometry: a branch of mathematics founded upon the geometry of triangles

triodes: nearly obsolete electronic devices constructed of sealed glass tubes containing metal elements in a vacuum; triodes were used to control electrical signals

Trojan horse: potentially destructive computer program that masquerades as something benign; named after the wooden horse employed by the Acheans to conquer Troy

tunneling: a way of handling different communication protocols, by taking packets of a foreign protocol and changing them so that they appear to be a locally known type

Turing machine: a proposed type of computing machine that takes inputs off paper tape and then moves through a sequence of states under the control of an algorithm; identified by Alan Turing (1912-1954)

1200-baud: a measure of data transmission; in this case the rate of 1200 symbols (usually bits) per second

twisted pair: an inexpensive, medium bandwidth communication channel commonly used in local area networks

ubiquitous: to be commonly available everywhere

ultrasonic: the transmission and reception of sound waves that are at frequencies higher than those audible to humans

Uniform Resource Locator (URL): a reference to a document or a document container using the Hypertext Transfer Protocol (HTTP); consists of a hostname and path to the document

Universal Product Code (UPC): the first barcode standard developed in 1973 and adopted widely since

UNIX: operating system that was originally developed at Bell Laboratories in the early 1970s

uplinks: connections from a client machine to a large network; frequently used when information is being sent to a communications satellite

vacuum tube: an electronic device constructed of a sealed glass tube containing metal elements in a vacuum; used to control electrical signals

valence: a measure of the reactive nature of a chemical element or compound in relation to hydrogen

variable: a symbol, such as a string of letters, which may assume any one of a set of values known as the domain

vector graphics: graphics output systems whereby pairs of coordinates are passed to the graphics controller, which are interpreted as end points of vectors to be drawn on the screen

vector processing: an approach to computing machine architecture that involves the manipulation of vectors (sequences of numbers) in single steps, rather than one number at a time

vector supercomputer: a highly optimized computing machine that provides high performance using a vector processing architecture

velocities: vector quantities that have a magnitude or speed and a direction

Venn diagrams: diagrams used to demonstrate the relationships between sets of objects, named after John Venn, a British logician

venture capitalists: persons or agencies that speculate by providing financial resources to enable product development, in the expectation of larger returns with product maturity

video capture cards: plug-in cards for a computer that accepts video input from devices like televisions and video cameras, allowing the user to record video data onto the computer

video compression algorithms: special algorithms applied to remove certain unnecessary parts of video images in an attempt to reduce their storage size

virtual channel connection: an abstraction of a physical connection between two or more elements (or computers); the complex details of the physical connection are hidden

virtual circuit: like a virtual channel connection, a virtual circuit appears to be a direct path between two elements, but is actually a managed collection of physical connections

Virtual Private Networks (VPNs): a commercial approach to network management where privately owned voice and data networks are set up on public network infrastructure

virtual reality (VR): the use of elaborate input/output devices to create the illusion that the user is in a different environment

virtualization: as if it were real; making something seem real, e.g. a virtual environment

visible speech: a set of symbols, comprising an alphabet, that "spell" sounds instead of words

visualization: a technique whereby complex systems are portrayed in a meaningful way using sophisticated computer graphics systems; e.g., chemical molecules

volatile: subject to rapid change; describes the character of data when current no longer flows to a device (that is, electrical power is switched off)

waveform: an abstraction used in the physical sciences to model energy transmission in the form of longitudinal or transverse waves

web surfers: people who "surf" (search) the Internet frequently

wide area network (WAN): an interconnected network of computers that spans upward from several buildings to whole cities or entire countries and across countries

wireless lavaliere microphones: small microphones worn around the speakers' necks, which attach to their shirts

wireless local area network (WLAN): an interconnected network of computers that uses radio and/or infrared communication channels, rather than cables

workstations: computers (usually within a network) that interact directly with human users (much the same as "client computers")

xerography: a printing process that uses electrostatic elements derived from a photographic image to deposit the ink

XML: the acronym for eXtensible Markup Language; a method of applying structure to data so that documents can be represented

Topic Outline

Weather Forecasting
World Wide Web

BUSINESS

Accounting Software
ATM Machines
Chip Manufacturing
Computer Professional
Computer Supported Cooperative Work
  (CSCW)
Computerized Manufacturing
Credit Online
Data Mining
Data Processing
Data Warehousing
Database Management Software
Decision Support Systems
Document Processing
E-banking
E-commerce
E-commerce: Economic and Social Aspects
Economic Modeling
Electronic Markets
Office Automation Systems
Process Control
Productivity Software
Project Management
Spreadsheets
SQL
SQL: Databases
Word Processors

CODES

Binary Number System
Codes
Coding Techniques
Cryptography
Information Theory

COMPUTING TECHNIQUES

Analog Computing
Digital Computing
Digital Logic Design

CORPORATIONS AND ORGANIZATIONS

Apple Computer, Inc.
Association for Computing Machinery
Bell Labs
Census Bureau
IBM Corporation
Institute of Electrical and Electronics
  Engineers (IEEE)
Intel Corporation
Microsoft Corporation
Minitel
National Aeronautics and Space Administra-
  tion (NASA)
Xerox Corporation

DECISION SUPPORT

Artificial Intelligence
Decision Support Systems
Expert Systems
Knowledge-Based Systems

EDUCATION

Computer Assisted Instruction
Digital Libraries
Distance Learning
E-books
E-journals and E-publishing
E-mail
Educational Software
Electronic Campus
Virtual Reality in Education

ENTERTAINMENT

Animation
Chess Playing
Computer Vision
Fiction, Computers in
Film and Video Editing
Game Controllers
Games
Home Entertainment
Home System Software
Hypermedia and Multimedia
Music

Music Composition
Music, Computer
Photography

FILM, VIDEO AND PHOTOGRAPHY

Animation
Digital Images
Film and Video Editing
Hypermedia and Multimedia
JPEG, MPEG
Photography

GOVERNMENT

Census Bureau
Computer Fraud and Abuse Act of 1986
Copyright
Government Funding, Research
Information Technology Standards
Minitel
National Aeronautics and Space Administration (NASA)
Patents
Political Applications
Privacy

HARDWARE, COMPUTERS

Analytical Engine
Cache Memory
CAD/CAM, CA Engineering
Central Processing Unit
Chip Manufacturing
Computer System Interfaces
Digital Logic Design
Integrated Circuits
Mainframes
Memory
Memory Devices
Microchip
Microcomputers
Minicomputers
Storage Devices
Supercomputers
Tabulating Machines
Vacuum Tubes
Virtual Memory

HARDWARE, TELECOMMUNICATIONS

Bandwidth
Bridging Devices
Cache Memory
Cell Phones
Cellular Technology
Communication Devices
Fiber Optics
Firewalls
Information Technology Standards
Laser Technology
Networks
Optical Technology
Telecommunications
Telephony
Transmission Media
Wireless Technology

HISTORY, COMPUTERS

Analytical Engine
Babbage, Charles
Early Computers
Early Pioneers
Generations, Computers
Hollerith, Herman
Internet
Jacquard's Loom
Mainframes
Microchip
Microcomputers
Minicomputers
Pascal, Blaise
Supercomputers
Tabulating Machines
Turing Machine
Vacuum Tubes
Virtual Memory

HISTORY, LANGUAGES

Algol-60 Report
Assembly Language and Architecture
Compilers
Generations, Languages
Java Applets

JavaScript
LISP
Logo
Markup Languages
Object-Oriented Languages
Procedural Languages
Programming
SQL
SQL: Databases
Visual Basic

HUMAN INTERACTION

Computer System Interfaces
Human Factors: User Interfaces
Hypertext
Integrated Software
Interactive Systems
Speech Recognition
User Interfaces
Window Interfaces

INFORMATION RELATED TOPICS

Information Access
Information Overload
Information Retrieval
Information Systems
Information Theory
Library Applications
Search Engines
System Analysis
Systems Design

INNOVATION

Artificial Intelligence
Artificial Life
Data Mining
Data Visualization
Data Warehousing
Desktop Publishing
Digital Images
Digital Libraries
Embedded Technology (Ubiquitous
    Computing)
Fiber Optics
Global Positioning Systems

Laser Technology
Mobile Computing
Molecular Computing
Nanocomputing
Optical Character Recognition
Optical Technology
Pattern Recognition
Personal Digital Assistants
Robotics
Robots
Satellite Technology
Scientific Visualization

INPUT AND OUTPUT DEVICES

Display Devices
Game Controllers
Graphic Devices
Input Devices
Keyboard
Magnetic Stripe Cards
Mouse
Pointing Devices
Printing Devices
Reading Tools
Sound Devices
Touch Screens
Video Devices
Word Processors

INTERNET

Authentication
Browsers
Credit Online
Cybercafe
E-banking
E-commerce
E-commerce: Economic and Social Aspects
E-journals and E-publishing
E-mail
Electronic Markets
Entrepreneurs
Internet
Internet: Applications
Internet: Backbone

Internet: History
Intranet
Search Engines
Virtual Private Network
Wireless Technology
World Wide Web

LIBRARIES

Digital Libraries
Distance Learning
E-books
E-journals and E-publishing
E-mail
Electronic Campus
Library Applications

MATHEMATICS

Binary Number System
Boolean Algebra
Codes
Coding Techniques
Cryptography
Information Theory

MEDICINE

Artificial Life
Biology
Cybernetics
Digital Images
Image Analysis: Medicine
Knowledge-Based Systems
Laser Technology
Medical Systems
Molecular Biology
Molecular Computing
Neural Networks
Pattern Recognition
Scientific Visualization

MUSIC

JPEG, MPEG
Music
Music Composition
Music, Computer
Sound Devices

NETWORKS

Asynchronous and Synchronous Transmission
Asynchronous Transfer Mode (ATM)
ATM Transmission
Bandwidth
Boolean Algebra
Bridging Devices
Communication Devices
Embedded Technology (Ubiquitous
    Computing)
Fiber Optics
Firewalls
FTP
Global Positioning Systems
Information Technology Standards
Information Theory
Intranet
Network Design
Network Protocols
Network Topologies
Networks
Routing
Satellite Technology
Security
Security Applications
Security Hardware
Security Software
Serial and Parallel Transmission
Service Providers
TCP/IP
Telecommunications
Telephony
Telnet
Transmission Media
Virtual Private Network
Wireless Technology

PEOPLE

Amdahl, Gene Myron
Asimov, Isaac
Babbage, Charles
Bardeen, John (See entry: Bardeen, John,
    Brattain, Walter H., and Shockley, William
    B.)
Bell, Alexander Graham

PRECURSORS TO COMPUTERS

PROGRAMMING

PUBLISHING

SECURITY

SOCIAL ISSUES

Compatibility (Open Systems Design)
Computer Scientists
Cookies
Copyright
Credit Online
Cybercafe
Digital Libraries
Digital Signatures
Distance Learning
E-banking
E-books
E-commerce
E-commerce: Economic and Social Aspects
E-journals and E-publishing
E-mail
Electronic Campus
Electronic Markets
Entrepreneurs
Ergonomics
Ethics
Fiction, Computers in
Global Surveillance
Government Funding, Research
Home Entertainment
Information Access
Information Overload
Journalism
Library Applications
Medical Systems
Mobile Computing
Open Source
Patents
Personal Digital Assistants
Political Applications
Privacy
Service Providers
Social Impact
Software Piracy
Technology of Desktop Publishing
Telephony
Urban Myths
Virtual Private Network
Virtual Reality in Education
World Wide Web

SOFTWARE

Agents
Browsers
Compilers
Database Management Software
Geographic Information Systems
Human Factors: User Interfaces
Integrated Software
Office Automation Systems
Open Source
Operating Systems
Procedural Languages
Productivity Software
Search Engines
Simulation
Spreadsheets
User Interfaces
Window Interfaces

STUDY AREAS

Artificial Intelligence
Artificial Life
Expert Systems
Information Theory
Molecular Computing
Nanocomputing

TECHNOLOGY, DEVICES

Abacus
Analytical Engine
ATM Machines
Bandwidth
Bridging Devices
Cache Memory
CAD/CAM, CA Engineering
Cell Phones
Cellular Technology
Central Processing Unit
Communication Devices
Computer System Interfaces
Display Devices
Game Controllers
Global Positioning Systems
Graphic Devices

TELECOMMUNICATIONS, PEOPLE AND ORGANIZATIONS

TELECOMMUNICATIONS, TECHNOLOGY AND DEVICES

Volume 2 Index